TouchIT

TouchIT

UNDERSTANDING DESIGN IN A PHYSICAL—DIGITAL WORLD

ALAN DIX
Professor and Director, Computational Foundry,
Swansea University, Wales, UK

STEVE GILL
Professor and Deputy Director of Research & Graduate Studies, Cardiff
School of Art and Design, Cardiff Metropolitan University, Wales, UK

JO HARE
Director of Education and Head of Computer Science,
Huddersfield Grammar School, UK

DEVINA RAMDUNY—ELLIS
Senior Lecturer, FET- Architecture and the Built Environment,
University of the West of England, UK

OXFORD
UNIVERSITY PRESS

OXFORD
UNIVERSITY PRESS

Great Clarendon Street, Oxford, OX2 6DP,
United Kingdom

Oxford University Press is a department of the University of Oxford.
It furthers the University's objective of excellence in research, scholarship,
and education by publishing worldwide. Oxford is a registered trade mark of
Oxford University Press in the UK and in certain other countries

Published in the United States of America by Oxford University Press
198 Madison Avenue, New York, NY 10016, United States of America

British Library Cataloguing in Publication Data

Data available

Library of Congress Control Number: 2021949459

ISBN 978-0-19-871858-1
DOI: 10.1093/oso/9780198718581.001.0001

Printed and bound by
CPI Group (UK) Ltd, Croydon, CR0 4YY

Contents

part 1

Introduction

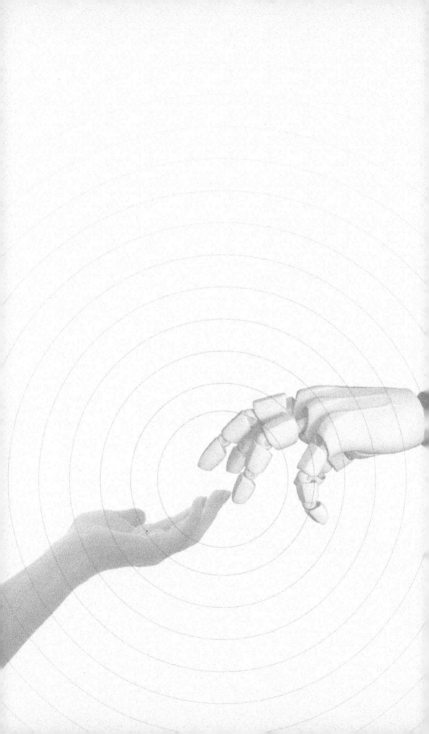

Elements of Our Hybrid Existence

This is a book about understanding the physicality of people and of technology, and how studying these can help us to improve the design of physical technology for people.

1.1 Why Study Physicality

Historically there has often been a dualistic view of mind and body, with cognition and thought being seen as quite separate from physical muscle and bone. Computation has a similar abstract feel, a world of algorithms and pure reason.

However, humans and computers are embodied respectively in flesh and silicon, and if we wish to communicate with any computational device, we do so through that flesh and silicon, through the physical world: tapping keys, pushing a mouse, or stroking an iPhone screen. Not all these interactions involve fingers and touch. Speech involves tongue and mouth creating pressure waves through the air to vibrate the microphone in the computer. Gesture recognition involves moving arms, photons, and optics. Even direct brain interfaces use electrodes and wires. There is no connection at the level of pure abstraction but always in the physical world.

As more devices around us have digital aspects it becomes essential that we understand the way physical and digital interactions meet. Traditionally, the physical form of a product was the domain of the industrial designer (sometimes also called product designer), whereas the digital interaction belonged to the usability or human–computer interaction specialist. Now, however, in products from mobile phones to washing machines, the physical design and the digital design must come together to create a single experience for the user.

Box 1.1   How many computers in your home?

How many computers are in your home? Think about the answer—you may need a quick run around to count. Later in the chapter, we'll return to this and see how you compare with the authors.

1.2 Components of the Physical World

The physical world can be seen in many ways, for example through biology, physics, or geography. To focus on those aspects that influence the design of hybrid digital/physical devices, we are organizing the central parts of this book around four main themes of the physical world.

- Part II. *The Body and Physiology*—Our bodies are physical, as are our brains. However numinous our thoughts, they have their life in the material substance of neurons. Our bodies too can be part of digital interactions, whether gaming on an X-Box or using an advanced gesture recognition interface.

- Part III. *Material Artefacts and Design*—The world is full of 'things', both natural things like stones, and constructed things, such as scissors, books, and mobile phones. Our understanding of the former is germane to the design of the latter.

- Part IV. *Space and Spatial Arrangement*—When we interact, we do it in physical space. This space may be where we perform physical movements. For example, a few years ago living rooms around the world were briefly reorganized to accommodate the Wii [315, 404]. Physical space also has social dimensions. For example, the Hermes system at Lancaster University uses small displays outside office doors where visitors can leave notes [65]. There have never been problems with abusive messages, perhaps because anyone leaving a note is aware that they can be observed in the public corridor—the spatial location changes the use [131].

- Part V. *Digital Artefacts and Virtual Physicality*—Sometimes we emulate aspects of the physical world in the digital: virtual reality creating whole parallel worlds, the desktop metaphor, dragging images on an iPhone, or even the idea of 'visiting' a website. Do we understand enough about the physical world to be able to capture the right aspects? And computation itself is embodied in silicon and magnetic surfaces and bound by that materiality (see the PalCom project 'making computing palpable' [322]). There can only be a finite amount of computation in a finite space, and information flows take time, hence the star-like pattern of supercomputer circuits.

These themes are not independent. As we have seen, as humans we interact with computation through the physical world, most commonly through devices and always set within space, whether in offices, homes, streets, the countryside, or the open sea.

Of course the physical world has other aspects: living organisms, like animals and plants, or the natural forces of fire and storm. We have chosen the four themes that seem most intimately connected

with digital devices—although there have been proposals to help
people interact better with their pets! [388, 286]

1.3 Kinds of Things: From Stones to Silicon

While this book is about the confluence of digital technology and
physical design, in fact digital technology is the latest step in a long
process whereby humankind has shaped its world. With the exception of the fourth (Part V), each of our major themes encompasses
both natural and artificial phenomena. Figure 1.1 lists some of the
kinds of things we find in the world, divided left to right by whether
they are natural or artificial, and grouped into their themes, where
they fit into one.

Note that the distinction into natural and artificial is itself slightly
problematic. After all, we are part of the natural world, so in one
sense a computer is as natural as cow dung: both are products of

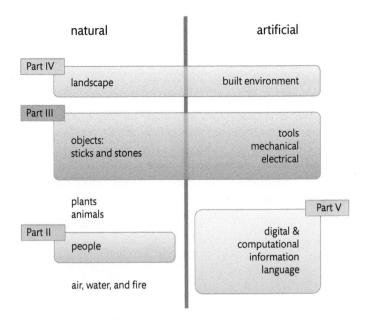

Figure 1.1 The natural and artificial world

animals in the world. If we exclude bodily functions, then certainly a bird's nest should be included as an artificial construction. Similarly, we have put language on the artificial side of the divide, yet birdsong could equally well sit there. Both lines and language have a tendency to impose discrete distinctions upon continua, a point we will discuss later in the book.

1.4 The Natural Order

The Ancient Greeks had four basic elements, earth, water, air and fire, though Aristotle added a fifth—ether—for the material of the heavens. Similar systems occur across the world. While earth represents the solid things of the world, water, air, and fire are increasingly numinous, hard to hold or contain, or even see.

Of the kinds of things listed for the natural world in Figure 1.1, most are things of earth, the solid things we can see, touch, and hold: the landscape, stones, plants, animals, and other people. Yet while each is solid, they differ dramatically in the way we understand them and the ways in which we can interact with them.

The most 'earthy' of natural things is the ground itself beneath our feet and the landscape that stretches out around us. This forms the matrix within which we live and act, hence the importance of 'space' in the organization of this book.

The landscape, near and far, is not bare but full of inanimate and living things. The inanimate, whether 'never living' like stones, or 'once living' like sticks and shells, is our starting point when we look at material artefacts. In some ways it is the simplest of things, within our control. Inanimate objects do not change unless they break. When we want a child to learn we often give them simple blocks of wood (or plastic) to play with: they can experience and create order, or be the agent of their own chaos.

Plants are not so different from stones except that these living and once living things tend to be more pliable, changeable in form, not just location; even wood becomes more solid as it ages. Animals, however, change the rules. Just like people they move and act of their own volition. In contrast, just like stones, the ground or dead bones, a tree will stay where it is. Interaction with stones and plants depends only on your own actions, but to interact with an animal (whether chasing it to eat, or running away to avoid being eaten) you need to consider what it will do.

We recognize that any attempt to distinguish people from animals based on essential attributes, whether consciousness, self-consciousness, intention, intelligence, or moral sense, is bound to lead to debate if not argument. However problematic such distinctions are, we will treat humans as special in this book as it is humans who create digital technologies and primarily humans who use them.

Turning to water, air, and fire: of the three, water seems most well behaved, tending to leak if given a chance, but otherwise controllable, holdable, movable. No wonder the liquid metal in *Terminator 2* is so frightening and the water horses in *Lord of the Rings* so awe-inspiring. Uncontained, the crashing sea or flowing stream have also always held that sense of 'otherness' and mystery. But it is air that is most often associated with life itself, and even spirit. The blowing wind apparently gives vitality to trees and even dead leaves, and in the Book of Genesis, God breathes life into man.

Fire, on the other hand, is the destroyer, perhaps the most mysterious element of all. From a scientific point of view it is just hot, glowing, burning gas, but it seems to defy day-to-day rules, with apparent edges yet constantly forming and reforming. As water seeks to escape downwards, fire constantly flows upwards to the sky, never reaching it but disappearing, leaving a dark dirty smoke from its pure glowing heart.

It is fire that gives us the best metaphor for many of the more abstract notions of language, society, and computation. Fire is essentially an emergent phenomenon. While earth, water, and air are, in the end, composed of molecules and atoms, a fire is defined not by a particular set of molecules—these are constantly changing state from fuel to smoke. The identifiable flame is more about the self-sustaining form and structure in which these passing molecules find themselves. We will return to this idea in Chapter 15.

This quality of fire, constantly changing yet also fixed and bounded, was germane to the philosophy of Heraclitus, who in turn influenced the views of later Greek philosophers including Aristotle. Heraclitus saw that change was the essence even of things that appear unchanging, or, as Karl Popper phrased it in more modern philosophical language, Heraclitus sees everything as process [329].

Our bodies are, of course, similar. We eat food and shed skin, we have all heard that each breath we take contains an air molecule once breathed by Julius Caesar. As with fire, it is not the particular molecules that make us who we are, but their arrangement. Flocks of birds, multinational companies, files on a magnetic disk: each has identity in an arrangement of changing parts. However, now we have moved on to the artificial world, the world forged by human hands.

1.4.1 The artificial—works of our hands

The roots of the word 'artificial' are from the Latin 'ars' meaning art and 'facere', to make: the artificial is the made. The Chinese elements differentiate earth, wood, and metal: although small amounts of precious metals occur naturally, metal is largely a product of human labour. We not only shape the earth, we add materials to it that do not previously exist, or rarely exist in natural form. Arguably, fire itself should have been in the category of the artificial; while natural fires exist on earth as the result of lightning or volcanoes, the majority of terrestrial fire is manmade. Along with stone tools and skeletons, fire circles characterize the oldest remains of hominids. Fire allows the smelting of metal, fire drove the Industrial Revolution, and it is the carbon dioxide from that fire which threatens to destroy us now.

When we think about the work of our hands, however, it is the remains of buildings that are often the most persistent signs of past artifice: the Acropolis in Athens, the Coliseum in Rome, the Great Wall of China, the hilltop city of Machu Picchu in Peru, and the remnants of Neolithic post-holes. Indeed, of the ancient Seven Wonders of the World (Box 1.2), five are buildings and the other two giant statues. Buildings change our relationship to the environment. We can shelter from the weather and be protected from animals, and other humans. Large-scale building also requires sophisticated human organization and planning. Many of the four-tonne stones used in the construction of Stonehenge were transported hundreds of kilometres from Pembrokeshire in south Wales over a period of many decades.

Box 1.2 The Seven Wonders of the World

- Great Pyramid of Giza
- Hanging Gardens of Babylon
- Temple of Artemis at Ephesus
- Statue of Zeus at Olympia
- Mausoleum of Halicarnassus
- Colossus of Rhodes
- Ishtar Gate of Babylon (earliest lists)
- Lighthouse of Alexandria (later lists)

This list was compiled by the Greeks as a sort of 'Lonely Planet Guide', so it is not surprising that all are in or near to Greece. More recent lists include wonders from other parts of the world. Only one of the wonders exists today, the Great Pyramid of Giza, which was also the oldest at around 2500 BC.

Pyramids at Giza   The Ishtar Gate

It is not only buildings that influence our relationship with the natural landscape. Large works of civil engineering, such as the Roman roads that cut across Europe, the Suez Canal, and the trans-Siberian railway, shape both landscapes and lives. Indeed, the Suez Canal shows how powerful a political issue these remouldings of geography can be. The Roman roads were there precisely to enable fast movement of troops to conquer and to control; and, in the United States in the nineteenth century, it was the railroad, as much as the US Cavalry, that enabled the expansion of the western frontier and the eradication or displacement of many indigenous American tribes.

In many areas of the world, agriculture provided the surpluses that enabled the growth of large social units. However, the public works needed to maximize production also led to political and physical change. In Egypt, the whole civilization is believed to have arisen in order to harness the annual floods of the Nile through massive works of embankments and channels. Even what we now consider to be natural environments are often the result of large-scale agricultural interventions: the Lake District in northern England (Figure 1.2) is shaped partly by the work of nature—ice and rain—but would be wooded if it were not for the sheep.

In later chapters we will see that humans are not the only toolmakers, but we are certainly the most prolific and sophisticated. The earliest tools were axes and spears to hunt, fish, and prepare food, and bone needles to fashion clothes. In fact, textile production has

Figure 1.2 The Lake District

always been one of the most technically sophisticated activities, from early handlooms to the Spinning Jenny, which was the catalyst for the Industrial Revolution.

As technology advanced, both mechanical and electrical artefacts were seen, in their time, as almost magical. This may be partly because through hidden mechanisms and harnessed power, they seem to defy the laws that hold for simple physical objects. And in each age humankind has imagined itself formed by these technologies, with artificial humans driven by clockwork, then steam, now electronics. From Pygmalion to Golem to Frankenstein, literature and folktale have stories of constructed humans becoming alive. In science and philosophy we use the images of the day to make sense of our bodies and minds. Descartes imagined tiny movements of the nerves carrying information from fingers to brain, and today we cast the brain in information-processing language.

It is precisely this computational and digital technology that is the focus of this book, technology that can be numinous, like air and fire, difficult to put your finger on and touch. However, we shall see that notions of information have existed from the earliest stage of modern humanity and are intimately tied to language itself. Information and language are carried by particular words on a page, sounds in the air, or electrons in a wire. Just as the constituent molecules of fire change from moment to moment, words are passed on from person to person. Each tongue of flame is unique, but the fire itself has a persistent, dynamic form. The words are, in a sense, different in each telling, but the power of language and the power of information is that they also have a meaning beyond the particular wax tablet, parchment, or silicon chip.

1.5 Coming Together

This book comes as the confluence of two areas of research and practice: human–computer interaction and industrial design. Industrial design is about generating ideas and solutions for physical products, whether in the home (kettles and corkscrews), in the workplace (adjustable chairs, paperclips, and filing cabinets), or in the world

Box 1.3 Revisited: How many computers in your home?

How many did you count in Box 1.1? Probably several, depending on how many people live in your house. Maybe, if you are very geeky, you have separate development or gaming machines, perhaps even old machines for nostalgia's sake.

Well, our counts were:

Alan	28
Steve	99
Devina	20
Jo	21

(and she lives on a boat!)

Yikes, are we total geeks? If you haven't guessed already, think again. Do you have a HiFi, microwave, TV, washing machine? Each of these typically contains one or more computers, so how many computers in your home?

Try looking around your body too. How many computers do you wear, have in your pockets, or carry around in your wallet, or handbag? Phones, Fitbits, chipped credit cards, cameras, even car keys, all have computers or some form of computer technology in them.

(cat's eyes on roads, waste paper bins on the high street). Human–Computer Interaction (HCI) is concerned with any place where people interact with technology. This may be a one-to-one interaction between a person and single computer (like the person typing on a laptop to write this), or a situation where the computer is a mediator in a human–human communication (Skype calls and instant messaging).

For many years, those working in HCI largely had to treat the hardware of computing (keyboard, screen, and mouse) as a 'given' and focus almost exclusively on the design of software and on understanding the cognitive, social, and organizational impacts. In contrast, industrial design was confined to objects with (at most) relatively simple mechanical or electrical activity. However, as devices such as washing machines and mobile phones became more complex in terms of their interactivity, industrial designers started to attend HCI conferences, and as computers became embedded in everyday devices those in HCI started to look to industrial designers for insight on physical design.

1.5.1 Making things usable—Human–Computer Interaction

The roots of HCI can be traced back at least fifty years. In 1959 Brian Shackel published probably the first HCI paper, on the ergonomics of displays [358, 239], and the early 1960s saw the development of landmark systems including Ian Sutherland's Sketchpad (Figure 1.3) [384] and the work of Douglas Engelbart's Bootstrap Institute [154]. The Bootstrap Institute was home to the development of concepts that took many years to become mainstream, including video conferencing and hypertext, and, perhaps most iconic, the first computer mouse. However, it was in Sketchpad that we saw the first use of the computer screen to create an interface that was in some way like the physical world, with a light pen used to edit diagrams on screen.

The late 1970s and early 1980s saw the emergence of a recognisable discipline of HCI, Shackel again was critical in establishing the international community. This expansion was largely driven by the emergence of the Engelbart's personal computer and in particular

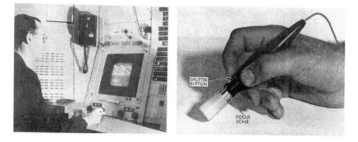

Figure 1.3 Left: SketchPad in use; Right: SketchPad light pen(from [384])

the Apple Macintosh, still seen as a design icon as well as an enabling technology. The visionary element was still there, especially in the work of Xerox PARC Laboratory, which pioneered many of the interaction techniques that found their way into the 'Mac'.

Box 1.4 What's in a name

In the early days HCI was known by different names, including the 'Man–Machine Interface'; This term had various problems: 'Man' is gendered, 'Interface' fails to give regard to broader interaction and context, and 'Machine', well, just sounds dated. However, the adoption of 'Computer' instead has its own problems, as 'Machine' suggests a broader view of technology. In these days, when computers are in everything, it may be a moot point, and the name has not prevented the field of HCI from embracing the broader issues whenever and wherever people interact with technology. However, for this book, we wish the field could be called Human–Technology Interaction, since the computer, while present in almost all modern technology, is not the focus of human interaction with it.

For many years HCI research focused almost exclusively on interaction through the graphical user interface, itself a physical metaphor at use in the flat digital world of a pixellated screen. However, there has always been a strand that looked at physical interactions, especially in the design of improved or novel input devices, including squashable balls, foot-based interaction and numerous devices for navigating in 3D environments. Studies of technology in context have always emphasized the importance of the physical layout of work environments; for example, the different ways practice nurses, general practitioners, and hospital consultants oriented their screens to include or exclude their patients. However, it is only in recent years, with the development of mobile technology, ubiquitous computing and tangible user interfaces that physicality has become a core issue in HCI.

1.5.2 Of designers, computer-embedded devices and physicality

What do we mean by design? It is a word that means many things to many people. The *Cambridge Advanced Learners Dictionary* defines it as 'to make or draw plans for something, for example clothes or buildings; [288], a definition that leaves plenty of room for its application in a range of areas by a very broad range of professionals and amateurs from chefs to chemists and from electronic engineers to ergonomists. Not only that, its meaning has also changed over the years: 'mass-production has evolved and has been perfected, and in the course of this evolution the designer has been variously an artist, an architect, a social reformer, a mystic, an engineer, a management consultant, a public relations man and, perhaps, now a computer engineer' [15]. For the purposes of this book, we shall be concentrating on one area of design: the design of physical objects, particularly, though not exclusively, those intended for production (industrial design, more on this later in this chapter).

Arguably, design is as old as people, whether fashioning flint arrowheads or building a broch. Generally speaking, what separates modern design from design before, say, the Victorian era, is that earlier design tended to be based more on individual output rather than mass or even batch production. There are exceptions. The Romans, for example, produced pre-laid mosaics that could be bought 'off the shelf' for installation in the home. Examples of 'mass production' may even be found in Neolithic times: Skara Brae is a Neolithic village on the principal island of Orkney, Scotland (Figure 1.4). It consists of

Figure 1.4 Stone dresser, Skara Brae

ten dwellings dating to around 3100 BC. They are very well preserved, being largely intact with the exception of their roofs. The buildings themselves are of a standardized layout with furniture, cooking area, beds, and dressers all in the same relative positions in each dwelling. The stone furniture itself is also of a standard design.

For most of recorded history, 'design' tended to be within single disciplines such as crafts (pottery, jewellery), engineering (bridges, canals), or architecture. Again, there are exceptions such as the detailed drawings of da Vinci and the Renaissance confluence of arts, science, and (albeit anachronistic to say) engineering. Throughout the later Middle Ages, in the increasingly mercantile society, the craft guilds grew, though largely to protect the secrets of their crafts, not to critique or develop them; and more aesthetic traditions in high-end furniture, fashion and architecture have flourished from the Renaissance onwards.

Design and manufacture began to separate in the mid-eighteenth century when mass production began to be used. Josiah Wedgwood was among the first to bring in sculptors to 'design' the form of the ceramics manufactured in the Wedgwood factory [15]. The ability to reproduce forms accurately meant that the quality of the end product was determined by the quality of the design at the beginning. It was in the late nineteenth century that more reflective and modern design traditions had their roots. Just as today, design philosophies varied greatly. On the one hand, John Ruskin's works led to the nature-inspired and handcraft-focused Arts and Crafts movement. Whereas Ruskin and the Arts and Crafts movement were partly acting in reaction to the mechanism of the Industrial Revolution, others embraced the utilitarian lines of new materials and methods, giving rise to Modernism. The architect Louis Sullivan was one of these, both developing the steel-structure high-rise and also coining the design maxim; form ever follows function;. This period also saw the first mass-produced electrical appliances, with irons, toasters, cookers, and electric fans all appearing before 1910 [173].

According to Bayley and Conran, the term 'industrial design' first appeared in 1919 in America, introduced as a method by which products could compete essentially through 'styling' when their prices were 'stabilized' during the Great Depression. The profession quickly expanded its role to embody product function as well (e.g. Dreyfuss' home phone in 1937, Figure 1.5). The International Council of Societies of Industrial Design (ICSID) no longer attempt to define industrial design—a term somewhat interchangeable with product design. However, in 1963 they did define it, as 'a creative activity whose aims are to determine the formal qualities of objects produced by industry. These formal qualities are not only the external features but are principally those structural and functional relationships which convert a system to a coherent unity both from the point of view of the producer and the user. Industrial design extends to embrace all the aspects of human environment, which are conditioned by industrial production.' [414].

Another key influence in the development of industrial design as we know it today was the Bauhaus. Founded in 1919 by an architect, Walter Gropius, the Bauhaus was a ground-breaking art school that sought to bring arts, craft, and design together in a single modernist movement.

Figure 1.5 Iconic industrial design—Home Phone by Henry Dreyfuss (1937)

Adopting Sullivan's 'form follows function' approach, important Bauhaus designers such as Mies van der Rohe designed products and buildings that exploited new materials and processes that relied on simplicity and mechanical integrity for their structural and aesthetic success.

Box 1.5 Design approaches: defying, exposing, and denying physicality

Defying: Bauhaus designers sometimes sought to use new materials that appeared to defy physicality. The *Brno* chair (1930) by *Mies Van Der Rohe* uses steel to create a cantilevered structure employing a minimum of material to create the impression of a 'floating' structure. Jonathan Adams used a similar trick with the design of the Wales Millennium Centre in Cardiff, UK, the apparent physical structure—in this case glass, appearing to support the bulk of the building.

continued

Box 1.5 *continued*

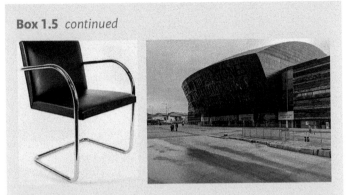

Exposing: Richard Rogers, Renzo Piano, and Gianfranco Franchini designed the Pompidou Centre (1977) to expose its service infrastructure on the outside, ostensibly to clear space inside. Lifts, stairs, escalators, water, air, and electrical services are each colour coded: electricity in yellow, water in green, air in blue. Not only are the building's innards exposed but the physical purpose of each is highlighted. This change in the physical presentation of the building alters the viewer's perception of the importance of structure (which normally has primacy) over service, which we might also see as support for the occupants.

continued

Box 1.5 *continued*

Denying: The Millennium Bridge in York, UK offers an apparent physical, aesthetic, and structural confluence while actually separating structure from the other two. The bridge is in fact held up by its curvature and the large girders that make up its main span. The arch which first appears to be a part of the structure not only contributes little to the strength, it places a twisting moment on the rest of the structure!

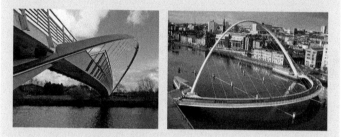

The Gateshead Millennium Bridge, on the other hand, offers a true confluence between the three elements. Here the physicality and aesthetics of the structure are neatly combined and the balance of forces are just as they are presented.

Industrial design's importance grew through the twentieth century alongside industrial production, including the foundation of the American Union of Decorative Artists and Craftsmen in 1927, the British Council of Industrial Design (now the Design Council) in 1944, and ICSID in 1957. Together these various movements and societies shaped a profession whose role was to cohere a design solution that answered the needs of all stakeholders to create the finished item with which the user interacts. Within that process they were required to understand the user's limitations, abilities, desires, and frustrations. A good industrial designer should, it follows, design products with an appropriate cognizance of their context of use.

In 1980 Heskett pointed out that one of the outlooks that separate the industrial designer from the artist is how the form is realized [217]. An industrial designer will not make the objects they design.

However much they may use physicality in the development process, it is merely a means to an end, yet the act of making is fundamental to an artist.

A mixture of physicality, cogitative, and drawing-based techniques has served designers well for decades (or millennia, depending on your definition of design). However, the ascendance of the transistor has created challenges that the design community have yet to satisfactorily integrate into those tried and tested methodologies. As far back as the early 1990s designers started to realize that the products we now know as computer-embedded devices were going to pose challenges because much of the human interaction with them occurred on the physical–digital border. Steve once had a conversation with an interactive appliance design expert who told him that in his experience, industrial designers tend to address user interfaces, particularly the graphical user interfaces of computer-embedded devices, with a 2D mentality. Considering industrial design is all about 3D output that is a damning criticism, but should it surprise us? This enforced disjunction in the design process for products with computers in them is key to the theme of the book and so it will be a strand we pick up later in more detail.

1.6 Different Ways to Touch

There are a number of related areas that study the meeting of physical and digital worlds. Each overlaps either HCI or industrial design to some extent. We will look in more detail at these areas in the next chapter and we will encounter them all at different times during the rest of this book.

- *ubiquitous computing (ubicomp)*—In 1991, Mark Weiser painted a vision of computation permeating the world, woven seamlessly into life [416]. His thinking was based on early prototypes at Xerox research centres in Palo Alto and Cambridge, mostly involving displays of various sizes from 1-inch 'tabs' to yard-scale wall displays and explicit interactions. More recent work often also uses forms of implicit sensing (e.g. cameras) and less 'in your face' ambient displays. Despite Weiser's vision, in fact, technology often seems far from seamless, but certainly both our body-load of devices and the number of digital devices in our homes suggests that they are ubiquitous, if not invisible.

- *tangible user interfaces* (TUI)—In contrast, tangible user interfaces attempt to make computation both visible and touchable, where physical tokens represent digital things, embodying computation [238]. For example, a town planning application can use small models for planned buildings placed on a table on which a map is projected. As the planners move the models their location is tracked, a simulation works out projected traffic volumes, and projects the resulting flows onto the map.

- *mobile and personal devices*—Of all the physical devices in everyday life, it is probably the mobile phone that has transformed lives most over recent years. One of the reasons they are so powerful is that they are location aware, and the physical location of the phone is central to applications such as maps or 'find a friend' applications.

- *virtual reality*—Whereas ubicomp, TUI, and mobile applications all involve actions in the physical world, virtual reality attempts to emulate the physical world within a digital environment. This may be a representation of a real or planned physical setting, as in tourist applications or an architect's fly-through; it may create a realistic, but artificial world as in the Sims or Second Life; or it may use a physical world metaphor to represent information artefacts such as the computer 'desktop', or more sophisticated systems such as the Tower project that created an urban city-scape where each building and area mapped to files and folders (Figure 1.6) [333, 334].

- *augmented reality and mixed reality*—Augmented and mixed reality systems blend the physical and digital worlds, overlaying digital imagery or other outputs (sound, tactile) on top of the real world, using spectacles, projectors or mobile devices. For example, a tourist guide device can show reconstructions of buildings overlaying archaeological ruins. Core to all is some form of registration between physical and digital worlds, so that digital content can only be accessed at physical locations. We will be revisiting some of these, especially in Chapter 14.

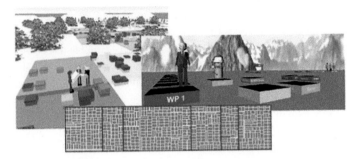

Figure 1.6 Tower creates a 3D city of information

Figure 1.7 Kevin Warwick wired for interaction [412]

- *physiological computing*—While most of the above use the physicality of the device and the world as their connection point to the digital, there are also people whose very body has become the computational device. In assistive technology, small muscle movements and even nerve impulses are used to drive and sense prosthetic limbs [248]. Physiological signals such as heart rate can be used in therapeutic settings or even to modify or control game play [181]. In Chapter 3 we will be noting the extremes the likes of Kevin Warwick (Figure 1.7) and Stelarc have gone to in this regard.
- *human–robot interaction*—Robots are slowly finding their way out of science fiction, and even out of the factory and into human lives:

Figure 1.8 Sony AIBO

they include autonomous vacuum cleaners, the Sony AIBO, (Figure 1.8) and Philips iCat. Some robots are designed to do useful jobs, for example carrying cleaning equipment for an elderly person allowing them to continue to remain in their homes. Others, such as the AIBO, are designed for their emotional aspects: they are like a small cute pet. The Philips iCat (Figure 1.9) ([54]) is somewhat similar but does not move around like the AIBO; instead its complexity is focused on its facial expressions and related features.

- *telepresence robots* —In addition to being used in one's own home, the iCat can be networked, so that stroking an iCat in your home can make your friend's iCat react: social robotics. More direct telepresence robots allow a remote operator in a limited way to 'feel' socially present somewhere else. These use technology that is similar to the remotely controlled drones that are so much part of modern warfare but is instead applied to enhance social relations. Telepresence robots usually include a video camera and screen so that the remote operator can both see and be seen. However, unlike a video conference, the robot

can be driven by the remote operator so that they have a degree
of movement.

After these visions of our cybernetic future, the confluence of industrial design and human–computer interaction may seem prosaic,
merely concerned with those mundane devices that fill our pockets and homes: MP3 players, mobile phones, washing machines, and
Sat Navs. However, these are the things we actually live with, not
simply gadgets in research labs. As ubiquitous, tangible, and mobile
technologies become used technologies, they also become part of industrial design, and then the challenge is how to turn them into
things that can become part of our lives.

1.7 Learning about Physicality

So, where do we turn to learn about the nature of physicality?

Most obvious are the sciences of physics and applied mathematics,
which study the properties of the physical world, human physiology
for the body, and cartography or geography for space. We will draw
on knowledge and literature from all of these. They can tell us how
a device will behave when acted on with a certain force, or whether
a certain movement is possible or likely to cause injury. However,
this is only part of the story. It may be possible for me to open a
box, but will I do it? Do I understand that I can do it and *how* I can
do it? To be able to analyse and design even non-digital products we
need to understand how people understand. Understanding people
is more the domain of the human sciences, psychology, sociology,
and anthropology, although they have very different methods. Psychology, on the whole, tends to use laboratory experiments, or other
forms of controlled experiment, whereas sociology tends to study
people in real life by various means, from simple questionnaires to
direct observation. All of these have proven useful in HCI in general and particularly for those who study phenomena associated with
physical interactions.

In Chapter 9 we will discuss experiments targeted at understanding the 'natural inverse', the way some bodily movements are the

Figure 1.9 Philips iCat

opposite of others (push–pull, left–right). Because this involves low-level and often involuntary movements, it is close to the stuff of traditional psychology and amenable to laboratory experiments. Elsewhere we make extensive use of knowledge gained from ethnographic studies, both our own and those of others. Ethnography, a technique drawn from anthropology, is about studying people in as near a natural environment as possible (albeit that simply having some form of observation inevitably causes changes). While the laboratory experiment is about creating a closed, controlled environment, ethnography embraces an open and sometimes chaotic world, which very often reveals the subtle and complex ways in which people get mundane things done.

Archaeologists often have little to work with except the material remains of cultures and yet they manage to work out, from those, much about the ways people lived and worked. In a similar way, objects themselves tell us a lot about the way they have been used and the way they have been designed. Studying artefacts can be used as an ethnographic technique, and in Chapter 15 we will see the way documents can be analysed to understand office practice. However, because artefacts have been designed, in a sense they embody the knowledge of the designer, and in Chapter 9, we will see how studying everyday consumer electronics can tell us about heuristics for physical interaction.

In both cases, implicit knowledge and practices can often be discovered through analysing the artefacts, knowledge that a person is not even aware of possessing, or which is so 'obvious' that they would never think to mention it if asked. For example, ask a person about their job and they will often tell you the 'rule book' version, but if you pick up a piece of paper from their desk and ask them how it got there and what would happen if you moved it, a far richer story will often emerge.

The very everydayness of physical interaction can make it difficult to study. When you put a cup down, you assume it won't walk away (and would be surprised if it did!), but normally you would not tell someone that this and other basic properties of the physical world are part of your implicit understanding of it. The problem here is that these things are not only obvious to the person being studied but also to the analyst who is trying to study them. In order to see through this 'obviousness' of everyday things you need to make them in some way strange or odd.

In diverse areas, including neurology and nutrition, it is when things go wrong that scientists begin to understand how they normally work. For example, the discovery of the role of vitamins often arose from recognizing the deficiency diseases (see Box 1.6). Where the effects aren't harmful to health, it is possible to deliberately 'break things' in order to understand how they work. For example, the ethnographer Garfinkel encouraged his students to perform 'breaching experiments' such as standing really close to people while having an ordinary conversation. By breaking the social norms they exposed how important these are [176].

Similarly, we have found various forms of 'breaking' have helped us in the necessary 'estrangement' of the ordinary. The experiments on the natural inverse, which we will describe in Chapter 9, are of this kind, creating situations where pushing back and forwards on a joystick does not have opposite effects on the interface. This technique can also be used in more qualitative studies; for example, in one study of group design we forced groups to use particular materials even if they weren't the most appropriate [338].

Fairytale, myth and science fiction are also rich resources that can reveal which elements of reality are necessary to human understanding of the world [106, 117]. If we examine these stories we find that some parts of reality are bent or broken. For example, fairytales often have magic doors that take you into different worlds, and science fiction has portals or teleportation, all breaking the normal contiguity of space. However, if everything is broken we then have chaos, and if we look carefully we see that the story-makers retain certain properties, suggesting that these are more crucial to our internal models of the world. As designers this tells us what we should retain and what we can afford to lose in our own emulations of, or interventions with, physicality.

Box 1.6 Of the prevention of the scurvy

The role of vitamin C was only discovered because of the prevalence of its deficiency disease, scurvy.

A ship's surgeon, James Lind, gave an early account of a quite rigorous experiment to determine the best treatment for scurvy [263]. He took twelve patients with severe scurvy, 'putrid gums, the spots and lassitude, with weakness of their knees', divided them into pairs and gave each patient one of six different treatments. It was the patients who had access to oranges and lemons who recovered most quickly and completely.

> The consequence was that the most sudden and visible good effects were perceived from the use of the oranges and lemons; one of those who had taken them being at the end of six days fit for duty. The spots were not indeed at that time quite off his body, nor his gums sound; but without any other medicine than a gargarism or elixir of vitriol he became quite healthy before we came into Plymouth, which was on the 16th June. The other was the best recovered of any in his condition, and being now deemed pretty well was appointed nurse to the rest of the sick.

It was not until the twentieth century that vitamin C was isolated and fabricated, but the understanding of vitamin C and its importance for health were the results of early studies like this of disease and deficiency.

What's Happening Now

There are a number of related areas that study the meeting of physical and digital worlds. Each overlaps either HCI or industrial design to some extent and we will encounter them all at different times during the rest of the book.

2.1 Computing in The World

2.1.1 Ubiquitous computing (ubicomp)

The most profound technologies are those that disappear. They weave themselves into the fabric of everyday life until they are indistinguishable from it. [416].

Mark Weiser was head of the computer science laboratory at Xerox, which has often been at the leading edge of new developments in computing. Reflecting on a number of projects, Weiser realized that they represented a shift in computing, from something that happened sealed inside the computer to something that permeated the world. His 1991 *Scientific American* article 'The computer for the 21st century', from which the above quotation is taken, inspired a new area, which he called 'ubiquitous computing', although it is often known by different terms, including pervasive computing and the invisible or disappearing computer.

Weiser's seminal article was principally about displays and the ways these were proliferating—look around your workplace or home and count the displays! He identified three scales of display, all of which have since become common in day-to-day life:

Inch scale—the smartphone, washing machine, or printer: while smartphone displays are general purpose, most displays embedded into appliances have quite specific purposes, sometimes displaying only a single number or setting.

Foot scale—the size of a traditional computer display or television: also think about self-service check-in at airports or pre-order kiosks at fast-food outlets.

Yard scale—for example, shared digital whiteboards, which have never really taken off in offices as Weiser envisaged but have become a common part of teaching practice in schools, and at many railway stations or tourist destinations larger information displays allow small groups to interact.

2.1.2 Internet of Things

Weiser was writing before the creation of the World-Wide Web, when global networking was still only emerging, and few people outside large organizations or universities had access to the Internet. Nowadays, though reliable networking can still be problematic outside affluent urban centres, for many purposes the Internet can be regarded as part of the infrastructure of life, like electricity. Weiser's vision was about the way people would interact with computers or, to be precise, the way that interaction becomes seamless. The Internet of Things is more about the way smart objects interact with one another using networking, and often web technology.

For example, a smart kettle may have a small display (inch scale) that allows you to set different temperatures, but an Internet-enabled kettle may allow you to turn it on via a phone app while you are on the bus home so that it is ready to make a cup of tea when you arrive.

The true power of these smart Internet-connected devices is the way that they work with each other. Imagine a web service, ' myHouse'. On the bus you tell the myHouse app that you are on your way home: it not only turns on the kettle at the right moment but also adjusts the heating ready for your return. As you enter the house and turn on the Internet-enabled lamp in the hall it tells myHouse it has been switched on, so myHouse starts to play background music and switches on ambient lighting in other rooms. Of course, there are less welcome aspects of connected devices, as we'll see in Chapter 13.

2.1.3 Invisible intelligence

In some ways Weiser's discussion of displays seems at odds with his focus on the invisible nature of computing, but in fact the core concept is not that the computer is literally invisible but that it is simply unseen, so much part of everyday life that we do not explicitly notice we are using it.

In the 'myHouse' scenario, we see examples where the computers really are invisible: the hall lamp has no display and even the house heating may rely on a phone or TV app to control it.

Some of this truly invisible computing may still be under your direct control, but much will be 'intelligent'. Some call this ambient intelligence, and the boundaries between this and ubiquitous computing are somewhat loose, as some level of intelligence is increasingly present in all ubiquitous computing.

Sometimes the intelligence is about trying to understand your *context* (where you are and what is happening around you) and activity (what you are doing). An example of *context-aware computing* would be your phone automatically changing to vibration ringing when it works out from your diary and location that you are in a concert. An example of *activity recognition* might be the myHouse system using the location, direction of movement, and accelerometers in your phone to deduce that you are jogging home, and adjusting the heating to be cooler when you first arrive while you are hot from the exercise, then slowly raising it as you rest. Context and activity may be combined: for example, myHouse might use knowledge of the current weather as well as activity recognition to set an appropriate temperature.

Notice that the phone changing to 'vibrate' in the context example does not initiate any substantive action, it simply alters the style of your interaction with the phone to vibration rather than speaker. However, in the myHouse examples the system autonomously turns on heating, the kettle, or the lights. An early BBC schools programme described the computer as a 'Totally Obedient Moron', but such autonomous interactions are more like a guardian angel operating in the background. Crucially, these interactions may be mediated by the physical world: your actions in the world are monitored and interpreted and the computer acts on the physical world in order to make your life better; it may never directly interact with you at all.

Although there is extensive work on the technology to enable these kinds of computer systems, we still have only a rudimentary understanding of how to manage and understand human interaction with them [126]. The direct manipulation metaphor, which has driven more than 30 years of user interfaces, tries to represent digital items as if they were passive physical objects (see below), while robotics and virtual agents are more like interacting with artificial people, but these diffuse forms of ambient interaction sit in a different sphere, more like a primitive world-view where physical things and the world itself are imbued with agency—ghosts in the walls!

2.1.4 Sensors, surveillance, and smart cities

Invisible interactions are made possible by an increasingly sensor-filled world. There is a wide variety of sensors in phones and other devices (see 'Up Close and Personal' section), Closed-Circuit Television (CCTV) cameras monitor shops, airports, and ordinary streets, and home security allows you to watch for unexpected movement when you are on holiday. At a small scale, proximity sensors open doors for us, while at a large scale, satellites image the earth on a daily basis. Old maps show dragons at the margins, Sir Arthur Conan Doyle imagined dinosaurs in a lost world in the upper reaches of the Amazon; now we simply look on Google Earth.

The proliferation of sensing can make life easier or safer but it raises concerns about privacy. In the digital domain, many have accepted that nothing is private and nothing is ephemeral, yet when we sit in our homes or walk in the streets we have expectations based on the physical properties of the world: closed doors keep us secure, distance makes us invisible. Artificial, and especially digital, sensors change all this, making it possible, for example, to record a private conversation with a camera and a pot plant [91]—more of which in Chapter 13. Digital technology is literally changing the properties of the physical world. Even those of us brought up with digital technology do not always appreciate issues of digital privacy, and legal frameworks struggle to cope.

Beyond the personal, sensors are making it possible to monitor and manage transport and other services at a city scale. For established cities, this is a retro-fit, adding sensing, networks, and data management, typically in a piecemeal fashion. However, in some countries with rapidly growing economies, whole cities are built from scratch with digital monitoring and control as part of their fundamental infrastructure. That is, at the scale of the built environment, the digital/physical divide is fundamentally bridged.

2.1.5 Nanotechnology and smart dust

Using Firefly technology (Box 2.1), a Christmas tree just a couple of metres tall might have 1,000 individual computers all networked together. In military and environmental sensing applications, large numbers of tiny sensing devices, often called 'smart dust', are distributed over an area to be monitored. Each individual device is dispensable, but together they create an image of the area as a whole.

Smaller again, one can imagine smart spray-paint that turns your wall into a display, while nano-machines are already being built with molecular-scale gears and motors. Blends between nano-machine and biotechnology are also being developed to allow the targeted delivery of drugs, in particular for cancer treatment. At these tiny scales the fundamental nature of the physical world starts to change: gravity becomes almost imperceptible, but surface tension turns damp surfaces into tar traps. Soon we will need to learn ways to understand and interact with technology so small it flows in our blood, or falls between the tufts of a carpet.

Box 2.1 Firefly—intelligent lights like fairy dust

Firefly is a technology that embeds tiny computers behind individual LEDs, effectively turning each LED into a single pixel networked computer [63, 164].

Conventional lights have to be carefully positioned, but the smart nature of Firefly means that each light can flash out its own unique identifier during a calibration stage. Cameras enable a three-dimensional (3D) model of the position of the lights to be built using triangulation. Lights can be freely wrapped around complex shapes such as a Christmas tree and still used to display precise messages or images.

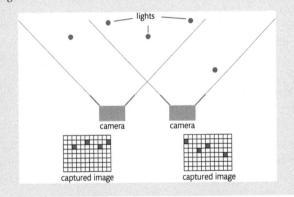

2.2 Technology at Our Fingertips

2.2.1 Tangible user interfaces (TUI)

In the mid-1990s it seemed as if everything was becoming digital: famously, academic and futurologist Nicholas Negroponte suggested that many things now made of atoms would become bits. However, at nearly the same time as this radical digitization vision was being popularized, a new member of Negroponte's MIT Media Lab was exploring a different concept, tangible bits, where computational structures took physical form [238].

Typically, tangible bits involved some form of physical token representing something in the digital world. Moving, positioning, rotating, or connecting these tokens would create corresponding digital effects, often taking advantage of the physical form of the token to suggest or constrain actions, and also often allowing two-handed or even multi-person interactions in a shared space. For example, in a town planning application one might have physical models of buildings and a map of a town on a tabletop screen. Moving the physical models would drive a traffic simulation, which would then show the simulated rush hour traffic on the screen beneath them.

Tokens are instrumented in various ways in order to track their position and orientation: some use a form of visual code often called a fiducial marker (details in Chapter 18), others a form of electronic tracking.

It is uncommon for there to be physical feedback as motors or other means to move physical objects tend to be more difficult to operate reliably. Instead, feedback is almost always in the form of some sort of projection. A notable and iconic exception is Durrell Bishop's 1992 marble answering machine [31], which we will discuss in Chapter 19.

2.2.2 Haptics and smart materials

Other forms of technology focus on physical feedback also known as 'haptic feedback'. Typically this may mean using some sort of motor to create resistance or physically push back against your own movements, or vibrating pads to give a sense that you have touched something. Haptic technology enables virtual reality applications that combine visual imagery with tactile sensation.

Simulators for keyhole brain surgery were an early example. Keyhole surgery is relatively straightforward to emulate visually, since it involves a camera, and the device used is some form of tube controlled by twisting and pushing, so sensors can easily be added to a mock-up to produce a realistic interactive visual experience. However, surgeons also use the resistance of tissue to help them work out whether they have cut far enough. Because the device was simple, it was possible to add small motors to generate realistic resistance, driven by models of the actual brain derived from scans.

More 'open air' virtual reality requires more complex devices. One method is to use special articulated gloves, powered to give a sense of physical resistance, a bit like putting your hand inside a robot hand. More recent developments use arrays of ultrasound speakers, which can be tuned so that their interference patterns produce peaks of low-frequency vibration at specific points in the air. This is similar to the effect you might see in a harbour where the small waves bouncing back and forth create little peaks in the open water. If these peaks in air vibration are set to be where your hand is, it feels as if there is something solid in the air [377]. The ultrasound can even be used to levitate small, light objects such as polystyrene balls [280].

Haptics is also used in more mundane technology. The BMW iDrive has a resistance motor added to its control knob. This gives the impression of small 'clicks', as you would get from a mechanical knob, but the number of click positions depends on the number of items in a menu. There are smartphones that utilize the vibration motor in the phone, which is normally used for silent ringing: as you move your finger over an onscreen button, the vibrator gives a little kick. Although the whole phone has moved, not the point where your finger is, your brain interprets this as the effect of your own movement and hence it feels as if the button is raised.

2.3 Up Close and Personal

2.3.1 Mobile and personal devices

There are more mobile phones than people in the world. As well as a phone, you may well carry with you a laptop or tablet, perhaps a camera or dedicated music player.

For the purposes of this book, this proliferation of devices raises three main issues.

First, they are with us all the time, they are personal. This means we often develop an attachment to them and they can be used to measure or monitor us. We'll return to wearable and physiological computing later in this section. In terms of the ontology introduced in the last chapter, which drives the structure of this book, they connect to the *body*.

Second, these are often physically small devices, with a large range of functionality, so there is a close interplay between the digital design of functionality and interface, and the physical design of the shape, placement of buttons, and so on. These are precisely issues we will return to in Part III of this book on *objects and things*.

Figure 2.1 BMW iDrive haptic controller

Third, mobile devices are often intimately connected with *space* and location. Although it may initially seem like a tautology, we can divide mobile applications into two classes: (i) those where location doesn't matter and (ii) those where it does [30]. The first of these is where the device removes the need to be in a specific place to perform an activity: we can send email *anywhere*, edit a file *anywhere*, or access the web *anywhere*. However, the other class is where the precise location is specifically what makes the application important: a map that guides us, a tourism app telling us about the statue in front of us, a review site telling us what people think about the restaurant we have just entered.

2.3.2 *Wearable computing and fashion*

Wearable technology includes smart jewellery, fitness sensing devices, and even smart clothing and fashion. Whereas a smartphone sits in your pocket or bag where it is separate though at hand, a smart watch is physically attached to your wrist.

You wear a device on your wrist because it is convenient to access and always present, just like a traditional wristwatch, in fact. However, being worn on the wrist immediately enables another use of the device: to measure your pulse or skin temperature. Of course smartphones also make use of the fact that they are normally carried on your person to measure aspects of you (e.g. physical activity from accelerometers), or your environment (Global Positioning System (GPS), compass), but being in contact with your skin and at a known position on your body means the wrist-worn device can measure more things about you, more accurately.

Those involved in sport, professional or amateur, may also wear semi-medical devices such as chest straps for more accurate heart rate, pedometers, or exercise measurement devices such as Fitbits. More and more of our physical bodily activity and function is being captured online and even shared with friends. This has the potential to enable future personalized medicine, but with consequential risks for privacy or intrusive demands about intimate details of your life from, say, an insurance company or potential employer.

Smart jewellery and clothes tend to focus on intimacy of a different kind, the sense of closeness and identity we invest in our appearance and the things we wear. Even those who claim not to care about what they wear often take a pride in the fact! Technology may be used as part of the construction of objects, for example spray-on fabric or 3D-printed jewellery. Products may use electronic elements as part of their aesthetics; for example, LEDs woven into hair braids, or electroluminescent or shape-changing fabric. The most sophisticated may combine sensing or interactive elements to create new kinds of bodily experience: for example, adjusting the colour of jewellery based on skin conductivity, or stroking an Internet-connected brooch to cause a whiff of scent on a partner's device, allowing loved ones to communicate intimately and surreptitiously.

2.3.3 Physiological computing

Some of the technologies we've already discussed measure aspects of the body such as heart rate, skin conductance, and gait. In physiological computing, the body is the computational device.

Medical devices may not only measure but also stimulate or control aspects of the body. Some of these deliberately do not give the person wearing them control over the device, for example devices that restart the heart if it enters an unhealthy rhythm. In contrast, assistive technologies usually try to enhance the person's control of their body or environment; for example prosthetics activated by small muscle movements or nerve impulses, or even just by thinking.

Physiological state and emotion are closely linked, so games and art have often used physiological sensors as part of designed experience. This includes various games based on heart rate or brain waves, but also more sophisticated gameplay strategies [188].

Many of the sensors used are intrusive. For example, the best electrocardiogram (ECG) devices to measure detailed heart activity need small patches to be stuck across the chest, and brain–computer interaction typically needs special electroencephalogram (EEG) skullcaps with gels to improve conductivity. However, this has been changing; for example the Kinect can measure heart rate from a distance, based on the changing colour of your skin. This non-intrusive technology has been deployed in experimental cars and aircraft cockpits in order to detect tiredness or lapses of attention.

However, there are also moves to embed technology more deeply into our bodies for non-medical reasons. Extreme 'transhuman' augmentations of the body through implantation of mechanisms and computing will be discussed in the next chapter but there have also been more prosaic uses with surprising levels of uptake. A number of nightclubs have offered regular customers the option to have a small chip, the size of a grain of rice, embedded near their shoulder. The chip can be read by the staff to admit entry and to pay for drinks so that the customers do not have to carry cash.

2.4 Blending Digital and Physical Worlds

2.4.1 Simulated reality

The modern digital computer was born out of the extreme needs of the Second World War, which involved two major uses. One was in cryptography, notably the work of Alan Turing at Bletchley Park breaking the Enigma code. The other was in ballistics, calculating the paths of shells: in other words, simulating limited aspects of the physical world.

Today we don't just simulate the path of a single artillery shell but the evolution of the whole cosmos from the Big Bang, global weather systems, or the complex twisting and folding of DNA. Indeed, computation is now so abundant, and so cheap, that mobile phone menus appear to 'roll on' for a while when moved, giving us the sense that they have weight and friction, and snooker apps send photo-realistic pixel balls bouncing between virtual cushions.

Computers are used not only to simulate physical objects but the behaviour of people, from emergency evacuation plans to characters in video games. Cognitive scientists will try to model aspects of a single mind in high fidelity, but many simulations use more simplistic models of people and their interactions, and though each may be relatively crude, together they have a massed behaviour that is sufficiently close to a human crowd.

2.4.2 Virtual reality

Some simulations, such as the 2D path of a missile, can be visualized easily on a flat screen or paper printout. However, for more complex 3D simulations, you would like to be able to 'get inside' the simulation, perhaps watching simulated air flows over an aircraft wing, or prodding and spinning a twisted protein molecule.

Virtual reality (VR) enables us to view such 3D objects and worlds, whether real or fictional, by creating visual, sometimes multi-sensory, experiences that allow us to become immersed as if we were really inside the VR.

Some virtual reality, such as first-person shooter games, uses desktop or other forms of screen; as long as the interaction is smooth enough, we can become lost in even a 30-centimetre view of a virtual world. Larger displays, such as CAVEs, where you are surrounded by full-height screens, can make the experience even more realistic.

However, the iconic image of VR is of a head enveloped in goggles, arms apparently blindly grasping empty air. Early VR used heavy displays, one for each eye, with their weight counterbalanced on complex expensive bespoke gantries. Now changes in display technology have brought down the cost and weight of products such as Oculus Rift and smartphone-based goggles so that they can be used by ordinary gamers as well as for professional uses such as walking through an architect's plan of a new building.

The effective design of VR requires a deep understanding of the way we as humans interact with the physical world, and correspondingly some of the failures of VR have helped us to develop that understanding. For example, one of the seminal early papers in VR showed that interactive responsiveness is far more critical than visual fidelity [326]. Even small delays in reacting to head movement rapidly lead both to loss of a sense of reality and to a form of sea sickness.

2.4.3 Augmented reality and mixed reality

While virtual reality tries to create a self-contained world, augmented reality (AR) technology overlays digital information or simulations on top of the physical world. Typically AR uses some form of semi-transparent glasses. You look at the real world through them, and they simultaneously display additional objects or information. For example, when you look at a person at a large meeting, the glasses might recognize the face and show the person's name and when you last met, displayed above their head.

Other forms of AR use portable displays such as tablets or smartphones. The camera on the device allows the screen to be a bit like a viewfinder, except that some of the things shown in the view are not 'really' there, as if the phone were acting as a magic glass revealing hidden objects or characters. An example of this, still popular as this book is being written, is Pokémon GO, which displays Pokémon characters in the real world. However, this technology can also be used for 'serious' applications, for example showing a reconstruction of an historical building when looking at the physical ruins.

In any augmented reality application the computer system must be able to recognize objects in the real world well enough to place the virtual objects and information appropriately in the image. This may require a form of orientation reference, such as the combination of GPS and compass to know where a phone camera is pointing. Alternatively, the real world may be identified using image recognition, sometimes aided by fiducial markers.

Mixed reality is similar, except that the digital reality is in various ways projected onto the physical world. In one example, an installation titled *Desert Rain*, the arts group Blast Theory used a veil of water as a projection surface so that the audience could literally walk into the projected image [32, 361]. A simpler example can be found at some airports: close to walkways the image of a person giving instructions is projected onto flat, human-sized and shaped frosted-glass panels.

2.5 Robots and Automation

2.5.1 Human–robot interaction

From Robby the Robot in *Forbidden Planet* to Asimov's Laws of Robotics and Ava in *Ex Machina*, robots have captured the imagination: sometimes amusing, sometimes enigmatic, often frightening. Most real robots are, at least at present, more down to earth, sometimes no more than an automated arm bolted to a factory production line. However, robots are beginning to find their way out of the pages of science fiction and off the factory floor into our homes, in the shape of autonomousvacuum cleaners and toy-like devices such as Sony AIBO and Philips iCat, discussed in the previous chapter.

While robots are in fixed locations in factories they are simply 'automation', but once they can move, or need to do flexible tasks alongside people, especially in the home, then they must be able to interact with humans. This may involve responding directly to commands, albeit rarely in the kinds of conversations beloved of science fiction. More importantly, perhaps, it requires a level of physical collaboration. As humans we are able to pass a flower to another person without a thought. That is well beyond current practical robotics, but one can imagine achievable goals such as a 'second pair of hands' that responds to small pushes and pulls to help you manoeuvre large objects.

A key issue is to work out what we would want robots to do. One project looked at assistive robots for older people. The researchers suggested a robot to clean the windows, but the people interviewed said, 'no', they would like a robot to carry the water and brushes to help them clean the windows themselves. Getting this right is particularly critical as appropriate assistive technology can allow people to remain independent longer in their homes.

One of the most surprising uses of robots, given their aggressive image in films, is as social companions. There is substantial effort taking place to make robots for practical assistance more human-like, simply because most houses and workplaces are structured for humans with two arms and two feet. In contrast, companion robots are usually more like animals. The core computational effort goes

Figure 2.2 Roomba autonomous vacuum cleaner

to make them emotionally and physically responsive, with appealing facial expressions or bodily movements.

While this social use of robots may seem frivolous, in fact it can bring important benefits. It is known that people with pets are healthier, even if the pets do not require physical exercise. Furthermore in a society where families and friends are dispersed, loneliness is a major problem, which companion robots may alleviate.

2.5.2 Not being there—telepresence robots

Remote-controlled toy cars and the Mars Rover allow you to operate at a distance. In simple cases such as the cheapest drones, you are there watching, effectively from the outside, but once the drone has a wireless camera you are virtually within it.

This form of remote-controlled robotic was originally developed for 'serious' applications including unmanned submarines repairing telecommunications cables, bomb disposal and rescue robots to go into situations too dangerous for a human, and military drones

Box 2.2 Artificial companions

In densely populated Japanese cities, it is hard to keep a pet. So interactive dolls and pet-like robots have been designed as companions for elderly people who look after them and often will not be parted from them, taking them out shopping or to see friends [16]. The most well-known example of this is Paro, a companion robot modelled after a baby harp seal, which has been extensively studied and is available as a commercial product [405].

While Paro has various patterns of movements, artificial companions do not need to move to be effective. Cathy Treadaway and other design researchers at Cardiff Metropolitan University ran a series of participative workshops with carers and experts to see how art and craft practice could enhance the life experiences of those suffering advanced dementia. This led to the design of HUG by LAUGH, a sensory device, somewhere between a baby and small animal, with long arms that naturally hug the wearer. It is designed to be cuddled and has a beating heart within its soft body. It can play music from a favourite playlist or audio files (stories, poetry, nature sounds) that can be easily personalized to suit the individual user [227, 398].

HUG by LAUGH (photo Cathy Treadaway)

designed to strike targets too difficult for humans to reach by other means. However, they are now used for leisure as well as less extreme functional applications such as monitoring crops.

There are other forms of telepresence robotics. Some of the social robots can be networked, for example so that actions on a robotic pet in one person's home can affect the behaviour of the robot pet of a friend or family member. Here the robot is helping to maintain human emotional connections at a distance. Telepresence robots can also be used to participate remotely in meetings or other forms of remote collaboration. Typically there is some sort of screen, set lollipop-style on top of a wheeled robot (see Figure 2.3), and this is controlled from a remote desktop interface with a camera and microphone, not unlike a Skype call. The screen shows the face of the remote participant and you can talk to the person through the robot, as if they were actually present, while they can see what the robot is 'seeing'.

In the near future remote tourism companies plan to let you fly a drone or operate a telepresence robot in exotic locations, perhaps exploring a Mayan temple from a sofa in Macclesfield.

Figure 2.3 Suitable Technologies Beam Telepresence

2.5.3 Robots you live in

In the United Kingdom, many people recall hiding behind the sofa as a child whenever the Daleks came on television in *Dr Who*. The Daleks initially appear to be robotic creatures, but are in fact a casing for radiation-withered creatures within. In a more benign example, Anne McCaffrey's The Ship who Sang series envisages a time when babies born physically deformed but mentally viable are given an alternative life as the brains of space ships, forever encased in metal, but feeling and acting in the world through the sensors and thrusters of the ship. HAL in '2001' and the Enterprise computer in 'Star Trek' are not identifiable 'robots'; rather, the space travellers are effectively within a computer-controlled ship: in other words, inside a robot.

Have you ever been inside a robot? Not scrunched up inside R2D2 on a film set but a real autonomous robot. The answer is almost certainly, 'yes'.

Outside the pages of science fiction, technologies similar to those used in independent robots are also used in assistive technologies to offer mobility and autonomy, and various forms of exoskeleton are beginning to move from the research lab to practical applications. In fact most of us have been within a Dalek-like outer skin as we drive a car, an experience that is itself becoming more robotic as existing automatic assistance, such as Anti-lock Braking System (ABS) braking, gives way to fully autonomous cars.

In the built environment, when you step into a lift you are effectively getting inside a robot and, while still far from the complexity of HAL or the Enterprise computer, current and close-to-market smart buildings and smart cities put you inside a place where much of the physical environment is digitally controlled.

2.6 Digital Fabrication and DIY Electronics

2.6.1 Digitized industry

Industrial automation dates back centuries. Indeed, the Jacquard loom inspired Babbage's Analytical Engine, and numerically controlled machines were commonplace long before digital technology flowed into the office and invaded personal products and household appliances. There are still discussions on whether computers will eventually replace the jobs of lawyers, artists, or computer programmers, but the impact on physical labour is evident. The seeds of this were sown in pre-digital days, when Adam Smith's division of labour and Taylorist time and motion studies effectively reduced people to biological robots, leaving just a small step to exchange muscle for metal.

The earliest automation, dating back to the Industrial Revolution, was often inflexible, relying on human operators to set up and monitor machines. Digital technology has, in part, simply replaced these human roles, for example monitoring the vibration of a drill bit to detect when it is likely to break and should be replaced. These predetermined processes led to mass production of uniform products compared to the variability of handcrafts.

However, numerical control also allowed the same machine, say a lathe or plasma cutter, to be programmed to create different products. This meant that production lines could rapidly swap between product lines by simply reprogramming the various machines. Instead of spending months installing new equipment, the factory could be reconfigured overnight and what once required physical reorganization could now be accomplished digitally.

Of course some industries have effectively been replaced by digital equivalents. The demise of Kodak is an iconic example of this, the production and developing of celluloid film replaced by bits on a silicon memory card. For others it is more that the logistics of producing the same or a similar physical product have changed: Ford's 'any colour so long as it is black' gives way to mass customization, and print-on-demand has both removed the need for large warehouses of books, and created new opportunities for self-publishing. Industrial-scale versions of 3D printing mean that automotive manufacturers can start to reimagine their spare parts logistics.

2.6.2 3D printing and digital fabrication

It is hard to have missed the revolution in 3D printing, from plastic toys to prosthetic limbs and even buildings. Industrial 3D printing has been available for many years, but reductions in the cost of both 3D printing and small laser cutters have transformed digital fabrication from industry to an often subversive do-it-yourself (DIY) culture. Arguably the defining point of this transformation was the development of MakerBot, not only a low-cost 3D printer but one that could be constructed almost entirely using low-cost digital fabrication.

Some 3D printers, including most professional-grade printers, work by depositing thin layers of a substrate and then selectively hardening areas of it. As the layers build up the hardened parts become a solid object, and when the printing is completed the unwanted, non-solid substrate is removed, leaving the object. For plastic objects, layers of liquid resin are selectively hardened with an ultra violet laser, while for metal objects fine layers of metal dust are deposited, and selected areas melted using a powerful laser. The resulting objects may be either used as prototypes or usable products. For example, metal printers can be used to create metal skull plates designed to fit perfectly using head scans, or to print a fully working gearbox for bespoke cars.

DIY-level printers work more like icing a cake by pushing small amounts of hot plastic through a nozzle on a digitally controlled arm. The new layers of plastic stick to the old, slowly building up a complete object. If there are several nozzle heads, multi-coloured objects can be made. This process can be used for any substance that can be extruded and then solidifies, and the same technique has been used to print food, objects with embedded electronic circuits, and human tissue. At a very large scale, crane-like machines pour concrete to '3D print' entire buildings.

2.6.3 DIY electronics and hacking

In parallel to DIY (do-it-yourself) physical fabrication, there has been a growth of DIY electronics. Just as MakerBot was the defining technology for 3D printing, the Arduino became the breakthrough electronics technology. There had been previous toolkits and development boards designed to make it easy to create smart devices, especially in the ubicomp area [198], but these had mainly been limited to research and education settings. Arduino captured the imagination more widely, particularly among artists.

There was already a long tradition of artists using computers, initially limited to obvious 'computer' outputs and and visuals. Over time, audiovisual installations, including reactive exhibits, became more common (see also the section on mixed reality above), but these were complex to produce, typically requiring collaborations with programmers.

Crucial to 'handing over' the technical expertise to artists was the growth of a number of development environments and coding methods targeted at the non-coder. In the music domain, MAX/MSP uses a wiring-diagram-style interface (building on the way musicians needed to plug physical devices together), and in the visual domain, Processing looks more like a conventional language, but with a faster path to results. In many ways these are not particularly simpler than conventional languages and environments, but because they are not branded as 'programming', they gained traction among a generation of artists and musicians who were already beginning to be digitally savvy.

Arduino and various follow-on technologies, from the Raspberry Pi to MakeyMakey and BBC micro:bit, built on this growing digital coding culture to allow physical sensors and control. With an Arduino, a small 'breadboard' and an instruction sheet, it is possible to create lights that flash or motors that move when you wave your hand over a proximity sensor or touch a contact.

The ability to create interaction beyond the keyboard and screen has opened up a hobbyist market from small robots to home automation. Lilypad, a washable and stitchable variant of Arduino, has made smart fashion accessible, connecting into a textile community where the handmade has long sat alongside mass fashion and haute couture.

2.6.4 Maker culture, from coding to crafting

The growth of DIY digital fabrication is due not simply to cost and availability, but to a culture and community. Universities and community organizations have created workshops with a range of machines including 3D printers, laser cutters, and plastic benders. Many are FabLabs, following a particular equipment list, so that designs fabricated on one can be shared with any. More generally a range of websites have grown up for sharing 3D printer files, or other forms of DIY technology plans.

Similarly the DIY electronics community has benefitted from sites that allow the sharing of code and web-based applications for developing, testing and critically 'modding' other people's code. These web environments often also sidestep the need to install development code onto your own computer, which has often been a daunting initial hurdle when using a new coding technology.

These new digital crafting communities join and in some cases overlap with traditional craft, where sharing experience and working together have long been part of normal practice. Physical working together continues to be important both in traditional craft (sewing bees and 'knit and natter' groups) and in the digital sphere with hackathons and maker meetings. However, these are supplemented with vast digital networks such as Ravelry for fibre communities, or Etsy for selling crafts.

The DIY communities that connect digital and physical design are not going to go away, but it is less clear whether this democratization of design will simply spawn a hobbyist industry, or whether it will have a more transformative effect on large-scale manufacture. The internal changes in spare-part logistics and mass customization are clearly going to happen, but for those buying products, this will have limited impact beyond possibly more product choice and faster and cheaper maintenance. It is less clear whether, like the music industry, we will see a radical reorganization and the emergence of 'digital artisans' such as the car mechanic who can simply download a file and print a spare part on demand, probably paying some small royalty. If this were to happen it would open the way for customization of basic appliances at the level of the local craftsperson, and possibly the emergence of app-like marketplaces where you construct the table lamp, phone, or washing machine from shareable and modifiable designs sent to your local 'print shop', or printed in your own garage.

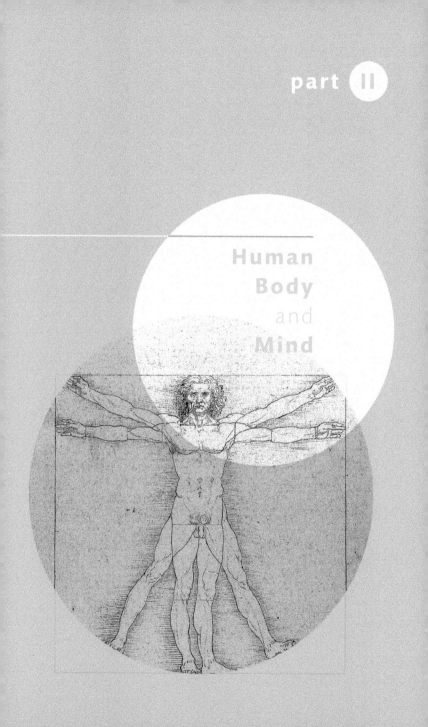

part II

Human
Body
and
Mind

Body

3.1 Body as a Physical Thing

Our bodies are clearly physical things, skin and bone, muscle and tendon. Some of our physiology can be understood in terms of the physics or engineering of the body. Muscles in our upper arms operate on the lower arms using pivots (joints) and levers. When we run fast our muscles need more oxygen, so we breathe faster and deeper in order to get more air and our heart beats faster to distribute oxygen.

We have limits on how far and fast we can go, how accurately we can point, how strongly we can grasp. Sometimes we do not notice the limits of our own bodies as we surround ourselves with chairs of the right height, steps that are not too steep, objects that we can lift (limited by health and safety regulations). However, if we step beyond the bounds of our constructed environment, to climb a mountain or swim in the sea, our limitations are brought sharply home to us. We work within them or perish. Even in the safe environment of our home it only takes a small muscle strain to realize how complicated everyday actions are, how many movements we make to accomplish the simplest task.

For the elderly, or those with physical disabilities, these complications are ever-present and often require special aids, from electric stairlifts to rubber cloths for opening jars. However, it is not only the elderly and infirm who use technology to go beyond the limits of their own bodies. When you drive a car, ride a lift, or even press the button on a TV remote, you are substituting mechanical, electrical, or digital means for simply walking. A forklift truck helps you to lift more, a mobile phone helps you talk over distance, and a spreadsheet helps with calculation.

> **Box 3.1** Assistive technology
>
> Assistive technology in the home has tended in the past to be relatively low-tech, but that is changing with automatic windows and doors operated by remote control, and sensors carried on the person or in the environment, triggering alarms for relatives or carers. For example, video cameras can be programmed to learn normal movement patterns and so detect unusual activity, perhaps after a fall.
>
> This technology is often installed with the promise of greater independence, especially important when most Western countries face an ageing population and potential 'demographic time bomb'. Allowing people to live longer in their own homes, or in specially designed independent living units, can improve quality of life and reduce demands on human services. However, the impact can often mean reduced face-to-face contact with real humans, and for those under the surveillance of motion detectors and under the glare of automatic lights, the very technologies intended to promote independence can seem more like intrusion.

Sometimes we can use the limitations of the body as an explicit resource in design. The sweetie jar is on a high shelf to put it out of reach of a small child, and the lids of medicine bottles are designed to make them difficult for a child to open. For adults too, physical limitations can enforce constraints: in a nuclear bunker the two 'firing' buttons are placed too far apart for a single person to press both. In a digital world, sometimes things are just too easy, anything can happen at the press of a single button. It is easy to do things and it is easy to do things wrong; as in the nuclear bunker, we can deliberately use physical constraints to prevent errors, for example using recessed buttons to prevent accidentally pressing them. Perhaps computer keyboards could use haptic technology and have more resistance placed on the 'delete' button when you have a whole document selected, compared with just a few words?

3.2 Size and Speed

The physical size of our body is crucial in determining how we can interact with the world. Birds can grip a wall and stand horizontal, but even the most practised trapeze artist, rock-climber, or skier could not hold their bodies horizontally using their ankles alone.

This is because as an animal gets smaller its weight gets smaller proportional to the cube of its height, and the distance of its body from the wall decreases with its leg length. Therefore the force needed to support it falls off as the height to the power of 4. So if you were half as high you would only need 1/16 of the force to hold your body horizontal, and if you were 1/3 of the height only 1/81 of the force. Of course, if you were smaller, your muscles would also be smaller, but the ability to exert force is determined by the cross-sectional area of the muscle, which falls with the square of your height. If you were 1/2 the size, your muscles could exert 1/4 of the force, or if you were 1/3 of the height, 1/9 of the force—you can see that the muscle force gets smaller much more slowly than the required force so that it gets easier and easier to support your body. This also means that bones can be smaller, and lighter, thus increasing the effect. So that bird, perhaps 1/20 of your size, finds it 400 times easier to hold itself horizontal than you do.

Our physical size also influences the speed we can move. Try this experiment. Stand up and raise one leg in the air. Hold the raised leg with the knee stiff and start to swing it back and forth—see how fast you can move it before you feel yourself losing balance. Now do the same again, but this time keep your knee loose so that your leg can 'flap' back and forth. Notice how much easier it is to move quickly when your knee can bend.

This, again, is basic physics. With your knee fixed your leg is a *simple pendulum*, like the pendulum in a grandfather clock, whereas when your leg can bend it is a *compound pendulum*: one pendulum (your upper leg) with another (the lower leg) joined on to it. Each pendulum has a *natural frequency*, the speed it would move back and forth if you didn't force it with your muscles but just let it flop. It turns out that a long, stiff, simple pendulum has a slower natural frequency than if it is divided into two halves as a compound pendulum. In general, it is easy to make a pendulum work at its natural frequency. Think of pushing a child on a swing: you time your pushes to coincide with the natural movement of the swing. However, one has to work harder to make a pendulum work faster or slower; try making that child swing back and forth slightly faster or slower than the swing wants you to. This is why we bend our legs as we run: the natural rhythms of this compound pendulum are faster than a straight leg.

Box 3.2 Just walk

The natural frequency of a simple pendulum is $2\pi\sqrt{(L/g)}$, where L is the length of the pendulum. For our legs, the weight is relatively evenly spread, with slightly more in the upper leg muscles. So the effective length to the centre of gravity is around 30 cm, giving a natural frequency of about a second.

So, the speed we can move our limbs, and hence the speed with which we walk and run, is directly related to the length of our legs (and indeed our torso and arms as they keep pace). Bridge designers have to take these natural rhythms into account and try to avoid bridges that bounce up and down with a frequency of near a second. This is also why soldiers break step when crossing bridges; all of them walking at the same speed could cause a bridge to build up a wave of motion.

The designers of the Millennium Bridge over the Thames in London forgot that while the up-and-down pace of normal walking is about 1 second, the side-to-side pace as we swap weight from one leg to the other is twice that, around 2 seconds, or a frequency of 0.5 Hz. Unfortunately the bridge had a side-to-side natural swaying frequency of precisely 0.5 Hz! This would not have been so bad if not for the fact that when we are on a swaying structure we tend to fall into step with it, to keep ourselves upright, so that those walking across the bridge became rather like a single line of marching soldiers [382, 243].

In order for us to walk at around 1 Hz, or one pace per second, our brains must be able to drive muscles at this kind of pace (and faster for running). This may well affect the way we can keep time. Orchestral conductors say that the slowest beat they can reliably keep is about 40 beats per minute; that is about the same frequency as a very slow walking pace. While we often think that we dance to music, it may well be that it is the other way round; our natural sense of rhythm has its origins in the length of a typical leg. We don't dance to music, we music to dance.

3.3 The Networked Body

At the other end of the spectrum, the fastest speed at which a highly practised person can tap their finger is around 10 beats per second, with most of us much slower. Try it with a stopwatch. To get faster rhythms a drummer will use two hands, or a pianist several fingers. Even our tongues can't move arbitrarily fast. Try counting out loud one to ten again and again as fast as you can. Can you get an average of much faster five or six counts per second? Here the limits are to do with the raw speed of muscles, not the combination of length and gravity in a pendulum. However, this is related to another set of physical processes in our bodies. When you want to move your hand, signals pass from your brain down your spinal column to the fifth to the eighth vertebrae, then along a nerve to the muscles in your arm. If you watch your hand you can see where it is, or if it touches something you can feel it touch. However, it also takes time for signals to pass from your eyes through several layers of nerves to your brain, or for the signals from the touch receptors in your hands to pass up to your brain. Altogether the round trip from sending the signal to seeing or feeling what happens takes around 150–200 milliseconds (ms).

These delays in your body are similar to those in a computer network and about the same as the round-trip time taken by Internet signals when you are accessing a website in your own country (intercontinental times are more like 150–200 ms in each direction). Although 200 ms sounds fast, your arms can move a long distance in that time, and a fast tennis ball, baseball, or cricket ball would move 8 metres. Because of this, skilled sports players work predictively, their

Box 3.3 How quick are you?

You can measure for yourself the round-trip time from eyes to muscles. Take a sheet of paper (A4 or US letter). Hold the paper at the top, and ask a friend to put their fingers close to the bottom of the sheet and be ready to catch the paper when it falls. Then let go. Mark on the paper where they caught it. Do this several times, each time they will catch it a slightly different place.

The average distance between the bottom of the paper and where they catch it tells you the total reaction time, from seeing the paper move, to actually moving their fingers. You can work this out using the speed of fall ($1/2 \, g \, t^2$):

reaction time	distance fallen
100 milliseconds (ms)	5 cm
150 ms	11.25 cm
200 ms	20 cm
250 ms	31.25 cm

If your friend is very canny, they may notice your fingers start to move just before they open, so you may need to cover your hand with a second piece of paper.

As an alternative test, have them keep their eyes closed but start with the paper touching one of their fingers so they can feel it begin to fall. Are they faster or slower to catch it?

Then try doing a countdown: say out loud 'three, two, one', and then drop the paper. See how much faster they are when they can time their movement to coincide with yours, rather than waiting to see the paper fall.

brains working out where the ball will be when it is close to them and then 'telling' their arms where to move to meet the ball when it comes—there is simply not enough time to see the ball coming when it is close.

3.4 Adapting IT to the Body

The importance of understanding the human body in interacting with technology pre-dates digital technology. The field of ergonomics can be traced back to the mid-nineteenth century or even Ancient Greece [241, 276], but the modern academic field developed in the twentieth century especially during the Second World War. Ergonomics originally focused on the body and physical movement: the appropriate height of a desk or a kitchen worktop, and the layout of controls in a car are all in the purview of the ergonomist, and we are used to seeing products advertised with 'ergonomically designed' handles or controls. However, by the early 1980s a sub-area of 'cognitive ergonomics' had formed, including cognitive issues alongside the physical body.

Effective ergonomic design is important for comfort and enjoyment—we all know the feeling after sitting in an uncomfortable seat during a long meeting. However, more important are the implications for health and safety. For a pregnant woman or someone with back problems, poor posture is not simply a matter of comfort (Figure 3.1). If you are reaching a long way to access the HiFi controls on a car, you may not steer a straight course or be as fast to react. For regular computer users Repetitive Strain Injury (RSI) has become endemic and this has spawned a whole range of special 'ergonomic' keyboards, although the increasing use of laptops has made it more difficult to obtain the optimal screen and keyboard configurations.

While ergonomics was one of the foundation disciplines of human–computer interaction, it is perhaps less evident in recent years, when aesthetics of design often dominate over fit to the human body. For example, the older curvy Apple laptops had a trackpad in front of the keyboard with the 'mouse button' on the front edge of the computer. On later laptops, however, the button was

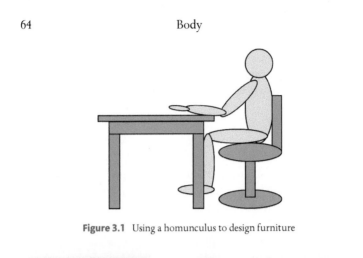

Figure 3.1 Using a homunculus to design furniture

Figure 3.2 Stone-like shape moulded in clay naturally fits the hand; then transformed from clay to computer-aided design (CAD) and from CAD to 3D printed resin.

moved next to the trackpad and on the top; later still it was integrated *into* the trackpad. The older design allowed the thumb to be used to squeeze the button in a natural grasping action, whereas the later designs required the thumb to press sideways and outwards, a very unnatural action. Furthermore, to avoid the thumb touching the trackpad the arm has to be held with the elbow twisted away from the body.

On the positive side, effective placement and shaping of controls can make physical tasks effortless and easy to learn. In an experiment Jo used different design tools to create several designs to the same brief [141]. One of the designs started out using hand-moulded clay (Figure 3.2) and ended up rather like a small pebble with a depression on one side. When you pick up the 'pebble' it naturally falls into the right direction in your hand, without the need for instructions.

3.5 The Body as Interface

Archaeologists often try to understand a society from its material remains; in this vein, more than 20 years ago Bill Buxton imagined what a visitor from another planet would infer about the human species from the evidence of a standard graphical user interface. There would of course be a single large eye (single because a normal screen does not require binocular vision), a single hand for moving the mouse and a single finger (for the Mac), or perhaps two fingers for pressing mouse buttons. There would be other fingers for typing (although most of us manage with three) and a rather limited ear for hearing the odd beep. In contrast, most musical instruments use a nearly full range of fingers, and in the case of the organ and drum kit, also two feet.

Buxton was early in advocating the use of both hands (and sometimes other limbs) for input, but in recent years multi-finger and multi-hand interaction has started to become mainstream. The iPhone and similar devices use two-finger gestures to shift, stretch, and scroll content, and large displays such as Microsoft Surface can use fingers on both hands, or indeed several people's hands.

Touch-based devices have a natural scale determined by the size of the human body: hand contact limits one to stretches of around a metre or yard from the body for horizontal surfaces, and a little more (allowing for knee bends and arms stretching) for vertical ones. Larger displays require physical movement along the display, or some form of indirect interaction.

Effectively any display has a natural distance for viewing so that it does not take too wide or too narrow a viewing angle, typically between 20 and 45 degrees (Figure 3.3). Too wide means you have to move your head excessively with, if the display is flat, a very oblique viewing angle. Too narrow means only limited information can be displayed. There are exceptions, a wrist watch has a small display

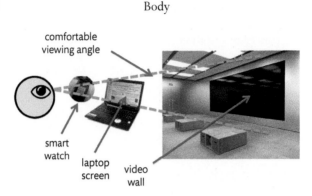

Figure 3.3 Comfortable viewing angle—closer devices can be smaller

because it has to fit on your arm and correspondingly has limited display resolution. At the other extreme a virtual reality CAVE can produce 180 to 360 degree panoramas, although you need to look around to see it all fully, as peripheral vision is far less detailed than central vision.

The combination of distance and angle creates a rhomboidal space, usually from one to three screen widths wide, within which it is sensible to view the display (more details in Chapter 14). If the distance to the display is too large, interaction will normally need some sort of remote control device, for example the TV control at home or the long sticks used to move aircraft across maps in Second World War Air Force control rooms (Figure 3.4). The size of the area also determines how many people can see a display at the same time.

The body is not just used for touching and seeing. In gesture-based interfaces, cameras track the position of arms and hands so that one can make gestures to control a computer system, either alone or in combination with voice commands: 'put that there (*points*)'. Gestures can also be tracked using devices we hold, for example the Wiimote and phones with accelerometers.

Global Positioning System (GPS) enabled devices and instrumented public spaces allow a level of interaction that is governed by the movement of your body through space. With a Google map on a fixed PC you navigate through the map by using zoom and pan

Figure 3.4 The Operations Room at RAF Fighter Command's No.
10 Group Headquarters, Rudloe Manor (RAF Box), Wiltshire, showing WAAF
plotters and duty officers at work, 1943. Imperial War Museums (image CH 11887)

controls, but with a SatNav the navigation on the map is driven (literally) by the motion of the car. Proximity-based technologies, such as Bluetooth, WiFi, mobile phone cell, or NFC readers, also offer ways to create interaction that is either modified by the context or triggered by it (e.g. location specific adverts). This kind of system has clear uses in tourist guides and is also finding applications in various forms of games.

Although not very 'interactive', biometrics are another way in which the body is used as part of technological interactions but for authentication rather than control. Such interactions all depend, to some extent, on the large range of individual differences between people, physical features like a fingerprint or iris scan, and skills or habits like a signature. To be useful the feature needs to be (i) different enough between people and (ii) stable enough over time that the same person can be reliably recognized. What counts as 'enough' depends on the situation, and depends critically on whether one is seeking (i) to verify someone is who they say they are, or (ii) to locate someone or identify who they are, based on the feature.

These issues have become critical in several cases where DNA evidence is used in court. If a DNA 'fingerprint' is unique to one person in a million, then matching the DNA found at the crime scene with a known suspect is ample evidence. However, the UK police database contains over 5 million samples [222]. Matching against this would be likely to find a match by random chance and might result in a few people to check, but would certainly not be strong evidence.

Likewise, the 'stable enough over time' criterion also depends on context. For example, US border controls use biometrics to match the entry and exit points of those who visit the country; this only requires stability over weeks or months. However, stability of features over many years is essential for the use of biometric identity cards, whether or not one regards that as desirable anyway.

3.6 As Carrier of IT—The Regular Cyborg

For many years some researchers in wearable computing, Steve Mann being a notable example, have conducted their daily lives with cameras strapped to their heads, screens set in eye glasses, or computers in backpacks (Figure 3.5). Over time, the technology has become smaller and more discreet, but for most observers there is still something odd about these 'cyborgs', who so intimately tether technology to their bodies. This disquiet was famously expressed during the alleged altercation between Mann and McDonalds staff when Mann refused to remove his digital eye glass in a Paris restaurant [275, 197].

But is it so unusual?

In the introduction we asked how many computers are in your house? You might also ask, how many computers on your body? Empty your pockets, bag, or whatever you carry with you normally. Count the computers. You will probably have a mobile phone, USB (Universal Serial Bus) memory stick, or maybe a smart watch. If you carry a separate camera it too will have computers even if it is a film camera; a car key with remote locking has a computer

Steve Mann: Evolution of Wearable Computing + Augmediated Reality in everday life

1980 | 1995 passport | 1999 | 2004 with firstborn child

Figure 3.5 Steve Mann—three decades of early cyborg research

to generate unique changing key sequences. Reach into your wallet and you will find smart chips and a magnetic stripe on each card. You may even have a hearing aid in your ear, or if you have heart problems a computer inside you, in a pacemaker. How many computers?

We are all cyborgs.

Box 3.4 The riddle of the Sphinx

The Sphinx asked passing travellers, 'What creature walks on four legs in the morning, two legs at noon, and three legs in the evening, but is weakest when it has most legs'. Oedipus replies that the answer is a man, who crawls on all fours as an infant, two legs as an adult, and needs a walking stick when old.

The use of physical prostheses is, of course, not new; walking sticks have probably been around as long as people, and the first use of splints dates back to the fifth Egyptian Dynasty nearly 5,000 years ago [23]. The core difference is that the new technologies are mainly information prostheses, helping us to think or communicate better. However, the two have been coming together with increasingly sophisticated medical prosthetics that use digital technology to sample tiny muscle movements or nerve signals and use these to control robotic limbs.

In gaming, head-mounted displays in eye glasses are becoming common. For 'serious' mobile computing these offer the potential to create virtual screens far larger than can be accommodated on a phone. These displays can now be almost indistinguishable from ordinary glasses. However, discreet cyborg technology can have its own problems.

Some years ago Jennifer Sheridan studied users of wearable technology at Georgia Tech. Because the display in the eye glass was only visible to the cyborg, the cyborg could be talking face-to-face with someone while simultaneously browsing web pages, reading email, or even carrying out a parallel instant messaging conversation. Sometimes this was simply rudeness, but often the virtual interactions were connected in some way to the face-to-face dialogue, just as one might look up a web page about a topic while talking to a friend. Sheridan found that the cyborgs had developed various ways to manage potential conflicts. They might say something like 'hold on while I check that' before focusing on the web page or email. One cyborg had his head-mounted display arranged so that he had to look upwards at the 'screen', so it was obvious when he was not 'there' in the conversation as his eyes gazed heavenward.

Sheridan became interested in these three-way interactions and as an exploration she and technology art group .:thePooch:. developed a performance, 'the schizophrenic cyborg', at an arts event [364]. 'Normal' cyborgs are in the centre and in control of the three-way interactions, but the schizophrenic cyborg shattered this control. He wore a small display strapped to his waist and wandered round the exhibits at the event. Another performer, hidden up in a high gallery, provided the content of the display. The hidden performer could see from a distance but not hear what was going on. The hidden performer would display inviting comments, like 'hug me', 'I'm lonely', or make comments—'you in the red dress'.

When people came to talk to the cyborg they would not at first believe that it was not the cyborg himself controlling the display, and even when they did accept that it was a third person, they still interacted in ways that did not fully take into account the distinction. Some began to ignore the cyborg wearing the display and focus on the screen instead. We normally expect a single area of space to hold just one person. The participants were faced with a single space that in a sense 'held' two people, the cyborg himself and the hidden performer. In self-reports later, the cyborg repeatedly used language that alternated between first- and third-person accounts of himself, suggesting that it was equally confusing to experience someone else apparently occupying the same space as oneself.

On an even more intimate level, while people with a pacemaker or internal insulin pump have these implanted for medical reasons and would undoubtedly choose to have them removed were it medically safe to do so, there are those who choose to have computers permanently implanted in their bodies.

Various artists, notably Stelarc, an Australian performance artist, have explored the relationships between technology and the body: ingesting devices, strapping them to their bodies or in various ways insinuating metal into flesh. In one performance Stelarc had electrodes strapped to his skin so that they stimulated the muscles of his arm [380]. Measurements of network activity were used to drive the electrodes, so that people could use computers across the Internet to make his arm jerk and move without his control.

Kevin Warwick, Professor of Cybernetics at the University of Reading, believes that the embedding of digital technology into our bodies is a next inevitable step, and that before long we will all do this through choice [412]. Putting this into action, he has had various implants including one that linked nerves in his arm to those of his wife. While he was away on an overseas trip they could feel each other's movements (but only when the device was turned on).

It may seem unlikely that people would willing do this outside an academic experiment, but in fact it is already happening. In Glasgow, Barcelona, and Rotterdam, nightclub goers can have a small chip implanted that allows them to enter quickly and to pay for drinks without having to carry money [278]. Compared to this, Steve Mann's cyborg technology begins to look mundane!

Mind

4.1 Mind as a Physical Thing

Our brains are also physical, apparently inert grey goo, yet full of electrochemical activity running through networked neurons and flooded with neurotransmitters. Three different kinds of physical process working together: electrical, structural (connectivity), and chemical.

In the nineteenth century, many believed that one could tell a person's character and skills through the shape of the skull, reading 'bumps'. This study of 'phrenology' did make sense: if the brain is the seat of character and intellect, and if some parts of your brain are bigger then normal, then surely this should be able to tell you about the person (Figure 4.1). In fact, we now know that even gross measurements do not correlate well with specific abilities. For example, the total volume of the brain typically varies between individuals by up to 50%, but there is no connection between this and intelligence.

However, while the raw size of parts of the brain is not related to specific traits or abilities, the physical parts of the brain do perform different jobs; there is functional separation. This was first discovered through accidents involving traumatic injuries to parts of the brain, or through tumours that affected specific parts of the brain. Nowadays the locations of these would be determined by X-rays or brain scans, but in the early days doctors often had to wait for the patients to die to study the brain during an autopsy.

Brain surgeons now use this knowledge to avoid damaging areas associated with critical functions such as Broca's area and Wernicke's area, which are essential for different aspects of language. However, the same surgery has also offered fresh knowledge. While the broad

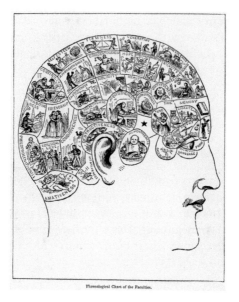

Phrenological Chart of the Faculties.

Figure 4.1 Phrenology—early attempts to understand the brain

structures of the brain are roughly similar between individuals, the details vary, and in order to determine precisely the limits of critical areas surgeons will often use a probe to administer tiny electrical impulses to different parts of the exposed brain. The patients, still awake despite having part of their skull removed, perform simple tasks. If the impulse disrupts the task, this tells the surgeon which areas to avoid, and in the process reveals more about the fine structure of the brain. For example, stimulating an area may trigger a particular memory of an experience.

Modern brain scanning has allowed scientists to study the patterns of activity of the brain less invasively. In one example, which reveals the rich nature of imagination, subjects are placed in a brain scanner and then shown a picture. The scanner shows the parts of their brain that are active in response, including the visual system and the other parts connected with the interpretation of the picture. Then the picture is removed and the subjects are asked to *imagine* the picture. A few new parts light up, but there is much in common with the pattern when seeing the actual picture. In particular, parts of the visual cortex light up—the imagining of the picture stimulates parts of the sensory system in a similar way to actually seeing it.

4.2 Memory and Time

If we consider memory we see the importance of all three forms of brain physicality: electrical, connective, and chemical [245]:

- *short-term memory*—Our fleeting thoughts are carried electrically, ionic discharges across synapses transferring information from neuron to neuron, as is measured through electroencephalogram (EEG) monitoring. This is the basis of all our immediate perception, and also short-term memory with its $7+/-2$ chunks of information [292].
- *long-term memory*—In contrast, long-term memory is normally assumed to be stored in the physical connections between neurons and the strength of these connections. This storage literally grows. Even the strength is determined by the size of the synapse.
- *mezzanine memory*—There are things that lie between short-term and long-term memory: the general sense of where I am and what I am doing, and the memories of what I have been doing over recent minutes and hours that have not had time to 'grow' long-term memory and yet last longer than the effervescence of short-term electrical activity. This is less well studied in the psychological literature except for work in situation awareness [152] and 'long-term working memory' in studies of reading comprehension [155]. Indeed there is no name for this medium-term memory, and the name 'mezzanine memory' is Alan's own. It seems likely that this form of memory is stored using chemical build-up with neurons, a process known as 'long term potentiation'. [74, 266]

Chemicals in the form of neurotransmitters are also constantly produced in our brains, and hormones flood through our bodies. Some of these chemical processes are quite fast, in the order of seconds, but some, especially those in our bloodstream, may take many minutes to return to their normal state—think how long you feel 'jumpy' after a scare. Adrenaline and other chemicals flood through your body and do not disappear equally fast once you realize there is no danger.

While not part of our explicit memory systems, these chemicals act as a slowly decaying trace of past feelings and activity. In particular, many of these relatively slow-acting chemicals are critical to mood and emotion, and this has its impact on digital design.

Imagine visiting a friend who is about to have a party, then moving on to another who has lost a parent. We adapt and react differently to each, but in between our bodies have had time to 'reset' the chemicals that influence mood.

Now imagine the same scenario but using instant messaging chat windows. On one side of the screen, planning a party; on the other, a funeral. While the electrical parts of our brains may be able to adapt rapidly between situations, the chemical parts cannot.

Box 4.1 Miller's 7+/−2

Look at the following number: 4216. Hide it and try to write it down. That wasn't hard was it?

  Here's another: 286657. How was that? Maybe a little more tough.

  OK, now try this number: 919188467508

Unless you have unusually good memory you won't manage this at all. In one of the most widely cited psychology papers ever, 'The Magical Number Seven, Plus or Minus Two: Some Limits on Our Capacity for Processing Information', George Miller reported on experiments with subjects remembering lists of words, numbers, and letters, and found that the maximum was round about seven items [292].

  Crucially, it is 'chunks' we remember, so six words such as 'banana phone tree wheel curtain pan' is not significantly more difficult than six letters 'b p t w c p'. This can sometimes be used as a memory aid; for example you might find the sequence of six two-digit pairs easier to remember than the original twelve-digit number: '91 91 88 46 75 08'. Maybe some will be significant years, or you'll notice the first two digits repeating.

4.3 Just Numbers

Because long-term memory is stored physically in the connections between neurons, it is possible to calculate just how much a single brain can remember [113]. We have approximately 10 billion neurons and each neuron connects to between 1000 and 10,000 other neurons, giving around 100 trillion connections. It is this pattern of connections that is normally assumed to encode our memories. Each of these neurons also has a strength of connectivity given by the size of the synapse.

Now imagine a brain scanner in the far-off future that can trace each neuron, including how strong they are. As it reads the neurons it gives each one a number (needing about 34 bits) and records the connections and strength using a scale of 0 to 63. Together these require 5 bytes per connection. So with 100 trillion connections, our scanner of the future would need 500 trillion bytes, or half a petabyte, or approximately 500 hard disks, to store the neuron connectivity of a single human brain. Oddly, when the Internet Archive was set up in 1996, the dump of the web was about the same size [113].

You can do a similar calculation for the speed of processing, to see how fast a computer would need to be to simulate the brain running in real time. The figure turns out to be about 10 petaflops, that is 10 thousand million million calculations per second. Sounds a lot, but yes, you guessed, if you add up the processing power of all the PCs connected to the Internet, it is about the same.

So in storage capacity and processing power the Internet is roughly similar to a single human brain!

However, although the raw numbers are roughly similar, the web is not really like a brain (and the brain is not like the web). Our brains are relatively slow (around 100 'cycles' per second), but very highly parallel — lots of things happen at once. Each PC works much faster, several billion cycles per second, but serially, one thing at a time (although a 100 million PCs on the web is quite a lot of parallelism in itself!). Furthermore, the brain has a lot of non-local connections, that is neurons in one part of the brain talk to neurons in distant parts. This would make it very hard to actually emulate a brain on all those PCs, as the Internet in between would both be too slow and buckle under the load.

Does the idea of simulating a brain worry you? It is possible to simulate fluid flows, so one could model a glass of water, but running the computer simulation of the glass of water would not make you less thirsty any more than looking at a painting of a mountain stream.

The difference between simulating water and simulating our brains is that some would say that our thoughts, minds, consciousness, indeed who we are, reduces to the memory patterns and 'execution' of the brain functions. In other words, a computer emulating your brain is 'just the same' as you thinking it in your head.

Of course, these are things hotly contested in the philosophy of consciousness, with some arguing that the special nature of neurons makes a difference [352]. Roger Penrose even argues that it is the quantum effects of sub-cellular microtubules that allow us to think in ways that are not computable and therefore not able to emulated by a computer (except perhaps in a quantum computer) [327].

When we discuss 'mind and body' we shall see a different view that places the human body as a crucial part of the picture, and some argue that no emulation of the mind could be truly a mind without being connected to a living, acting body.

4.4 Multiple Intelligences

We will discuss the particular ways in which we think about objects and about space later in this book, but it is interesting to note that there are specific ways in which we think about objects that are not the same as the way we think about space, and different again from the way we think about other people. We pick up objects, move them around, and expect that they may be moved by others or natural forces. In contrast, with space, buildings, and the topography of hills and mountains, we are thinking about moving ourselves around and within them.

To some extent these can be seen as workings of the same sort of reasoning applied to different kinds of situation and indeed this is certainly the case for more logical thinking. However, there is strong evidence that we also have quite specialized ways of thinking about different aspects of the world, sometimes called 'multiple intelligences' [174, 175]. Some evidence for this comes from brain science, which shows there are specialized areas of the brain related to particular aspects of perceiving, thinking, and acting (to the extent that these are separate), and some evidence from experimental studies which show that effectively identical problems are solved differently if presented in ways which appeal to our different 'intelligences'.

Imagine a pack of cards, each with a letter on one side and a number on the other. Four cards are selected and placed on a table like this:

You now need to verify whether the following rule is true of the four cards:

> if there is a vowel on one side then there is an even number on the other

Which cards do you need to turn over to verify the rule?

This puzzle is called the Wason card test [413] and variants of it have been used heavily in psychological experiments.

In fact, about three-quarters of people get the answer wrong. The most common answer given is the 'E' and '2', but the 'correct' answer is actually the 'E' and '7'. The reason for the 'incorrect' answers is that we have a tendency to look for 'confirming' evidence, so we look at the back of the '2', even though if it were not a vowel it would not invalidate the rule. We also focus on the cards most similar to concepts mentioned in the question, namely the vowel and the even number. In the real world, full of irrelevant information, these are sensible heuristics, but they do not work so well for artificial logic problems like this one.

Now consider a different problem. A newspaper stand has an 'honesty box' in which to put your money when you take a newspaper. A social psychologist watches people walking by. For each person the researcher writes on a small card. On one side she writes whether the person paid any money, on the other whether they took a newspaper. She even records a card for people who simply walk past.

Four of these cards are placed on the table:

You now need to verify whether the following rule is true of the four cards:

if the person takes a newspaper then they have paid money

Just as in the Wason card test, your task is to turn over as few cards as possible to verify the rule. Which cards do you turn over?

The problem is formally the same as the normal Wason card test, just substitute 'newspaper' for vowel, 'money' for even number. However, this time about three-quarters of people get the right answer. The explanation given for this is that this variant recruits knowledge about fairness and cheating and so is able to tap into our social intelligence, rather than abstract logic.

Some 'evolutionary psychologists' talk about our brains being not so much a general-purpose tool (like a survivalist's machete), but more like a Swiss Army Knife, with specialist tools to tackle special tasks (Figure 4.2) [76, 397].

In *The Prehistory of the Mind* [294] Steven Mithen argues that one of the crucial human developments has been the integration of these different intelligences, which in other animals, including early hominids, are distinct and unable to 'communicate' with one another. In other words the defining human cognitive accomplishment is joined-up thinking!

Mithen's analysis is not merely speculative but based on detailed analysis of the palaeontological record. Early hominids over a million years ago were able to shape flint tools, showing advanced forethought. Indeed even chimpanzees do this in the wild, selecting sticks of an appropriate size and shape, stripping them of leaves, and

Figure 4.2 Is the brain like a Swiss Army Knife—special parts for special purposes?

breaking them to length so that they can later be used to dig out termites. Tool-making itself is complex but not uniquely human. However, it was not until 60,000 to 70,000 years ago that modern Homo Sapiens tied flint heads to wooden handles to make better axes or spears. This is seen as evidence that wooden sticks (previously living things) could now be thought about together with physical (non-living) stones.

Similarly it is only recently that we see the emergence of cave art and the making of clay or stone objects to represent animals or people. The representation of an animate thing (creature or human) using an inanimate medium (clay, stone or paint) again shows evidence of joined-up thinking.

To describe the cognitive architecture of the mind, Mithen uses the metaphor of a cathedral with (in order of evolutionary development) a nave of 'general intelligence', several chapels for the specialized intelligences, and a 'super chapel' of meta-representation where the differing intelligences can intermingle with each other leading to 'cognitive fluidity'. The form of this meta-representation is not elaborated, although Mithen suggests it is in some way related to language, and this accords with the social changes occurring at around the same period, 50,000–60,000 BC, which are also often attributed to language development, a sort of socio-linguistic Eden.

Indeed the most obvious meeting point of different kinds of intelligence is in rational logical thought mediated by language. Words by their nature make things equal. While very different in meaning, 'stone', 'spider', 'speed', 'society', and 'science' are all 'just' words, tokens that can be put inside similar constructions. We can reason equally with all, and can mix them together, leading to a level of integration across intelligences (Figure 4.3).

However, as you may have guessed, with our focus on physicality that is not the end of the story.

Simpler creatures than ourselves, such as dogs, birds, and fish, do not lead fragmented existences but are integrated because they live in the world. When we act based on a single kind of intelligence, the *results of the actions* are available to all of our modes of thinking, not just the one where they originated. If you want to go to see a colleague (social intelligence) and they are in the next room, you may start to walk towards them, but the fact that a wall is in the way will immediately be obvious to your spatial understanding (and if you do walk

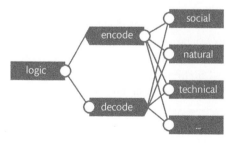

Figure 4.3 Logic as the focus

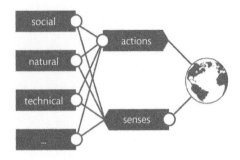

Figure 4.4 The world kicks back

forward the actual presence of the wall will make it even more obvious). Things do not need to be linked in the head because they are linked in the world (Figure. 4.4).

However, while we do not always need to link forms of thinking in our heads of course we often do, but apparently without lots of intense logical thinking. Partly this is due to imagination. As soon as you consider going to see your colleague next door an image of going starts to form. However, recall that imagination works its way right back into the sensory system, so it is almost as if you are actually seeing it, and this is available to your spatial intelligence just as with the real world. The physical intelligence says 'no' without you ever getting up from your chair. The 'virtual world' in your head kicks back just as hard as the real world (Figure 4.5).

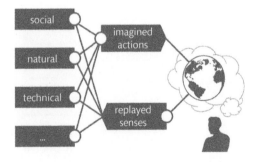

Figure 4.5 Imagination like the world

4.5 The Brain as Interface

Most of our interactions with computers use our limbs, or maybe our voice, for input to control the computer, and sight, hearing, or occasionally touch to get feedback from the computer. However, there are a number of technologies that more directly connect computer to brain, bypassing our voluntary body movements and our normal senses.

We have already seen one example of this, the implants into Kevin Warwick's arm nerves that enabled him to control devices and directly connect to his wife. It is normal to use these nerves to control muscle movement and bodily feelings. So in a way this *is* bodily interaction—just bypassing the actual body!

With different technology one can even bypass the nerves and tap directly into the brain. This is often called 'brain–computer interaction'.

We have discussed how different parts of the brain perform different functions. Brain scanners can reveal this but are a little large for use in computer interfaces. However, simpler EEG equipment can be used instead. EEG (electroencephalography) is used for medical diagnosis and involves placing large numbers of electrodes on the skull and measuring the electrical activity induced in the scalp by the corresponding activity within the brain due to the firing of neurons. Clinical apparatus may involve many dozens of electrodes, but in computer interaction research useful information can also be obtained using just a small number, often fitted into a skullcap.

For many years EEG has been used in simple bio-feedback equipment, perhaps playing a different tone or projecting colours. In particular it is often used together with the detection of particular frequencies of activity (alpha and beta waves) associated with states of alertness or relaxation. While we do not normally have conscious control over these states of the brain, once they are made visible or audible in some way, subjects can often learn to influence them.

Bio-feedback is more about allowing the user to monitor their own body. However, if the outputs of EEG equipment are put into a machine learning algorithm, it is possible for the computer to recognize some of the user's 'thoughts', though only from a small pre-chosen set. For example, there has been some success using apparatus of this kind to control an onscreen pointer by having subjects simply think about moving it one way or another. The recognition rate is still relatively poor so this is not currently an option for day-to-day computing. For those patients with severe disabilities, particularly those with 'locked-in syndrome', both non-invasive use of EEG (or similar apparatus) and direct brain implants offer a chance to be able to communicate with the world.

There has also been some limited success in work with brain implants for visual impairment. Visual images are transferred from the retina to some parts of the visual cortex in a fairly direct way: there is something like (but not exactly like) a little image of the scene that you can see in front of you in the visual cortex. By working the other way round, brain implants that stimulate the visual cortex appear as points of light.

Less invasive means can be used for more everyday interactions, especially in affective gaming, that is games that respond in some way to the user's emotional state. Most of these make use of heartbeat, or GSR (Galvanic Skin Response—basically sweating as used in lie detectors). Both are related to the general level of arousal of the body, and so can be used as a rough measure of emotion. The most common form of game is 'relax to win', as you become more relaxed you get more speed or energy. This may be combined with social situations in which your friends try to make you less relaxed!

These physiological measures tell you how strong an emotion is, but not whether the person is very happy, or very angry, nor do they detect subtle emotions such as apprehension. Typically, more detailed emotion detection needs to use facial expression or tone of voice, both of which are more complex yet still only deliver a fairly small palette of emotions. Kiel Gilleade's research has tried to bridge this gap by using the fact that as humans we are successful (when we are!) at detecting other people's emotions, because we also know the context [188]. In games one has a lot of information about the context, as it is a simulated world, and hence it is possible to make some inferences even from simple physiological measures.

The trouble with attempting to ascertain brain state from body state is that the body is affected by many things as well as what you are thinking and feeling. A researcher at Bristol University, Cliff Randell, designed a small camera that he wore connected to a heart-rate monitor. He reasoned that the important events one might want to record would be marked by periods of heightened emotion, so a camera was triggered to take a photograph when his heart rate peaked. The technology worked in the lab, but when he wore it elsewhere he found the photos were full of the tops of flights of stairs.

While the lacuna between pure mind and computation remains, it is perhaps not as wide as it once was. The means of contact are still very physical (silicon chips in the brain, wires and electrodes on the skull), but intimate and direct.

4.6 Creativity and Physicality

Creativity is surely a defining cerebral activity. Artists wait upon the inspiration of their muse and the results are translated into words, images, or sound. But of course it is not quite like that. Painters rarely sit for hours and then paint, they just paint. They seem to think with their brush. Similarly a composer will write their score sitting at a piano and a poet will jot down phrases. We will discuss this embodiment of thought more generally in the next section, but certainly there is some connection between creativity and physical manifestations.

The same is true of problem solving. Some problems can be solved analytically, by decomposing the elements of the problem and then going fairly mechanically through cases. However, others are not amenable to procedural solutions. Psychologists talk of 'insight problem solving', puzzles that seem intractable, but where there is a sudden 'aha!' moment and they become obvious. Look at the matches in Figure 4.6. If you remove the seven matches from the top boxes, it is easy to leave just three squares. But can you remove five matches to leave exactly three squares?

You may try and 'do it in your head', but it is more likely that you will experiment and play with real matches. You might need some

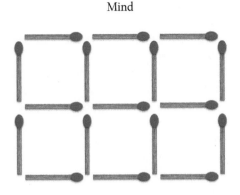

Figure 4.6 Match puzzle (answer at the end of this chapter)

time away from the problem too, what the psychologists call 'incubation', and when you return the problem may have become easy. Both time engaged in the physical form of the problem and time completely divorced from it seem to be necessary.

One such psychologist, Ronald Finke, studied this very physical 'playing with materials' stage in more creative design [163]. In a series of experiments he studied simple problems where subjects were asked to perform simple creative tasks: creating things (e.g. means of transport) from shapes such as rods and circles. In some conditions the subjects were first given the shapes to play with for a period and then asked to come up with a design. In others they were simply presented with the shapes and immediately asked to come up with a design. He found that those who had time to play in a non-goal-directed way were able to produce more 'creative' designs.

This series of experiments by Finke and his colleagues was the basis of the 'geneplore' model of creativity [162], which has two stages. The first is a 'generation' phase (corresponding to the play), which is not directed towards the goal, during which the subjects develop 'pre-inventive structures', patterns and relations of the materials to be used. This is followed by an 'exploration' stage (slightly confusingly named) when the pre-inventive structures are put together to deliver the creative solution. While there have been criticisms of both the model and the methods, the work underlined the benefits of the

Figure 4.7   Design exercise (i) materials (ii) clay group at work

use of physical materials (although interestingly people could also perform purely mental 'play' as well).

In our own observations of group design activities we have also seen some profound effects of the choice of design materials on the results obtained. As part of a workshop on the topic of physicality, attendees were divided into small teams and given a design brief: 'a hand-held device for producing light'. Each team was given one of three kits of design materials to use, either (i) paper and pencils, (ii) card and glue, or (iii) modelling clay (plasticine) (Figure 4.7). Participants were only supposed to use their own materials (although some cheated!). Beyond this they were not told how to use the materials, but in fact the materials implicitly suggested ways of use. For example, no team in the paper and pencil group chose to fold or mould the paper to make a model. In normal design, any or all of these materials would be used according to the preferences of the designer at a particular moment. However, in this exercise, teams of participants were given just one kind of material to work with. Thus we were performing something similar to the 'breaching experiments' [176] discussed in Chapter 1: a deliberate disruption of human activity in order to bring to light aspects that are tacit or taken for granted. In this case we were disrupting the ability to choose appropriate materials.

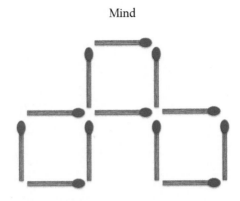

Figure 4.8 Solution to match puzzle in Figure 4.6

Analysis of this design exercise and other work reveals the subtle ways physical materials influence design [338]. In particular, we saw differences in the way groups investigated depth versus breadth of ideas (paper and pencil sketches and lists generated more ideas than physical materials, but the latter were elaborated in greater detail). There were also subtle ways in which the materials both constrained and also suggested ideas (rolling of paper, deformability of clay), reflecting the importance of constraints, seen in the creativity and problem-solving literature [320].

Note we carefully use the word 'influence', as the materials do not fully *determine* outcomes. For example, one group given physical materials 'cheated' and used paper and pencil to sketch, reflecting Buxton's focus on the importance, in early design, of the indeterminacy of the sketch [52] over the more concrete prototype. And human ingenuity can conquer the obstinacy of the material world: one group made a cuddly teddy bear out of paper by tailoring the paper as one would a suit of clothes.

5

Body and Mind

5.1 Whole Beings

It has already been hard to write about the body without talking about the mind (or at least brain) and perhaps even harder to talk about the mind without involving the body. We are not two separate beings but one person where mind and body work together.

In the past the brain was seen as a sort of control centre where sensory information about the environment comes in and is interpreted, plans are made, then orders are sent out to the muscles and voice. However, this dualistic view loses a sense of integration and does not account for the full range of human experience. On the one hand, we sense not only the environment but our body as well, and in some ways we understand what we are thinking because of how we feel in our body. On the other hand, much of the loop between sensing and action happens subconsciously. In both cases the 'little general in the head' model falls apart.

While there is clearly some level of truth in the dualist 'brain as control' picture, more recent accounts stress instead the integrated nature of thought and action, focusing on our interaction with our environment.

5.2 Sensing Ourselves

When we think of our senses, we normally think of the classic five: sight, hearing, touch, taste, and smell. Psychologists call these exteroceptive senses as they tell us about the external world. However, we are also able to sense our own bodies, as when we have a stomach

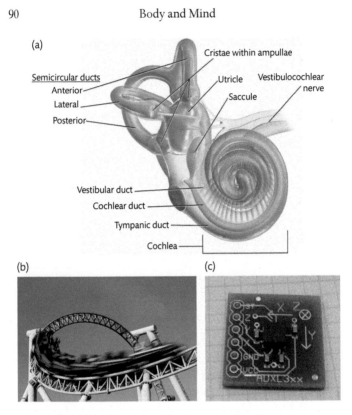

(a)

Cristae within ampullae

Semicircular ducts
Anterior
Lateral
Posterior

Utricle   Vestibulocochlear
                           nerve
Saccule

Vestibular duct
Cochlear duct
Tympanic duct
Cochlea

(b)   (c)

Figure 5.1 (a) inner ear; (b) rollercoaster; (c) accelerometer

ache. These are called interoceptive senses. The nerves responsible for interoception lie within the body, but in fact some of these senses also tell us a lot about our physical position in the world.

We are all familiar with the way balance is aided by the semicircular canals in our ears. There are three channels, filled with fluid that is sensed by tiny hairs. This allows us to detect 'up' in three dimensions. Of course, if we spin or move too fast, perhaps on a fairground ride, the churning fluid makes us dizzy. A similar mechanism is used in mobile devices such as the iPhone: three accelerometers are placed at right angles, often embedded in a single chip (Figure 5.1).

However, this is not the only way we know what way up we are. Our eyes see the horizon, and our feet feel pressure from the floor. Sea-sickness is caused largely because these different ways of knowing which way is up, and how you are moving, conflict with one another. This is also a problem in immersive virtual reality (VR) systems (see also Chapters 2 and 12). If you wear VR goggles or are in a VR CAVE (a small room with a virtual world projected around you), then the scene will change as you move your head, simulating moving your head in the real world. However, if the virtual world simulation is not fast enough and there is even a small lag, the effect is rather like being at sea when your legs and ears tell you one thing, and your eyes something else.

It is not quite correct to say we detect which way is up. Most of our senses work by detecting *change*. Our ear channels are best at detecting changes in direction, so when someone is diving, or buried in snow after an avalanche, it can be difficult to know which way is up. Because there is equal support all the way round and they can see no horizon, their brains are not able to sort out a precise direction. Divers are taught to watch the bubbles as they will go upwards, and avalanche survival training suggests spitting and trying to feel the way the spit dribbles down your face.

The physics of the world also comes into play. Newtonian physics is based on the fact that you cannot tell how fast you are going without looking at something stationary (see also Chapter 11). You may be travelling at 150 kilometres an hour in a train but while you look at things in the carriage you can easily feel that you are still. We even cope with acceleration. As we go round a sharp corner we simply stand at a slight angle. It is when the train changes from straight track into a curve or back again that we notice the movement. Likewise, in a braking car, so long as we brake evenly we simply brace our body slightly. It is the change in acceleration that we feel, what road and rail engineers call 'jerk' (see Box 11.3).

Again, in virtual reality the same thing happens. You are controlling your motion through the environment using a joystick or other controller and then stop suddenly. The effect can be nauseating. All is well so long as you are moving forward at a constant speed, or even accelerating or decelerating or cornering smoothly. Your ear channels and body sense cannot tell the difference between standing still and being on a uniformly moving or accelerating platform. However, if you 'stop' in the VR environment, the visual image stops dead, but your body and ears make you feel you are still moving.

As well as having a sense of balance, we also know where parts of our body are. Close your eyes, then touch your nose with your finger—no problem, you 'know' where your arm is relative to your body and so can move it towards your nose. This sense of the location of your body, called proprioception, is based on various sensing nerves in your muscles, tendons, and joints and is crucial to any physical activity. People who lose this ability due to disease find it very difficult to walk around or to grasp or hold things, even if they have full movement. They have to substitute looking at their limbs for knowing where they are and have to concentrate hard just to stay upright.

Proprioception is particularly important when using eyes-free devices, for example in a car where you can reach for a control without looking at it. In practice we do not use proprioception alone during such interactions, but also peripheral vision and touch. Indeed, James Gibson [182] has argued that our vision and hearing should be regarded as serving a proprioceptive purpose as well as an exteroceptive one because we are constantly positioning ourselves with respect to the world by virtue of what we see and hear.

5.3 The Body Shapes the Mind—Posture and Emotion

It is reasonable that we need to sense our bodies to know if we have an upset stomach (and hence avoid eating until it is better) or to be able to reach for things without looking. However, it seems that our interoceptive senses do more than that: they do not just provide a form of 'input' to our thoughts and decisions but shape our thoughts and emotions at a deep level.

You have probably heard of smile therapy: deliberately smiling in order to make yourself feel happier. Partly, this builds on the fact that when you smile other people tend to smile back, and if other people smile at you that makes you feel happy. But that is not the whole story. Experiments have shown that there is an effect even when there is no-one else to smile back at you and even when you don't know you are smiling. In a typical experiment researchers ask subjects to sit while their faces are manipulated to either be smiling or sad. Although there is some debate about the level of efficacy, there appear to be measurable effects so that even when the subjects are not able to identify the expression on their faces, their reports on how they feel show that having a 'happy' face makes them feel happier [255, 281]!

This may seem odd, since it makes sense that unless we are hiding our emotions we look how we feel, but this suggests that we actually feel how we look! In fact, research on emotion suggests that higher-level emotion does often include this reflective quality. If your heart rate is racing but something good is happening, then it must be very good. Indeed, romantic novels are full of descriptions of pounding hearts. Effectively, some of how we feel is 'in our heads', but some is in our bodies. These can become 'confused' sometimes. Imagine a loud bang has frightened you and then you realize it is just a child who has burst a balloon. You might find yourself laughing hysterically. The situation is not really that funny but the heightened sense of arousal generated by the fear is still there when you realize everything is fine and may be a bit amusing. Your body is still aroused, so your brain interprets the combination as being VERY funny.

In the previous chapter we discussed creativity and physical action, which is as much about the mind and body working together as about the mind alone. There are well-established links between mood and creativity, with positive moods on the whole tending to increase creativity compared with negative moods. One of the experimental measures used to quantify 'creativity' is to ask subjects to create lists of novel ideas; for example, 'how many uses can you think of for a brick'. In one set of experiments the researchers asked subjects either to place their hands on the table in front of them and press downwards, or to put their hands under the table and press up. While pressing they were asked to perform various 'idea list' tasks. Those who pressed up generated more ideas than those who pressed down. The researchers' interpretation was that the upward pressing made a positive 'welcome' gesture, which increased the creativity, whereas the pressing down was more like a 'go away' gesture. Again, body affects mind.

5.4 Cybernetics of the Body

We have seen how the body can be regarded as a mechanical thing with levers (bones), pivots (joints), and pulleys (tendons). However, with our brains in control (taking the dualist view), we are more like what an engineer would regard as a 'control system' or 'cybernetic system'. The study of controlled systems goes back many hundreds of years to the design of clocks and later the steam engine.

There are two main classes of such systems. The simplest are open loop control systems (Figure 5.2). In these the controller performs actions on the environment according to some setting, process, or algorithm. For example, you turn a simple electric fire on to keep warm and it generates the exact amount of heat according to the setting.

This form of control system works well when the environment and indeed the operation of the control system itself are predictable. However, open loop control systems are fragile. If the environment is not quite as expected (perhaps the room gets too hot) they fail.

More robust control systems use some sort of feedback from the environment to determine how to act to achieve a desired state; this is called closed loop control (Figure 5.3). An electric fire may have a

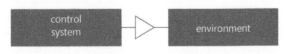

Figure 5.2 Open loop control

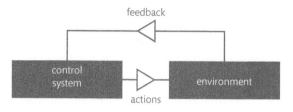

Figure 5.3 closed loop control

temperature sensor, so instead of turning it on and off to produce a predetermined heat, you set a desired temperature and the fire turns on if it is below the temperature and off if it is above.

One of the earliest explicit uses of closed loop control was the centrifugal governor on steam boilers (Figure 5.4). Escaping steam from the boiler is routed so that it spins a small 'merry-go-round' arrangement of two heavy balls. As the balls swing faster they rise in the air. However, the balls are also linked to a valve, so as they rise they open the valve, releasing steam. If the pressure is too high it makes the balls spin faster, which opens the valve and reduces the pressure. If the pressure is too low, the balls do not spin much, the valve closes, and the pressure increases.

This is an example of negative feedback, which tends to lead to stable states. It is also possible to have positive feedback, where a small

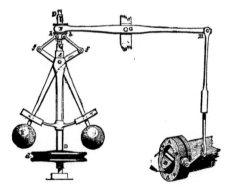

Figure 5.4 Centrifugal governor

Figure 5.5 Dot to touch—sense your finger movements

change from the central state leads to more and more change. Imagine if the universal governor were altered so that the rising balls closed the valve and vice versa. In nature, positive feedback often leads to catastrophes such as an avalanche, when small amounts of moving snow make more and more snow move.

At first, positive feedback may not seem very useful. However, it can be used to produce very rapid 'hair trigger' responses. In our bodies we find a mixture of different kinds of control mechanism. For example, the immune system uses positive feedback loops to produce different kinds of cells in sufficient quantity to fight infection or to create antibodies. In a healthy immune system there is also a negative feedback loop to regulate production of these kinds of cells before they start to attack the body itself. In an auto-immune disease, this balancing system has failed.

When we want to position something we use hand–eye coordination, seeing where our hands are and then adjusting their position until it is right. Look at the dot in Figure 5.5, then reach your finger out to touch it. You may be able to notice yourself slow down as you get close and make minor adjustments to your finger position. That is closed loop control using negative feedback.

Of course, recall that our bodies are like networked systems with delays between eye and action of around 200 ms (milliseconds) (Chapter 3). As these minor adjustments depend on the feedback from eye to muscle movement, we can only manage about five adjustments per second.

These time delays are one of the explanations for Fitts' Law, a psychological result discovered by Paul Fitts in the 1950s. Fitts drew two parallel target strips some distance apart on a table. His subjects were asked to tap the first target, then the second, then back to the first repeatedly as fast as they could [165].

He found that the subjects took longer to move between narrower targets, not surprising as it is harder to position your finger or a pointer on a smaller target. He also found that placing the targets further apart had the same effect, again not surprising as the arm has to move further.

However, what was surprising was the way these two effects precisely cancelled out: if you made the targets twice as big, and placed them twice as far away, the average time taken was the same. All that mattered was the ratio between them; in mathematical terms it was scale invariant.

In addition, one might think that for a given target size the time would increase linearly, so that each 10 cm moved would take a roughly similar time, just like driving down a road, or walking. However, Fitts found instead that time increased logarithmically: the difference between moving 10 cm and 20 cm was the same as the difference between moving 20 cm and 40 cm—when the targets got further apart the subjects moved their arms faster. This gave rise to what is known as Fitts' Law

$$time = a + b * \log_2(distance / size)$$

Fitts called the log ratio the 'index of difficulty' (ID).

$$ID = \log_2(distance / size)$$

Fitts' Law has proved very influential in human–computer interaction. The precise details of the formula vary between different sources as there are variants for different-shaped targets, and for whether you measure distance to the centre or edge of a target and size by diameter or radius. However, it appears to hold equally both when a mouse is used to move a pointer on the screen to hit an icon or when moving your hand to hit a strip. Each device has different constants 'a' and 'b' depending on their difficulty, and individuals vary, but the underlying formula is robust. Further studies have shown that it also works when 'acceleration' is added to the mouse, varying the relationship between mouse and pointer speed, or when other complications are added. The formula has even been embodied in an ISO standard (ISO 9241-9) for comparing mice and similar pointing devices [235].

When Fitts was doing his experiments, Shannon had recently finished his work on measuring information [360, 359], where log terms are also used. This led Fitts to describe his results in terms of the information capacity of the motor system. He measured the index of difficulty in 'bits' and when 'b' is 'throughput' (1/b) gives the information capacity of the channel in bits per second, just like measuring the speed of a computer network.

An alternative (and complementary) account can be expressed in terms of the corrective movements and delays described in Chapter 3: that is, a cybernetic model of the closed loop control system.

Our muscles are powerful enough to move nearly full range in a single 'hand–eye' feedback time of 200 ms. So when you see the target, your brain 'tells' your hand to move to the seen location. However, your muscle movement is not perfect and you don't quite hit the target on the first try, you just get closer. Your brain sees the difference and tells your arms to move the smaller distance, and so on until you are within the target, and you have finished (see Figure 5.6). If you assume that the movement error for large movements is proportionately larger, then the 'log' law results.

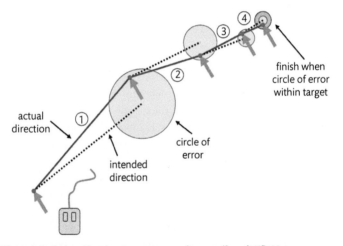

Figure 5.6 Series of hand movements towards target (from [112]). Note, exaggerated distances: the first ballistic movement is typically up to 90% of the final distance.

The 'information capacity' of the motor system measured in bits/second is generated by a combination of the accuracy of your muscles and the delays in your nerves—the physical constraints of your body translated into digital terms.

Box 5.1 Forever cyborgs

We saw in Chapter 3 that prosthetics, including the simple walking stick, are very old. More fundamentally, hominid tool use pre-dates Homo Sapiens by several million years—from its very beginning, our species has used tools to augment our bodies. This is particularly evident in Fitts' Law, which is often seen as a fundamental psychological law of the human body and mind.

Draw a small cross on a piece of paper and put it on a table in front of you. Put your hands on your lap, look at the cross and then, with your eyes closed, try to put your hand over the cross. Move the paper around and try again. So long as it is in reach you will probably find you can cover it with your hand on virtually every attempt.

Now do the same with just your finger and wrist. Rest your hand on this book, and focus on a single letter not too far from your hand. As before, close your eyes, but this time try to cover the letter with your finger. Again, you will probably find that so long as the letter is close enough to touch without moving your arm (wrist and finger only), you can cover the letter with your finger almost every time.

Fitts' Law is about successive corrections, but in fact your arm is accurate, in a *single* ballistic movement, to the level required by your hand, its effector, and this is also true for your finger and its effector, your fingertip. The corrections are only needed when you have a tool (mouse pointer, pencil, stick) with an end that is smaller than your hand or fingertip.

In other words, Fitts' Law, a fundamental part of our human nature, is a law of the *extended* human body.

We really have always been cyborgs.

5.5   The Adapted Body

When something is simple, people often say, 'even a child could do it'. For computers and hi-tech appliances this is not really

appropriate as we all know that it is those who are older who most
often have problems! However, one can apply a different criterion:
'could a caveman use it?' Now by this we do not mean some sort of
time machine dropping an iPad into a Neolithic woman's hands but
rather to recognize that there has not been very much time since the
first sophisticated societies, barely 10,000 years, not enough time for
our bodies or brains to have significantly evolved. That is, we live in
a technological society and learn very different things as we grow up
in such a world, yet we still have bodies and brains roughly similar to
those of our cave-dwelling ancestors. If we did have a time machine
and could bring a healthy orphan baby forward from 10,000 years ago,
it is likely that she would grow normally and be no different from a
baby born today.

However, while humans were hunter-gatherers 10,000 years ago,
Homo Sapiens as a species had over 100,000 years of development
before that, and our species is itself part of a process going back many
millions of years. Given this, it seems likely that:

1. we are well adapted to the world, and
2. the world we are adapted to is natural, not technological.

James Gibson, a psychologist studying perception and particularly vision, was one of the first to take this into account in the development
of what later came to be called ecological psychology. Previous research had considered human vision as a fairly abstract process turning a 2D pattern of colour into a 3D model in the head. However,
Gibson saw it as an intimate part of an acting human engaged in the
environment. [182]

Gibson argued that aspects of the environment 'afford' various
possibilities for action. For example, a hollow in a stone affords filling with water, a rock of a certain height affords sitting upon. These
possibilities are independent of whether we take advantage of them
or whether we even know they exist. An invisible rock would afford
sitting upon just as much as a visible one. However, if our minds
are bodies are adapted to be part of this environment then our perceptions will be precisely adapted to recognize and respond to the

visual and other sensory effects caused by the affordances of the things in the world. We will be revisiting Gibson and affordance in Chapter 8.

Evolutionary psychologists, whom we mentioned earlier in the context of the 'Swiss Army Knife' model of specialized intelligences, try to understand how our cognitive systems have evolved and hence what they may be capable of today. The 'social version' of the Wason card test we saw in Chapter 4 comes from these studies. Reasoning from possible past lifestyles and environments to current abilities is of course potentially problematic, but can also be powerful as a design heuristic. If you are expecting the user of your product or device to have some cognitive, perceptual, or motor ability that has no use in a 'wild' environment, they are likely to find it impossible to use, or require extensive training.

One example is when we have pauses in a sequence of actions. In the wild, if a sabretooth tiger appears you run at once, you do not wait for a moment and then run. However, various sports and various user interfaces do require a short pause, for example the short pause needed between selecting a file onscreen and clicking the file name to edit it. Click too fast and the file will open instead. While we can do these actions by explicitly waiting for some indication that it is time for the next action, it is very hard to proceduralize this kind of act–pause–act sequence. It requires much practice in sport and, in the case of file name editing, is something that nearly every experienced computer user still occasionally gets wrong.

Another example is the way we can 'extend' our body when driving a car or using a computer mouse. Our ability to work 'through' technology like this is quite amazing. A mouse often has different acceleration parameters, may be held at a slight angle so that it does not track horizontally, may even be held upside-down by some left-handed users so that moving the mouse to the left moves the screen cursor to the right. However, after some practice we can achieve the Fitts' Law behaviour, slickly operating the mouse almost as easily as we point with our fingers. The sense of 'oneness' with the technology

is evident when things go wrong. Think of driving a car, of the moment when traction is not perfect on a slightly icy road, or when you
rev the engine and the car does not accelerate because the clutch is
failing. Whether or not the situation is dangerous enough to frighten
you, you experience an odd feeling as if it were your own body not
responding properly. You and the car are a sort of cyborg [109].

In fact, we go on adapting during our lifetime. One of the great
successes of the human is our plasticity: the ability of our brains to
change in order to accommodate new situations. We may start off
just like a cave-baby, but as adults growing and living in a technological world our minds and bodies become technologically adapted.
Brain scans of taxi drivers show whole areas devoted to spatial navigation far larger than in normal (non taxi driver) brains. This is not so
much physical growth but more that the part dedicated to this function is making use of neighbouring parts of the brain, which would
otherwise have been used for other purposes.

Such remapping can work very quickly. If a child is born with
two fingers joined by a web of skin, brain scans show a single region
corresponding to the joined fingers. However, within weeks of an operation to separate the fingers, separate brain areas become evident.
Similarly, in experiments where participants had fingers strapped together, the distinct brain areas for the two fingers began to fuse after
a few weeks.

In comparison, change in the body takes longer, but of course
we know that if we exercise muscles grow stronger and larger. In
addition, any activity that requires movement and coordination creates interlinked physical and neurological changes. If you do sports
your hand–eye coordination for the relevant limbs and actions will
improve.

Dundee University Medical School measures the digital dexterity
of new students. Well-controlled hands are especially important in
surgery where a slip could cost a life. While individual students would
vary, overall dexterity did not vary much from year to year until the
mid-2000s, when students (on average) displayed greater dexterity

in their thumbs than in the past. Indeed their thumbs now had the same dexterity as index fingers, rather than being a relatively clumsy digit, useful only for grasping. This was attributed to the effect of PlayStation use on a generation (Figure 5.7).

Figure 5.7 Game controllers in action

5.6 Plans and Action

One morning Alan was having breakfast. He served himself a bowl of grapefruit segments and then went to make his tea. While making the tea he went to the fridge to get a bottle of milk, but after getting the milk from the fridge he only just stopped himself in time as he was about to pour the milk onto the grapefruit (Figure 5.8)!

What went wrong?

Older models of cognition focused on planned activity. You start with something you want to achieve (a goal), then decide how you are going to achieve it (a plan), and finally do the things that are needed (execution). There are many very successful methods that use this approach. Two of the oldest and most well known in HCI are

GOMS (goals, operators, methods, and selection) [57] and HTA (hierarchical task analysis) [7, 363]. GOMS is focused on very low-level practised tasks, such as correcting mistakes in typing, whereas HTA looks more at higher-level activity such as booking a hotel room. Making tea is somewhere at the intersection of the two, but we will focus on HTA as it is slightly easier to explain.

HTA basically takes a goal and breaks it down into smaller and smaller sequences of actions (the tasks) that will achieve the goal. The origins of hierarchical task analysis are in Taylorist time-and-motion studies for 'scientific management' of workspaces, decomposing repetitive jobs into small units in the most 'efficient' way. Later, during the Second World War, new recruits had to be trained how to use relatively complex equipment, for example stripping down a rifle. Training needed to be done quickly in order to get them onto the battlefield, yet in such a way that under pressure

Figure 5.8 Automatic actions at breakfast

they could automatically do the right actions. Hierarchical task analysis provided a way to create the necessary training materials and documentation.

While HTA was originally developed for 'work' situations, it can be applied to many activities. Figure 5.9 shows an HTA for the task for making a mug of tea (with a teabag, not proper tea from a teapot). The diagram shows the main tasks and sub-tasks.

The task hierarchy tells you what steps you need to do, and in addition there is a plan saying in what order to do the steps. For example, for Task 4 the plan might be:

```
Plan 4.
   if  milk not out of fridge do 4.1 then do 4.2
```

If you follow the steps in the right order according to the plan, then you get a mug of tea. Easy—but why did it go wrong with the grapefruit?

You might have noticed that the world of task analysis is very close to an open-control system. Not entirely, since the plan for Task 4 includes some perception of the world (`if milk not out of fridge`), but predominantly it is a flow of command and control from inside to out. It assumes that we keep careful track in our heads of what we are doing and translate this into action in the world, but if this were always the case, why the near mistake with the grapefruit?

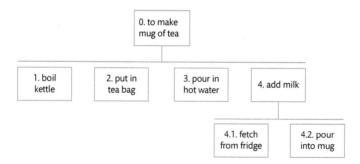

Figure 5.9 HTA for making a mug of tea

One explanation is that we simply make mistakes sometimes! However, not all mistakes are equally likely. One would be unlikely to pour milk onto the bare kitchen worktop or onto a plate of bacon and eggs. The milk on the grapefruit is a form of capture error: the bowl containing the grapefruit might on other occasions hold cornflakes. When that is the case and you are standing in the kitchen with milk in your hand, having just got it out of the fridge, it is quite appropriate to pour the milk into the bowl.

Staying close to the spirit of HTA we can imagine a plan for making tea that is more like:

```
if milk not out of fridge do 4.1 when milk in hand do 4.2
```

However, if we were to analyse 'prepare bowl of cornflakes', we would have a rule that says:

```
when milk in hand pour into bowl
```

So when you have milk in your hand, what is the 'correct' thing to do: pour into a mug or pour into a bowl? One way is to remember what you are in the middle of doing, but the mistake suggests that actually Alan's actions were driven by the environment. The mug on the worktop says 'please fill me', but so also does the cereal bowl. Alan was acting more in a stimulus–response fashion than one based on pre-planned actions.

Preparing breakfast is a practised activity where, if anywhere, forms of task analysis should work. In more complex activities many argue that it is a far too simplistic view of the world. Nowadays most people using such methods would regard task analysis as a useful, but simplified model. However, in the mid-1980s, when HCI was developing as a field, the dominant cognitive science thinking was largely reductionist. A few works challenged this, most influentially Lucy Suchman's *Plans and Situated Actions* [383]. Suchman was working at Xerox and using ethnographic techniques borrowed from anthropology. She observed that when a field engineer tried to fix a malfunctioning photocopier, they did not go

	internally driven	**environment driven**
explicit	(a) following known plan of action	(b) situated action, means–ends analysis
implicit	(c) proceduralized or routine action	(d) stimulus–response reaction

Figure 5.10 Types of activity (from [115])

through a set process or procedure but instead would open the photocopier and respond to what they saw. To the extent that plans were used, they were adapted and deployed in a situated fashion driven by the environment: what they saw with their eyes on the machine.

Cognitive scientists have developed their own responsive methods of problem-solving analysis where tasks can be adapted based on what is encountered in the environment. In artificial intelligence new problems are often tackled using means–ends analysis. Beginning with a goal (e.g. make tea), one starts to solve it, but becomes blocked by some impasse (no milk), which then gives rise to a subgoal (get milk from fridge). However, this still does not capture the full range of half-planned, half-recognized activities we see in day-to-day life.

In reality, we have many ways in which individual actions are strung together: some we are explicitly aware of doing, others are implicit or sub-conscious. Some involve internally driven preplanned or learned actions, others are driven by the environment (Figure 5.10). It is often hard to tell which is at work by watching a user, and hard even when we introspect, since once we think about what we are doing we tend to change it! This is why errors like the grapefruit bowl are so valuable as they often reveal what is going on below our level of awareness.

In most activities there will also be a mix of these types of activity and, over time, frequent environment-driven actions are thoroughly learned and end up being proceduralized or routine actions—practice makes perfect. Anyone who has practised a sport or music will have found this for themselves.

Box 5.2 Iconic case study: Nintendo Wii

When Nintendo launched the Wii in 2006, it created a new interaction paradigm. Like the iPhone that followed it, the Wii allowed us to bring learned gestures and associations from our day-to-day physical world into our physical–digital interactions. A two-part controller translated body movement into gaming actions, and in doing so opened computer gaming up to a completely new market. The Microsoft Kinect took the Wii concept further by literally using the gamers' bodies as controllers. The Wii/Kinect revolution brought with it a lot of interesting case material on how we perceive physical space. Consider for example the case of two players standing side by side playing Kinect table tennis. One serves diagonally to the other across the net. If we assume, for example, that the player 'receiving' is right-handed and on the lefthand side of the court (from their perspective), will they be forced to receive the ball 'backhanded'?

5.7 The Embodied Mind

Like our perception, which is intimately tied to the physical world, our cognition itself is expressed physically. When we add up large numbers we use a piece of paper. When we solve a jigsaw puzzle we do not just stare and then put all the pieces in place, we try them one by one. Researchers studying such phenomena talk about distributed cognition, regarding our cognition and thinking to be not only inside our head but distributed between our head, the world, and often other people [221, 228]. Early studies looked at Micronesian sailors, navigating without modern instruments for hundreds of kilometres between tiny islands. They found that no single person held the whole navigation in their head but it was somehow worked out between them [229, 228].

More radically still, some philosophers talk about our mind being embodied, not just in the sense of being physically embodied in our brain, but in the sense that, all together, our brain, body, and the things we manipulate achieve 'mind-like' behaviour [68]. If you are doing a sum on a piece of paper, the paper, the pencil, and your hand are just as much part of your 'mind' as your brain.

If you think that is far-fetched, imagine losing your phone: where are the boundaries of your social mind?

Theorists who advocate strong ideas of the embodied mind would argue that we are creatures fitted most well to a perception–action cycle and tend to be parsimonious with mental representations, allowing the environment to encode as much as possible.

> In general evolved creatures will neither store nor process information in costly ways when they can use the structure of the environment and their operations on it as a convenient stand-in for the information-processing operations concerned.   ([69] as quoted in [68])

Clark calls this the '007 principle' as it can be summarized as 'know only as much as you need to know to get the job done' [68].

In the natural world this means, for example, that we do not need to remember what the weather is like now because we can feel the wind on our cheeks or the rain on our hands. In a more complex setting this can include changes made to the world (e.g. the bowl on the worktop) and even changes made precisely for the reason of offloading information processing or memory (e.g. ticking off the shopping list). Indeed this is one of the main foci of distributed cognition accounts of activity [221].

It is not necessary to take a strong 'embodied mind' or even 'distributed cognition' viewpoint to see that such parsimony is a normal aspect of human behaviour—why bother to remember the precise order of actions to make my mug of tea when it is obvious what to do when I have milk in my hand and black tea in the mug?

Of course parsimony of internal representation does not mean that there is no internal representation at all. The story of the grape-fruit bowl would be less amusing if it happened all the time. While eating breakfast it is not unusual to have both a grapefruit bowl and a mug of tea out at the same time, but Alan had never before tried to pour milk on the grapefruit. As well as the reactive behaviour 'when milk in hand pour in cup', there is also some practised idea of what follows what (plan) and some feeling of being 'in the middle of making tea' (context, schema).

Parsimony cuts both ways. If it is more efficient to 'store' informa-tion in the world then we will do that. If it is more efficient to store it in our heads then we do that instead. Think of an antelope being chased by a lion. The antelope does not constantly run with its head turned back to see the lion chasing after it. If it did it would fall over or crash into a tree. Instead it just knows in its head that the lion is there, and keeps running.

A rather more everyday example involves workers in a busy cof-fee bar at Steve's university. Two people work together at peak times: one takes the order and the money while the other makes and serves the coffee. Orders can be taken faster than fresh coffee can be made and so there is always a lag between taking and fulfilling the or-der. There are a lot of combinations: four basic types of coffee order (espresso to latté); four possible cup sizes; one or two coffee shots; no milk or one of three types of milk as well as twelve types of optional flavoured syrups. Then there is the sequence in which the order is to be fulfilled: customers get upset if they are made to wait while the person behind is served.

The staff devised the following solution: the person taking the order selects the appropriate paper cup (large, medium, small, or espresso). They turn it upside down and write the order on the base (Figure 5.11). This creates a physical association between the cup and the order that simultaneously takes care of the size of the coffee and the exact type of coffee to go in it. The cups are then 'queued' on the counter in the order in which they are to be made, with the most

Figure 5.11 Embodied information on a coffee cup

immediate order being closer to the staff member making the coffee. The end result is that a great deal of information is efficiently dealt with through physical associations and interactions.

Box 5.3 External cognition: lessons for design

In design this means we have to be aware that:

1. people will not always do things in the 'right order'
2. if there are two things with the same 'pre-condition' (e.g. milk in hand), then it is likely that a common mistake will be to do the wrong succeeding action
3. we should try to give people cues in the environment (e.g. lights on a device) to help them disambiguate what comes next (clarifying context)
4. where people are doing complex activities we should try to give them ways to create 'external representations' in the environment

6

Social, Organizational, and Cultural

6.1 Personal Contact

Not only are we individually physical beings, living and acting in a physical world, but our contacts with one another are played out in that same physical world, whether in a formal handshake or in sexual intimacy. Even our spoken words, gestures, and facial expressions require physical proximity if not direct contact.

However, over the years, layers of technology have allowed us to establish contact while we are temporally or geographically remote: letters, the telegraph, paintings, and photographs. Today opportunities for remote contact often seem to swamp face-to-face encounters, with the growth of Facebook, Instagram, WhatsApp, and even plain old-fashioned video conferencing. During the COVID-19 global pandemic, these technologies showed their value yet also emphasized for many the importance of physical presence. We will discuss virtual reality in Chapter 12, but forms of video conferencing belong here, as it is the image of the real human body that is projected across space, even though its transport is by pixel and wire.

Face-to-face conversation is enabled not just by spoken words but by continual gestures and movements of the face and eyes. While video preserves these better than text-based media or avatar-based virtual reality (VR) meetings, still the glass barrier of the screen not only separates us psychologically but may also lose some of the subtle cues that help us to communicate.

One problem is that when you look straight at the image of the person you are talking to, the camera is slightly to one side or above the screen, so that your conversant sees your eyes averted or looking down. An early solution, the video tunnel, used two-way mirrors to enable the camera to be effectively placed in the middle of the screen [372]. However, though useful for experiments it was an impractically large contraption. Current laptops and screens often have a built in charge-coupled device (CCD) camera close to the top of the screen, which reduces the angle compared with older 'bolt-on' arrangements, though still not entirely.

The situation is worse still for multi-person conversations as it may not even be clear to whom one is talking. One early solution, Hydra (see Box 6.1), tackled this by having a number of tiny screens each with its own camera, so effectively each screen on the desk 'stood' for one of the participants.

Box 6.1 Digital–physical peculiarities 2—sense of place

While video conferencing tools such as FaceTime, Zoom, and Skype have their strengths, their social dynamics are different from those enabled by physical presence. In the early 1990s Bill Buxton attempted to tackle this issue of video presence [355]. While it may not have succeeded, there is much to recommend his concept, which combined the advantages of physicality with those of video-conferencing.

Buxton: 'First, I wanted to get the image of the remote people off of my computer screen. It already has too much stuff on it, no matter how big it grows. Second, I wanted to be able to do things in video conferences that I did in live meetings, such as whisper in someone's ear, or break off into a brief side conversation, yet still be able to keep track of what was going on. And, I wanted people to know who or what I was looking at, just as I wanted to know the same about them. Such things are the underpinnings of our face-to-face social interactions, and they are typically awkward (at best) or absent (at worst) in electronic communication.'

Hydra consisted of a number of physical screened devices, each showing a video image of a single participant. The device also housed a microphone, speaker, and camera, and so, in effect, became a physical–digital avatar of the person: the camera represented that person's eye, the microphone their ears, and so on.

continued

Box 6.1 *continued*

Buxton: 'Because each person's voice comes from their own unique location, you can exploit what is known as the "cocktail party effect" and hear them all, but attend to the one that you want. Plus, everyone knows who is looking at who. Why? Because the whole thing was designed to exploit the very same skills that you had built up from a life time of living in the everyday world.'

More recent systems, including HP HALO (now incorporated in Polycom Immersive Telepresence), are more sophisticated, with identical rooms at different locations designed so that the video of the remote room seems to fit seamlessly into your own meeting room, but of course at the cost of a dedicated and expensive installation.

6.2 Intimacy

It is easy to think that everything virtual and Internet is new and has never been seen before. The point at which technology finds its way into mainstream media is often telling. The film 'You've Got Mail' [411] did that for online romance, but virtual love affairs are now common, with Internet dating sites and meetings in chat rooms, and there have even been weddings in cyberspace dating back to Multi-User Dungeons (MUDs) in the 1990s [86, 237].

However, romance by letter dates back hundreds of years and it was 1848, not 1998, that saw the first tele-wedding [379]. The daughter of a wealthy Boston businessman fell in love with one of his employees. To prevent the affair from developing the father posted the unwelcome suitor to the European office and he duly went. However, the daughter was not to be foiled in love so easily. While her beau was still *en route*, his ship called in at New York, where she sent him a message telling him to bring a magistrate to a telegraph office. With each at opposite ends of the telegraph line, they were married. Her father contested the marriage but the courts upheld it. Love conquers all.

Whether or not they were forged online, many couples and families are forced to have long-distance relationships due to their jobs. Email, instant messenger, and webcams have now joined or supplanted the traditional love letter, but are not a substitute for physical closeness. A number of more tangible ways of establishing physical contact have been exploited, some in artistic settings, some as research probes [267].

One early example consisted of two rollers linked to one another by the Internet [42]. If the user at one end spun her roller, the roller at the other end would also spin, and if her remote partner spun his, she would see hers move. If they both touched the roller at the same time they could feel the pressure of the other, either working with them or against them, like holding hands beneath the tablecloth. Others have experimented with clothes, for example using electrically reactive materials to create a hugging shirt that lets you send 'hugs' to your partner via a mobile phone [87]. Of course, Kevin Warwick's direct nerve implants attempt to establish a form of intimacy that, as far as possible, bypasses physical means entirely (see [412]).

Perhaps most common have been various forms of connected jewellery that release fragrant smells, pleasant sounds or comforting glows from a piece at one location when the connected piece at the other end is touched or stroked. Such artefacts might connect lovers or partners or indeed anyone with a close personal relationship. One piece, 'Journeys between ourselves', focused on a mother, aged 75, and daughter, 45 (Figure 6.1):

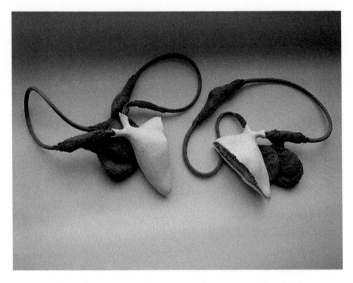

Figure 6.1 'Journeys between ourselves', Jayne Wallace [407]

> Light sensors in each piece detect a wearer touching and holding the porcelain form. The partnering piece then softly trembles in response. We developed this haptic and tactile way of interacting with the neckpieces with the hope of facilitating a gentle, human centred mode of communication. (from [407])

Yet as well as bringing remote people together, technology often gets in the way of direct human contact. Central heating replaces being together round a winter fire, and even family TV watching has been replaced by per-person devices and apps: mobile phones, iPads, YouTube.

6.3 Mediation and Sharing

Ethnographies of work settings repeatedly find that both the physical things *and* the arrangement of people in an environment are crucial to enabling coordination and collaboration.

One classic example is a study of a London Underground Control Room (Figure 6.2) [208]. The room contains a large display, the 'fixed

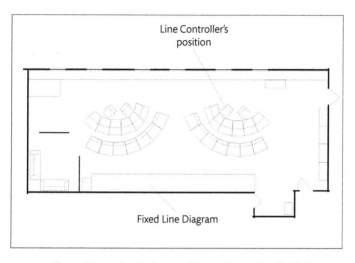

Figure 6.2 London Underground Control Room from [208]

line diagram', which is visible to everyone and shows the locations of trains, track and signals. Not only does this give explicit information but its common availability is essential to the staff's understanding of each others' behaviour. As well as the fixed line diagram, which is updated by the actual movement of trains, the cellophane pages of a printed timetable are edited in felt pen by the Controller, a publicly visible act and one emphasized by talking out loud. In fact 'overhearings' of one sort or another are critical for numerous activities in the control room and are enabled by each member of staff being distant enough to be able to get on with their own job, but close enough to be able to monitor other people's actions and words.

Studies of other 'command and control' situations, such as the bridge of a ship, airport ground services, and , reveal different details, but similar importance of the mediating artefacts. Air traffic control has been particularly well studied in several countries because it is necessary to automate more due to increasing volume, and yet difficult to do so in a way that does not compromise established practices and so threaten safety [225].

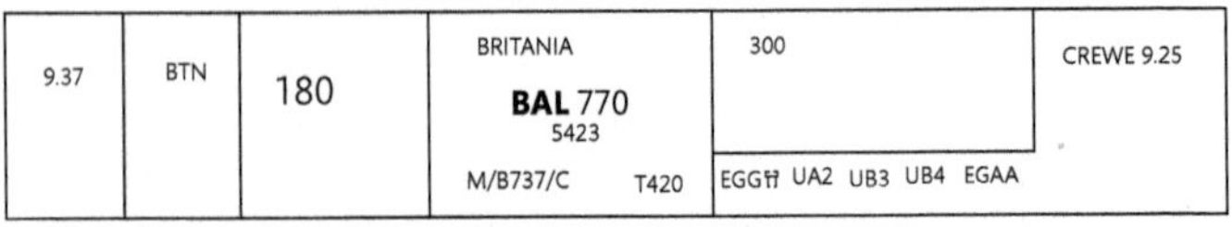

9.37	BTN	180	BRITANIA **BAL** 770 5423 M/B737/C T420	300 EGGↂ UA2 UB3 UB4 EGAA	CREWE 9.25

Figure 6.3 Flight strip (schematic)

Until very recently, a critical part of the traditional air traffic control system was the 'flight strip', a small slip of paper printed out when a plane entered the airspace (Figure 6.3). These carried information such as the flight number and altitude of the plane. The air traffic controllers sat in pairs, each with their own screen, and the flight strips were placed in a rack between them. As well as updating the flight strips when, for example, the altitude changed, they would also slightly pull out strips that were of particular interest for any reason. This was partly to act as a reminder for the controller working with the plane, but also implicitly allowed the other controller to monitor the general situation, since lots of tweaked strips might indicate problems.

It is not just in work life that we use the physical world to coordinate with others. In the home we have message boards and notes stuck to the refrigerator door; we notice that a coat is in the hall or keys on the table and know that a family member is home. Many of these signs are implicit and we would be hard-pressed to articulate all the ways in which we use them, but they are crucial in giving us a sense of 'what is going on'.

With the coat in the hall it is the presence of the object that is the 'message', unlike, say, the London Underground timetable, where the message was written explicitly on the object. We will discuss the different forms of these 'accidental' properties of objects in more detail in Chapter 14, but in this chapter we are interested in the way the presence, movement and exchange of objects facilitates social interaction.

During a meeting one person may pass a report across the room. The report was there all along but the act of passing it says 'this is now for you to read'. When sitting near someone, even changing the orientation of a paper may say, 'you read this too, but I'm still holding on to it'. When working remotely with digital media, we may be able to see someone on a webcam, hear them, and be able to send documents, but it is hard to replicate the subtle interactions that take place around shared paper.

For people working together, shared screens can be one means of establishing that rapport while using digital technology. One example involved using a large horizontal screen or multiple smaller screens for planning Australian travel itineraries with a travel agent (Figure 6.4) [345, 346]. The shared point of reference and side-by-side orientation allowed many of the same subtle bodily interactions as a paper-based meeting, while still making use of the power of the digital planning software, including interactive maps, hotel and tourist information.

Interactive tabletops, such as the Microsoft Surface, allow more subtle interactions as the digital documents can be shuffled around, not unlike real papers. One system, UbiTable, uses a tabletop display that can link to users' own laptops [362]. Although only a prototype, the idea is that it could be used in public places like airports, where people may have an ad hoc meeting and want to share some information, yet keep other information private. With paper, you might have papers in your briefcase, papers on your side of the table, or papers moved so the other person can see them. UbiTable emulates this by

Figure 6.4 The Oz travel planner [345, 346]

Figure 6.5 Different parts of a web page displayed using multiple devices in 'Better Together' [344]

connecting to your own laptop (private) and allowing documents to be moved to the shared tabletop display. Once on the display they can be on your side of the table facing you (personal) or moved into the centre of the table and rotated around so the other person can easily see them (public).

The need to be able to bring physical devices together in ways that create an enhanced experience also emerged from a series of design workshops amongst emerging users in Kenya, India, and South Africa and led to a system 'Better Together' (Figure 6.5) [344], which allows users to bring their own multiple phones or tablets so that, for example, the parts of a web page can be distributed over the devices allowing a view that would otherwise only be possible on a much larger screen.

6.4 Socio-organizational Church–Turing Hypothesis

Some organizations clearly have a physical purpose: a factory making cars, a bus company carrying passengers, or a theatre presenting a play. Others, while having physical premises, have less physical outputs: a bank, an insurance company, or a travel agent (as opposed to an airline or hotel). However, even those with physical outputs also have ancillary functions more like the bank or insurance company: processing orders, paying staff, managing stock. An organization has many roles, but one of them is some form of information process-ing either, like the travel agent, as its principal role, or, like the car factory, as a secondary one.

In computing, the Church–Turing thesis asserts that in the end all computers can do the same things, given sufficient memory and time. Strictly, this refers to what can be achieved or what is com-putable; in principle, computers could be very different in the way in which they perform computation. However, in practice most computers are very similar in terms of the major components and structure. If you have a new computer you can ask questions like 'where is its memory?' and usually get a sensible answer. In fact com-monalities are also found between the human brain and computers, and this brain–computer analogy lies at the heart of much of cogni-tive science. There are limitations to such a view, indeed our brains perform a substantial amount of associative thinking, linking ideas together by similarities, whereas digital computers tend to be largely sequential. However, it has proved a very useful analogy for both disciplines.

Given this, and the fact that organizations perform information-processing functions, it seems reasonable to look for structural sim-ilarities between the organization and the computer (Figure 6.6), a form of socio-organizational Church–Turing hypothesis [145]. In fact, distributed cognition (see section 5.7) uses precisely this sort of computational language when discussing individual and small group activity in their environments [221].

The most obvious two elements in a computer are the program and the data.

	computer	human	organisation
process	program	procedural memory	processes
data	data	LTM	files
placeholder	program counter	STM/activation	location of artefacts
initiative	interrupts, event-driven programs	stimuli	triggers

Figure 6.6 Parallels between information processing in computers, humans, and organizations

Computer programs are always explicit (the code) and expressed formally. Similarly the organization will have some formally written processes and rules of operation. These rules are not, however, followed in a lock-step fashion across the organization but by each department and each individual doing their job and together achieving the overall organization's objectives (one hopes). That is, in terms of the computational analogy, it is a distributed system. However, not all the rules are formally written down. The clerk just knows that when she gets a blue form ZK9b it needs to be signed and passed on to the Accounts Department.

Data is usually easier to locate than process: some is stored physically in filing cabinets and ring binders, some digitally in databases. This aspect of the organization has been most consistently subjected to computerization, although the process side is also automated in some workflow systems. Even here some of the data is in people's heads, particularly more personal sales knowledge about customers and clients.

While such implicit data and process knowledge may work well, for the organization it can become a problem when an employee leaves or is sick. The desire to record, preserve, and pass on this knowledge has been a major impetus in several areas of management science, such as organizational learning and customer relation management.

However, what about the more ephemeral aspects? A computer has a 'program counter' that says where in a program it is operating. So how does an organization 'know' and remember what it is doing? Imagine it is night, everyone has gone home, and the office lights are turned off. The records of the organization are preserved in filing cabinets and databases, the processes in rule books, and, intangibly, in people's job knowledge. But in the morning how does the organization 'pick up' where it left off the night before? Somewhere, there must be placeholders that say what is to happen next.

Just as with the processes and the data, some of this may be explicitly written down, perhaps ticks on a timetable of activities or 'to do' lists left on people's desks. Some will be in people's heads:

they remember where they left off the day before. However, typically much is stored in the physical locations of documents, records, and forms. You know you were partway through filling out form ZK9b yesterday because this morning it is sitting there on your desk half complete, and the organization 'knows' that that form is at a particular point in its processing because it is on your desk and not somewhere else.

6.5 Culture and Community of Practice

When we think of culture, particularly past culture, it is likely to be in terms of physical artefacts and buildings: the Mona Lisa, Stonehenge, the Pyramids and Acropolis, McDonald's burgers, and Marvel comics. For oral cultures studied by archaeologists there are indeed only the material traces. The society that created the cave paintings of Lascaux (Figure 6.7) may have had a sophisticated oral culture with folk tales and song for which the familiar running horses and aurochs were just a backdrop. But if so, the words and music died with them. All we have is the paint on the walls.

Figure 6.7 Cave painting Lascaux, France

Our view of our technological past is likewise informed by, and often relies solely on, preserved or discarded artefacts, from Neolithic axe heads to Victorian shovels. Even in relatively recent times when the records of the great and the letters of the middle classes preserved their legacy, the lives of mundane craftsfolk are poorly documented; we only know them through what they made.

In a literate age, print and music stave have preserved words and music although even now the knowledge of things can easily be lost (see Box 6.2).

Box 6.2 Nearly lost

The Tornado, a reproduction Peppercorn class 'A1' steam locomotive, was completed in 2008 after eighteen years in construction. The original engines had been built in 1949 but scrapped fifteen years later as diesel locomotives took over. The last surviving plans for the Peppercorn were only just saved when they were rescued from a skip, their discovery leading to the establishment of the A1 Steam Locomotive Trust (http://www.a1steam.com/), which reconstructed and now runs the Tornado.

The things we have around us, from the TV set to the electric kettle, shape our understanding of who we are, and how we see the world. However, the Soviet philosopher Ilyenkov went further. He saw 'ideals' (ideas or concepts) as being both embodied in artefacts and also giving those artefacts meaning [232]. So, a chair is a chair and not simply pieces of wood because the ideal of the chair has been made material through the labour of a carpenter, and it has become a chair. However, equally it is our idea of the chair that enables us to make sense of those pieces of wood arranged in that way and see that they are for sitting on.

6.6 Political

The physical world is central to politics. The land itself is at the core of the notion of the nation state, whether protected by walls and border controls, or simply measured out on a map. However, when we consider national identity it is often the symbolic nature of physical things that becomes important: the Houses of Parliament, Capitol Hill, or the Kremlin, waving flags, and national costume.

Digital technology has challenged the physical form of the nation state, making borders permeable. In the demise of the Soviet Union, the Allied bombing of Baghdad, the 2016 US Presidential Election, and numerous G8 summits, the openness of the Internet challenges the power of arms and police.

Yet perhaps the most radical subversive power of the digital is that it destabilizes the control of information. As Orwell's *1984* highlights, what we have most to fear is not the physical power of states but the more insidious psychological repression [321]. Again and again, totalitarian states have diminished physical distinctiveness to de-individuate and depersonalize and have used control of the press to control people's minds. In *1984* even the dictionary was rewritten so that only the 'right' information could exist. Blogs make the faceless human, and tweets undermine propaganda, although conversely these can also be the source of 'fake news' or state-sponsored manipulation.

However, the digital world also provides the very tools of state that Orwell imagined. In the United Kingdom, there is one closed-circuit television (CCTV) camera for every fifteen people, and while steaming open letters was laborious and hard to hide, the digital scanning of a nation's email is silent, invisible, and swift [426].

In other ways, globalization is reducing the integrity of the nation state, which was historically rooted in space and geography. Groups have always claimed allegiances before and beyond the nation state. Some groups are regional; for example, Italy is a young nation so many Italians feel a stronger regional than national identity, even down to the town (a sort of local nationalism called 'campanile' or 'campanilismo' [59]. Beyond the nation, multinationals, campaign groups, non-governmental organizations (NGOs), and social networks all claim loyalty; if Facebook were a country it would be the most populous in the world. Other allegiances are non-geographic, based around religion, trade, sport, or fandom.

In nature, computation, and human society there are two ways in which something can obtain integrity and identity. One way is through boundaries: cell membranes, city walls, or barbed wire fences. The other is through shared attributes: ant pheromones, bird song, or tagged photos in Instagram. Where groups have no

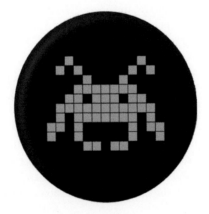

Figure 6.8 Physical symbols in a digital age

geographical boundary to define them, they often resort to physical symbols to identify themselves: coats of arms on the medieval battlefield, hoodies in the shopping mall, or brightly striped scarves in the football stadium. In the digital world there are no boundaries and no physicality, but blogs and social media pages are skinned and decorated, and it is possible to buy badges and T-shirts based on your favourite computer games (Figure 6.8).

Objects and **Things**

Physicality of Things

7.1 Physics and Naïve Physics

We all learnt Newton's laws of motion in school.

1. Every object stays still or moves at a uniform speed in a straight line unless acted on by an external force.
2. The rate of change of momentum is equal to the force applied $(F = ma)$
3. For every action there is an equal and opposite reaction.

But do you recall how confusing these were when you first heard them? They may be 'true' but they don't seem like 'real life'. Two millennia earlier when Aristotle considered motion, he asserted that the speed of an object, not the acceleration, was proportional to force. You push something harder, it goes faster. This accords with day-to-day life. If you are pushing a heavy box, when you push harder it moves faster and when you stop pushing it stops moving. But this contradicts Newton's first and second laws, which suggest that the object should keep on moving at a constant speed.

Of course, the two accounts can be reconciled. The box stops because of the frictional force that acts against its motion, and according to the third law there is an equal and opposite reaction, so that the friction also 'pushes' the floor, which itself pushes against the ground, and ultimately the earth spins a little slower or faster (yes, really). Happily for the future of the earth, the effects of pushing are negligible (the earth is a LOT bigger than any box you push) and moreover, as you originally pushed it, your feet pushed against the earth in the opposite direction, neatly balancing the effects!

While the physics of Newton and the physics of everyday life are not actually at variance, they are different. To apply Newtonian physics to complex phenomena requires complex analysis, so we have rules for the world that are simpler to apply. These common-sense rules are often called naïve physics [205, 371] or folk physics.

Here we are most interested in what this means for human understanding of physical things, but researchers in artificial intelligence and robotics are also interested in naïve physics since it often allows more efficient and robust automatic reasoning than attempting to use 'proper' Newtonian physics. With Newtonian physics, a robot wanting to move a box would have to know how heavy the box was, the characteristics of the surface of the floor and box (to work out the friction), and the exact power output of its own motors. If it encountered a tiny bump or imperfection in the surface it would have to start over again. With naïve physics it simply begins by pushing a little, and then pushes harder until the box moves.

We have naïve physics rules for objects and gravity, 'what goes up must come down'; for space and containment, 'if a room has only one entrance, what goes in must stay in or come out'; and for fluid substances, 'the amount of liquid stays the same when you pour it'. Many of these rules are learned from a very early age; one of the stages noted by Piaget, the founder of developmental psychology, is when a child learns about conservation of number, volume, and area.

Even the basic start point is different. Newtonian physics tends to reduce objects to equivalent 'point masses', ignoring all their other attributes. In contrast, James Gibson, the ecological psychologist of perception and action, argued that a person's immediate perception of objects is holistic; they are surfaces (the floor of a room, the outside of a ball) [182]. The physicist breaks objects down into their smallest constituent parts and most basic properties to analyse, whereas our naïve physics deals with the ways these parts and properties normally interact as a whole. The word 'normally' here is crucial. When faced with very unusual or unnatural situations the rules of naïve physics tend to go awry: think of walking on ice, a smooth frictionless surface, or pictures of space walking. Crucially, technology disrupts 'normal'.

Box 7.1 Naïve physics: weight and worth

A good general rule of thumb is that things of similar substance weigh more when they are bigger. A large sack of potatoes weighs more than a small one. However, if you are moving house the boxes all look similar, yet hide very different contents. You may find yourself almost falling over when you try to pick up a large box that is nearly empty, as your muscles were prepared for a heavy weight. If you actually weigh the boxes, you find that when you have a larger box that is exactly the same weight as a smaller one, the smaller one *feels* heavier than the large. Because you expect the large one to be heavier, your brain says, 'this is lighter than I thought'.

Likewise when you pick up a small metal item, it feels weightier than a larger plastic one that is actually identical in weight, and because it feels weightier physically, it also often feels weightier in terms of importance or quality.

7.2 Rules of Physical Things

In contrast to Newton's three laws there are many, many rules of naïve physics. However, here are three simple 'rules' of physical things. They were originally formulated to help explain to students why it is harder to design software than to engineer physical objects:

- *directness of (or proportional) effort*—Small effort produces small effects, large effort produces large effects. If you push a pebble a little, it moves a little; if you push it a lot, it moves a lot.
- *locality of effect*—The effects of actions occur where and when you act. If you push something and then it moves later you are surprised, and only a magician would try to move something without touching it.
- *visibility of state*—Physical objects have complex shape and texture, but this is largely static. The dynamic aspects of state are very simple: location, orientation, velocity, and rate of angular rotation. However, as humans we are not very good at assessing even the last of these!

These rules do have exceptions. For example, if a rock is precariously balanced a small push might send it rolling down the hillside (breaking directness of effort). Or if you accidentally put a glass down on the edge of a table and turn round you may be surprised to hear it fall and shatter a few moments later. The interesting thing is even these very natural breakings of the rules cause us surprise or, like magnetism's action at a distance, seem like magic.

All of these rules are systematically broken by human technology, and in particular digital technology. Consider a mobile phone:

- *no directness of effort*—Dial one digit wrong and you may ring someone in a different country, not just next door.
- *no locality of effect*—The whole purpose of a phone is to ring people up—spatial non-locality; the alarm you set at night rings in the morning—temporal non-locality; and text messages break both spatial and temporal locality!
- *no visibility of state*—The phone is full of hidden state, from the address book in the phone itself to the whole Internet (which while not 'in' the phone, can appear on the screen and therefore appears to be part of it).

As noted, it is not only digital technology that breaks these rules. Even the most basic technology often seems to give us supernatural power. For example, a simple saw means that a small amount of effort allows one to cut through a large piece of wood that would be impossible to split by hand (breaking directness of effort), and a bow and arrow allows action at a distance. Mechanical items like a car have complex invisible state (look under the bonnet) and a chemical plant is very like digital technology in terms of complexity (open a valve at one end of the plant and pressure goes up at a vessel at the other end).

It is interesting that in many areas of modern life where there is physical complexity, such as in the chemical plant, digital technology is being used to augment or substitute some of the unnatural activities. In a plane where cables once ran from cockpit to wing flaps, wires now carry signals to actuators. In the chemical plant not only are many valves operated electronically but sensors allow one to see the impact across the plant.

The last example is particularly significant as the sensors and visualizations in the chemical plant control room allow visibility at a distance and reveal things inside the vessels (pressure, flows) that one would not see by eye. The technology, by extending our senses, ameliorates the disorienting effect of the broken rules of physicality. Things distant and hidden become close and visible, so that the virtual world of the control room is closer to 'normal' physical reality than the situation a few years previously where the impact of actions was unseen.

7.3 Continuity in Time and Space

Each of the above rules is connected with some form of *continuity*. In scientific terms, digital computation is naturally discrete and discontinuous whereas physics (above the quantum level) tends to be about continuous processes. Indeed, there is a special area of computer science, 'hybrid systems', which focuses on models that allow these two worlds to meet [231]. More radically, within HCI, 'status–event analysis' tries to treat both kinds of phenomena on an equal footing [102, 130, 142].

Continuity is often broken in magic worlds and in science fiction where portals and teleportation allow us to move across space, or in the case of the Tardis [386] across time, without touching the points in between.

7.4 Conservation of Number and Preservation of Form

In the story of the Frog Prince (Figure 7.1) [202], the princess eventually kisses the frog and it turns into a handsome prince. Although this transmutation is odd, we accept it in the magic world. However, imagine if the story had three frogs which, when the last was kissed, became a single prince. Somehow this is much more surprising.

Figure 7.1 Jessie M King, 'The Frog Prince'

Conservation of number seems more primitive than conservation of form.

In fact, this difference is borne out by studies of very young babies. Newborns cannot focus clearly, but as soon as a baby is able to focus it is possible to obtain a measure of interest or surprise by recording how long the baby stares at something before moving its eyes.

One experiment involves having a barrier and putting objects one by one behind the barrier. In the baseline condition, the experimenter puts two mice behind the barrier and then opens the barrier and the baby sees two mice. In other conditions the experimenter puts two mice behind the barrier, but when it drops there are three mice, or just one mouse. In the conditions where the number revealed does not match the number put in, the baby will stare for longer, is more surprised: the tiniest babies can assess number (well, at least up to three). Experiments with animals find a similar effect: many animals can assess number (though not count).

An alternative test involves putting, say, a truck behind the barrier, but when the barrier is removed, a duck is there. In such cases the babies show less surprise and need to be much older before they realize something is 'wrong'. In other words conservation of number is more primitive than conservation of form [95]. The Frog Prince's transformation is not a surprise at all for a very young baby. This is of course very sensible for a developing baby: a single object, such as a toy or a mother's face, looks different from moment to moment as it moves, catches different light, or when the mother smiles. We have to learn over time which differences are simply differences of perspective and which really represent different things.

7.5 Emotion and Nostalgia

E-cards have been around for more than 20 years and in 2008 were estimated to be growing by 200% per year, so much so that there were fears that traditional cards would become a thing of the past [1]. Yet in the United Kingdom, over a billion paper Christmas cards were purchased from bricks and mortar stores in 2018, and millions more from electronic sites offering print-on-demand customizable cards [200]. Most of us have mementos, either on display on a mantelpiece, or in a box in drawer: a ticket from a football match, earrings you got for your 18th birthday, love letters, or a milk jug that belonged to your mother; physical things that you can touch and pick up, often things that were touched and held by someone else. They mean something because of what they are, who has given them, and the memories they hold.

Physical characteristics like weight and texture are critical in our emotional reaction to objects. If a device feels too light it may be perceived as fragile, whereas weight is often associated with value. So industrial designers have to worry as much about the feel of an object as its appearance. Car designers can create three-dimensional (3D) computer-aided design (CAD) models, view them in virtual reality environments, see what they look like as the sun catches their curves, but still there is something else beyond the look, the speed, and the accessories. Just stroke a hand along the bonnet; does it feel right?

Theories of experience and emotion have different terms for this. McCarthy and Wright's analysis of technology as experience includes a sensual thread of experience [285], the way the look and feel of an artefact or product creates thrill, excitement, or even fear. Don Norman, writing about emotional design, refers to visceral design [313], that immediate, in-your-body, reaction where 'physical features—look, feel, and sound—dominate'. And it works: users of the first iPod still talk about the feel of that scroll wheel [55].

Not only is the feel of an object a strong part of its aesthetic appeal but likewise the way we act on an object expresses our own emotions. When we are upset we may slam doors or clatter cutlery. And not only doors and cutlery; have you ever kicked your car or thumped the keys on your computer? Of course, such displays of emotion can be unfortunate if we actually dent the car or break the computer but they are an important part of expressing ourselves, and something we can use in design.

Certainly physical movements in Xbox interactions are used to control the gameplay, but they can also be expressive, perhaps swinging a virtual tennis racket between shots, or cornering over-sharply in a car race. However, just like the danger of breaking things in real life, if emotionally expressive actions overlap with those used to control the game the two may conflict. So, it can be beneficial to leave certain actions or gestures deliberately uninterpreted in order to provide space for expression.

Alternatively the user's expressive actions can be deliberately sensed in order to use that emotion as part of the device's behaviour. For example, researchers at Glasgow Caledonian University used the fact that gamepad buttons include pressure sensors. They hypothesized that the pressure with which a button is pressed will give an indication of the level of arousal, and indeed found that increasing the difficulty of the game increased average button pressure [385].

This form of implicit detection of mood was used in the design of the Key Table as part of the Equator 'curious home' (Figure 7.2) [179]. This was a small table placed just inside the door where people would put their keys when coming in. The force with which they put them down was measured, from gentle placement to slamming them down. Behind the table was a picture frame with a small motor. If the keys were put down hard the picture frame would move slightly, almost as if they were slammed with enough force to shake the whole house. People were left to interpret as they liked the angle of the picture.

Stephan Wensveen, Kees Overbeeke, and Tom Djajadiningrat went a step further in their design for an alarm clock [420, 419]. Instead of a conventional means to set the time, twelve sliders were

Figure 7.2 The emotionally expressive Key Table [385].

used (Figure 7.3). When all the sliders were in the middle the alarm would ring 12 hours from the time it was set. However, if you wanted eight hours sleep you had many options, you could put eight of the sliders in the middle, or put them all two-thirds of the way to the middle, or indeed use any pattern where the sliders 'added up' to eight. The mapping to the functionality of the alarm (the time to ring) only used some of the potential space of settings of the clock, leaving the rest free for emotional expression. Studies of how patterns of slider movement related to emotional state allowed the system to build a model of how the owner was feeling when going to sleep and this was used to adapt the alarm sound in the morning.

7.6 All Our Senses

While the fine arts tend to separate senses—oil painting for the visual, orchestras for the aural—the emotive and visceral reaction to physical objects is typically not confined to one attribute like

Box 7.2 SenToy—playing with emotions

Researchers in the European Safira project produced a small stuffed toy called SenToy [323]. SenToy is a bit like a rag doll but has no features, simply limbs and head. However, inside SenToy is a box of electronics, including accelerometers to sense shaking and movement, and cables for measuring flexing of the arms. SenToy is used to control a game of magic, but unlike a normal video game you cannot directly influence your character's actions. Instead you control its emotional state; for example, if you stretch SenToy's arms wide, your character is surprised, if you shake it violently it becomes angry. Inside the game a program then creates appropriate behaviour dependent on the emotion.

After playing with SenToy, people do not want to give it back. Some of this is to do with the fact that the whole experience is about emotion, but that is not the entire story. A careful design exercise compared potential designs and found that the soft cuddly designs were chosen over hard plastic. The feel is as important as the behaviour.

Figure 7.3 Emotionally expressive alarm clock [420, 419]

appearance, sound, or feel, but is about the way they work together. An initial sense of the quality and robustness of a device loses its integrity if it is too light when you pick it up, or squashes under your fingers. Contrast the tinny clatter of cheap saucepans with the duller thud when you put down a cast-iron casserole dish. Our senses have adapted to react to a range of facets of the physical world and, without realizing it, we come to expect a close integration between them all.

Sound is our second sense and crucial for speech. It is also a part of almost every interaction with a physical object. The oddness of silent films is not so much the lack of speech but the lack of everyday sounds, and the eeriness of fog scenes in movies is not just that you cannot see but that sound too is dulled. Players of video games know that the sound is an essential part of the play, both the ambient soundtrack and the noises of things: the roar of an engine, the boom of an explosion, or the thwack of a ball hitting a tennis racket.

Box 7.3 Silent battles

Think of the space fights in a film like 'Star Wars'. There is a constant sound of gunfire and explosions. However, in a real space fight you would only hear your own engines and gunfire. Enemy kills and the destruction of your own side would be silent except perhaps for the occasional clunk of debris against your hull. The only time you would hear an explosion would be your last.

Mechanical devices make noises (the click of a switch, or purr of a motor), often also linked to vibrations, and while we usually strive to reduce how noisy things are, total silence can be unnerving. We 'read' the sonic environment without noticing that we do so. Think of an old jungle film, they wake in the night and feel that something is wrong, only slowly realizing it is because of the silence, all the animals have fled. Total silence can also be dangerous; indeed some electric cars make an artificial noise to avoid accidents.

In general, digital devices tend to be more silent in terms of physical action. For example, many buttons on small devices use flexible underlays and dials do not audibly click. The importance of hearing the sound of pressing a key is evidenced most strongly by the fact that many keyboards generate a simulated key-click. In fact, sound is one of the easiest senses to recreate digitally and has been used very effectively to make digital actions emulate physical ones. Think about the 'crunch' when you throw a file into the virtual desktop rubbish bin.

In the real world the sound an object makes is closely associated with its physical properties. Hard materials tend to make stronger and higher pitched sounds than soft materials: the sharp clang of a dropped spanner versus the dull thud of cricket ball and bat. Large and full vessels make deeper pitched sounds while small or empty vessels make high-pitched sounds. The sound also depends on the kind of action: tap a table gently and the sound is different than if you hammer it with your fist.

Some years ago, in the spirit of Gibson's analysis of visual perception, Bill Gaver proposed an ecological approach to auditory sound perception, analysing the different sound patterns in neutral environments, whether from solid objects (bumps, bangs, scrapes), liquids (bubbles, flows, splashes), or gases (explosions, wind). Figure 7.4 shows his typology of different kinds of sounds [180].

Gaver suggested that these natural relationships between sound and physical action and material could be used to generate better digital sounds. For example, if you discard a small file it should make a higher note than throwing away a large file, or during the download of a large document the progress bar could be accompanied by the sound of water filling a container with the sound becoming lower pitched as the download nears completion. The utility of this approach was verified by later experiments [303], but the application of physical sounds in the interface is still minimal. For example, macOS does include a number of sounds such as a 'crunch' when files are thrown in the trash but the sound does not depend on the size of the file.

The feel of objects is obviously crucial when we cannot see or look at them directly: reaching out for a glass of water in the night or switching radio stations when driving a car. However, even when we

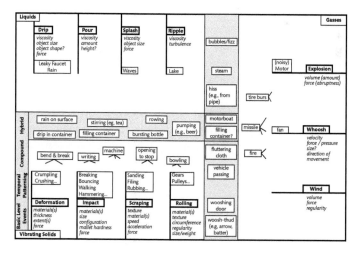

Figure 7.4 Typology of ecological sounds from [180].

can see the object and our hands, we still rely on tactile properties. In experiments with different prototype mobile phone keyboards, the most profound differences in behaviour were found when real keys were replaced by a flat membrane [202] (see the Equinox Case Study in Chapter 20). While the membrane still allowed tactile feedback as you pressed a button, you could not simply feel the buttons under your fingers as you tried to locate a key.

Recent digital technologies often replace the projecting buttons and knobs of older consumer electronics with sleek flat panels or touchscreens. Some touchscreen phones attempt to ameliorate this by using the vibrator motor to give little 'kicks' as your finger moves over onscreen buttons and keys. The effect is not the same as feeling a real button but is remarkably effective, given the simplicity of the mechanism.

Another example comes from the iDrive found in some BMWs, first mentioned in Chapter 2. A single dial was to be used for many different menu functions, each of which could have different numbers of options. The iDrive uses a haptic feedback device, a small motor that gives slight resistance as you try to turn the knob.

These are both examples where a loss of tactile or haptic feedback is being replaced with digital emulation. However, tactile and haptic properties can be a significant design resource. By choosing surfaces with different characteristics (smoother, rougher, sticky), or controls with the right level of resistance, the user's hand can be naturally guided to the most important controls, or learn the layout by touch alone. Furthermore, vibrotactile technology (arrays of tiny vibrating pins), which has been used for some years in electronic Braille displays, is beginning to become a feasible alternative for many devices, allowing the possibility of dynamically adjusting textures of surfaces.

Interacting with Physical Objects

Objects in the world may have all sorts of properties and impact on our senses in many ways, but when thinking about design the most critical are what we can do with them (e.g. pick up, throw), or what they may do to us (hit us!). When we interact with objects they become part of our own activities and lives.

8.1 Affordance Revisited—What We Can Do and What We Think We Can Do

We briefly mentioned James Gibson's affordance theory in Chapter 5. Recall that affordance is about what it is possible to do with a thing, the potential for action of an object or the world in general [182]. Note that what the environment affords depends on the person or animal looking at it. Whether or not a rock shelf affords sitting upon depends on your leg length; whether a large stone affords throwing depends on whether you are an Olympic shot-putter or not. The differences between humans are relatively small, but certainly what the environment affords a song thrush is very different to what it affords a snow tiger. Affordance is fundamentally relational and can only be understood by considering both the environment and the agent who can act (or be acted upon) in the environment. It is for this reason that Gibson's approach is often called ecological psychology: it is about the creature in an environment.

However, we are creatures adapted to our (natural) environment, and so Gibson argued further that our whole perceptual system is attuned to seeking out the action potential of the environment. Our eyes, our ears, indeed all our senses and the brain processing that goes with them, are designed in order to act. This is precisely the emphasis of embodied mind philosophy introduced in Chapter 5.

Because of this adaptation to the environment, Gibson argues that the perception of affordance is *immediate*. We do not need to go through abstract reasoning steps:

> rock is about 10 centimetres across and rock is in reach, therefore rock can be picked up

Instead we are immediately aware of the pertinent qualities of both the object itself, our own bodies in the environment, and the available affordances. Even that awareness may itself be subconscious. We do not explicitly think, 'that cup can be picked up', we just do it and drink.

8.2 Affordances of the Artificial

Gibson's illustrations of affordance include artificial phenomena and objects as well as natural ones. However, there is a crucial difference. It is reasonable to believe that the human species has adapted over millennia to the natural world and hence its affordances are directly available to us. The low-level discrimination of our eyes, the range of frequencies that our ears pick up, the turning of our eyes and head in response to movement at the edge of our vision, the ways in which our brains process these and react to them—they are all there to support acting in this natural environment.

It is not so clear why we are able to ascertain that a cup can be picked up, let alone that a television can be switched on using a remote control. Indeed, in the human-crafted world things often go awry. Norman highlighted many examples in his book *The Design of Everyday Things*[1], which popularized the word 'affordance' within the Human–Computer Interaction (HCI) and design communities, albeit with a somewhat different meaning than Gibson's [314].

---

[1] Norman's book was originally entitled *The Psychology of Everyday Things*, but when it moved into paperback the publishers obviously thought 'design' was a better draw than 'psychology'

Many building doors look symmetric. Though they only open in one direction, the handles look the same from whichever side you approach. You see the door in the distance and as you get closer you can see a sign attached to it. The sign says 'Push'. You read the sign, acknowledge it, and reach for the handle. Then you pull the door and nearly jar your arm out of its socket. If you *have* done this, the good news is that it's not your fault. Essentially, the door carries two signs: the handle itself, telling you to pull, and the written one telling you to push. The physical feel of the handle triggers your immediate response to it, and you pull. It is possible to overrule this urge but only if you are concentrating, and this is not the type of task we generally concentrate on!

The problem is that the perceived affordance is different from the actual affordance.

Sometimes these disparities between appearance and action are deliberate, as in the joke of gluing a coin to the pavement in order to see people struggle to pick it up. However, more often, as in the case of the door handles, it is an accident or poor design (Figure 8.1).

While our senses are tuned to the affordances of the natural world, there is no *a priori* reason why the affordances of constructed (and hence unnatural) objects should be apparent, unless they are designed to be so. That is we have a design heuristic:

Figure 8.1 Glued coins and door handles

design so that the affordances suggested by appearance match those
actually afforded by the artefact

The surprising thing is not that there are problems like confusing
door handles in the constructed environment, but that there are not
more. How is it that we manage at all?

It is partly to do with the objects themselves, and partly with the
skill of the designer.

- *necessary physical correlates*—The purpose and use of an artificial object, that is what it affords, are constrained by the properties of
  the physical world (including people) in which it will be used.
  If you design a cup to hold drinks then it will need to have a
  suitable hollow in it, and this hollow will be similar to those in
  natural objects that afford holding fluid. Likewise, if the cup is
  designed to be picked up, it will tend to have a size and shape
  similar to natural pick-up-able objects.
- *design selection*—Successful designs can be used easily. Therefore it
  is reasonable to suppose that over time, traditional designs will
  end up with perceived affordances that match their actual affordances. The pace of mass manufacture means that this is not
  necessarily the case for more explicitly designed goods, though
  it is still likely that those with successful sales match appearance
  and affordance, whether deliberately or accidentally.
- *by design*—A good designer may either explicitly realize that
  they need to match perceived and actual affordance, or simply
  'know' what is right.
- *imitation and artefact ancestry*—Often artificial objects mimic natural
  objects, or derive from previous artificial objects that themselves mimicked natural ones or were subject to physical correlates, design selection, or plain good design.

8.3 Adapted for New Actions

Not only are objects adapted to people, we also adapt to the world.
Some creatures operate almost purely by instinctive reaction. Frogs

have dedicated visual areas that respond to a small *moving* dot (that is, flies) and trigger the tongue to dart in the right direction to catch it. If you try to feed the frog dead flies, no matter how fresh, it will never even notice but will starve even with food in front of it.

Higher animals and especially humans are much more adaptable and learn both during infanthood and also as adults. Rather than being born pre-programmed for the affordances of a particular natural environment, we are instead able to *learn* these affordances. In other words, the immediate perception of (natural) affordances is not entirely innate, but we are born with the ability to form new associations between perception and action. This has given us the ability to adapt ourselves to different natural environments from savannah to tundra and also to artificial environments of our own making.

Note that this adaptability and ability to learn does not mean we are born without innate responses. The idea of the child's mind being a *tabula rasa*, a blank slate ready to be written upon by experience and education, was present in some of the earliest philosophy, but is most closely associated with John Locke's 'An Essay Concerning Humane Understanding' [265]. However, more recent philosophers and psychologists, especially those taking a more embodied view of the mind, suggest that there is far more that is 'inbuilt'.

Evidence for this includes the fact that babies can perform mirror actions from an early age, imitating facial expressions and movements before there has been any chance to learn the association [172, 290]. Similarly, they can move their heads in the direction of sounds and in other ways that suggest that a basic model of the physical self and an egocentric 'model' space are there from birth or develop spontaneously soon after.

Brain imaging has shown the existence of so-called mirror neurons. When we see another person doing an action it fires particular parts of our brain (the mirror neurons), but these in turn connect to exactly the same parts of the brain as when we perform the same action ourselves [172, 336]. Seeing someone else doing something is nearly the same as doing it oneself!

It is possible that the relationship between our proprioceptive sense of body position and the actions of muscle movement is effectively 'learned' through association, maybe even in the womb. However, the ability to see another person and mirror their actions, that is the development of the mirror neurons, cannot be learned before we see others and so appears to be born in us, part of our initial neural wiring.

Looking at other animals, it is clear that they too have an innate sense of body presence and movement, and indeed their 'initial wiring' seems if anything far stronger than our own. The young of most animals, including those that exhibit learning, can function to some extent either from birth or at a young age; think of those Bambi-like pictures of young fawns standing and running with the herd moments after birth. However, animals with more complex

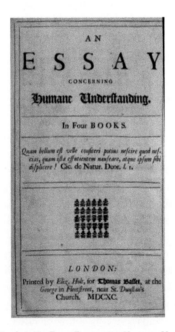

Figure 8.2 John Locke's 'An Essay Concerning Humane Understanding' [265].

social behaviour (dogs, elephants) often have infants who are more dependent for longer, suggesting that a stronger role for life-long learning necessitates weaker innate instincts.

Humans are the extreme, and indeed Clive Bromhall's book *The Eternal Child* [43] suggests that we are effectively always infants, not so much naked apes as ones that never mature enough to have hair! He argues that the infantile features and behaviours in some species allowed them to be more social because they avoided the extremes of territoriality that come with adulthood. In humans this effect may have been amplified by runaway sexual selection. Following this argument, our cognitive flexibility is simply a side effect of our per-petual neonate status; we retain the neural plasticity of a pre-born and the curiosity and sociability of a child, while having the physical size and strength of an adult.

Others would perhaps swap these round and see the cognitive ad-vantages coming first, but in both views it would be a big step from weaker instincts to no instinctive understanding. While the price of sociability and cognitive flexibility may be that human infants do not have the ability to run like a deer, it seems likely both from empirical evidence and common sense that we all start with a level of innate grasp of the body and world that acts as a bootstrap for later learned understanding.

The problem of distinguishing innate understanding from under-standing developed early as an infant arises precisely because of our rich ability to learn, especially if we are 'hard-wired' to learn cer-tain kinds of things easily. As tiny infants we reach out, touch things, push beads and blocks. Are we born with the understanding that if we push things they move, or is it that we pick this up in our first few months of life? Whichever it is, our grasp of the physical world is a form of birthright, available to every child brought up in normal circumstances, anywhere in the world and at any time in history.

The end-point of this ability to cope with savannah and tundra is that we are also able to learn about light switches and TV remotes. We are natural born affordance-seekers, learning new ways to act in the world and then adding these to our repertoire. The conventions that we learn, whether turning a water tap or switching on a light, are cultural affordances which then become part of the way that future action potential is perceived.

However, while the basic properties of the physical world do not change, these conventions do. Cultures vary geographically and travellers find it difficult to relearn how to turn on a shower, or even a light. Cultures also change over time. Sometimes old conventions are maintained long after the physical reasons for them have faded; for example, the play/pause/fast-forward/rewind buttons of the old analogue tape recorder (Figure 8.3) are now preserved in digital controls. However, changing conventions can disenfranchise. For example, elderly people may have difficulty in grasping the action potential of onscreen menus that seem second nature to those who have grown up with computers.

Our cognitive flexibility also allows us to reason, even when the appearance of things does not immediately suggest use.

1. There is a water tap, but no handle to twist or press.
2. There is a foot pedal and it is attached to the water pipe.
3. Therefore try pressing the foot pedal.

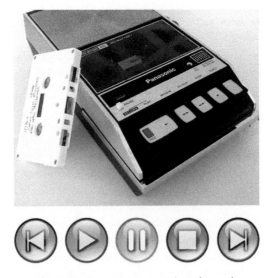

Figure 8.3 Screen icons imitate physical controls

Of course, this reasoning itself makes use of a combination of basic properties of the physical world, learned associations, and culturally specific clues. There is a hierarchy here, from those things that are either innate or learned as a tiny infant, to those that we learn culturally, to those that we have to work out in the situation. As we move up this hierarchy to more and more complex behaviours, our reactions tend to be slower, require more mental effort, and potentially become more error-prone.

It is perhaps the times when errors occur 'lower down' the hierarchy that things go most dramatically wrong. A short while ago, Alan was in a stairwell at night. There was no natural light and in the dark he felt around close to the door from which he had just emerged. Eventually he found a small square pad, rather like (cultural affordance) the timed light switches that you press to give you a few minutes of light. He gently pressed, it did not instantly move, so he pressed a little harder (physical understanding—if it doesn't move press harder). A moment later he felt and heard a crack beneath his fingers and the fire alarm rang!

Earlier we suggested that a good heuristic for affordances was to design things so that the perceptual affordances suggest the actual action potential, but even more important as a design rule is:

> make sure that the perceptual affordances (natural or cultural) do not suggest erroneous and harmful behaviour

If you can't get it right, don't make it too wrong!

8.4 Action as Investigation

Situation 1: You are in your own home and wake early in the morning. You go to your kitchen, open a cupboard, and take out the coffee. A few minutes later you return to bed with a mug of coffee and a book.

Situation 2: A few days later you are visiting a friend. You wake early in the morning and go to the kitchen to make a coffee. In front of you is an array of identical cupboards, but which contains the coffee? You have various ways of finding out. You could go and wake your friend to ask. You could reason it out, maybe selecting the cupboard nearest the stove. However, what you are likely to do is open a few doors until you find the coffee.

In Situation 1 you know where the coffee is, since it is your own kitchen (the knowledge is in your head), but in Situation 2 the knowledge is in a sense 'out there' in the kitchen, so you need to explore to find out. In both situations you open a cupboard, but in your own kitchen the action is pragmatic, it achieves a concrete purpose, whereas opening the cupboards in Situation 2 is an epistemic action, an action intended to give you knowledge.

You can probably think of many epistemic actions: looking in the fridge to see what you need to replenish, turning a tomato over in a supermarket to check it is not damaged on the hidden side, tugging the leaves of a pineapple to see if it is ripe, craning your neck to check the road is clear before driving off. Many of these are incidental to the main purpose of your activity (shopping, getting from A to B, drinking a mug of coffee), but in some cases, such as turning the pages of a book, the primary purpose of the activity is purely informational.

We have already discussed how perception and thinking are not disembodied but are intimately tied to our being creatures who act in the world: we perceive in order to act. Epistemic actions are in a sense the other side of this, in that we act in order to perceive. Indeed, Gibson argues that the boundaries are largely artificial, so that seeing is not just about a single image on our retina, nor even the flow of images as our eyes scan in front and our head rotates to see behind, but is part and parcel of an integrated sensing-acting system that includes our hands and bodies.

Just as we saw when discussing the embodied mind in Chapter 5, Clark's '007 principle' of parsimony applies [68]. In general, we do not bother to hold information in our heads that can be more quickly or easily seen, heard, or felt in the environment.

One aspect of this that has been studied in detail is mental rotation; that is the ability to turn an object round in one's head in two or three dimensions. This is often tested by asking people to decide whether two shapes shown at different angles are the same. The time taken to make the decisions is directly proportional to the angle you have to 'turn' the objects in your head in order to match them. Players of Tetris typically turn the fresh pieces as soon as they appear, as it only takes a few hundred milliseconds to do an onscreen rotation, (taking into account visual and motor delays) whereas the equivalent mental rotations may take over a second [250]: it is quicker to turn over the actual pieces than to think about it. Likewise with physical puzzles, if you are completing a jigsaw you will not just stare at a piece trying to decide if it will fit but instead spin it round and try it in position.

It may seem odd that we are not better at mental rotation, which is effectively about the physical world of which we are part, but in fact drawing is a fairly new skill, in evolutionary terms. Before we drew, we could always 'try things out' or move to see an object from a different angle, so we did not need to develop better mental skills. Note this is a cost–benefit trade-off again, but at a longer timescale. The 'choice' in Tetris or the jigsaw puzzle to manipulate objects in the environment instead of the head is something we do moment to moment and largely unconsciously Figure 8.4. The fact that we are not better at mental rotation is about our development as a species.

Of course, acting to perceive is sometimes costly or dangerous, especially if the act of investigating has irreversible consequences, as was the case with Pandora's Box. In such circumstances, we often have consciously to stop ourselves from acting, for example reaching out to open a door if there is smoke coming through, or looking over your shoulder instead of at the road when driving past a car accident.

The boundaries between action and perception blur further because many actions that are about 'getting things done' also give us fresh information as a side effect. As you drive down the road you can see further round the corner, as you pick up a box you feel how robust and how heavy it is. Equally, epistemic actions often become the effective action for which they are seeking information. You turn the jigsaw puzzle piece round, try it in position, and find it fits, so you leave it there. Finding out if it fits and putting it in place are one

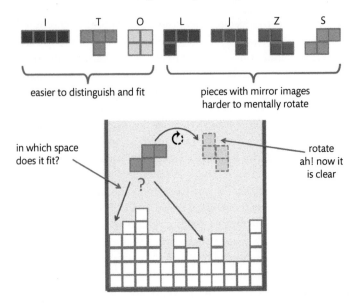

Figure 8.4 Embodiment in Tetris (top) mirror image pieces are especially hard to rotate mentally (bottom) where does it fit? Rotating the piece makes it easier to tell.

and the same action. If you were to ask your friend where to find the coffee in their kitchen, the acts of finding out (asking) and getting the coffee would be separate. When you investigate yourself, the point at which you open a cupboard to see what is inside and find the coffee there is coincident with opening the cupboard to take it out.

8.5 Letting the World Help

Our bodies are covered in soft skin, our tendons and muscles are elastic, even our bones have some flexibility. This flexibility is important for many reasons. It protects us from injury: we are less likely to break limbs when we fall, or strain muscles when we exercise. It is also efficient; when we run, the foot that lands absorbs the energy of your body and leg hitting the ground and then 'bounces back', helping you on your next stride and meaning you can run faster with less energy.

This flexibility also helps when we interact with objects in the world. Imagine a classic science-fiction robot with a pincher grip picking up a crystal vase. It needs to exert a very precise grip: too tight and it will shatter the glass, too loose and the vase drops. However, when you grip the vase the flexibility of the pads of your fingers gives a small margin.

The objects that we manipulate also make a difference to how easy it is to work with them. More natural materials typically have more flexibility: think about putting on a woollen jumper compared with a suit of armour! Tight, precision fit is often important in mechanical items but is typically harder to assemble.

While humans cope with this type of action, robots do not, and those designing automated production lines have to design some of this natural flexibility back into both the robots and the items being assembled. Take the example of locating a screw in a hole. If the screw is a tight fit, it may be very difficult to position it in precisely the right position. However, if the screw is slightly pointed at its end, or the hole is drilled with a slight countersink, the screw will find the hole even if the location and angle are not entirely perfect (Figure 8.5). The robot arm also has to 'give' a little so that the screw can guide itself into position; in robotics this is called 'compliant action'.

Box 8.1 Tight screws

If you are putting in a small screw yourself, you may have similar problems to the robot. If you tighten the screw when it is in the wrong position you might 'cross-thread' the screw, spoiling either it or the work piece or both. Instead try holding the screw in the hole and with slight pressure turn it backwards (counter clockwise for a normal screw). At some point you feel a slight click into position. When you feel this you can then start to turn the right way and (usually) it fits easily.

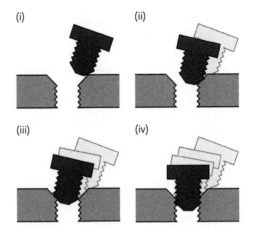

Figure 8.5 Compliant action: (i) screw slightly misplaced, but naturally (ii) slides, and (iii) rotates, (iv) into place.

In Chapter 5, we noted how one solves mathematical problems using paper, and in Chapter 4 how match puzzles usually require playing with the matches, not just thinking about them. In both these cases the problems are rather discrete (unless one breaks the matches!) and cerebral (even if enacted with physical materials). However, we often use the more analogue properties of materials to help us solve problems or 'compute' things.

It is laundry day and you have just taken the freshly cleaned sheets off the washing line. You want to fold the sheet in half. Do you carefully measure the mid-point? No. If there are two of you, you each take opposite corners and then bring the corners together, hold them with one hand, put your finger in the fold, and then pull tight. Your finger naturally slides into the middle position. To fold end to end one of you brings their end to the other and the weight of the sheet again neatly halves it. Even thirds are quite easy using variants of the finger-and-slide techniques (Figure 8.6).

As well as helping us to do things, physical properties can prevent us doing things. Think of the time-set button on a wristwatch; it is

Figure 8.6 Folding clean linen in perfect thirds

usually small and recessed so that you have to use a pen point or something similar to hold it in position. While this makes it rather difficult to set the time deliberately, it also makes it almost impossible to accidentally do so. In a similar way, flip phones have a flap over the keyboard so that you cannot accidentally ring a number. Phones with physical keys but no keyboard flap need to have an explicit keyboard lock function, usually pressing several keys in combination. Notice the choice: the flip phone works by exploiting the physicality of the phone, the keyboard lock uses digital interaction.

There are clearly many issues in play when making design decisions, but when a physical constraint can be used, such as the keyboard flap or the recessed time-set button, it is often more intuitive and robust.

The flip phone flap does not just prevent accidental phone calls. As you open the flap, new opportunities for interaction are made apparent. In terms of affordances, the flap affords opening and the buttons afford pressing. When using a digital keyboard lock for a phone with physical buttons, the buttons are still visible, and so it is possible to start to enter a number before one realizes the phone is locked. In this case the perceptual affordance of the keys is there whether or not they actually afford entering a phone number, in contrast to the flap, where the perceptual affordances of the buttons are only revealed when they can be used.

Gaver calls this process sequential affordance, where performing an action corresponding to one affordance makes new affordances available and apparent. He gives the example of a twist door handle. The handle itself (if designed well) is hand-shaped and sized and affords grasping. Once you have grasped the door handle, it then affords twisting, and finally having twisted the door handle, the door affords opening.

Note that the actual affordances have a sequence: you cannot twist the handle unless you are grasping it, you cannot pull open the door unless you have twisted the handle. The door handle also has perceptual affordances: the hand size and shape is visually apparent. But what about the twisting and opening affordances? How do we know what to do?

Obviously there are cultural issues in play. We know door handles often twist and that doors open, and that typically (though not always) door handles twist downwards. There may also be subtle visible signs in the shape of the door surround or the visibility of the hinges, which tell us whether the door opens inwards or outwards. Yet we do cope remarkably well when we do not know and indeed if we initially get it wrong.

One reason is that the door handle 'gives' a little if you put pressure in the right direction—that is, you can work out what the affordances are by feel. This 'give' is common in physical situations. You are not sure whether a box is full, and too heavy to lift, or empty, so you give it a little trial pull, not fully lifting it, but with enough pressure to see if it would lift if you really tried. You are not sure whether a door is locked, so you give it little trial pull to see if it starts to move, but not enough to open it fully.

In contrast, many digital controls lack this 'try-it-out' nature. For example, with many touchscreens if you put your finger on an area and it happens to be active, then you have already selected it. Additional visual clues may be provided, for example the mouse cursor changes shape, a screen area changes colour, or a tool tip appears, or when you depress the mouse button over an active area the screen object may change colour or highlight. All of these offer similar information to the small 'give' of the door handle, but they lack the intuitive and immediate feel of the physical feedback and rely more on the visual senses.

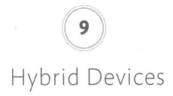

Hybrid Devices

9.1 Abstraction—Software as if Hardware Doesn't Matter

The computer being used to write this chapter is a laptop with a trackpad. The awkward angles needed to use the trackpad continuously lead to pains in the wrist and hands, so there is also a wireless mouse. However, when swapping between mouse and trackpad there is no need to change software, the same word processor works equally well with both. If this seems unsurprising to you, think again how different a mouse and trackpad are. It is like going to a restaurant and being given a fork instead of a soup spoon. Even more amazing, the same web pages you can use on the laptop with mouse or trackpad can also be used on the phone, clicking links using your finger alone.

Now this seems so obvious that you need to really step back to realize it is surprising at all. However, things were not always this way and the identification of abstract devices was crucial to the development of the modern user interface.

Early terminals had keyboards, so there was an easy first abstraction, *text entry*, as all had the basic alphabet and numbers. However, even here there were numerous differences, from plain keyboards to those with special keys for a particular function. Cursor keys came slowly, so early software often had different mappings from keys and key combinations to actions. Nowadays this is virtually obsolete, partly due to keyboard standardization and partly to increasing reliance on the mouse (or trackpad), but its remnants can still be seen in the slightly different key mappings of Mac and Windows software.

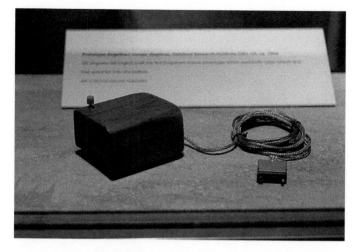

Figure 9.1   Douglas Engelbart's first mouse

The origins of the mouse date back to the early 1960s with Douglas Engelbart's innovative Augmentation Research Center (Figure 9.1). While the mouse was used in the very first Macintosh computer in 1984, it was in fact some time before it became more widely used in personal computers, largely because most did not have graphical windows-based user interfaces but instead were based on character maps.

However, before the desktop computer had become common-place there were a variety of high-end graphical workstations for use in specialized areas such as Computer-Aided Design (CAD) and scientific visualization. These often needed some way to draw and to select lines and areas on screen, but they varied tremendously in the devices used to achieve this. Some had light pens (Figure 9.2) which could be used to touch points on the screen directly, or draw on the screen as if it were paper. Others used tablets with 'pucks', a bit like a mouse except that the position of the puck on the tablet mapped directly to a position on the screen, whereas with the mouse it is only the movement that matters. Some CAD workstations had small

Figure 9.2 Light pen in use

joysticks, or two small thumbwheels: one controlling horizontal 'x' location and one for the vertical 'y' location.

This variety of hardware did not matter when computers were so specialized that software and hardware were delivered together as a package. However, in the late 1960s and early 1970s those working in computer graphics began to look for more generic ways to describe and build interactive graphical software, and identified a number of key functions, all of which could be achieved using a combination of a keyboard and some form of pointing device [308, 408]. Low-level software converted the varying signals generated by the different forms of pointing device into a uniform digital format. By the time the current windows-based operating systems (X/Linux, macOS, Windows) were developed, they all had generic 'mouse' devices, which in fact can be just about anything that generates an x–y coordinate and has the means to select through pressing a button or otherwise.

This abstraction away from hardware has been incredibly successful, and because of it, when laptops appeared that used alternative devices instead of the mouse—trackballs, keyboard nipples, and trackpads—there was no need to develop new software, just a 'driver' for the new device that made it appear to the software the same as the mouse. Likewise, direct screen devices such as styli on tablets or direct finger touch interactions are 'just like a mouse' to the word processor or web browser with which you are interacting.

This process has continued as radically new hardware capabilities have appeared. For example, both Mac OS X and Windows now provide the programmer with generic scroll wheel events. Multi-touch devices, such as the iPhone, that use two-finger gestures have proved challenging, since two fingers are definitely not the same as two mice (and anyway, not many systems use two mice). Apple, providing both software and hardware, were in a similar position to early graphics workstation manufacturers, able to tune the software to particular hardware characteristics, whereas Microsoft wished to provide a variant of Windows that could run on any multi-touch hardware and so had to work out new abstractions over the common features [425].

9.2 The Limits of Hardware Abstraction

It would be very surprising in a book about physicality if we ended up saying the precise nature of hardware doesn't matter. Abstractions are both theoretically elegant and practically useful, and the importance and utility of suitable ways to abstract away from the specificity of devices should not be underestimated. However, there are limitations: a mouse is *not* the same as a trackpad (if it were there would be no reason to buy a mouse to go with the laptop), and phone keypads, TV remotes, and washing machine controls are not all the same.

Very early on in the quest for abstractions over keyboards and pointing devices, there were voices who warned about these limitations. Bill Buxton was one of these. He pointed out differences in both the intrinsic capabilities of the then popular pointing devices and also in the ease with which different devices could be used for specific tasks.

For the first of these, the intrinsic capabilities, Buxton showed that pointing devices differ even at a very abstract level. He distinguished three states [53]:

- State 0—no tracking, no pointer shown on screen; for example, a light pen or touchscreen when the pen or finger is far from the screen.
- State 1—tracking, pointer shown on screen, but just to show you where it is; for example, a mouse when no buttons are pressed.
- State 2—dragging, pointer shown, and something happening such as a window being moved, or a line being drawn; for example, a mouse when the button is held down.

A mouse is only ever in States 1 or 2, whereas the light pens available at the time could have all three states: not in contact with the screen, so no tracking; in contact with the screen and tracking; and in contact with the screen with the button pressed for dragging. Of course, you can lift a mouse off the table, but this simply leaves the cursor on the screen where it is, whereas if you lift your finger off the screen and then down somewhere else, the 'pointer' jumps to the new position.

In fact this particular difference is not too much of a problem. Most applications are designed for the mouse, and the light pen had more capability than the mouse, so unless the programmer did not deal well with sudden jumps in mouse position, all was well.

More problematic is that many touchscreens, both stylus-based and finger-based, only operate in States 0 and 2. When you are not in contact with the screen there is no detection of location, and when you are in contact it is treated as a 'selection'. There is an argument that State 1 is only needed because the mouse is an indirect device, moved on the table top to affect the screen. You don't need State 1 with the stylus as you can see where it is on the screen. However, State 1 allows pixel-precision positioning of the mouse cursor, whereas with touch-based interfaces fine positioning is very difficult (the 'fat finger' problem).

There are ways round this. For example, the iPhone adds an extra layer of interaction: if you touch and move, it is treated as State 2 dragging, but if you touch and stay still, a small magnified view is shown and movement treated as State 1 with the lifting of the finger acting as selection. However, this allows no way to perform a drag action with pixel-level accuracy for the start and end points, so the text applications all have text selections where the end points can be individually dragged.

Even when devices are capable of the same things, it does not mean they are equivalent to use. Buxton showed this by comparing children's drawing toys. Like the early CAD workstations, Etch-a-Sketch has separate knobs for horizontal and vertical movement (see Figure 9.3). This makes it really easy to draw the sides of a rectangle, but hard to draw a smooth diagonal line or circle. The mouse of course has the opposite characteristics, fine for any movement, but without the precision of separate x–y controls. Indeed, in a

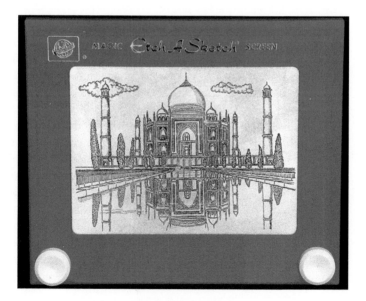

Figure 9.3 Etch-a-Sketch

drawing program you may have found yourself sizing boxes by separately dragging the side and top edges (x or y, one at a time) instead of the corner, or using text-entry boxes to give precise x and y coordinates.

Even the mouse itself differs considerably between brands. The earliest mice often had the buttons on the sides or end whereas most modern mice have buttons on the top (or in the case of the Apple mouse the whole top surface). This is fine when clicking or dragging for short distances. However, if you need to drag, say, an icon across a large display, you may have to pick up the mouse to scroll the whole distance. Doing this while gripping a button at the side or end is fine, but it is almost impossible while pushing *down* on the mouse button. It is worth mentioning that early Macs had very small displays, so this issue did not arise.

Such differences between devices affect performance. In Chapter 5, we described Fitts' Law, which predicts how long it takes to make positioning movements with a pointing device.

$$time = A + B \log (distance/size)$$

While any single device tends to follow the logarithmic law when comparing different distances and sizes of target, *between* devices the constants A and B can differ markedly, and this is used as the basis of the ISO 9241 standard to measure 'non-keyboard' devices.

The differences are even more important when considering specialized tasks. Many computer artists prefer to use a tablet and pen instead of a mouse as the combination of the angle you hold the pen and the fact that there is a direct mapping between location on the tablet and screen location makes it seem more 'natural', more like a real pencil or brush.

It is also significant, not least when comparing different 'equivalent' devices, that some have different ergonomic characteristics. The reason for using an additional mouse with the laptop is to alleviate the muscle and joint strain of relying solely on the laptop trackpad.

9.3 Specialization—Computer-embedded Devices

While it is possible to regard computers as pretty much similar to each other, the same cannot be said for kitchen appliances. The controls for a cooker, washing machine, dishwasher, microwave, and food mixer all look different, with specialized dials and buttons for particular functions. Because the computer is 'general purpose', it has a one-size-fits-all collection of devices (mouse, keyboard, screen), whereas more specialized consumer goods have controls designed specifically for purpose.

There is still a level of similarity, with individual controls on each device having recognizable buttons and dials. However, the number of controls and the way they are laid out are individual and specific. The computer uses a single physical device (the mouse or trackpad) and makes it serve many purposes, often by showing virtual 'buttons' on the screen. Larger consumer appliances are more likely to have several buttons or dials, each with a single or small number of functions. Furthermore, even the dials differ: some can be moved continuously within some range, others have a number of 'clicks' relating to the number of options they control.

While dials and buttons are generic, there are sometimes very specific controls designed for a particular purpose, such as the steering wheel on a car. These may have a seemingly arbitrary connection to the function they perform. For example, the gearstick on a car has a particular form due to the mechanics of the gearbox, but for the ordinary driver that is just the way it is. See Chapter 19 for more about physicality and car controls.

Other controls, however, are intimately connected with the act of using the device, for example the food mixer that turns on when you press down on it, or the digital scales that automatically turn on when you step on them. The latter can be particularly intuitive, to the extent that the user may not even think 'now I'm turning this on'; it just happens at the right moment. Volkswagen-built satellite navigation systems usually show an uncluttered screen, but when a user moves to interact with it, a proximity sensor triggers to reveal a set of options. Most users don't even notice!

Sometimes users are completely unaware of the carefully designed-in functions of a particular set of controls. When Steve was building the kitchen we saw in Box 1.1, he installed a new dishwasher. The dishwasher was of the 'integrated' type—designed to be hidden behind a panel matching the kitchen cupboard doors—so the controls were mounted on the top edge of the door. Once it was all plumbed in, Steve tried to switch it on, only to find that it was completely unresponsive. The very sympathetic repair man had to explain to Steve that the countertop would normally hide the panel when the door was shut, so closing the door also switched off the panel.

9.4 What Does It Do?

It is easy to know what to do with a device that only has an on/off button, but when faced by dozens of buttons on a remote control it may not be so obvious. Cases where it is not evident that something can be controlled at all are equally difficult.

Figure 9.4 shows a pepper grinder. A hapless guest might spend some time trying to work out what to twist to get it to grind. In fact it is an electric grinder and the metal disk on top is not decoration but a switch that turns on the motorized grinder and a small light to boot.[2] This highlights that there are at least three things you need to know before you can even attempt to use a device:

1. know what the device is capable of doing, its functionality
2. know what controls are available to you
3. know the mapping between the controls and the functions

The pepper grinder fails on both (2) and (3)!

The first of these may seem most fundamental, but in fact if you can grasp (2) it is often possible to work out (1) and (3) through experimentation, albeit with potential embarrassment or damage along

---

[2] The grinder is part of a pair, pepper and salt, but the makers clearly forgot the effect salt has on electrical wires; the motor still works on the salt grinder, but its light has, alas, failed.

Figure 9.4 Pepper grinder

the way—think of the consternation of 'Q' as James Bond playfully presses every button on the missile-packed sportscar.

In fact we have encountered these issues already in the form of affordances. Just as the rock of a certain height affords sitting, so also the pepper pot affords grinding pepper; however, it may lack the perceptual affordance that tells you how to achieve that.

One might think these are only issues for the newcomer to the device, such as the house guest, but they can affect even frequent users. Alan was once giving a talk about physicality and using the light switches in the room in order to illustrate a point. They were the kind that you press and the light goes on, you press again and it goes off. To illustrate that the action of pressing the light is in fact two parts, press in and then release, he pushed the switch in and held it for a few moments while talking. To his surprise and that of the rest of the people in the room the lights began to dim. What had appeared to be a simple on/off switch was in fact a dimmer. What was particularly surprising was that none of the people at the talk, several of whom taught regularly in the room, knew of the extra functionality. A more traditional dimmer switch would use a rotating knob to control the internal electronics directly. The knob suggests that it controls something variable, and would make it more likely that the users of the room would have discovered the dimmer functionality for themselves.

Such problems are particularly common with those flat buttons where a thin plastic sheet covers a contact below, or which operate by touch alone. Because these are easy to clean they have advantages in public areas as well as parts of the home, such as the kitchen, where hands may be dirty. However, it is common to see people pressing the sign beside the button instead of the button itself, since both are flat, plastic, and covered by many previous people's fingermarks. This is not helped by notices that say, 'press here'!

We will return to item (2), 'know what controls are available to you', later in the chapter, but for now let's assume you have some idea of what the device does, and can see what controls are available. You are then faced with problem (3): 'what does what', often called 'mapping'.

9.5 Mapping

The mapping between physical controls and functions has been a point of interest since the earliest days of human–computer interaction research. One of Don Norman's examples is the electric cooker. There are four dials and four rings, but which dial controls which ring? Often the controls are placed in a line on the front of the cooker or above on a separate panel. The two dials on the left control the left two rings, but what about back and front? Some cookers instead place the controls alongside the rings in a line from back to front— now it is not even obvious which is left and which right (Figure 9.5). Of course, the dials each have a little image beside them, intended to make this clear, but even if you can work out what they mean do you manage to do this quickly enough when the pan is about to boil over?

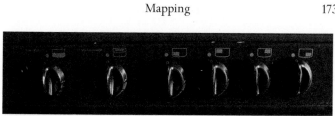

Figure 9.5 Cooker hob knobs—note picture above each to attempt to clarify mapping

Physical placement helps users understand mapping. If controls are on or near the item they control then you at least know which device they apply to. You may sometimes get confused about which remote control is which, but you're unlikely to go to the controls on front of the TV when you mean to turn on the HiFi. There are limits to proximity. The remote control may confuse you, but it saves you getting out of the chair. With the cooker, you could imagine having a separate dial for each ring placed right next to the ring, but of course you would burn yourself whenever you tried to use them.

Where the things that are being controlled have some form of physical layout, reflecting this in the controls themselves can help. For example, if there is a line of lights in a room, we can organize the light switches to be in the same order (see Figure 9.6). With the

Figure 9.6 (left) power socket switches have clear physical correspondence, but (right) what do these light switches do?

cooker, we could imagine laying out the dials in a square to reflect the layout on the hotplate, but of course this would take more space than placing them in a line.

For more abstract functions, such as the time and power settings of a microwave oven, or channel and volume selection on a TV remote, there is no direct physical correspondence. However, physical appearance and layout can still help users to establish a mapping. Look at the microwave oven controls in Figure 9.7. Related controls have similar appearance and are grouped together.

There are also metaphorical positions associated with some concepts. Up, loud, large, and forward are 'positive', so on a TV remote where there are arrow buttons for volume control we expect the upward-pointing arrow to make the sound louder; for the channel selection, up would increase the channel number and down decrease it.

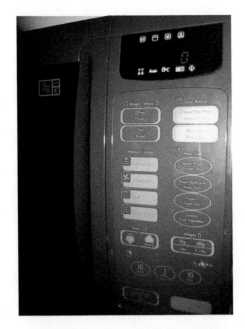

Figure 9.7 Microwave oven control panel

Left and right are somewhat more complex. In a dextra-oriented society, right is usually the 'positive' direction, but this is complicated by reading order. In left-to-right languages, such as European languages, the two agree, and in particular notices, images, and controls that need to be read or operated in a sequence should flow left to right, but where the language flows right to left sequences will also flow in that direction.

Interestingly the top-to-bottom reading order of English and other languages also causes a conflict for temporal ordering. Is forward in time up or down? You will find examples of both being used for information display, but where you want someone to use a sequence of controls in a particular order, the left-to-right and top-to-bottom reading order wins (for English and European languages).

The observant reader may notice another positioning conflict in the microwave controls in Figure 9.7. Along the bottom of the panel are three buttons, which add ten minutes, one minute, and ten seconds respectively to the total cooking time—that is bigger to the left, the opposite to the general right=positive=bigger rule. However, this reflects the order that the digits are written in the display—when you write numbers it is the digit corresponding to the biggest unit that comes first.

Box 9.1 Why are software scroll bars on the right-hand side of the screen?

Think of the reason for using a scroll bar. You have a document or list and want to find something. So you scroll a bit, examining the document as you go until you find the required position in the text or list. Now consider your eye movement during this process. It is usually the first few characters or words that are significant in identifying whether you are at the right place. These occur on the left, so your eye has to scan constantly from the scroll bar on the right (which you are controlling with a mouse and thus need to look at) to the start of the text on the left.

Early scroll bars in the Smalltalk and Interlisp environments (the direct ancestors of our current WIMP (windows, icons, menus, pointer) interface) had user-configurable scroll bars, which could be made to appear either side. But the default and norm was on the left. Yet

continued

Box 9.1 *continued*

the Lisa, then Macintosh, followed by almost all Windows interfaces, adopted Rank Xerox's GlobalView, the Xerox Star desktop interface that had scroll bars on the right. So why did scroll bars start appearing on the right?

The right-hand side seems 'right' because for most users (those who are right-handed), to grab a scroll bar on the left or to press a button on the left would mean your hand would have to move across the screen. Of course your hand doesn't really have to move across the screen, the mouse does, but it feels as if it would have to! But in fact, though for right-handed users of a touchscreen, light pen, or stylus the right-hand side is a good idea, for users of a mouse pointer the left would be better.

So, as you design you need to be aware that there may be several potential correspondences and the one the user assumes may not be the one you intend. Where there is potential for confusion you can either:

1. attempt to remove one of the ambiguous correspondences by repositioning controls; for example, putting time controls vertically rather than horizontally;

2. increase the physical connection of one control so that it dominates; for example, placing time controls directly below a display to make the correspondence between digits on the display and the button order more obvious;

3. add additional labels or other decoration to disambiguate; for example, make 'mins' and 'secs' a little more salient, though this shift from physical to symbolic may fail when users are stressed—just like the cooker control labels when the pan is boiling over; or

4. perform a user study to see whether one of the physical correspondences is the natural interpretation; in fact, the time controls on the microwave appear to work without any errors, so in this case the digit order is clear.

Even if physical correspondences have not been explicitly designed, users will often perceive them. Recall the story of the fire alarm in Chapter 8. In that case, the fire alarm button was next to the door. This is a sensible position for a fire alarm, but it is also where you normally expect a light switch to be.

All the examples so far have been of very 'ordinary' interfaces. However, the same issues arise when designing more innovative interactions. The 'expected, sensed, and desired' framework was developed as part of the Equator project in order to analyse and generate mappings in novel devices [28]. Figure 9.8 shows one device analysed, the Augurscope, which was used to view 3D virtual worlds. The user either pushes the small trolley or holds the detachable screen in their hands while walking around Nottingham Castle. When they point

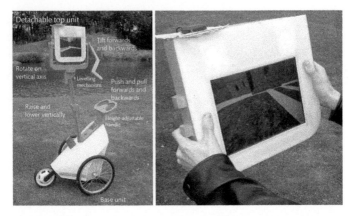

Figure 9.8 The Augurscope II, stand-mounted and hand-held (from [28]

the screen at a location they see a reconstructed 3D view of what was there in the past.

The framework considers three things:

- *expected*—What actions is the user likely to perform on the device? For example, the device may be pointed in different directions, or used while walking around.
- *sensed*—What manipulations of the device can the sensors embedded in the device detect? The Augurscope was equipped with a GPS (Global Positioning System) and an electronic compass (now common in mobile phones and other handheld devices, but not at the time).
- *desired*—What functionality is wanted for the device? For example, the ability to look at the scene from different directions.

Having identified elements in these three categories one can use the analysis to look for potential matches, mismatches and opportunities. Figure 9.9 shows the space of possible overlaps and gaps between these categories.

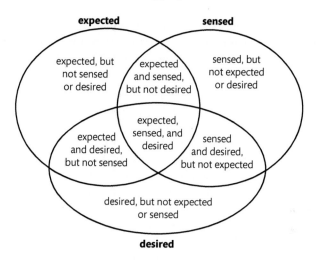

Figure 9.9 Overlaps and gaps identified by the framework (adapted from [28]

In the centre are the things for which the device is already catering well: desired functionality for which there is an expected user action, which can be sensed using the existing sensors. The simple act of turning the device around fits in this area: if the user is looking in one direction and can see the historic reconstruction in that direction, it is natural to turn the device to face other ways. This can be sensed using the compass and so the desired functionality of exploring the 3D reconstruction is achieved.

Other parts of the framework suggest potential problems. On the right are things that are desired and sensed but not expected. The seminar room light switch we mentioned earlier is an example of this. Part of the desired functionality was to dim the lights and this was mapped onto holding the switch down; however, this was not an expected action for the user and so it remained undiscovered until Alan's lecture.

However, the framework can be used as an inspiration or to identify opportunities for design. At the bottom is desired functionality that is currently not supported at all in the device, while at the top are actions that are expected and sensed but for which there is no currently desired functionality: can the latter be used to offer ways of achieving the desired functionality? One of the desired, but not supported, features of the Augurscope was to explore caves beneath the castle grounds. The Augurscope permitted 'flying' above the ground (to see a bird's-eye view of an area) by tilting the Augurscope screen downwards, but while it may be expected that users might make the opposite upward movement and this could be sensed with the compass (top area), there was no desired function mapped to that movement. This suggests a potential way in which the unsupported cave-viewing functionality could be mapped onto the upward tilt, like 'dropping' into the ground, and then reversed by a downward tilt which would 'fly' back up to the surface.

9.6 Feedback

Feedback—letting the user know what has happened—has been another key issue since the earliest days of human–computer interaction. When you type on a proper keyboard you can hear that you have typed a key as you hear the sound it makes—the sound is natural feedback. However, in a noisy street you may not be able to hear this click of the key and so cash machines often make an additional loud beep for each key that you press. Without this feedback you may press the key again because you are unsure whether you really pressed it the first time. In some circumstances this may be fine, if the second press does nothing, or at least does no harm, but often pressing a key twice is not what is wanted at all.

In *The Design of Everyday Things* [314], Don Norman suggested that human action can be seen in terms of a seven-stage cycle. Four of the stages relate to the execution of an action: deciding what to do and doing it.

- Stage 1. establishing a *goal* or desired state of the world (e.g. have document secure)
- Stage 2. forming an *intention to act* (e.g. save the document)

- Stage 3. producing a *sequence of actions* (e.g. move mouse to 'save' button then click)
- Stage 4. *executing* the action (e.g. actually move hand and fingers)

These stages can be used to diagnose different kinds of problem. In particular, James Reason [339] distinguished two kinds of human error: (i) mistakes, where the user is trying to do the wrong thing and (ii) slips, where the user is trying to do the right thing, but in some way fails to achieve it. The former are effectively failures in Stage 2 whereas the latter are failures in Stages 3 and 4.

However, it is the second part of the cycle which is of interest here, the three stages of evaluating an action: working out whether it did what was intended.

- Stage 5. *perceiving* the state of the world (e.g. see alert box 'file already exists')
- Stage 6. *interpreting* the perceived state (e.g. understanding the words)
- Stage 7. *evaluating* the resulting situation with respect to the goals and intentions (e.g. deciding that the document needs to be stored in a different place)

All these stages critically depend on feedback, having sufficient information available from the world (including a computer system or electronic device) to work out whether the right thing happened. As in the execution stages, failures can happen at different points. A small red light on the car dashboard may not be noticed at all (failure in Stage 5), or if noticed the driver may think it means the petrol is nearly empty whereas it in fact means the engine is seriously malfunctioning (failure in Stage 6).

Physical objects often create feedback naturally because of what they are: you lift a mug and you can feel its weight as it lifts off the table, drop it and you hear the crash as it hits the floor. However, with electronic and hybrid devices it is often necessary to add feedback explicitly for digital effects. For example, you do not hear the sound of an email squashing its way through the network cable but software may add a sound effect.

Box 9.2 Physicality-based digital input

The Apple iPhone changed the way we use mobile phones. The multi-touch screen technology it embraced and the physical gestures used to control it have become virtually ubiquitous, so it is hard to recall that they were once revolutionary. Apple made it possible to input using physical gestures that map well onto our 'natural' sense of how the physical world works. Multi-touch screens allow us to utilize gestures from our real, physical world as human digital interaction methods. Thus we are able to zoom in on a picture by placing our thumb and forefinger on the screen and expanding the space between them, in a signal we might physically use in, say, a game of Charades to indicate expansion (in the Charades case, of a word). The iPhone's ability to accept the inputs of more than one touch at a time and to interpret the physical movement between touches into meaningful digital inputs transformed our ability to interact with a digital product in a physical sense, despite the lack of many of the tactile qualities we would usually associate with a satisfactory physical interaction with an artificial device.

Imagine you are about to make a call on a mobile phone and start to enter the number. You will experience several different forms of :

- you feel the key being pressed;
- you hear a simulated key click sound;
- the number appears on the screen.

The first of these is connected purely with the physical device; you still feel it even if the battery is removed. The second is a simulated real sound, as if the physical keys made a noise, and the last is purely digital.

Figure 9.10 shows some of these feedback loops. Unless the user is implanted with a brain-reading device, all interactions with the machine start with some physical action (Figure 9.10 (a)). This could include making sounds, but here we will focus on bodily actions such as turning a knob, pressing a button, or dragging a mouse. In many cases this physical action will have an effect on the device: the mouse button goes down, or the knob rotates and this gives rise to the most direct physical feedback loop (Figure 9.10 (A)) where you feel the movement (Figure 9.10 (c)) or see the effect on the physical device (Figure 9.10 (b)).

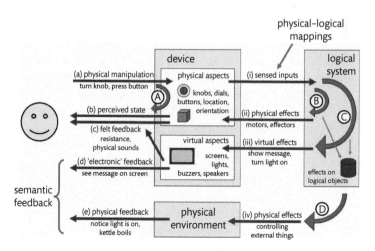

Figure 9.10 Multiple feedback loops

In order for there to be any digital effect on the underlying logical system the changes effected on the device through the user's physical actions must be sensed (Figure 9.10 (i)). For example, a key press causes an electrical connection detected by the keyboard controller. This may give rise to a very immediate feedback associated with the device; for example, a simulated key click or an indicator light on an on/off switch (Figure 9.10 (ii)). In some cases this immediate loop (Figure 9.10 (B)) may be indistinguishable from actual physical feedback from the device (e.g. force feedback as in the BMW iDrive discussed in Chapter 2). In other cases, such as the on/off indicator light, it is clearly not a physical effect, but proximity in space and immediacy of effect may make it feel like part of the device.

Where the user is not aware of the difference between feedback intrinsic to the physical device and simulated feedback, we may regard this aspect of loop (B) in Figure 9.10 as part of 'the device' and indistinguishable from (A) in Figure 9.10. However, one has to be careful that this really is both instantaneous and reliable. For example, Alan often used to mistype on his old multi-tap mobile phone, hitting four instead of three taps for letters such as 'c' or 'i'. After some experimentation, it became obvious that this was because there was a short delay (a fraction of a second) between pressing a key and the simulated key-click. The delayed aural feedback was clearly more salient than the felt physical feedback and so interfered with the typing; effectively, he counted clicks rather than presses. Switching the phone to silent significantly reduced typing errors. These interactions between visual and aural feedback can be quite complex; we will return to this in Chapter 20 when we discuss the McGurk Effect.

The sensed input shown in Figure 9.10 (i) will also cause internal effects on the logical system, changing the internal state of logical objects; for a Graphical User Interface (GUI) this may be changed text, for an MP3 player a new track or increased volume. This change to the logical state then often causes a virtual effect (Figure 9.10 (iii)) on a visual or audible display; for example an LCD showing the track number (Figure 9.10 (iii)). When the user perceives these changes (Figure 9.10 (d)) we get a semantic feedback loop (Figure 9.10 (C)).

In direct manipulation systems the aim is to make this loop so rapid that it feels just like a physical action on the virtual objects.

Finally, some systems affect the physical environment in more radical ways than changing screen content. For example, a washing machine starts to fill with water, or a light goes on. In addition there may be unintended physical feedback, for example, a disk starting up. These physical effects (Figure 9.10 (iv)) may then be perceived by the user (Figure 9.10 (e)) giving additional semantic feedback and so setting up a fourth feedback loop (Figure 9.10 (D)).

9.7   The Device Unplugged

When something stops working, you might give it to a child as a plaything, if it is safe to do so. Or perhaps you are waiting for a bus and have a restless baby; you might give your phone to the baby to play with (after turning it off so that she does not accidentally call the police).

With a smartphone the baby could perhaps use it as a mirror, feel the weight of it, look at its shininess. With an older phone, the baby might press buttons, perhaps open and close the lid (Figure 9.11).

When we think of a device such as a phone, we quite rightly treat it as a whole: 'I press this button and it dials a number'. However, as we started to see at the end of the last section, and as the playing

Figure 9.11   (left) A nice mirror; (middle) buttons to push; and (right) slide the phone in and out

baby demonstrates, the physical device has even when unplugged, disconnected from its power and digital functionality.

Think of the phone without its battery, or tearing a central heating control off the wall and snipping its wires. What can you do with them? What do they suggest to you?

As the baby would discover, the iPhone on the left in Figure 9.10 has very little interaction potential without its power: there is one button at the bottom of the screen, and a few small buttons on its edge, all artfully placed so as not to obscure the clean lines of the phone. In contrast, the phone on the right has a variety of actions that can be performed: pressing buttons, sliding the keyboard in and out.

In the remainder of this chapter we will work through a number of examples of devices showing different kinds of interaction potential when unplugged, and discuss how these physical actions map onto the digital functionality. The 'unplugged' behaviour will in most cases be illustrated using a *physigram*, a diagrammatic way of formally describing physical behaviour [132, 140]

9.7.1 Exposed state

One of the simplest examples of a physical device is an on/off light switch. In this case, the switch has exactly two states (up and down) and pressing the switch changes the state (Figure 9.12). Note that even this simple device has ; you can do things with it.

Even this is not so simple, since the kind of press you give the switch depends on whether it is up and you want to press it down, or down and you want to press it up. For most switches you will not even be aware of this difference because it is obvious which way to press the switch. It is obvious because the current state of the switch is immediately visible.

Note that the switch has a perceivable up/down state whether or not it is actually connected to a light and whether or not the light works—it has exposed state.

The phone in Figure 9.11 also has some exposed state in that you can see whether it is open or closed, but the buttons are not the kind

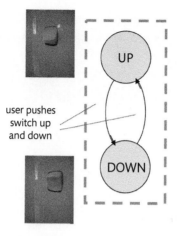

Figure 9.12 Light switch: two states—visible even when the light bulb is broken

that stay down. The iPhone has no exposed state at all. Here are some more exposed state devices (Figure 9.13).

The sockets are similar to the light switch except that the red colour on the top of the switch is also designed to give some indication of the mapping; this is known as feedforward. The washing machine control dial is more complex, but again it is immediately obvious by looking at the dial that it has many potential states. Like the power switch it also tries to provide feedforward through words and symbols around the dial. We will return to the washing machine dial later as it has a particularly interesting story to tell.

Figure 9.13 Exposed state devices

Figure 9.14 Volume knob on CD player—no visible state

The central heating control is more like the mobile phone as it has a flap that moves up and down. Like the light switch, this means there are two very visually and tangibly obvious states: open and closed. However, this is a very particular form of exposed state as its effect is to hide or reveal other controls. In this case the purpose is to hide complexity, but it may also be used to protect against unintended actions—when the phone is closed it is impossible to dial a number accidentally. In the case of the phone there is of course yet another purpose, which is to change the form factor: when closed the phone is smaller, to fit in your pocket or bag.

9.7.2 Hidden state

In contrast to these exposed state devices, consider this volume control on a CD player (Figure 9.14). It has clear action potential, perceptual affordance: you can see that it sticks out, is round, it invites you to pull, push, and, in particular given its roundness, twist it. However, remember the power is unplugged and so there is no sound (or imagine twisting it during a moment of between movements). There is no indication after you have twisted it of how far it turned. The washing machine and cooker knobs were styled and decorated so there was an obvious 'I am pointing this way' direction, but here there is no feedback. In fact, things have changed inside, but on the outside, nothing is detectable; it has hidden state.

Hidden state might be irritating on a music player, but there are occasions when it can have much more serious consequences (See Box 9.3).

Box 9.3 A physicality approach to infusion pumps—some thoughts

In 2008, Harold Thimbleby [392] noted that the annual death toll from medical errors was roughly similar to the combined annual toll of car accidents, breast cancer, and AIDS combined. He went on to describe a case study of an infusion pump that had caused at least one patient death. Thimbleby concentrates mostly on programming factors but we would argue (and indeed Thimbleby suggests) that the pump's physical design is an equally important factor. The accident in question involved a chemotherapy drug called diluted Fluorouracil. The bag's label described the contents, the size of the dose and so on. In this case 5250 milligrams (mg) of fluorouracil was to be diluted to 45.57 mg per mL and delivered over a four-day period. It was delivered twenty-four times too quickly, killing the patient. While 2008 is some time ago, infusion pump designs at the time of writing nearly all still follow a very similar layout to the one Thimbleby inspected, with the key difference being larger, colour screens on a minority of models.

A catalogue of issues had led to the patient's death, from failure to employ guidelines on how quantities should be notated to problems with employing calculators to work out dosages (bear in mind that the context here is a hospital ward where a nurse making the calculations and programming the pump may well be interrupted, and where there may also be a lot of background noise and activity). Thimbleby identified several issues with the design of the pump itself (which will have had to pass a series of very strict 'due diligence' design exercises to be allowed into production). Among these issues was the ease with which a button that changed doses by single units could be confused with one that changed the dose by tens of units. Thimbleby also noted that computer-based medical devices such as this infusion pump are frequently rebooted when problems arise, at which point they lose previously stored data. It was at this point that many errors tended to happen.

Thimbleby developed an iPhone app designed to overcome the flaws in the processes involved in programming the machine, but there is no reason the device itself couldn't be designed to reduce the potential for error. Could storing information via a device's physicality offer potential design solutions in cases such as this?

continued

Box 9.3 *continued*

In Chapter 7 we noted that computers appear to break some of the laws of the natural (physical) world where many of our gut level understandings and 'instincts' are rooted. As a quick reminder, those rules of thumb were:

1. directness of effort—Small effort produces small effects, large effort produces large effects.
2. locality of effect—The effects of actions occur where and when you physically initiate the action.
3. visibility of state—Physical objects have complex shape and texture, but this is largely static.

Just like the mobile phone in Chapter 7, our infusion pump breaks all of these physical world rules:

1. no directness of effort—One wrongly inputted digit (say a decimal point) and an effect can be multiplied 10 or 100 times.
2. no locality of effect—The whole purpose of an infusion pump is to supply a dosage over a period of time—temporal non-locality.
3. no visibility of state—The infusion pump is full of hidden state. It has a small screen driven by buttons which must be used to interrogate the computer one function at a time (e.g. dosage and rate of delivery).

Could physicality be used to develop a more 'natural' interface? Consider the following suggestions for changing the traditional infusion pump arrangement:

1. Use dials and sliders instead of buttons: these mechanical controls allow us to see a setting and judge if it is high or low (visibility of state). While there is no directness of effort as such with these controls, there is at least a correlation between effort and effect (e.g. to create ten times the dose I have to turn the dial ten times as far). The fact that the controls are physical would mean that the pump can reprogramme itself to its last setting in the event of a power cut or a reboot. This would remove a major and common risk area identified by Thimbleby.

continued

Box 9.3 *continued*

2. Place the controls in the order that the nurse generally needs to input them (e.g. from left to right or from top to bottom). This should reduce user error by providing logical sequencing. Remember that this arrangement might vary according to culture (e.g. in Arabic countries it would seem natural to read from right to left).

3. Assign one control device per task: this creates a direct, visible, and physical link between the control input and what it is controlling, removing hidden state.

4. The size or location of the controls can be used to denote their relative importance. This helps the user to concentrate their efforts where they are most critical.

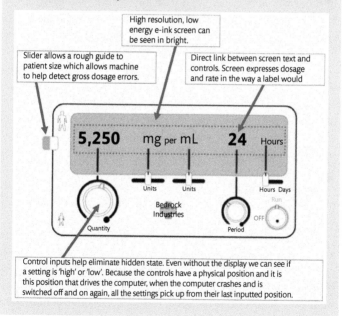

High resolution, low energy e-ink screen can be seen in bright.

Slider allows a rough guide to patient size which allows machine to help detect gross dosage errors.

Direct link between screen text and controls. Screen expresses dosage and rate in the way a label would

5,250   mg per mL   24   Hours

Units   Units   Hours   Days

Bedrock Industries   Run   OFF

Quantity   Period

Control inputs help eliminate hidden state. Even without the display we can see if a setting is 'high' or 'low'. Because the controls have a physical position and it is this position that drives the computer, when the computer crashes and is switched off and on again, all the settings pick up from their last inputted position.

Another common example of hidden state is bounce-back buttons, such as often found for the on/off switches of computers. Consider the TV and dishwasher button in Figure 9.15. Superficially they look similar, but when you interact with them their behaviours differ markedly. With the dishwasher button you press it and it stays

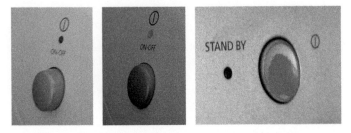

Figure 9.15 (left and centre) dishwasher with exposed state, out=off, in=on; (right) TV hidden state push-back button

in (in fact, this is the 'on' position when the power is on—see the little red light, the power was actually on when the photo was taken). In other words, it has exposed state. In contrast, you press the TV button in and as soon as you let go, the button bounces right back out again. Of course, the TV turns on or off as you do this, but the button on its own tells you nothing; this is hidden state.

If this seems a minor thing, maybe you have had the experience when the TV screen is blank but you don't know why. Is it because it is off, because it is in standby, because you have just turned it on and it is warming up, or because the DVD (Digital Versatile Disk) player connected to it is off? In principle, it is often possible to see, because small red LEDs are added—in this case you can see the Light-emitting Diode (LED) next to the button labelled 'STAND BY'. However, in reality, do you really look at all those little red lights or do you simply press a few buttons at random on the different boxes until something happens?

Maybe you have even lost data from your computer because you accidentally turned it off when it was in fact just sleeping? On many computers, both desktop and laptops, there is a single on/off button (Figure 9.16). To turn it on you press it, to turn it off you press it, but it simply sits there looking the same. You open the laptop or look at the blank monitor (which itself may be because the computer is asleep or because the monitor is asleep). Thinking the machine is off, you press the power button to hear, too late, the little whirr of the disk starting to spin as it wakes from sleep, followed rapidly by the dull thud as it turns off and starts to reboot. What was onscreen before

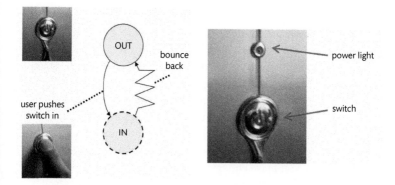

Figure 9.16 Computer on/off button: hidden state with power light

it went to sleep? Did you save the draft of that chapter on annoying hidden state buttons?

As you contemplate several hours' lost work, you can take comfort in the fact that the designer has often foreseen the potential problem. In Figure 9.16, you can see that this computer button, like the TV button earlier, has a small light so that you can see that the power is on, in this case a tiny green (unlabelled) LED. If you had been observant, if you had realized this is an indicator meaning 'turned on' rather than 'connected to the power', if you hadn't got confused in the moment, then you could have worked out it was on and not lost all that work—small comfort indeed.

Now there are good reasons for using a bounce-back switch, which we will discuss in detail later, one of which is when the computer can also turn itself off through the software. However, these bounce-back buttons are often found on computers when this is not the case (indeed the one in Figure 9.16 does not have a software 'off') and an old-fashioned up/down power switch might be more appropriate, or a switch which, like the dishwasher button, stays depressed when in the 'on' position. Even where the software can switch the power off, why not simply have an 'on' button and then an additional 'emergency off' button for the cases when the software is not shutting down as it should? This could be small and recessed so it is not accidentally pressed, rather like a wristwatch button for setting the time.

Sometimes the reason for not doing this is lack of insight, and sometimes plain economics—the cents or pence it costs to add an extra button are worth more to the manufacturer than your lost work! However, often it is aesthetics: your lost work is weighed against the flawless smooth casing with its single iconic button. And if you think the designer made a poor choice, what do you think about when you buy a new computer? It is a brave designer who is willing to focus on the long-term benefit of users, which improves their lives, rather than the immediate appearance that makes them buy the product. Are you brave enough? Or perhaps it is possible to achieve both aesthetics and safety. Certainly the additional small 'emergency off' button could be located slightly out of sight (although not so hidden the user can't find it), or made into an essential part of the aesthetic of the device.

9.7.3 Tangible transitions and tension states

When you twist the CD knob shown in Figure 9.14 it is heavy to turn, giving it a feel of quality, but there is no sense of how far you have turned it. However, not all knobs and dials are like this.

Figure 9.17 shows three experimental prototypes that were produced for a photo viewer. All have an area where a small screen would go and all have a rotary control. The one on the left has a very obvious retro dial, the middle a more discreet dial, and the one on the right an iPod-like touch surface. In all the prototypes, rotating the dial enables the user to scroll between different menu options, although never more than seven at any level.

Figure 9.17 Three prototype media players

While they all use rotary controls, they feel very different in use. On the right the touch surface offers no at all, your finger goes round, but without the display you cannot tell there is anything happening. In fact, it is perhaps only because one is used to devices like this that one would even try to stroke it—the cultural affordance of the iPod generation! In contrast the more clunky looking prototype on the left has a far richer repertoire of tangible feedback. It already has exposed state, since you can tell what direction it is pointing, and it also has end stops so that you can feel when it has got to one extreme or other of the menu. In addition, the mechanics of the mechanism mean that there is slight resistance as you move between its seven positions: it has *tangible transitions* between states.

Tangible transitions are particularly important when considering accessibility for people with impaired vision, or for occasions when you cannot look at the screen, such as when driving. The left-hand device has both end-stops and tangible transitions; this means that once someone has learned some of the menu layouts, the device can be used without looking at the screen at all. Even when you can see, the tangible transitions give additional feedback and the resistance between the positions makes it difficult to accidentally select the wrong option.

The device in the middle has a form of tangible transition: there is a very slight sensation as one moves between positions. However it has no end stops and there is no resistance before it moves to a new position. The lack of resistance makes errors more likely and the lack of end stops means it is harder to orient oneself except by looking at the screen, but at least it is possible to tell how many steps one has taken.

It is not only knobs that can have tangible transitions. The light and power switches we discussed earlier not only have a visible state, but there is definite resistance as you push the switch down: it gives a little, and then there is sudden movement as it flicks down. If you release the pressure of your finger before it flicks down, it simply bounces back to where it started. In a sense the device has at least four states; as well as the obvious up/down there are also part-up and part-down states as one pushes the switch, although only the up/down states are stable when you release your finger pressure.

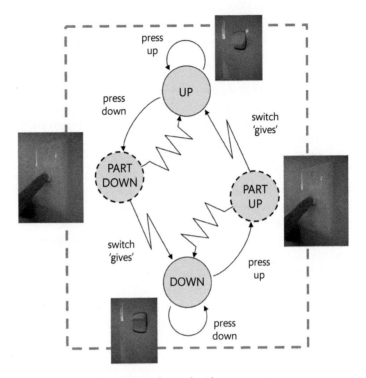

Figure 9.18 Light switch with partway states

Bounce-back buttons, such as the computer power button in Figure 9.18, can similarly be seen as actually having two states, out and in. Only the out state is stable, but while you press with your finger it remains in a pressed-in state. This is a tension state, one where you have to maintain a continuous effort in order to maintain the state. In the case of the computer power, the tension is never maintained, you just press and release. However, tension states are often used as part of interaction, for example, dragging with a mouse.

Keeping your hand or other muscles in tension can cause fatigue if continued for a long period, and it also affects accuracy and timing. Indeed, Fitts' Law measurements show measurable differences in performance between ordinary mouse movement and dragging [271].

However, the advantage of a tension state is that you are very aware that you are in the middle of doing something. When typing it is possible to break partway through a sentence and leave it incomplete, but it is impossible to go away partway through dragging the mouse, you have to release the mouse button and end the drag. This can be particularly important in safety-critical situations, such as the use of the 'dead man's handle' in trains.

9.7.4 Natural inverse

It's the summer holidays, and you are driving down a small country lane where the sides of the lanes are high earth banks and the lanes themselves winding, narrow and with no room for cars to pass one another. The car is packed full with suitcases and tents, spades and swimming costumes, so you cannot even see out of the back window. Suddenly, round the bend ahead another car appears, coming towards you. You both stop; one of you must go back. There is a relatively straight part of the lane behind you with nowhere to pass, but you do recall passing a gateway just before the last bend, so you shift the gear into reverse and begin to edge backwards, with only your wing mirrors to see where you are going.

At first you drive very slowly, everything is back-to-front and unless you think very hard you will turn the wheel in the wrong direction. However, after a bit you find yourself confidently driving backwards at a fair speed down the straight lane behind. Every so often you suddenly 'lose' it, end up getting too close to one of the banks and have to stop, and, as if from the beginning, work out which way to turn the wheel, but each time you quickly get back into the flow.

Even if you are a very experienced driver and find reversing is no longer difficult, maybe you have tried to reverse a trailer or caravan and had a similar experience.

It is reasonable that this is difficult if you are not used to reversing a car for long distances, but what is remarkable are the periods in between, when it becomes easy. It is not that you have learned the right thing to do, as you find that when you get out of the flow you have no better idea which way to turn the wheel than when you started.

The reason for these periods when reversing becomes easy is that the steering wheel exploits very basic human responses—the natural inverse. When you draw a line on paper and decide it is in the wrong place, you need to find the eraser and rub it out. It is not difficult, it is something you'll do without thinking, but it is something you've had to learn. If, however, you are trying to put the pencil inside a desk-tidy and you move your hand a little too far to the right, you'll automatically move it slightly to the left. In the world there are natural opposites, up/down, closer/further, left/right, and our body mirrors these with muscles and limbs hard-wired to exploit them.

Work by Rodolfo Llinás showed that some of this is very low-level indeed, with sets of mutually inhibitory neurons that allow pairs of opposing muscles to be connected [264]. Although higher-level brain functions determine which pairs operate, some of the actual control even happens in the spinal column, as is evident in the headless chicken that still runs around the farmyard. These paired muscle groups allow both rhythmic movement such as walking, and the isometric balancing of one muscle group against another that is needed to maintain a static position, such as holding a mug in mid-air.

When you first start to drive in reverse, you have to think to yourself, 'if I want the car to move to the left which direction do I need to turn the wheel?' However, when you have started to move the wheel and discover it is going in the wrong direction, or you are about to overshoot and go too far, you do not have to think again, you instinctively move it in the opposite direction (see also Box 9.4). The natural inverse takes over and you do the opposite of what you were doing before.

Unplugged devices often have buttons, knobs and other controls that have natural inverse actions: twist left/twist right, push/pull. The minidisk controller in Figure 9.19 was intended to be clipped onto clothing while the user was walking or running. Since it will be used eyes-free it is particularly important that the physical format helps make it easy to use. The device has two different kinds of control and both of them exhibit natural inverse.

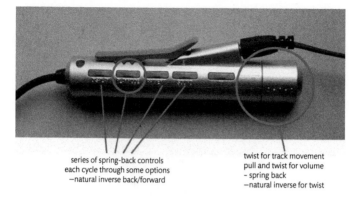

series of spring-back controls
each cycle through some options
—natural inverse back/forward

twist for track movement
pull and twist for volume
– spring back
—natural inverse for twist

Figure 9.19 Minidisk controller

On the end of the device is a knob. Twisting the knob in one direction moves on to the next track, twisting it in the other direction
moves it back a track—natural inverse. The knob can also be pulled
out and this changes its function: twisting it one way increases the
volume, twisting it in the opposite direction turns the volume down.
Note also that this is a tension state. It is obvious whether you are
changing track or changing volume, not just from the immediate
aural feedback but also because the knob wants to spring back into
place, and to adjust the volume requires continuous tension.

Along the side of the device are a number of spring-back sliders;
they can be pushed forward or backward. Each slider controls a different function, but all of them use the same principle. There is an
ordered list of options for each setting; pushing the slider moves between the relevant option settings one way through the list, pulling
it back moves it the other way. Note that the natural inverse reduces the impact of mistakes. If you choose the wrong option and
change it, you instinctively move the slider in the opposite direction
and restore the setting.

Using the natural inverse can obviate the need for explicit 'undo'
operations, and can make a control usable even when you don't
know what it does. The phone in Figure 9.20 belonged to Alan some
years ago. On the top left-hand side of the phone was a small slider.
This slider did different things in different modes: when in a call

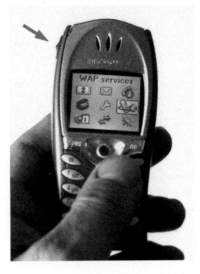

Figure 9.20 Phone with slider at top left

it adjusted volume, when in the address book it scrolled through the names. Alan never knew exactly what it did, yet he used it extensively. This was because it always respected the natural inverse property and so he could use it without fear; if it didn't do what he expected he just did the opposite movement and carried on.

Box 9.4 Why driving backwards is hard: expectation, magnification, and control theory

Of course, when you are driving using mirrors things are not really back-to-front. If, as you look in the mirror, you see the left-hand side a little too close to the bank, you turn the wheel to the right—this is exactly the same as when you are driving forwards. So if you could somehow 'switch off' the knowledge you are driving backwards and pretend that the mirror is really just a very small windscreen, things would be easier—however, we do not have the power to fool our own minds so easily!

The other difficult thing is that the wing mirrors are designed so that you can see the whole road behind in a tiny mirror, whereas the same portion of the road ahead fills the entire windscreen. Using the

continued

Box 9.4 *continued*

mirrors is a bit like driving forward looking through the wrong end of a telescope[a].

Finally the mechanics of the steering work differently in reverse. Whether driving forward or backward, it is always the front wheels that turn. This makes it (in principle) easier to reverse into a narrow space, but makes the car much harder to drive backwards in a straight line. The front wheels of a car also have a small 'toe in': they point slightly together. This has the effect of making the car tend to stay in a straight line going forwards, but the opposite effect when driving backwards.

Chapter 5 discussed open and closed loop control; these are part of a wider area of mathematics called 'Control Theory'. One general principle in control theory is that there is always a trade-off between control and stability. For example a light beach ball is easy to control. You can roll it exactly where you want it, but it is unstable: the slightest breeze and it rolls away. In contrast, a large cubic block of concrete is very stable, but boy is it hard to move where you want it. The forward and reverse movements of the car demonstrate different points in this trade-off: going forwards you have a high degree of stability, the car keeps on going in a relatively straight line unless you work hard to change direction, whereas in reverse the opposite is true, it is easy to control in the sense that you can manoeuvre into very tight spaces, but it is highly unstable.

Because digital and mechanical systems do not exhibit proportional effort (Chapter 7) it is possible to engineer situations that are at extreme points in this trade-off space. It is also occasionally possible to 'break' the trade-off, to have your cake and eat it. Modern fighter jets are deliberately designed to be unstable while flying, rather like the car driven in reverse. This allows very rapid movements when required, but makes them unflyable by a human pilots alone. However, the pilot's control is augmented by very fast, automated systems, which constantly trim the aerofoils to keep the plane flying where it is intended to go.

[a] N.B. not to be attempted on the open road if you value your life

10

Tools, Equipment, and Machines

10.1 Tools and the Development of Humankind

In Stanley Kubrick's '2001', the opening sequence shows an ape learning to use a bone to kill; the bone, thrown into the air, spins and the film cuts to an orbiting space station. The message is clear. Tools, or maybe weapons, define us as human beings, and the path from bone and shaped flint to spaceship is simply one of time.

Alongside language use, which we shall discuss in Chapter 15, tool use and tool-making are often seen as quintessential human activities. However, the story is both more complicated and more fascinating than a transition in a movie.

In fact, though it is rare, a small variety of non-human animals do use objects as tools. For example, several kinds of bird either use a stone like a hammer to break a snail shell, or select an 'anvil stone' against which to smash the snail. Tool making is rarer still, but remember the chimpanzees in Chapter 4. They select a stick as they move though the forest, and *later* use it to extract termites from a log. This is more than tool-making in response to an immediate need. The chimpanzees are choosing and modifying the sticks well before they encounter the termite site. Even chipped stone 'axes', the image that springs most readily to mind when thinking of human tool-making, though exclusively hominid, are certainly not modern human. The earliest stone axes date back 2.5 million years when the early hominids who made them were nothing like modern

Homo Sapiens, who only came onto the scene in the relatively recent 200,000 to 300,000 years.

The actual purpose of early stone axes is unclear. Not suitably shaped for connecting to a shaft, they cannot have been thrown like a spear. Some think they were only used for scraping meat from carcasses, and indeed it is the evidence of cut marks on ancient bones that helps identify them as human kill, or at least food. However, most stone axes are sharpened all the way round and many have a well-defined point, neither of which are necessary for a simple flesh scraper. One could imagine using them as hand-held hunting weapons, but this would require chasing the animal, leaping and catching it by hand while thumping it on the head with your stone axe—possible, but certainly risky with a large animal.

The neurophysiologist William Calvin in his book *The Ascent of Mind* [71] suggests an alternative: stone axes are, in fact, perfectly shaped to be thrown like a discus. He verified this idea by getting both expert discus throwers and ordinary students to throw replica axes. The axes behaved aerodynamically, rather like a frisbee, as they spun through the , and then embedded themselves on their point as they landed. Calvin envisages early hominids throwing axes into the middle of a herd of animals at a water hole (where many axes are found). The axe would strike the back of an animal, and as it rolled across the skin the point would snag or stick into the flesh, causing pain. The aim would not be to kill the animal with the blow but to cause it enough pain to stumble. As the herd stampeded away, the fallen animal might be trampled by its fellows, or at least left lying on the ground where it could be tackled by the band of hunters.

Simply lobbing a stone into the middle of a herd would be relatively easy. Greater strength might allow throwing from a greater distance, with harder impact, but accuracy is not an issue. In contrast, precision throwing at a single animal requires a degree and speed of muscle control unknown in other creatures. Calvin suggests that it is precisely this control that developed during the period of the Ice Ages, when hunting became not merely one among a number of food sources but the only means for winter survival. As a neuroscientist, Calvin is interested in what this implies for the development of the modern brain. Precision throwing requires two things:

- a level of complex sequential rather than reactive processing;
- co-opting and coordinating large areas of the brain to obtain accurate timing.

Calvin suggests that these requirements for complex throwing not only drove the development of the brain but furnished exactly the elements needed for complex cognition and language, and indeed laid the grounds for consciousness itself.

Recall from Chapter 4 that it was this period in the midst of the Ice Ages, 50,000—70,000 years ago, when there was a step change in tool use from plain stone 'axes' to spears where a wooden shaft was tied onto a stone head. At the same time social changes are evident in the traces of settlements, and before long there are clear signs of cultural development with early art. We saw that Steven Mithen takes these developments as signs of the meeting of our different forms of specialized intelligence [294], and we suggested that our multiple intelligences meet in both the logic of language and the pictures of imagination, the latter being needed to plan for future action.

Calvin's account of mental development is at present tentative, but both language and planning require just the kinds of sequential processing that he suggests were the outcome of tool use. While tool use may not be the sole prerogative of human intelligence, it may be its provenance.

10.2 Affordance, Understanding, and Culture

In Chapter 5 we discussed the important role of affordance. In particular, we carefully distinguished the intrinsic affordances of an object or device from its perceived affordance. The former describe its action potential in relation to you, what you can do with it, whereas the latter is the way in which those potential actions are made manifest: visual, aural, or other sensory appearance. However, as one digs deeper the story becomes a little more complex.

Western visitors to Tokyo often report confusion when they try to navigate. The writing is so different that they cannot even match the names on maps with those on street signs. This is especially confusing on an underground train as the stops come and go faster than they can match the letters of the station names. The underground clearly affords travelling, in that it is physically possible to get on and off the trains, but at a practical level it only affords transport to those with some understanding of Japanese.

Now imagine a person from 500 years ago suddenly deposited in the middle of a major present-day city. Does the underground system afford them transport? Similarly take a group of twenty-first-century design students and carry them back 200 years into a wheel-wright's workshop (Figure 10.1). Around them are numerous specialist tools of the trade. Clearly for the nineteenth century wheel-wright these tools afford the production of wooden wheels, but what about the time-travelling students? With the right knowledge and

Figure 10.1   Reconstruction of a wheelwright's shop, Amberley Museum, West Sussex, United Kingdom

skills they could use these tools, but without such knowledge and skills the tools afford little more than holding and throwing.

This is not just about sophisticated technology and tools. Going back 10,000 years, imagine you are looking at a wild boar moving through the woods. Does the boar 'afford' eating? Well, it does if you have stone axes tied to wooden shafts to make spears and are part of an organized social group that can hunt together.

Recall that the term 'affordance' was coined as part of an 'ecological' approach to psychology, an approach that takes seriously the fact that we live and act in an particular environment. Our potential for action is relational: a fit between the properties of the things around us (rocky shelves or wild boars), our physical size and abilities, our own knowledge and understanding, the tools and artefacts we have to hand, and the social group within which we live. Only when the right combination of these occurs can we choose whether or not to act.

Of course many of these things are dynamically changing over weeks, years, and generations. At one extreme are the adaptations by natural selection that occur over many thousands or millions of years, so that our perceptions and abilities become well suited to the more slowly changing parts of our environment. However, humanity's success in populating (and maybe destroying) the earth is less to do with our optimal fit for an environment—the 'naked ape' is not intrinsically suited for Arctic climes. Instead, it is our ability to adapt rapidly to changing situations and, in the longer term, to shape and change our environment, that makes us who we are.

Imagine yourself in the wheelwright's workshop 200 years ago. At first the tools and wood are a complete mystery, but after a while you may, through trial and error or reasoning, work out how to cut wood, shape it, join it. You build up knowledge over time through learning. A large stone may afford throwing to an adult but not a child, simply because of their physical immaturity. Similarly the wheelwright's tools may afford wheel-making after intellectual maturation.

But if instead you were an apprentice with the wheelwright, there would be more to the story. The accomplished wheelwright would teach you their methods and techniques, and after a long time, when you had learned them yourself, you would teach the next apprentice. Perhaps as you saw carts from other areas or met fellow craftspeople you would learn their tricks and they would learn yours.

Anthropologists talk about 'communities of practice': people engaged in related crafts or professions who share experience. Sometimes these are formal, like the medieval Craft Guilds; sometimes less so, like parents chatting at the school gate. These communities of practice both pass on existing knowledge across generations and also share and generate new knowledge.

Some of this knowledge may stay as 'head knowledge': techniques and methods of working transmitted orally or translated into written instructions, diagrams, or textbooks. This head knowledge is culture. However, sometimes this shared experience also leads to adaptations of the available tools, perhaps a special plane to make grooves of a particular shape, or pattern pieces for a different style of wheel. The wide variety of specialized tools in the nineteenth-century wheelwright's shop is the end result of hundreds of years of culture embodied in physical artefacts (c.f. Chapter 6). It was never static, and even today master craftspeople pass on new ideas and create new tools and rigs for future generations.

10.3 Heidegger, Hammers, and Breakdown

Heidegger's concept of 'ready-to-hand' has been influential within Human–Computer Interaction (HCI), and in particular his use of the hammer as an example. In Heidegger's philosophy, ready-to-hand refers to the way in which a tool becomes invisible to you as you focus on the work to be done with it [211, 210]. Think about eating soup with a spoon, or (the archetypal example) knocking in a nail with a hammer. You do not even consider the spoon unless something goes wrong, until you mislay it, or spill some soup. When all goes well you are 'thrown' or lost in the activity, the tools (spoon and bowl) 'withdraw' and become unnoticed in the act of eating.

> The peculiarity of what is proximally to hand is that, in its readiness-to-hand, it must, as it were, withdraw … that with which we concern ourselves primarily is the work.…[210]

This is equally true of digital tools such as a word processor—do you think about the word processor or about writing a letter? Similarly, when you get used to a digital device like a phone, you may dial a number without thinking 'I'm using a phone', or 'I'm pressing the "7" key'. If you do, the phone has become 'ready-to-hand'.

Heidegger deliberately does not talk about a single tool in isolation but always within a collection of stuff or equipment that is being used to do something or achieve something. The spoon, bowl, table, and even the chair you sit on are all part of the equipment of soup eating. For the carpenter, hammer, nail, saw and plane are all at hand and used almost unconsciously.

Chapter 5 discussed philosophical concepts of the embodied mind and while this is not a phrase Heidegger used, his work is seen as one of its roots. This is largely because he stood out against the dominant philosophical and scientific traditions of his time, which sought to define objects individually as something entirely separated from us. Newton's laws are just like this, as are Einstein's theories of relativity; physical laws of objects which say how they behave with no relation to human activity. Heidegger instead tried to understand humans as being 'in the world'. When it came to the things around us, Heidegger wrote of conventional philosophy:

> If we look at Things just 'theoretically', we can get along without understanding readiness-to-hand. [210]

Instead, for him, the ready-to-hand is the primary way in which we experience these things. This is in fact intensely practical. was trying to get inside the everydayness of human experience and uncover a way of seeing the world that takes the mundane seriously as a starting point. Normally you do not spend time contemplating a spoon or bowl, you just reach for them and use them; their primary mode of being for us is when they are ready-to-hand.

Of course, this 'thrownness', being able to act without thinking about the tools, is not our perpetual state; things are not always 'ready-to-hand'. Bleary-eyed in the morning, you reach into the cutlery tray to get a spoon to eat your cereal, but you forgot to wash up and there is no clean spoon; you start to swing a hammer but then stop as you can feel that the head is loose on the shaft; you hear the sound of your mobile phone ringing but fumble because it is in a zipped pocket and the zip is hard to open.

At these times you have to start looking at the tools as separate things. You only think about the spoon when it is not in the drawer, you think about the hammer because it is broken. This shift of focus from the task at hand to the tools in hand is often called 'breakdown'.

Heidegger identified three kinds of breakdown:

- When the tool is unusable for some reason, such as being broken like the hammer with the loose head. Heidegger says it becomes *conspicuous*.
- When the right tool is absent, like the missing breakfast spoon. In this case Heidegger says it is *obtrusive*.
- When something stands in the way, such as the zipper when you are after the phone. Heidegger calls this *obstinacy*.

In all these cases, instead of having something ready-to-hand, it is only present-to-hand: there, but merely in the sense of being something about which we can think and ponder its attributes. We are no longer simply doing something but instead have had to start considering *how* to do it or *what* to do.

However, these immediate causes of breakdown need not lead to a complete break in the flow of work. The missing spoon does not lead to an intense philosophical contemplation of spoon-ness. Often we can equally quickly recover from the breakdown; we pick up a screwdriver, realize it is the wrong size, and instantly reach for a different one. Only when there is a continued failure of these semi-automatic recovery mechanisms do we start really to consider what to do next, what Heidegger calls *circumspection*, casting our eye around and realizing for the first time the equipment that lies around us, which we have been using all the time yet have hardly noticed.

Box 10.1 Experience: ready-to-hand vs walk up and use

The idea of being ready-to-hand is sometimes confused with what are often called 'walk up and use' systems, such as tourist information points or bank cash machines. These devices are designed for public use, and should, to an extent, be accessible without depending on prior knowledge (or at least only on generic knowledge and skills).

However, to be 'ready-to-hand' in the way Heidegger describes typically requires familiarity with the equipment and practice in its use. The hammer is a prime example of this. Even how to hold it properly is not obvious: look at this picture.

There is a hand-sized depression in the middle. Recalling Chapter 5 you may think, 'ah yes, perceptual affordance', and grasp it like this:

But no, that is not the way to hold a hammer! If you try to use it like this you end up using the strength of your arm, and not the weight of the hammer, to knock in a nail.

continued

Box 10.1 *continued*

Give it to a child, surely the ultimate test of 'walk up and use', and they often grasp the head like this:

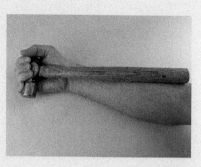

In fact this is quite sensible for a child, as a 'proper' grip would put too much strain on their wrist. Recall that Gibson's definition of affordance was relational, about the ecological fit between the object and the potential actions, and the actions depends on who is doing the acting. For a small child with weaker arms the hammer probably only affords use at all with this grip.

In fact the 'proper' grip is to hold it quite near the end where you can use the maximum swing of the hammer to make most use of the weight of the hammer and its angular momentum:

10.4   From Philosophy to Design: Designing for Failure

Heidegger's analysis raises two key challenges for designing digital artefacts:

1. how to make sure things are ready-to-hand
2. how to ensure that when breakdown occurs repair is rapid

The first of these is closely related to issues we have previously discussed: anything that makes a device easy and obvious to use, for example perceived affordances so we can immediately see or feel how to use the thing. It is most obvious when we test a device's usability, and it is what we are most likely to notice when choosing a product to buy. However, note that it is easy to focus on the very first use of the device, and forget the importance of long-term practised use.

This said, it is the second challenge, designing for when things go wrong, which is most often neglected yet has the greatest influence on long-term usability. When you try something out, or demonstrate its use, the tendency is to show what happens when it is working. Even testing with users is focused on minimizing the number of mistakes. However, day-to-day life is full of stumbling and fumbling, things not quite in the right place, the unexpected and malfunctioning. Yet somehow we usually muddle through without serious disquiet.

Physical tools and objects have particular qualities that ease repair from breakdown, qualities that may be missing from digital devices unless we take care.

Recall from Chapter 7 that physical things exhibit a visibility of state and locality of effect. These make it easy to detect that something is wrong, and early detection of failure is critical to ease of repair. In devices with digital functionality, we saw that there is less visibility and less locality, so it may not be obvious until much later that things have gone wrong. If you are hand-washing clothes and heat the water too much, you are likely to notice from the steam rising, or feel the heat as soon as you put your hands into the water. But if you select the wrong temperature setting on a washing machine, you will only notice an hour or so later when your favourite jumper comes out several sizes smaller than when it went in.

This can happen with more complex physical artefacts also. Imagine putting together a kit-pack wardrobe. You choose the wrong screw and it is slightly too big for the hole. You notice immediately and reach for another of the right size: minor breakdown and fluid recovery. Now imagine that early in the construction you chose a screw that was slightly too short. It fitted in the hole and you proceeded without noticing. Only at the end do you discover the sole remaining screw is too long for the last hole. Now you have to problem-solve, work out what is wrong, perhaps deconstruct the wardrobe until you find the other screw, or look for a drill to make the hole bigger.

Knowing that digital devices often lack visibility and locality means we can look for ways to 'put back' these aspects of physicality. This includes taking into account the different feedback loops discussed in the last chapter, and might involve redesigning physical or digital aspects of the device.

As an example, consider the problem of designing a remote control for a DVD (Digital Versatile Disk) player. The control typically has no display (no visibility of state), so the feedback is on the player, not the controller (spatial non-locality). Worse still, some operations, such as starting to power up the motor that spins the DVD, take time (temporal non-locality). There will also typically be multiple other connected devices with their own controllers. It may be confusing which controller is which (poor mapping), and furthermore if the television has multiple inputs then the output of the DVD may not be visible (no visibility of state). You pick up the remote and press a button but nothing happens: is it just a delay, is something blocking the infrared signal, did you press hard enough, is the TV on the wrong source, or are you just holding the controller the wrong way round?

To tackle some of these problems we might consider additional visual feedback, perhaps a little screen on the device, or a light on the player that flashes when it detects the controller. We might use vibrotactile feedback, maybe a small vibration while it is communicating with the player and a sharp 'kick' if communication fails. Alternatively, or in addition, we may change the physical design of the controller. For the issue of 'which device is which' we could simply design the player and controller with similar distinctive styling so they are obviously related; we could help orient the device by making the shape fall more easily into the hand in the right direction. Interestingly, adding the small screen on the controller would have the side effect of making the orientation clear irrespective of whether it works!

Having detected that something is wrong, you still need to repair it. Visibility is often useful here also as it makes it easier to work out how to fix a problem. However, the level of visibility required for repair is greater than for 'normal operation'. With the hammer, if the head becomes loose you can easily see this and work out how to fix it, perhaps by banging the hammer head further up the shaft or adding a small wedge. However, when the wireless network fails on your iPhone how do you work out what to do? With physical tools we can often obtain successive levels of information by simply paying attention to aspects we normally ignore (e.g. looking at the way the hammer head is attached to the shaft). With digital devices we may need to add means to reveal this explicitly (e.g. signal bars on a phone or trouble shooting modes).

The other barrier to easy repair is lack of proportionality. Recall that with physical things it is most often the case that small efforts create small effects, so if you make a small mistake only a small correction is needed. However, non-proportional effects may mean that your small slip is hard to fix. Desktop systems often deal with this by including an 'undo' button, but with physical objects we 'undo' by doing something else. This is why the 'natural inverse' discussed in the last chapter is so powerful. Whether the effect was small or large, controls with a natural inverse mean that you are able to fix mistakes, and often do so without noticing. Perhaps most importantly, the natural inverse means you make the right correction; if there is one thing worse than the mess caused by a mistake it is the mess caused by a botched attempt to fix it!

Not everything can be reversible; you can move flour back and forth between the bag and the scale pan, but not unbake a cake. The skilled tool-user has an awareness of reversible and non-reversible actions: positioning pieces of wood with a slow-setting glue vs sawing a plank in half. However, with digital devices this may not be so obvious. Again, skilled users develop knowledge and awareness of dangerous actions. For example, some users of the database query language SQL, knowing how dangerous 'DELETE' can be, may type 'WHERE id=37' and then backspace and insert 'DELETE FROM my_database', to prevent the potential problem of accidentally deleting everything by omitting the 'WHERE' clause.

Good design can make it easier to avoid irreversible unwanted actions. This can be achieved digitally, for example adding confirmation dialogues like 'are you sure?', though of course too many of these and we start to always click 'yes' without thinking! Physical design can also help: recessed buttons, colour coding, or flaps over dangerous controls as in the big red 'fire' button in action films, or clamshell phones.

Box 10.2 Protecting against dangerous actions

Consider again the two switches in Figure 9.15: there is another important difference apart from their visibility of state. The dishwasher button sticks out proud of the surface of the control panel when it is off while the TV on/off button is flush with the surface of the TV.

The dishwasher is in a kitchen at hip level where it is constantly brushed as one moves past or reaches across the worktop. Not infrequently the button is pressed 'on' by accident. This has the effect of spraying the dishes with cold water as a pre-rinse wash starts up. That's very annoying when the dishes have already been washed, and if not noticed immediately means they get washed again, at financial and environmental cost. If anything, it is the dishwasher that should have its button either flush or recessed to prevent accidents.

Small differences in physical design can make a big difference in life.

10.5 Breakdown and Reflection

It is easy to become so concerned about avoiding breakdown that the positive aspects can be missed.

Heidegger talks about the state that follows a breakdown which has not been instantly corrected. Rather than being ready-to-hand, part of your ongoing action, the tools around become purely present-to-hand, objects for inspection. However, the term he uses for this state is the circumspection: a casting around of the eye, seeing the multifarious equipment for the job scattered round, almost as if for the first time. Note how this state is still immersed in action, in the job at hand. It is not the speculation of the scientist looking abstractly at things in isolation, from the outside, as we often are in writing a book like this, but rather this circumspection has the actor and the activity still at its centre. It is a consideration focused on the needs of action.

Of course, you really want to get the job done, be it writing a book, making a cup of tea, or simply turning on the TV, so these breakdowns are an intrusion into everyday activity. However, they also offer an opportunity to reflect upon this everydayness, the tools we are using, and the activities we are doing. We might realize that we really need a new hammer, or that there is a better way of joining wood. Continual breakdown is bad, but occasional breakdowns are precisely what drive the cultural learning loops we discussed earlier in this chapter.

> New design can be created and implemented only in the space that emerges in the recurrent structure of breakdown. A design constitutes an interpretation of breakdown and a committed attempt to anticipate future breakdowns. [423]

This message is at the heart of Donald Schön's vision of the *reflective practitioner* [350]. For Schön, it is precisely levels of reflection that distinguish the novice or merely accomplished professional from the truly expert and innovative. He distinguishes several levels of knowing, including:

knowing-in-action—The clear knowledge, based on experience, that is there whether one is hammering in a nail, or sketching the design for a new bridge, but which is not explicit and may be hard to verbalize even when asked. This corresponds closely to 'thrownness', which Heidegger describes as when we are engaged in our everyday activity.

reflection-in-action—The reflection that we undertake while in the middle of an activity, often when we encounter breakdowns, similar to Heidegger's circumspection. The goal of such reflection is still job-focused, but by stepping back and out of the immediate task at hand often enables a fresh perspective and new way of tackling a problem that has become stuck.

reflection-on-action—The thinking after the event, going back over the decisions made, pondering the general lessons or novel solutions found, and reflecting too upon the processes we use, including the processes used during reflection-in-action.

These form a ladder of reflection where one can reflect on one's actions, one's process of reflection, and in a way Schön's own reflection is a very high-level reflection on the whole ladder. However, like Heidegger's circumspection, these levels of reflectionlevels of reflection are not divorced from praxis but are both based on experience and subject to frequent experimentation, trying out ideas, grounding ideas in action.

Schön studied a variety of professionals, but particularly those involved in various aspects of design. For a designer, reflection is particularly important as it is this that allows new solutions.

Often it is sufficient that a designer comes to a situation from the outside. You may have had the experience where a visitor asks a question about something in your neighbourhood or home and you step back, having never noticed it even though you have lived there for years. Of course, it is precisely because you have lived there for years and seen it every day that it is invisible to you. Our senses are tuned to ignore the familiar and so it is only the stranger who notices the things that are there all along.

It is often designing for a familiar environment that is hardest as here one has to find ways of estrangement such as Garfinkel's breaching experiments (see Chapter 1), designed to make the everyday rules of life obvious [176]. Of course, even to do this one has to be aware enough of the rules to deliberately contravene them! Experienced analysts may learn over time to look askance, to take the child's eye, and see the strange in the familiar, but that is a hard and long lesson—one that both expert ethnographers and comedians learn.

Estrangement can sometimes be aided by systematic actions: cataloguing everything. Every activity during the day, every object on a desk, items used daily, or infrequently, the unusual and the normal all become equal on the list. It is often surprising what you notice in a photograph that was not apparent when taking it, especially if you point the camera in an unusual direction.

Box 10.3 Counter tourism

Counter tourism involves doing the opposite of what a tourist would normally do, going to the places the guidebook tells you to ignore [8]. In particular, some counter tourists will deliberately visit a famous place and then turn their back on it and take a photograph in the opposite direction.

Looking at the unexpected, sideways, backwards, it is amazing what you see.

Fontana di Trevi is in every guidebook, splendid, glorious, and actually bigger than it looks in pictures. The small square containing the fountain is always awash with people.

continued

Box 10.3 *continued*

Fontana di Trevi in Rome, Italy

However, face away from the statues, the flowing water, the post-card and trinket sellers, and way to your right is a tiny alleyway, Vicolo del Forno. It is too small to be named on most maps; it goes nowhere. The narrow opening, part-shielded by the roast-chestnut seller, cuts out much of the noise, and its unprepossessing appearance puts off many visitors. But a short way within is a small side window to a shop, covered with wrought iron crossbars from the days before toughened glass and security alarms. On each bar there are tiny padlocks, and on the padlocks more padlocks, tumbling from one another, like rock plants growing from walls. Each padlock has names written on it, love trysts [114]

continued

Box 10.3 *continued*

Vicolo del Forno

Reflection is not just for designers. We may want ordinary users to pause and reflect too: on their health, on their neighbourhood, on the environment, or just on life. As well as designing to avoid breakdown, we may sometimes design artefacts that deliberately encourage breakdown.

In interaction design one is usually designing things to make them invisible, transparent, offering clear messages in the user's own language. However, Bill Gaver and colleagues turn this on its head and instead embrace ambiguity as a positive design value, creating pieces that provoke insight rather than provide information [178]. One example is the 'Sloganbench', situated in a Dutch housing estate as part of a project to increase the presence of older people in the community (Figure 10.2) [177].

The bench has a display built into the back, using electronically controlled fabric scrolls, as found in advertising billboards. But here, instead of slick messages encouraging you to buy toothpaste, are slogans hand written by older members of the community, capturing aspects of their feelings towards the estate. There is no explanation, no statement of purpose, nor brass plaque. Instead, those walking by or sitting on the bench are invited to create their own interpretations.

Figure 10.2 Sloganbench [177]

At a more prosaic level, pedometers, diet notebooks, and devices to monitor heartbeat are designed precisely to take you out of the activity of walking, eating, or exercising, to think about the activity and its implications for your health and well-being. Even a Twitter-enabled mobile phone, by encouraging you to tell others about what you are doing, also encourages you to notice. With electronic monitoring of temperature, electricity use, and other aspects of the home, it is becoming easier to provide a day-by-day and even moment-by-moment carbon footprint. Most current energy meters use standard liquid crystal displays (LCDs) or pass data direct to your computer, although some attempt to be decorative so that you actually look at them. However, it is possible to consider physically engaging devices such as a water column at the front door that shows the fifty-year sea-level rise if the world consumes as you did that day.

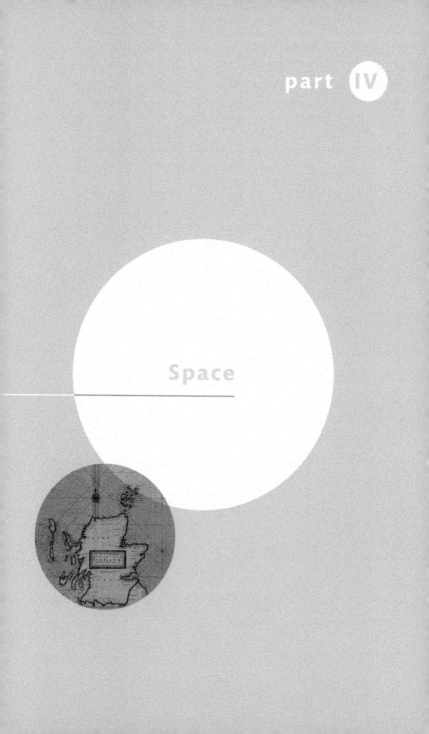

part **IV**

Space

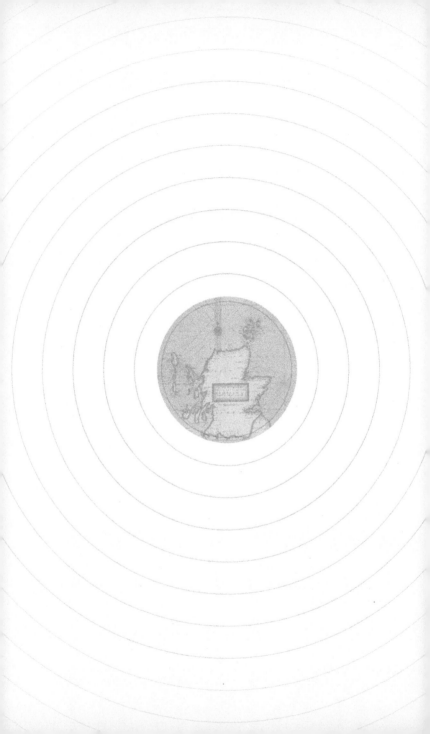

Physicality of Space

Space and time are the stuff of science fiction and yet so familiar that we hardly notice them. However, when we do think about them they are far more complex than we ever imagined. Sixteen-hundred years ago, Augustine of Hippo asked, 'What then is time?', and answered himself, 'If no one asks me, I know: if I wish to explain it to one that asketh, I know not' [12]. Space is no less strange. In this chapter we will look at how mathematicians and physicists have tried to make sense of space, and how some of the obvious properties are not at all what we first thought. In the next chapters we will see how many of these physical properties of space and time impact on the design of digitally augmented space, and indeed computation itself.

11.1 Void—Matrix or Myth

Aristotle said that nature abhors a vacuum. His reasons were partly ontological: if a vacuum is empty, then it is nothing, so it doesn't exist; partly pragmatic: without resistance objects would move with unbounded speed (given the physics of the day); and partly because if it were empty then things would naturally flow into it.

We are now all familiar with the idea of a vacuum, indeed we take a (partial) vacuum with us on a picnic. We also know that the viscous water and air that is our natural environment is but a thin film over the surface of the earth, and that between the planets and stars lie vast swathes of nothingness: we have seen film of suited people walking in space.

In fact, the air does continually evaporate into the vacuum but is largely held in check by the gravity of the earth, and if there is (ordinary) matter in the vastness of space it is no more than the equivalent of one-thousandth of a teaspoon of water in a volume the size of the earth. And because of Newton, we also know that the speed of movement is determined as much by inertia as viscous drag, so that objects move at constant, not infinite, speed in a vacuum.

Philosophically there is still a problem, though: as the astronauts float, in what do they float, and if there were no astronauts, no spaceship, no planets, no stars, would there still be space?

To some extent, the coordinates of Descartes solve this, at least mathematically. Even if there is nothing in space, we can still define it by its x, y, and z coordinates relative to some system. Space is still empty, but we can talk about it in equations, and property ledgers, filling it with an intangible web of notional graph paper.

There was once an argument that if someone owned a piece of land, then surely they owned the earth below and the sky above and far beyond the sky a piece of heaven. For the earth we might choose a polar coordinate system (one based on direction and distance from a centre) rather than rectilinear Cartesian coordinates as being slightly more convenient for celestial property speculation: longitude, latitude, and distance from the centre of the earth. At any moment we could give every point in the universe a unique grid reference, and while this would constantly change, if we owned our patch of land we could project our cone of ownership as a sweeping searchlight that encompassed stars, nebulae, and eventually, depending on your cosmology, an ever shifting patch of heaven itself.

If this sounds unlikely, on the 7 June 1494 in the Spanish town of Tordesilla, Spanish and Portuguese diplomats signed a treaty dividing the New World (America and Atlantic islands) between them along a meridian 370 leagues West of the Cape Verde islands—the reason why Brazil speaks Portuguese today and not the Spanish of most of South America. No-one from Spain or Portugal had ever walked that line, and determining it on the ground was never really solved, but from more than 7000 kilometres away, due to the power of coordinate geometry, the ownership of the land and the lives of the indigenous population was decided.

Over the years physics has intermittently challenged or championed the idea of the utterly empty void.

From Newton to Maxwell, notions of ether, a liquid-like medium filling all space, were posited, in particular as the medium through which light and electromagnetism propagated. If this were the case, then one would expect light to travel faster when shone in the direction of the earth's travel than when perpendicular to it, but the Michelson–Morley experiment in 1887 showed that this was not the case and that, counter intuitively, light travelled equally fast in all directions, paving the way for special relativity.

Done away with for a while, the fabric of space–time was given a more corporeal (albeit still empty) existence in general relativity with the idea of gravity being a bending of that fabric. Quantum mechanics introduced the concept of the vacuum as being a holder of an infinite potential of energy, virtually effervescing, and indeed the notion that our whole universe may simply be but one bubble in the foam of someone else's universe. With string theory, matter itself becomes mere loops and folds in space.

More recently still we have begun to fill the void yet more. A mismatch between the age of the universe as measured by the ages of stars, and the age as measured by the smoothness of background radiation led to the suggestion of a field of dark energy throwing the universe apart during a period of rapid expansion. Another mismatch, between the rotational speed and size of galaxies prompted notions of dark matter, ten times more than the visible matter, heaped in the space between stars and helping to 'glue' them together.

11.2 From Nothing—Points, Lines, and Circles

At school you will have studied geometry, following in the footsteps of the Greeks, and especially Euclid. The core definitions start with:

> Definition 1. A *point* is that which has no part.
>
> Definition 2. A *line* is breadth-less length.

Both lines and points, the basis of Euclidean geometry, are defined as much by their absence of size as by their presence. Yet, from

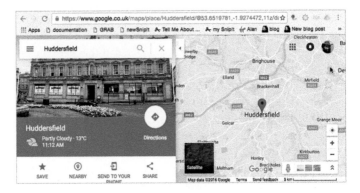

Figure 11.1 Huddersfield, United Kingdom, at high precision on Google Maps

these abstract nothings developed the system of thought and the mathematics that give us Global Positioning Systems (GPS) to guide smart bombs and Computer-Aided Design (CAD) to visualize our new kitchens.

Euclid's early definitions and postulates are meant in some ways to state the obvious, such as 'the ends of a line are points', but of course these sizeless points and lines, which are now familiar to us, are far from obvious in a world where every measuring rod or thread of wool has thickness, and stand in sharp contrast to the arguments of Euclid's predecessor, Zeno, who had concluded that all movement must be discrete.

This idea of sizelessness pervades many of the digital systems we use. If you search for Huddersfield on Google Maps, it is placed at 53.6519781,−1.9274472 (you can see this in the URL (Uniform Resource Locator)). Notice that the latitude is to seven decimal places, which works out as a *precision* of approximately 1 cm. Now Huddersfield is a town of around 150,000 people, but Google places it at a point with a purported accuracy of the fingernail of the statue of Harold Wilson that stands in its central square!

The Google Maps format for exporting and importing data is called KML (Keyhole Markup Language), and the tutorial includes

```
<?xml version="1.0" encoding="UTF-8"?>
<kml xmlns="http://www.opengis.net/kml/2.2">
  <Placemark>
    <name>Simple placemark</name>
    <description>Attached to the ground. Intelligently places itself
        at the height of the underlying terrain.</description>
    <Point>
      <coordinates>-122.0822035425683,37.42228990140251,0</coordinates>
    </Point>
  </Placemark>
</kml>
```

Figure 11.2 Example from KML Tutorial [192]

an example of a simple file with a single place (Figure 11.2). The longitude and latitude in this example are given to thirteen and fourteen digits respectively, the size of a medium molecule.

While somewhat ridiculous when applied to coordinates of everyday objects and locations, the idea of sizeless points and lines has been crucial in the description of physical systems from Newtonian physics to general relativity, though quantum mechanics challenges some of the limits.

As we read further through Euclid's elements, we find:

> Definition 13. A *boundary* is that which is an extremity of anything.
>
> Postulate 1. To draw a straight line from any point to any point.

These two encapsulate two critical roles of lines that we will encounter later when we look at the way we use linear structures in the built environment:

lines divide—they separate things: walls, moats, national boundaries

lines join—paths, roads, and fibre-optic cables

Of course, two special kinds of line dominate in geometry, the straight line and the circumference of a circle, constructed by ruler and compass respectively. For the Greeks the circle was often regarded as the perfect shape. A straight line was either finite, had fixed ends, and was therefore in a sense incomplete or imperfect, or was endless, infinite, a concept the Greek mind found curiously repelling. In contrast, the circumference of a circle (for Euclid, the circle was the figure within the circumference) stands complete in itself, self-similar, bounded yet endless. The story goes that Archimedes was so engrossed drawing geometric figures in the sand that he never noticed the Romans had invaded, and so was slain there amongst his circles.

Given this, it seemed natural to see the motions of the planets as lying on vast disks stretched out around the earth in Ptolemy's models of the universe. Even Copernicus merely replaced the epicyclical geocentric models of his day (circles upon circles) with a simpler circular heliocentric model. It took Newton to replace the perfection of the circle with the notion that all natural movement is linear, but that in the presence of gravity this linear tendency gives rise to both circular and elliptic orbits, as discovered empirically by Kepler.

The genius and wonder of Newton's explanation of orbits is that the planets are forever flying past the sun in their natural straight lines, whilst at the same time continually falling towards it and yet never getting closer; thinking back to the Greeks, not totally unlike Sisyphus eternally rolling a rock up a hill in Hades.

The idea of lines and points was critical in Descartes' reformulation of geometry in terms of coordinates. Cartesian coordinates, or variants of them, are ubiquitous, from the pixel locations on a computer screen to the longitude and latitude of GPS.

11.3 Flatness—The Shape of Space

In Euclid's seventh definition, we read that, 'A *plane surface* is a surface which lies evenly with the straight lines on itself', and a straight line itself is 'a line which lies evenly with the points on itself'. Flat, smooth, even: the ideals perhaps of a Greek stone floor as well as geometry.

Today, 'Flat Earther' is a synonym for someone who is ignorant or unscientific, yet for all of us it is our most natural first encounter with the world. Evidently, to our senses, the earth is flat and there is up and down.

As we grow, we learn that the world is in fact a sphere, or to be precise a flattened sphere bulging at the equator, but this always runs counter to that earlier common sense. Most of us brought up in Europe can remember, and perhaps still feel, the oddness that people in Australia are standing upside down. Presumably children in Australia feel the same about Europe, and likewise India about North America. In 1870, a vicar was walking to teach at a Mechanics' Institute and, struck by the wonder of the ever-turning globe, composed the evening hymn 'The day thou gavest Lord is ended', often played at funerals, which celebrates the endless cycle of prayer around the world where, 'As o'er each continent and island / The dawn leads on another day'.

In Euclid's time the idea of a spherical earth was well established, although it was not until after Euclid's death that Eratosthenes made the first calculations of its size. So Euclid was probably aware that his perfect flat surfaces were in fact as much an ideal or abstraction as his breadth-less lines.

On the curving earth, the shortest distance between two points is not a straight line, unless one wishes to undertake serious tunnelling, but a great circle, such as the apparently arcing path of a transatlantic flight above the Arctic Circle.

Of course, this only looks arcing on a standard global map because of the impossibility of mapping the spherical earth on a flat paper. For a small area, a city or even a smaller country, one hardly notices. The UK OS (Ordnance Survey) maps are based on a rectangular grid that gives an average fit for the country as a whole, but this means that 'grid north' may differ by several degrees from 'true north', depending on which part of the country you are in. As the earth is not even perfectly ellipsoid, the OS longitude and latitude system (OSGB36) can differ from the one used in GPS (WGS84) by up to 100 metres [319, 298].

Now we know that not only is the surface of the earth curved, but space itself has curvature. This is hard to grasp, as we envisage the curvature of the earth within a 'flat', three-dimensional space, but general relativity shows that gravity bends the very fabric of space. On the surface of the earth, if you draw a large circle, its area is

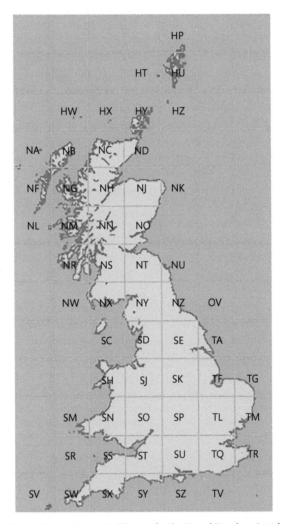

Figure 11.3 Ordnance Survey Grid System for the United Kingdom. Initial graphic made by Keith Edkins, modified by P Verdy and imported from English Wikipedia. CC BY-SA 3.0

slightly more than you would expect given its circumference, because the earth bulges in the middle. However, the equations of relativity say that if you were to create a perfect box, 1 metre in each

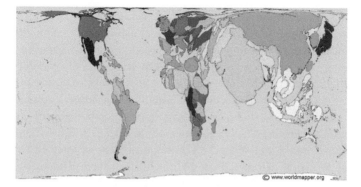

Figure 11.4 World map drawn with area proportional to population

direction, in the vicinity of any object exerting gravity (such as the earth), then the inside of the box would contain very slightly *less* than 1 cubic metre of space.

Most of this only matters if you are contemplating a career in cosmic physics, or very precise space engineering (such as the software for the GPS system itself). However, in practice, real space exhibits a non-flatness at even the ordinary scale. If two towns are connected by a fast road, they are 'close' for many purposes; but if there are few roads, or even a river or mountain range in between, then they become, in practice, distant. Maps are also sometimes drawn trying to capture these different ideas of distance, or modifying the areas of countries to represent features such as wealth, ecological footprint [214], or population (e.g. Figure 11.4).

11.4 Uniformity—Continuity and Fracture

Looking at Figure 11.4, the world is still recognizable even though the sizes and shapes have changed. *Closeness* relationships are also retained: India is still next to China, the United States is still next to Canada. Mathematics has a whole branch, topology, dedicated to spaces where what matters is closeness, but any amount of stretching and even sometimes folding is allowed—so long as you don't tear.

A tear means that two things that were once arbitrarily close become far away. In various branches of mathematics, continuity and smoothness are important concepts. Discontinuity changes require radically different mathematical tools, and are often seen as problematic. Notably, most of classical physics is based on ideas of continuity: small changes in input lead to small changes in output.

In the physical world, discontinuity is common but often disorienting. Sometimes it is caused by natural barriers: when walking round the coast of Wales [3], Alan frequently encountered estuaries, where the destination was no more than a couple of kilometres away but it took a whole day's journey upstream to find the closest bridge. Such barriers may also be human-made, such as the Berlin Wall during the Cold War. Mazes and labyrinths take this frustrating near-yet-farness and turn it into a game or spiritual journey.

A different form of non-uniformity occurs when distances are not symmetric. Again this can happen naturally; a distance uphill may feel further and take longer than the equivalent downhill journey. However, it is more common in constructed environments such as one-way road systems.

Digital systems can often create such fractures since by their nature they make things discrete, and this is often made more problematic because the computation is hidden.

One example you may have encountered is digital radio. The radio signal varies in different areas of the country and even some rooms of a house, and in the days of analogue radio the radio quality would also vary, from clarity, to crackling sound, to nothing. However, digital radio error-corrects degraded signal, giving apparently perfect reception—up to a point. If the signal is too poor for the error correction to work, you get nothing at all. If you are just on the edge of a region of reception, small changes to the environmental conditions or simply moving the radio a few metres may cause the reception to come and go but always completely: all or nothing.

Location-based systems often create similar effects by only showing material if the GPS or other sensed coordinates of the device are within a marked area or within a given distance of a location. Location sensing is often slightly inaccurate and may change from moment to moment, so that if you are at the edge of such an area, the material may flicker back and forth (see Box 11.1).

Box 11.1 Savannah

Savannah was an early experimental mobile game [159] where the virtual world of the Savannah was displayed on a mobile device, using a GPS in a backpack. Children were lions in the game and explored an open space looking for prey. However, they had to work together as a group and could only catch prey if they all acted in concert.

When examining the logs and video, the researchers noted that there were periods of frustration, when a child would spot prey, call the rest of their team, who would cluster close to one another, but one or other child would keep not being able to see the prey.

This happened because the area that showed the prey was determined by a boundary and only displayed if the child's GPS coordinates were within the boundary. The child would tend to stop at the edge of the boundary, where they first saw the prey, to call the other children. Because they were just on the boundary, whether the prey appeared for each child in the team became apparently arbitrary, much like the digital radio signal.

One way to deal with the problem is to introduce hysteresis, by expanding the area of influence a little once you are inside it, or having a minimum dwell time before the material changes. However, by doing this you get a 'one-way-street' effect. You step forward, see new material, think you would prefer what you were seeing before, but due to the hysteresis, stepping back does not return you to what you were seeing (see also Chapter 21).

Another approach is to make the boundary itself more evident. For example, your mobile phone shows signal bars, so that you can tell not only whether you can make a phone call but how reliable the call is likely to be.

Seamful design [62] takes this further, designing a game deliberately to make use of failings in the digital landscape, such as places between buildings that do not receive mobile signal or GPS, so that the player can hide in wait for other real or virtual players.

11.5 Scale—Size Matters

Part of Newton's genius lay in realizing that although they looked superficially different, the same laws of physics governed both the cosmic and the mundane. The same force that brings an apple falling three yards from its tree keeps the planets circling in their 100 million-mile orbits.

The belief that laws are universal, operating the same at all times and in all places, has become one of the fundamental tenets of science. In geology it was given a name as the 'Law of Uniformitarianism', standing against those who suggested special rules for times of past inundation or divine creation. Although the details of life vary at different times and in different places, they operate on the same underlying physical, cosmological principles. If scientists feel the need to call a portion of space or time special, for example the inflation period in the early universe, they start to look for yet deeper laws, rules that operate uniformly but for some reason exhibit themselves differently in the special portion. This principle can never be proven. While it has stood science in good stead so far, to go from that to universal validity is of course a circular argument.

Both Newton and Leibnitz used the new tools of calculus, but Newton expressed his results using geometry for fear that the common person would be able to understand calculus. It may be that geometry helped him grasp this invariance over distance and vast scales of magnitude. In Euclidean geometry most results are scale- and location-invariant. For example, a proof about a triangle with sides of 3 cm, 4 cm, and 5 cm, works equally for one of 3 km, 4 km, and 5 km. They are 'similar' triangles and the proof is true, independent of where the triangles lie.

This same invariance underlies the utility of architectural models in card and plaster and geographic information systems on computer screens. For digital fabrication, this means one can relatively easily take the design files for a small-scale model and simply magnify them to create a full-size version, although in practice small tweaks are usually needed.

Thinking again about Fitts' Law, discussed in Chapter 5, we can say that the time to point to a target was scale-invariant: if the target distance and size of target both double, it takes the same time to point. Our ability to draw also seems to be scale-invariant. Although it can be hard to sign within the small boxes on some official forms, on the whole you can sign your name equally well at the end of a letter or filling a whiteboard. Similarly, you can draw small circles or big ones, small squares or big ones. This is surprising in many ways as the muscle groups needed to write in the large are largely about arm movement, whereas signing a letter is all about wrist and finger movement. Clearly our brain stores shapes in ways that do not directly encode the physical actions needed to create them.

Perhaps most fascinating, although most simple, are the point and unbounded line of Euclidean geometry. They are self-similar: no matter how much you scale them up or down, they stay the same. Many phenomena in nature exhibit this self-similar scale invariance.

We have probably all been enamoured with fractals at some stage, the cold equations of the Mandelbrot set giving rise to exquisite, almost organic patterns of endless complexity. Although the precise details differ at different scales, the general statistical properties stay the same. Mandelbrot's own study of fractals was inspired by the work of LF Richardson, who suggested that coastlines, and in particular the west coast of Great Britain have ever greater complexity as you look more and more closely. Effectively coastlines are self-similar [274, 341]. The driving question was to determine the length of the coast, and the fractal nature means that there is no answer, the closer you look and the finer the curves you take into account, the longer it becomes!

Snowflakes, tree branches, and certain clouds all have this same fractal property and part of their beauty seems to stem from this, the modern equivalent of the Greek golden ratio which is itself related to self-similarity through the logarithmic spirals of sunflowers and snail shells.

Self-similarity also arises in temporal sequences, from the tumbling of piled sand grains in an hour-glass, to the occurrence of earthquakes, the drops running down a rain-spattered window, and

Figure 11.5　A snowflake and Romanesco broccoli

even the behaviour of pedestrians [244]. In many phenomena, stresses or instabilities build up over time until they are effectively always ready to fail, a process called criticality. Eventually there is some tiny fall, break, or fracture, releasing a little of the stress. Sometimes that is all, but sometimes the first small event triggers the collapse of a larger stress, and so on. The pattern of sizes of events may appear initially to be random but the sizes obey variations of the same power law: there are large numbers of small events, but small numbers of almost arbitrarily large events, with predictable frequencies. So common are these that some refer to this as universality [46, 410]. Crucially, many network systems, such as face-to-face friendships, web page linkages, and social media connections, obey the same power law dynamics. This is particularly important in empirical research as the statistics of power laws are very different from the normal (or Gaussian) distribution, which underlies many of the common techniques applied to experimental evidence.

We see, then, that scale may not always be important, but in certain circumstances scale matters critically. In older films, before special effects used computer-generated imagery (CGI), small models were often used for scenes involving vehicles and buildings, especially when they were to be crashed or destroyed. When constructed well, these could be virtually indistinguishable from their full-size counterparts, but when floating on water or burning there was always something about the shape of the waves or flames that gave away the size.

Even though the same laws operate at all scales, the balance of forces between surface tension, the weight and viscosity of the water, the wind speed, and many other factors interact differently. This is obvious when you watch a small bird cling to a wall or an insect skim across water surface, as we discussed in Chapter 3. Our body weight increases as the cube of our size, but the cross-sectional length of our muscles and other areas vary with the square of our size, so as size decreases weight becomes less important compared with things related to area. A human at 1.7 m tall is around 20 times larger than a wren, and 200 times larger than a spider. This means that the wren muscles, while 400 times smaller than our own, only have to support 1/8000 of the weight. This is one of the reasons adults are more likely to hurt themselves than small children when they fall.

This relationship between size, volume, and area is also why our lungs have such a convoluted (near-fractal) shape. Our oxygen needs increase with the volume of our body, but if our lungs were a simple open cavity, like our stomach, the blood–air connection would only increase with area, not volume, and it would be increasingly hard to get sufficient oxygen; the convoluted shape increases the surface area. Cities are the same, but on the flat; if you double the dimensions of the city, the land area and number of people goes up by four, but the perimeter length and the number of roads across the city boundary only doubles—there is a reason for gridlock, and it is scale!

Similar issues apply to computer circuit boards and chips. Indeed one of the reasons for investigating 3D or stacked computer chips is to reduce the physical distance data travel and the amount of data sent on-and-off chip through a limited set of connections [367]. This is rather like encouraging local transport within a city as opposed to long-distance commuting from outside. We will consider more issues related to the physicality of computing in Chapter 17.

Box 11.2 Chinese scale model

There is a community of people who scour Google Earth for interesting things. In 2006, KenGrok (forum handle) noticed a strange rectangular area in China [247]. It was big enough to show up on the satellite imagery, about 700 m × 900 m, but stood out against the rather featureless land around. It turned out to be an exact scale model of an area of disputed mountainous land on the border between China and India. Its purpose is unknown. Some think it is for military planning, others for hydro electric projects [203]. Either way, it is probably the biggest scale model in the world.

11.6 Relativity and Locality

Early mappae mundi placed Jerusalem at the centre of the world (Figure 11.6), a fixed and immutable point from which all other things were measured. Copernicus displaced the earth and positioned the centre of the universe towards the sun. Now we know that the sun itself is hurtling at three-quarters of a million kilometres an hour around the centre of our galaxy and our galaxy is itself just one among 100 billion more, all flying apart since the Big Bang.

In Euclidean geometry only the *relative position* of lines and shapes matter, the rules are the same everywhere. Newton took this one step further and his rules of motion are velocity invariant. It doesn't matter how fast you are moving; so long as everything else is moving

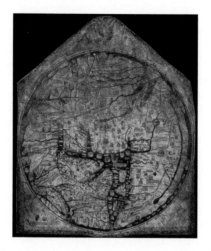

Figure 11.6 Hereford Cathedral Mappa Mundi [216]

at the same speed, everything still looks the same. If this were not so, you would find life very odd when walking down a train at 150 kilometres an hour, or in an aeroplane at 800 kilometres an hour. This is why it feels as if the plane is never going to stop when it lands on the runway. You feel the deceleration (braking) but interpret it as speed.

Einstein took yet another step in general relativity, which asserts that you cannot even tell the difference between acceleration and gravity, so that when the lift rises fast it is just as if gravity becomes stronger, and if the cable breaks, for those inside the falling lift it feels just the same as floating in a space station—until the lift hits the bottom. This phenomenon is used to train astronauts by having an aeroplane take a path where it free-falls for a short period.

Even though we know the earth is flying at 30 kilometres a second round the sun, we still use longitude and latitude. That may seem as if we have returned to the world of the Mappa Mundi, with Greenwich taking the place of Jerusalem. However, if there is no special centre

Box 11.3 Understanding jerk

The equivalence between gravity and acceleration explains some of the physiological effects we described in Chapter 5 and their impact on the design of railways and roads. So long as a train travels at a constant velocity (straight line and with no acceleration or deceleration), it is as if everyone on it were all stationary together. If you toss an apple to a friend, it does not hit them at 150 kilometres an hour, or to be strict, it does, but as they are also moving at 150 kilometres an hour, they don't notice.

When you go round a bend you do feel the acceleration throwing you sideways but this is effectively the same as if gravity had swung round to the side. So long as the bend is a constant circular arc, you can simply walk leaning slightly to one side and it is just the same as when the train stops on a slight camber. It is the point at which the curvature *changes*, from straight to curve, from curve to straight, or from right-hand to left-hand curve, that you notice the difference; you have to swing from standing upright to leaning and back, or from leaning one way to leaning the other. Track engineers call this change in curvature and hence acceleration 'jerk', and minimizing jerk is one of the major considerations when routing railway tracks.

then any centre will do, and even if there were a special centre to the universe, relativity means that choosing some other centre will still work (albeit with some caveats). The caveat here is that longitude–latitude is actually a spinning frame of reference, rotating once a day. So if you travel north–south you experience an (apparent) Coriolis force, pushing you sideways. This isn't a real force, but appears to be so. In fact, as you travel away from the Equator towards the poles, you end up spinning with less speed (still one rotation a day, but less far round the earth), so have to decelerate; similarly if you go from pole to equator you need to accelerate. To follow a 'straight' path on the earth, you must adjust your speed and this feels like a force.

This 'force' is too small to feel at human speeds, has a small effect on aeroplanes, but most significantly affects large ocean and air flows.

	miles/hour	km/hour	miles/second	km/second
spinning earth	1000	1600	0.3	0.5
earth around the sun	66,000	107,000	20	30
sun around the galaxy centre	483,000	792,000	135	220

Figure 11.7 Table of approximate cosmic speeds—spinning earth, earth around sun, sun around galaxy [168]

It also gives rise to the (near) myth that water changes the direction it goes down the plughole in the northern and southern hemispheres. It is true that if you create a very symmetric water tank full of very still water and very carefully remove the plug, the direction will be anticlockwise in the northern hemisphere and clockwise in the south, but for ordinary sinks the effect is so tiny that the direction is effectively random.

However, just because you can choose any frame of reference doesn't mean that the way you choose your coordinates doesn't matter. Physicists often choose a frame of reference that enables easier calculation, and if you are playing table tennis on a train, it is probably best to forget that you are all travelling at 150 kilometres an hour. Similarly, in robotics it may sometimes be easier to think about the coordinates of the room, sometimes easier to focus on coordinates centred on the robot and sometimes on the robot arm; part of the challenge is to transform between these different coordinate systems.

Perhaps more significantly, coordinates change the way you think about the world. The choice of Jerusalem as centre of the Mappa Mundi was not arbitrary; standard maps of the world place Europe or America in the middle for similar reasons. Mapping from near spherical earth to flat sheet also involves choices, as we've seen already. The most common world map uses the Mercator projection, which was chosen for navigational reasons since it preserves the *shape* of local areas. However, this is at the cost of distorting size, so that Greenland appears as big as all of Africa. For this reason some have suggested alternative projections, such as the Peters projection, which preserves area, although at the cost of distorting shape.

11.7 Time Too

The astute reader may well have noticed that we passed over Einstein's special relativity in the last section in our headlong rush from Euclid through Newton to Einstein's general relativity. That was because in many ways it draws on the same assumption as Newton—velocity invariance—but with the added information, due to Michelson–Morley, that the speed of light is the same no matter how fast you are going.

Imagine yourself on the train again, tossing apples to your friends. You are facing the direction of travel, your friends with their backs to it. You throw an apple at 2 kilometres an hour (a gentle toss), and they toss it back. Of course if the train is going at 150 kilometres an hour, someone outside the train would see an apple travelling at 152 kilometres an hour from you to your friends and at 148 kilometres an hour, but still in the direction of the train's travel, when they throw it back. Both you and your friends would, of course, be travelling at 150 kilometres an hour.

Now imagine the train goes dark and you shine a torch. Light is travelling at 1000 million kilometres an hour, so it seems that if you shine your torch on your friends' faces, the light should be travelling at 1000 million plus 150 kilometres an hour, but Michelson–Morley says, no, it is still 1000 million kilometres an hour. Something doesn't seem right.

Einstein's solution was to consider time itself and realize that it too is relative. You have probably heard two things about special relativity: first that time flows slower the faster you go, and second that things get shorter as they go faster. In fact the second is a consequence of the first. If a train is travelling rapidly past you, what does it mean to ask 'how long is the train', or more precisely to measure it. Just to make things a little more interesting, let's assume a foggy day so you can't see far along the track. One way to measure the length would be to have a number of friends stand every few metres down the track and note what time the end of the train passes them. You note when the front passes you and afterwards you compare notes with your friends. If one who was 500 metres away from you saw the end of the train pass them at the same moment the front passed you, you conclude the train is 500 metres long.

However, this all depends on synchronized watches, and what you mean by 'now'. Einstein's genius was to realize that 'now' is not a fact of the universe, but a human construct.

Let's go back a few hundred years before the invention of clocks. You measure time using a sundial. When the sun is at its highest, that is noon. Now roll on to the days of town hall and church clocks, which are set so that they agree with the sundial. Of course, people know that the earth is turning, so that it's noon in Rome nearly an hour before it's noon in London, and for navigation and particularly for the calculation of longitude, mariners use clocks set to Greenwich Mean Time (GMT), the time set by the midday sun in London. But that would be useless for day-to-day time elsewhere in the world, and certainly not a standard the French would agree to.

So at the start of the nineteenth century we have a universal time (GMT), used for marine calculation, and we have local time used for daily life. Then came the railways. The local time at Cardiff is more than 12 minutes behind the time in London, fine if you live in London and fine if you live in Cardiff, but with trains operating to a strict timetable, to which time should the train guard set his watch? Each train company in Britain adopted its own standard time, then, gradually, GMT as the single standard time, which effectively put London at the temporal heart of Britain, though it is not far from the most easterly point. Almost everyone else in the country has to start their day up to half an hour earlier (by the sun) than Londoners!

In fact, establishing a single time across different locations is difficult. A person cannot be in more than one place at once, so to synchronize clocks in different places they would either carry a clock from one to the other or communicate at a distance using signals (or later telegraph, the 'speaking clock', or the 'pips' on the radio). Of course, for convenience we have different time zones in different parts of the world but these are closely synchronized with one another and whenever there is doubt scientists will use universal time (UTC).

If you live in Swansea and you forget that the time zone is different in Australia, when you phone your aunt in Sydney at 7.30 in the evening, she will not be very pleased to be woken up at 4 o'clock in the morning. You will know that *at the same moment* the sun is setting in south Wales it is about to rise in New South Wales. But though we say 'at the moment', in fact we know there are slight delays in the phone lines. These are partly due to switching, and also because the speed of light (or electrical transmission, which is slower) puts an absolute limit of about 70 milliseconds (ms) on the time it takes. However, despite the delays, which you sometimes notice, you can *closely enough* hold a conversation that feels simultaneous.

Of course, 'close enough' for everyday human purposes may not be close enough for physics. Einstein realized that 'now' was not just hard to measure, but fundamentally meaningless. We can talk about the 'here and now', and for any person and any clock it is meaningful to talk about the rate of time passing, but there is no universality to that passage.

In pasta terms, classical physics sees the world rather like a lasagne: each sheet of pasta is like a moment of time, and by knowing what is true 'now', the state of the world at the next step, the next layer of pasta, is determined. In contrast, Einstein's time–space universe is more like spaghetti. Each of us has a strand of our own history and carries our own time. If we lie alongside another strand we will measure time passing at the same rate, but if we separate and reconnect there is no reason why we should agree.

Unless we are designing on a cosmic scale, with regard to light speed experiments or GPS satellites, the differences between the two will not affect us directly, but the larger lessons do affect us. The finite is important for the design of computer chips (see Chapter 17) and finite communication, for whatever reason, affects streaming video (yes, that 'buffering'!) and, even more, Skype, Zoom, and other video or audio communications.

When designing algorithms to synchronize data (e.g. address books on different devices), time as measured by local clocks may not be good enough, not because of special relativity but due to simple inaccuracies. However, the effect is the same, requiring great care in, for example, ordering events that occur on different devices.

Finally, as we saw with spatial relativity, the choices we make about time also have social and political importance. Northern Ireland and the Scottish Hebridean islands are about 20 minutes to half an hour behind GMT (London time), and both Cardiff and Edinburgh around 12 minutes behind; perhaps a time based around a Cardiff meridian would be a better average for the United Kingdom than London-based time?

11.8 Terra Firma

'The wise man built his house upon the rock' Matthew 7:24

Until Copernicus, the dominant view was that the earth was not only solid but also the centre of things, the point around which the arcs of heaven rotated. It was not until the early twentieth century that seismologists realized that the earth had a liquid outer core (with a smaller solid core), and until the mid-1960s, it was only fanciful schoolchildren who matched up the African and American coasts and imagine them fitting together like a jigsaw puzzle.

How fast science changes its ground truth!

Now we know that the earth is spinning around its axis each day, the ground beneath our feet thundering along at 1500 kilometres an hour (happily, we are likewise travelling at 1500 kilometres per hour in the same direction), and the earth hurtling at three-quarters of a million kilometres an hour around the galactic centre [304]. The continents shift like floating islands over a sea of magma, and land is constantly created in the mid-ocean ridges (coming to the surface occasionally in Iceland and the Pacific atolls) and destroyed in ocean trenches.

Yet still, despite these movements in geological time, or in our day-to-day lives, there is nothing as solid, as unmoving, as reliable as the ground beneath our feet. Metaphors remind us that we are 'on solid ground', in science we have 'ground truth', and if someone is well-balanced and reflective they are 'grounded'.

This is why it is so disturbing when the earth moves beneath our feet, itself a metaphorical statement, due to volcano or earthquake, or when a sinkhole opens and swallows cars and houses whole. Inge Lehmann, who discovered the earth's inner core in 1936, was driven towards the study of geology by the experience of earth tremors as a child [261]. During one winter while this book was being completed, storms reshaped many areas of the British coastline, exposing 6000-year-old drowned forests and smashing giant sea stacks and arches.

The earth is far from fixed and firm.

Alan used to live on the Isle of Tiree, a small island off the west coast of Scotland. The bedrock is Lewisian gneiss, some of the oldest rock on the planet, with no fossils—it was formed 3 billion years ago, way before the beginning of life on earth. Yet his house was built on sandy soil (like the foolish man!) that has formed and shifted within the last few hundred years. The whole of the British Isles is still tipping after the weight of ice melted from its northern half at the end of the last Ice Age, slowly drowning valleys in Cornwall and rising, a few centimetres a century, in Scotland. But this slow rise of the 'solid' Lewisian rock will not be fast enough to counter the rising sea levels due to global warming, within our own and our children's lifetimes.

Life has always been part of this movement. The sandy soil of Tiree is the remains of countless seashells, ground by wind and tide and mixed with peaty deposits of long-dead, semi-decayed moss. And it is only recently that scientists have realized that the movement of continents is made possible by the 'lubricating' effect in subduction zones of soft earthy deposits caused by the earliest flora and fauna.

Of course, we ourselves are the greatest shifters of land, from ancient earthworks such as Offa's Dyke, to modern open-cast diamond mines and artificial islands in Dubai and the South China Sea. But the biggest shift is, like Vulcan's workshop below Mount Etna, the result of fire. In Greenland, the rate of ice loss due to global warming means that within a few generations the land will bounce up, so that sea-edge settlements will rise faster than the rising sea levels and be left high and dry.

Traditional industrialization was and is the cause of this catastrophe, but digital simulations and modelling are at the heart of trying to understand the potential effects of our actions and may be part of the solution, helping us to tune our energy demands in a better way to what the earth can provide.

At even shorter time periods, areas of high and low air pressure literally suck the ground up and push it down. For precise architectural work one has to use relative point-to-point measurements rather than absolute earth-centred ones, because the earth really does shift beneath our feet and is more akin to a floating platform.

11.9 Patterns in the Landscape

Such change is often what forms our landscape around us: the Himalayas and Alps, created as vast continental plates crash into one another, throwing up mountains as if they were sea foam. In their wake other changes follow, rivers and sea and wind erode the weakest rock first, cutting deep valleys, hollowing caves beneath sea cliffs, or leaving precarious sculptures across deserted landscapes.

These processes of erosion often expose and amplify small differences in resilience. The tiny crack in the rock allows rainwater to flow and eventually becomes a karst sinkhole. On the rock of stream beds and beaches you often see small circular depressions, so perfect you would think they had been cut with a lathe. They start as a point of weakness or sometimes just a random fold in the rock, which captures pebbles and sand. These swirl in the current and dig the depression a little deeper so that more sand and pebbles are likely to fall in. As we've so often seen already, positive feedback can create large effects from the smallest of beginnings.

These self-reinforcing effects can be so strong that they defy the underlying drivers. In the south Wales valleys, rivers flow down from mountains north of Cardiff, feeding rivers that flow into Cardiff Bay. This is unsurprising, until you realize that the rivers cut across the underlying geology.

The whole of the mountain system is a syncline, where the rocks at the edges have been raised relative to the centre. This was crucial for the development of the south Wales coal industry in the eighteenth and nineteenth centuries, since coal was exposed at the edges, revealing its presence for early shallow mining, followed later by deep mines towards the centre. The river pattern we see to-day formed initially before the syncline but managed to cut its way through the rock faster than the rock raised up, leaving a superimposed drainage pattern, a relic of past geology.

Turn to Cardiff itself—at a confluence of rivers, it was always a place of importance with a Roman fort and later a cathedral and Norman castle. The coal and iron industries led to the growth of the port, with the first 1 million-pound cheque paid in Cardiff's Coal Exchange buildings in 1904, when it was one of the biggest ports in the world. As ships switched from coal to diesel and newer industries arose, the port became less important, but by this time the city had become a major centre of commerce. Secondary industries took on a life of their own and it is now the seat of Welsh government. The original factors of geology and transport have faded but the self-reinforcing human structures remain.

Cardiff Bay, once a hub of shipping, is now a vast marina. The old Coal Exchange is surrounded by the modern National Assembly, opera house, bars, restaurants, and waterfront apartments. It is clear when we look at the city that it is the work of human hands, less evident that the hills of the south Wales valleys were once covered in heaps of mining waste at what appeared to be geological scale. Only after one of these slid down the hill, killing over 200 children at Aberfan, were attempts made to stabilize, if not remove, these vast unnatural hillsides.

The aesthetic of the past often focused on controlling nature, even if human spaces were sometimes created to emulate the wild. This started to change with the growth of the Romantic movement in the early nineteenth century and today we value nature, possibly because there is so little left.

However, geological, environmental, and human influences are often hard to disentangle.

As exemplified by the growth of Cardiff, our human cultural, linguistic, political, and technical structures often follow the lines of the environment. Roads and railways skirt along contours and rise over mountain passes; rivers and mountain ranges often create linguistic divides and tend to form natural limits to national or other boundaries. The environment does not uniquely determine these things: roads and railways do not follow every contour but only those that connect significant cities or industry. National boundaries can lie along any of a number of natural barriers, but tend to be more stable if the boundary is physical as well as political.

And like the Welsh valleys themselves, what appears to be a natural environment may often be the product of human hands. The Lake District in the north of England was the birthplace of the UK's National Trust and is now a National Park. It was a source of inspiration for Wordsworth and the other Romantic poets as well as many painters who tried to capture, or exaggerate, on canvas its rugged *natural* majesty. The deep valleys, filled with its eponymous lakes, are the work of ice sheets that carved out paths through limestone, volcanic, and metamorphic rocks, presumably themselves following and deepening long past river courses. However, as we saw in Chapter 1, without the human introduction of sheep who graze its slopes, the rock-hewn landscape would quickly cover with scrub woodland, creating a different landscape, softer and perhaps beautiful in its own way, but no longer the wild 'natural' landscape that first attracted the Romantics.

Comprehension of Space

When considering human spatial abilities, psychologists distinguish body space, the area immediately around and in reach, from the larger space that we walk around. However, when we think about how our understanding of space relates to digital 'spaces' it is also worth distinguishing vista space, the space we can see, from the hidden spaces that are behind walls, through doors, around mountains, or over the horizon. Whereas we navigate vista space directly with our senses, we navigate these latter spaces through memory and imagination as well as actual locomotion. We use navigation space to refer to this partially hidden space of landmarks and routes, since we are not usually consciously aware of 'navigating' around vista space, unless it is exceptionally full, or we have a large overview, for example on a mountaintop.

In summary we have three kinds of space:

body space—things we can reach and touch without moving our feet
vista space—things we can see, but may have to walk, run or otherwise travel in order to reach
navigation space—places and routes that we cannot directly see, but encounter over time

We will return to these three types of space throughout this chapter, as we look first at how our understanding of space develops from infancy, then at our adult sensory and mental perception of space, and finally at how we transform and manage physical and digital space.

12.1 Early Understanding of Space

When a baby is tiny its focus is primarily on body space: what can be touched and felt. This is partly because its vision is poor, and partly because distant things are incomprehensible until explored and examined. As the baby grows, it starts to point to things that are out of reach, hoping that its parent will bring things closer, clearly knowing what something is, even when distant. But it is primarily when babies start to crawl and walk that space becomes a place of potential, as opposed to a backdrop or context.

Experiments with young kittens have shown that this active exploration of the environment is essential for normal development [213, 310]. Two kittens were used, one harnessed to a small carousel, and the other suspended opposite. The one that was able to move could wander around as much as it liked (in a circle). Whenever this kitten moved its suspended partner moved, and whatever this kitten saw its partner saw as well. They were kept like this for several weeks and then released to roam freely.

Despite being constrained to move in a circle, the kitten that was dragging the carousel suffered no ill effects, but the kitten that was suspended was unable to develop a normal ability to navigate its environment. Although it had seen the environment in exactly the same way as its mobile partner, it had not had any control. It was evident that active exploration of the environment was essential for the kittens to develop a connection between what they saw and what they felt and understood.

There is also evidence that in babies without early crawling experience, long-term spatial perception is deficient [172], and when congenitally blind humans have had surgery and gain sight, they find it very difficult to attain any normal sense of the larger visual field. We need to both see and actively explore our environment to develop our full spatial abilities.

12.2 Childhood and Larger Spaces

So the early child with sight and movement gradually develops a sense of the relation between what can be seen, and what can be walked around. However, the larger, unseen world is more complex.

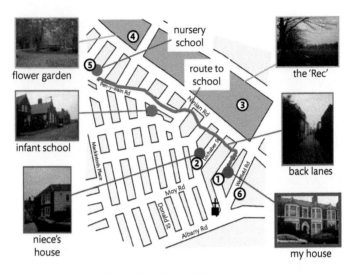

Figure 12.1 Alan's childhood world

Figure 12.1 shows a map of the area of Cardiff where Alan was brought up. Various places are marked: (1) is Alan's home and obviously the heart of his earliest memories. However, he also knew (2) well. It was the house in the next street where his (much older) half-brother's family lived until they emigrated when Alan was three years old. Yet while the place was well known, it was only as a young adult that Alan realized it had been in the next street—the outside of the house, the metal stairs up to the upstairs flat, were recognizable, but the route to it was not.

The parks nearby are marked (3) and (4) and were also places he visited as a young child and (5) is the nursery school which was reachable through a walk through back lanes, dropping his sister in school on the way. This route grew familiar over time, but on sunny days, the children from the nursery school were led across the road to play in the park (5). He learned that the same place was reachable by two routes. There was another crucial development stage when it became clear that the shopping street nearby (6) could be reachable by going out of the house in two different directions.

Note the stages in understanding: first places, patches of space that are recognizable and familiar, then paths or routes between those places, and finally the understanding of the network of connections. Also note that none of this involves the map shown in Figure 12.1. For most purposes the Cartesian layout of space is not important, it is the *connectivity* that is crucial (see the example of the London Underground map in Chapter 19).

In other words, our understanding of the larger spaces beyond our vision tends to begin as a network of linked places, not a Cartesian 'bird's-eye view' map. Much later, we may come to appreciate maps, and the ability to make use of them varies between people, but deep down the larger world is a network. It is this network understanding of space that we exploit when we navigate information spaces such as the Internet.

12.3 Feeling and Acting in Space

Recall Gibson's ecological understanding of perception and action (Chapter 5)—the way we act on the world influences the way we perceive it. This differs for the different kinds of space.

For body space, our main form of action is through our hands and arms; we twist and turn, pick things up, turn them over. This is a truly three-dimensional (3D) space, since, within the reach and strength of our hands, we can move them to any location, even pass things between our hands when they are behind our backs. Our ability to act in this space is driven as much by proprioception and touch as vision.

For the larger vista and navigation spaces, however, our mode of action, and thus our affordances, are determined by our legs, and take on a more two-dimensional (2D) aspect. We can of course climb walls or stairs, go underground in caves and tunnels, or even fly. However, it is clear that our ability to make sense of the walked world fully three-dimensionally is less than perfect.

The complexity of true 3D movement is rarely encountered in day-to-day life. However, pilots, especially helicopter pilots, do need to perceive the world in 3D. When walking around a field, or driving down a road, you only have to decide which direction to move in, left, forward, right. While we are moving about in a 2D world, we

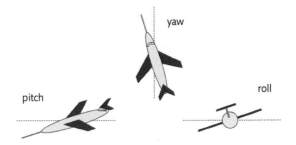

Figure 12.2 Moving in three dimensions: pitch, yaw, and roll

only have to consider one degree of freedom for direction, and, of course, how fast to move in that direction.

In contrast, a plane (or submarine) has three kinds of 'direction' (Figure 12.2). Yaw is the side to side movement we are familiar with, but the pilot also has to know about pitch, whether the nose is down or up, and roll, whether the wings are level, or whether one side is down, when the plane is banking. Pilots can develop some of this through practised use of their ordinary senses. For example, even as a passenger you can tell when the plane is banking steeply. However, as we saw in Chapter 5, it is soberingly easy to lose our sense of 'up', so pilots use instruments, for example the artificial horizon, which allow them to detect more subtle changes in roll and pitch.

In fact, when powered technology in the form of cars or trains takes over from our legs, our perceptions can also be fooled, even in 2D. As we've seen, Newton's laws of physics are based around the fact that you cannot tell the difference between moving at constant speed and being still unless you have some external point of reference. In a fast-moving train, you can forget you are moving at all until you look out of the window, and in a station you can sometimes think your train has started, when it is really the train on the next platform that is moving. When walking or cycling we know we are moving because we have to put in constant effort to keep moving, but when divorced from this effort we have little intrinsic sense of speed. Indeed, you may have had the experience while driving of looking down at the speedometer and realizing you are driving much faster or slower than you thought, especially if the road is straight and other cars are moving quickly also (poor physical and visual feed-back). When technology takes over locomotion we need additional technology for gauging speed, whether the simple speedometer, or the car computer beeping to tell you you have exceeded the speed limit.

12.4 Seeing Space—3D Vision

As we saw in Part II, we use all our senses in concert. However, nearly half of our brain is dedicated to vision, and vision plays a significant role in a sighted person's understanding of space, especially body space and vista space.

The lenses in our eyes direct light from the world onto the back of our eye, where the cells of the retina distinguish light from dark and separate out colours. These sensory images exit the eye at the optic nerve, the point of attachment to the eye giving us a blind spot, which our brain neatly fills in so that we are rarely aware that anything is missing. The nerve then splits, taking two routes. One route leads directly to the lower brain for instant flight-or-fight-style responses; one of the reasons why some people who have brain in-juries that leave them apparently blind can still catch a ball. The other route goes to the visual cortex, where it is processed further in complex ways, giving us the rich experience of vision.

Given the world is projected into the curved 2D back of the eye and ends up in a largely 2D visual cortex, it is a wonder that we have any ability to perceive in 3D at all. The ability stems partly from having two eyes. We effectively look at everything from two slightly differ-ent angles at once—stereo vision. However, if you cover one eye, the world does not immediately feel 'flat'; we actually have numerous ways in which we make sense of the full 3D nature of the world. Some originate in the eye itself. As we focus on an object, things in front and behind are blurred; the further in front or behind the more blurred they get. As our eye moves across a scene, the eye constantly refo-cuses and this gives us more information. However, this cannot be the whole story or we would not be able to interpret the flat image on a canvas or photograph as having depth. In fact we use a whole range of cues, based both on the physical nature of light, from occlusion to hazing for very distant objects, and on our semantic understanding of the world, from textures to just knowing that the tiny person is really a full-size person faraway.

Finally, but perhaps most importantly, our vision is not like a static camera. As ecological psychology suggests, it is part of a complete motor-sensory system. For example, when we see movement out of the corner of our eye, we move our eyes and head to look at it: an example of *epistemic action* as we discussed in Chapter 8. You may have seen 'what is this' images of familiar objects taken in close-up at odd angles such as Figure 12.3. Some can be very puzzling, but if you ever encountered them in real life, you would simply move your head slightly and it would all make sense.

At a larger scale, as we walk around, cycle, or drive in a car, distant objects appear to follow us, whereas close objects fall rapidly away due to parallax, and if we can't work out where we are, we may walk to a street corner in a city, or climb to a vantage point in the hills so that we can see better. Space syntax uses the way that different places have more or less good views, which in a city or building usually means junctions of roads or corridors, as a technique to model and interpret human sense-making in built environments. If one measures 'distance' by the number of turns, or in other words

Figure 12.3 Epistemic action in practice: (left) what is it? (right) move your head a bit—of course!

the number of times you obtain a new vista, then areas that are more 'central' by this distance measure tend to be more important parts of a city or building [218].

When it is dark and we cannot see, or for those who have little or no vision, the world is very different. We can still use other senses, such as the way our footsteps echo, to give some idea of the size of a space and even the location of objects and people, but with far lower fidelity than is possible with vision. In these circumstances, vista space effectively disappears, and even small spaces become part of navigation space, experienced as much by memory and imagination as by raw senses.

12.5 Mental Space

Psychologists study cognition of space in various ways. Informally, we are aware that some people are 'better' spatially than others, although it is also clear there are many different kinds of spatial cognition: people who are good at map reading may not be so good at estimating whether furniture will fit in a room, and the ability to follow instructions of landmarks and turns is different again.

Unless you have highly developed skills, it does not take too many twisting corridors to lose your sense of direction, not to mention keeping track of how rooms correspond to one another in a two-storey building. In the 'Alien' movie series, the aliens were able to burn through metal floors with acid secretions. If you were in an upper storey room in a building you know well, let alone a hotel bedroom, could you work out which ground floor room the alien would arrive in as it dropped down through the floor? This is one of the tests used by psychologists to determine a person's spatial ability. They are taken through real or virtual spaces and then asked to point their way home.

People who score well by this measure are deemed to have a good 'mental map' of the environment. Usually this is used as a single measure of navigational ability, but in fact there are different sorts of 'mental map' that would help one in these tests. The most obvious is the bird's-eye view of the floor plan. However, there is also the ability to mentally 'look through' walls, almost certainly what you would do if you just took a single turn in a corridor. In that case one's 'mental map' might take on a different virtual viewpoint, or imagine solid walls to be translucent.

Box 12.1 Sea Hero Quest

Experiments in spatial navigation can be time-consuming, so it is hard to obtain really high accuracy metrics over large samples of people. Problems with spatial navigation can be an early indicator of dementia, but to use this diagnostically requires an accurate comparison with the healthy population. In an Alzheimer's Research UK project, one group of scientists solved this conundrum by deploying a game, Sea Hero Quest, which is carefully designed so that each level requires greater levels of spatial skill [6, 230]. The game has been downloaded and played millions of times and many players have agreed to their usage data being collected for research purposes. This has created a vast dataset, which will prove invaluable both for its original diagnostic purpose and also for spatial cognition research more generally.

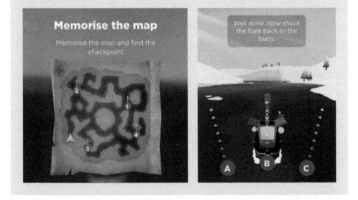

Mental rotation (Chapter 8) is a test of spatial ability more closely connected with body space. As we noted, it seems people literally slowly rotate an object in their head, but rotation may be achieved in different ways. This becomes obvious if you imagine being shown an image of a building and then asked questions about it from another angle. You might rotate it round, effectively treating it as a model building in body space. Or you might mentally walk around it, that is move your point of view in mental navigation space.

As noted, for very large spaces the simplest mental map may be more like the small child's model earlier in the chapter; a series of well-known places linked by routes, but without a single map that could be sketched.

12.6 Maps, Sketches, and Cartography

There is considerable scholarly disagreement about the interpretation of what may be some of the earliest stone-cut maps. These include a 14,000-year-old stone tablet from Abauntz in northern Spain, thought to depict local terrain, and what appears to be a 9000-year-old schematic plan of a village in Çatalhöyük, Turkey. However, whichever of these is the earliest true map, it seems likely that the first maps pre-date even the writing of numerals by several millennia.

The image from Çatalhöyük is thought to depict the village from the vantage point of a nearby peak, and this is certainly the form of most (though not all!) modern maps. Rather like the spatial cognition tests of the previous section, physical maps can be thought of in different ways once you are back on ground level. In one view you can use them mentally to float yourself far above the terrain, turning the network space of streets and houses, or rivers and forest, into the extended vista space of the eagle. Another way is effectively to see the map as a scale model, so that you have shrunk the village, town, or whole countryside into your body space and can place yourself ('you are here') and others into that model. Piaget found that children can interpret this sort of model with imaginary people on it from about seven years old, and when Martin Hughes modified the tests by making more realistic scenarios even four-year-olds were able to do this [226, 149].

The idea of the map as the bird's-eye view has become accepted as the normative or even 'true' view of cartography. Sometimes this is called a God's-eye view, which is perhaps especially germane now that satellite imagery is starting to replace on-the-ground surveying. Older maps are seen as quaint and fanciful in terms of decoration, but limited in their accuracy by the knowledge and technology of the time.

However, if you look more closely at older maps, and more recent hand-produced maps, a different story emerges.

James Cowen's *A Mapmaker's Dream* [78] tells the story of Fra Mauro, a monk in the sixteenth century. Fra Mauro never leaves his monastery in the Venetian lagoon and yet creates one of the major mappae mundi based only on the tales of merchants and adventurers who passed through the bustling port. His journals relate how he gradually comes to the realization that the map should not just be about mountains, cities rivers, and seas but that it should encompass the richness of the tales that he has been told. Viewed as a practical guide to navigation, it is all but useless, but as a record of the age of discovery, priceless.

John Speed's early maps of Wales show coastline that is cartographically 'accurate' in the way one would expect today, but inland, mountains, rivers, and towns are depicted pictorially, with only a sketchy relationship to precise geographic location. This is partly because the long sight-lines of the sea make large-scale Cartesian cartographic surveying *possible,* while the hills, cliffs, and forests of the land often make travelling in a straight line difficult or impossible. However, it is also because at sea this representation is useful, since it is possible to plot a straight-line course, and necessary to take sightings from landmarks on the coast; Cartesian accuracy is therefore important. In contrast, travel in the interior of Wales in the seventeenth century follows river valleys and passes, not straight lines, distance is not Euclidean, and a more network-oriented presentation of connectivity and routes is more important.

Neil MacGregor's book on the British Museum project *A History of the World in 100 Objects* [270] includes a map drawn on a buckskin by Piankeshaw Native Americans. In a more schematic representation than we are now used to, it embodies the conflicts of a crucial period of American history and the way maps have often been used to broker trade or enforce power. The map is thought to be part of a negotiation for a settler company to buy Piankeshaw lands, although the very idea of buying land would have been all but meaningless to the Piankeshaw. The actual sale was voided by the British colonial administration, whose refusal to allow settlement of Native American land west of the Appalachians went on to become one of the *casus belli* of the American War of Independence.

Today it is still true that what you choose or do not choose to show on a map affects the way the land is perceived. For example, in dual language countries such as Canada, Scotland, or Wales, which version of place names do you choose to use? On a tourist map, or a Google map, whether a business is included or not may make the difference between profit or bankruptcy.

Locally drawn tourist maps often depict town plans as if from a high hill rather than a bird's-eye view, with buildings drawn as small side-on images, as this is more comprehensible to many users. Critical areas, such as the town centre or beach front, are stretched relative to the periphery, both stressing what is important (political) and allowing the most frequented areas to have more detail (practical). Such maps are becoming less common as the web makes 'standard' cartography easier to access. Yet while Google Maps, Bing Maps, and OpenStreetMap have made it simple to include mapping even in amateur websites, they also enforce an external, non-local view. As Barbara Bender writes [26]:

'Post-Renaissance maps cover the surface of the world with an homogeneous Cartesian grip'

In fact, even standard maps do not always have the verisimilitude of the ideal. Borges' short story 'On Rigor in Science' (in Spanish 'Del rigor en la ciencia', [36]), based on an idea of Lewis Carroll, envisages a country whose geographers became so obsessed with the accuracy of mapping they created a map that was at the same scale as the territory itself. This was so patently useless that it led to the demise of the art of cartography as well as the neglect of the map:

In the Deserts of the West, still today, there are Tattered Ruins of that Map, inhabited by Animals and Beggars; in all the Land there is no other Relic of the Disciplines of Geography. [36]

Not only are real maps smaller than the space they represent but they distort certain aspects in order to be usable. For example, on a 1:200,000 scale road atlas (2 kilometres to the centimetre) a quite wide 10 m road would need to be an invisible 1/20 of a millimetre wide on the map, whereas roads are, of course, depicted at a scale that is useful for their purpose, car navigation. When producing digital maps it is very important to remember that different scales of the same map are not simply the same as zooming in or out of a detailed image. As well as purpose- and scale-related depictions of objects and marks on maps, the maps themselves may be distorted. We've already mentioned the way some tourist maps show the town centre at greater scale, a fixed distortion. Some digital maps and graphs make this dynamic, using fish-eye or other forms of distortion to give greater detail to the point of focus whilst allowing a broader but smaller context in the periphery.

12.7 Paths and Narrative

We have asked participants at a number of workshops to draw or use a sheet of paper to represent the way they came to the workshop (Figure 12.4). So far no-one has returned origami, or even folded the paper, but they do return, as you might expect, quite a wide variety of images. Some attempt to create a cartographically 'correct' map and plot their route on it, but they are in the minority. Others depict a wandering line that represents the general direction of their route, usually magnified at either end. For example, they show the turns to get out of the town from which they came, reflecting the space syntax idea that it is the turns that count. Others depict the way as a near straight line.

In fact, linear maps are a common way to represent routes or paths, from some of the earliest road maps to modern atlases. In the

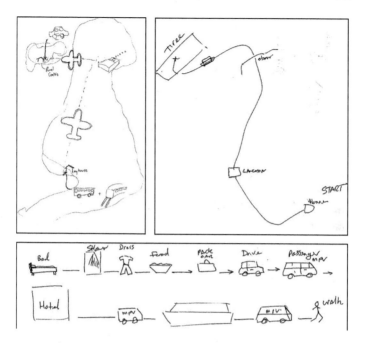

Figure 12.4 Journeys to Tiree Tech Wave, November 2011 [124]

Second World War, pilots had a rolled-up map of their route. They navigated by matching landmarks on the ground with the map, so the linear map was far easier to manage than trying to open up a flat map in a tiny cockpit. Of course, in straightening out the route certain liberties will have had to be taken with layout, compared with a traditional chart. A modern equivalent of this, *StripeMaps*, uses fragments of standard maps, but adds 'tears' to straighten the route sufficient to roll down a smartwatch screen [418].

All the maps produced in our workshops, even the more standard cartographic ones, show additional detail at key points on the journey, such as the beginning, the end, stopping points, or major intersections and landmarks *en route*. In other words, the maps people drew were as much about the events as the route.

From the *Odyssey* and Exodus to 'Thelma and Louise', the journey has been a common narrative form, and symbolic journeys are often used to reinforce significant stories, such as the Stations of the Cross in a Catholic church. Fra Mauro's map, while not a path map, used space to link to narrative, and when Alan was planning his walk around Wales he very quickly began to associate places with dates, even before he had actually walked there. Time, space, and story merge.

Digital locative media link sound, image, or narrative to space using mobile phones or similar devices. The two simplest forms privilege the journey and the space respectively. Many mobile tour guides force you to follow a particular path, possibly detecting when you have reached key points and triggering narrative when you do. Other apps take the opposite approach, associating particular snippets of sound, text, or image with particular locations, but enabling you to experience them in whatever order you encounter them spatially.

Tim Ingold [233] believes that modern society has privileged the point or place in preference to the line or route. This is intensified by sat navs, which remove any need to make sense of where you are on the way, and self-driving cars may exacerbate it further: some design proposals organize the interior almost like a small room that magically transports its passengers from start to finish with no need to be aware of the transition.

In Chapter 11 we saw that relativity transforms the lasagne-like layers of spatial moments into a spaghetti-like world view where we each carry our own unique temporal line. Post-modern literature often prides itself on non-linear narrative, but in the end each reader's experience, no matter how different in other respects, is a linear cut through time.

Exercise mapping applications like MapMyRun often provide both a map view of your route and an elevation view, showing the height you were at any point in time during the run. This is a particular example of the general way in which time graphs and time lines transform time into a spatial dimension in order to visualize it.

12.8 The Language of Space

Space and time are such a basic part of our understanding that we use spatial and temporal metaphors for many other things.

Sometimes the analogies are direct, so that 'bottoms up' is a reference to lifting the bottom of the tankard up. Piles of bricks or coins mean that number also inherits up-/down-ness, so that we count up our money, but count down to zero to take off. Similarly take 'off' itself is really about the spaceship leaving the ground, but 'on the button' pictures a finger placed on an actual button.

Most opposing terms have a valence, where one is seen as more positive. In the case of up and down, up is definitely 'good' [256]: if someone's prospects are improving we say they are 'on the up and up'; if you are depressed you are 'down'. This can be combative: 'getting the upper hand' is related to images of fighting where the person on top is typically winning.

Height in general is related to seniority in age (child vs adult) and often enhanced by a headdress or dais that makes the senior person physically higher. When we denote these structures in a hierarchy or organization chart, the most important person is always at the top, and the 'underlings' at the bottom. This then leads to secondary metaphors. In programming we talk about high-level and low-level programming languages, or more generally high-level and low-level descriptions. This draws on analogy with the hierarchy where the details appear to be at the bottom.

Left and right similarly have negative/positive connotations, as any left-handed person will attest: a villain is sinister (from the Latin *sinistra* meaning 'left'), but a talented craftsperson would be dextrous (from the Latin *dexter* meaning 'on the right side'). Some of the negative connotations of 'left' may be because the left hand seems less 'good' to the majority right-handed population, and perhaps because of the tendency to see the 'other' as dangerous.

Whereas up and down are relatively unproblematic (up is always up), left and right are relative. When we look at one another, one person's right is the other person's left (which is why the machine-centred notions of starboard and port are used on ships and aircraft).

Some of us cope with this from an early age, others may struggle well into adult life. However, even those who appear to have no problems with left/right are still measurably slower making left/right distinctions compared with up/down.

Time distinctions seem easier: you are either going back or forward. But of course our use of forward and back is itself a spatial metaphor for time. When we walk, the places yet to be reached, the future, are in front of us; the places we have been, the past, are behind. This leads to secondary metaphors: for example, we go 'back' in a book or skim 'forward'. But think of a book lying on a table. The page on top has the smallest number and the page on the very bottom has the largest. Going back in the book is typically moving up and forward is moving down. This weirdness is even greater in digital documents, which are laid out as if in a huge vertical scroll. If the page moves up the scroll bar moves down and vice versa [105].

12.9 Culture and Time/Space

The examples above come from English. While most, possibly all, languages make use of spatial metaphors, they do so in different ways. Furthermore, different cultures and languages can change the way we perceive both spatial metaphors and indeed space and time itself.

Western culture has had a linear view of time, either going ever forward and back, or having some finite start (creation or big bang) or end (cosmic freeze, second coming). In addition, there has been a tendency, at least during the twentieth century and probably due to teleological Christian influence, to see a line of progress, albeit one that was shaken by two World Wars.

Other societies have had a more cyclic view, taking the diurnal motions of the sun and the monthly motions of the moon as symbolizing a deeper periodic structure. For example, the Mayans combined a 260-day cycle with a 365-day solar year, leading to a fifty-two-year combined cycle when both repeated at the same time, and a series of longer and longer cycles, which led some people to believe the world would end in 2012.

Culturally, cyclic structures can be seen as suggesting stasis. If change happens the natural order will always reassert itself. However, even in Western linear teleological culture, we still say 'history repeats itself'. More practically, different cultures mark festivals and other such events purely by the sun (e.g. Diwali and Christmas), purely by the moon (e.g. Ramadan), or by a combination of the two (e.g. Passover and Easter)

Spatially, while up and down are universal, the use of left and right is not. In Bali, religious observances mean that everyone has a very good sense of absolute direction, so rather than using an ego-centric system and saying something or someone is in front, behind, left, or right of you, you would say they are to your north, south, east, or west. On another island with a single large mountain in the middle, people use mountain-ward and sea ward, with, one assumes, clockwise and anti clockwise for direction around the circumference.

Incidentally, labelling rotations and screw threads can also strain language. 'Clockwise' and 'anticlockwise' are based on the direction of the sun and its shadows in the *northern* hemisphere. In the south, a sundial would move 'anticlockwise'—effectively setting in language a north–south bias—and of course the placing of the Arctic at the 'top' of the world is arbitrary but not unproblematic for the therefore lesser south who are at the 'bottom'.

Even forgetting the words we use, basic spatial perception seems to be dependent on culture. A number of optical illusions make use of perspective, the effect where lines that converge to a point suggest disappearing into the distance. Whereas most visual effects can be understood in terms of phenomena that our more primitive hunter-gatherer ancestors would have seen, it is hard to think of many strong parallel lines in nature. Very straight tree trunks, perhaps, but they are vertical, not horizontal to create a vanishing point. In constructed environments straight lines are of course common: roadways, stone pavements. It transpires that for certain forest-living tribes the Müller–Lyer illusion (Figure 12.5) does not work [215]. Linear perspective, the great discovery of Renaissance art, is not an innate spatial ability but something learned by living amongst rectilinear buildings.

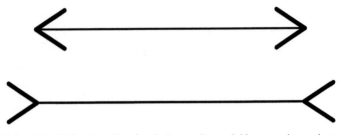

Figure 12.5 Müller–Lyer illusion—the bottom line probably appears longer, but in fact the two lines are of identical length

12.10 Virtual Space

As we saw earlier in this chapter, we come into this world with the raw ability to make sense of 3D space and our bodily and temporal existence within it. And unless we are devastatingly disabled or cruelly neglected, we all share a common heritage of learning to make sense of that world, albeit differing in the particular natural and constructed environment, cultural milieu, and natural abilities at our disposal.

It is therefore reasonable that various forms of virtual spaces exploit these innate or commonly learned spatial skills and understanding. Seeking a rich understanding of the way we make sense of physical space should help us as we design these virtual worlds.

The most obvious is virtual reality, which often very directly emulates the physical nature of space. Some, such as many first-person shooter games, are almost chillingly photorealistic. Others like Minecraft or Sims are more schematic visually, while having rich underlying social and physical models.

We have learned, both in Chapter 5 and in this chapter, how our senses work together when we act as embodied creatures in the physical world. When virtual reality is more or less purely visual, then there are bound to be problems, and indeed one of the drivers for virtual reality (VR) research has been the desire to have to clean the lab less often after participants develop motion sickness!

Early work showed that speed of feedback was far more critical than photorealism when head tracking [326], although now, with far faster hardware, both can typically be achieved. However, there is more than this. We discussed that we do not directly perceive speed. So if you are in a virtual car that is travelling very fast (virtually), then the fact that you are sitting stationary does not matter. The felt experience is the same. However, if the car stops suddenly, when the visual 'movement' stops, your body expects to be thrown forward suddenly, and the disparity can a cause a visceral tension in the gut. More complex VR systems may make use of rooms, surfboards, or bicycles that tilt on large hydraulic rams in order to emulate some of these feelings.

VR headsets also still struggle with the disparity between vergence (the angles your eyes make as they point to the object of interest) and focus. Focus in VR is typically in a fixed plane either at natural focal distance or at infinity. New headsets incorporating eye trackers and screens with a variable focal plane will eventually deal with these problems, but they are some way off, especially for low-budget VR such as in the use of smartphones.

Occasionally virtual worlds deliberately allow physics to be modified for educational purposes [373]. Being able to, say, switch off gravity or friction can help pupils understand the physical world better. This may seem odd, but in the real world various effects all operate at the same time, making it difficult to see the constituent forces and laws. We are able to function day to day, but it is hard to gain the experience necessary to understand physics and engineering. A good example is that if we are pushing a box across the floor it stops moving when we stop pushing. This is why Aristotle thought that constant force was needed to keep an object in motion. Newton realized that it was in fact the friction that made it stop, and that most of our effort is counteracting friction. Playing with these laws can help pupils to understand each effect on its own.

Spatial metaphors can also be useful even when the portrayal is far from realistic. The desktop metaphor and graphical user interfaces are key examples of this (as we'll see in Steve's 'Virtual School' Virtual Learning Environment in Chapter 19). Although the objects lack many of the dynamics of real work objects, being able to drag shapes around in a graphics application, or move files into a folder, recruits aspects of real-world understanding.

The desktop metaphor uses aspects of body space and VR, mostly vista space, but possibly the most important spatial metaphor of all is in the information spaces we inhabit, from folder hierarchies to social networks and the web. These recruit navigation space, the patterns of landmarks, paths, and open spaces, which enable us to find our way around cities or traverse mountain ranges.

Many of William Gibson's cyberpunk novels include virtual information worlds that are more like city blocks, using VR-style interactions to access information stored in virtual rooms of virtual skyscrapers. This makes engaging fiction, and some have tried to emulate this in research systems [334]. However, it is fortunate for those with limited sight that real information systems actually use navigation space, which depends more on memory and discrete cues than continuous vision.

12.11 Place and Non-place

In the last chapter we discussed the physical nature of space, and began to see its social and political importance, an importance which becomes more evident in this chapter. The patches that form an incipient childhood understanding of space are about well-known people, not mere Cartesian containers. Personal route drawings are structured by events. Local maps capture not just geographic features but what is important for a community. Geographers and social scientists distinguish the plain location in *space* from the rich socially imbued *place*. The former has coordinates and extent, the latter culture and norms (but note that some writers, including Certeau [61], use the words space and place in exactly the opposite way). When you visit a library you speak in hushed tones, which would be inappropriate at a rugby match in a stadium. When you visit St Paul's Cathedral you sense the weight of history: Christopher Wren, and the images of the dome standing unsullied in 1940 with smoke all about (Figure 12.6) but when you get home you kick off your shoes and collapse in an armchair.

Figure 12.6 St Paul's survives

When we create virtual spaces, these may have that sense of place. For many, Facebook or Instagram have a sense of presence, not a 300-year history, but the knowledge of salient events that have happened earlier, perhaps friends or family reunited. It could be that one of the defining features of successful social media is whether they get beyond being a communications medium, like air or telephone wires, and become a place.

The same is true of commercial spaces. *Shopping* is a rich social experience, whether in the rush of shopping frenzy on Black Friday, the sense of Christmas in Oxford Street in December, the exclusivity of an haute couture house, or the intimacy of an independent bookstore. *Buying*, in contrast, is ticking boxes on a procurement form. Amazon.com attempts to capture some of that sense of place in the use of wish lists to connect with family and friends, reviews, and 'Customers Who Bought This Item Also Bought . . .', but still it is hard to feel it is more than a very efficient order form. That may be one of the reasons why online sales, though often cheaper, are still only a tenth of the volume of walk-in sales.

The French philosopher Marc Augé identified spaces that are the antipathy of places. The soulless mall, the poured concrete bus station, the welfare benefits office—places often physically created *ex nihilo*, and lacking a social connection. Augé calls these *non-places* [11]. If nature abhors a vacuum, humanity seems to abhor the non-place, either being broken in spirit by its placelessness or, like a damaged seal on a vacuum chamber, flooding the non-place with 'placefull-ness'. In 'Brief Encounter' the railway station, a grey place of coming and going, of passing through, is painted with repressed passion, not only within the fiction but also in the way Carnforth Station, where it was filmed, becomes a place of pilgrimage for the romantic.

A project studying non-place had meetings in a variety of 'non-places' including an out-of-town B&Q hardware superstore and Stansted Airport [79]. The B&Q was like so many similar stores, it was hard to imagine shoppers feeling it at all as 'place', but in staying there for a day, rather than the mere half-hour of a guerrilla DIY shopper, there was an inkling of the rich social life of the employees who worked there day to day, sharing jokes, and gossip. Stansted Airport similarly had its multiple overlapping communities, shop workers, ground staff, and security. Even for Alan—passing through Stansted on a chaotic snow-bound December day, after a three-day diversion to Turkey on a flight home from Malaysia, long enough to wonder if he would ever get home for Christmas—a non-place?

12.12 Journey or Destination

In the 1945 film 'I Know Where I'm Going', a young woman, Joan Webster, has a clear knowledge both of her life goal, to be married to Robert Bellinger, a successful industrialist, and of her physical destination, the Scottish island where she and Bellinger are to marry. Of course, things do not turn out that way, and she does not reach her physical destination, the (fictional) Isle of Kiloran, until the closing minutes of the film. Meanwhile, the events of the journey have permanently changed her life destination. The maelstrom of the Corryvreckan on the final, near fatal, leg of her journey is reminiscent of the ordeals of Odysseus or Jason, and symbolic of the social upheaval in the latter days of the Second World War, notwithstanding that she eventually chooses the down-at-heel hereditary laird over the new-money industrialist.

We have already touched on the road-movie genre and while this movie is more one of the 'stranded traveller', it similarly picks up the theme that the process of the journey may be more significant than the destination. Some of Augé's non-places are 'on the way', the service station or bus station. Others, like B&Q, are simply passed through, useful for their functional purpose, a place you stop but do not stay. Crucially, except insofar as they may be a necessary mid-point of a journey, they are fungible. One B&Q is as good as another for a bag of nails, the choice of a service station governed solely by the emptiness of your petrol tank or stomach, or the fullness of your bladder.

In contrast, tourism theorists talk about the *destination*, not necessarily as a *final* destination, but somewhere you choose to go for itself, a real ale eighteenth-century inn rather than a service station, an art gallery rather than a DIY store. Sadly, the quick route of the motorway, or even the slow Wales Coast Path, may bypass off-path destinations, and in so doing, ignore and effectively displace them.

For Joan Webster, the Isle of Mull, the momentary stop, became a destination, with real people and life to be explored, like a peek behind the scenes at Stansted Airport.

This brings us back to Ingold's focus on the line as more than simply a connection between end-points [233]. This was brought home to him (an interesting spatial metaphor itself) by his anthropological study of nomadic reindeer herders in Lapland [234]. For the Skolt Lapps, as for summer afternoon berry-pickers and gatherers from the dawn of time, there is value in the way itself, rather than its end-points. The circular pleasure walk epitomises this; indeed when Alan walked around Wales, he took 102 days and 1000 miles to get back precisely to where he started. Note that this is not necessarily about process-oriented vs goal-oriented personalities. For the Skolt, the way is the goal.

When translating this idea to digital space, it is easy to jump from the road between towns to the link between websites. Both road and link have end-points, and follow predetermined or externally determined routes. The choice of which road or link to follow lies with you but is constrained by the past choices of planner or page author.

However, there are important differences. The road links end-points but passes through real terrain. It may skim that terrain, encouraging you to ignore it, or treat it as a mere backdrop to the important business of listening to the radio or discussing how to make the visit to Aunt May as brief as possible, but it is there, there is something you are missing. In contrast, the digital link really has nothing in between. It is precisely the thing that Ingold wishes the road not to be, the gapless interstice.

Possibly Google search is the closer analogy. It has traversed the lines and used them to determine the most likely end-point, so it transports you directly there, bypassing all the web pages and links between, without passing 'Go'. Contrast this both with the process of direct exploration through a series of web pages, which not only takes you to a final destination, but informs you of the context through the journey. Possibly everyone links to something to say it is wrong? Even web directories such as Yahoo! or Open Directory Project, while pre-selected, encouraged you to see a variety of other pages related by more than just keywords.

However, by forcing the analogy we may also look inward and interrogate the web link itself, perhaps look for its provenance: who put it there and why? Of course, we could do the same for a road or railway track, perhaps finding ways to trace the information terrain that is traced even by physical paths. Older hypertext systems often had multiple destinations for a single link, allowing you to choose between them. The Alan Walks Wales website does this for place links in its description of each day's travelling (Figure 12.7). They are still pre-chosen but suggest digital design moves that could make link traversal an experience in itself.

Roads and signposts are officially written into the landscape, or sometimes, as with signposts in the Second World War, expunged. However, there are also unofficial inscriptions. In the days when WiFi hotspots were rare and connectivity costly, small chalk marks were left on the walls of to mark places where unprotected could be found to gain free access to the Internet. This followed a long history of Romany patrins [375], tramp marks, and hobo codes [96] written in chalk or simply sticks and stones.

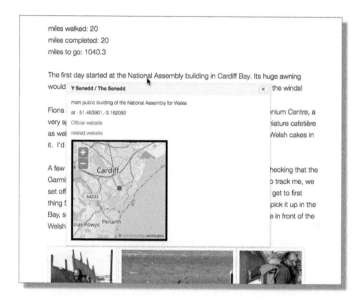

miles walked: 20
miles completed: 20
miles to go: 1040.3

The first day started at the National Assembly building in Cardiff Bay. Its huge awning

would · Y Senedd / The Senedd · the winds!

main public building of the National Assembly for Wales

Fiona · at · 51.463901, -3.162082 · nium Centre, a

very s| Official website · iature cafetière

as wel · related website · Welsh cakes in

it. I'd

Cardiff

A few · hecking that the

Garmi · b track me, we

set off · A4232 · get to first

thing S · pick it up in the

Bay, s · Penarth · e in front of the

Welsh · inas-Powys

Figure 12.7 Place links in Alan Walks Wales (https://alanwalks.wales/)

Although they constrain, roads and signs do not fully prescribe the *routes* that people take. A bus tour or guidebook may traverse multiple roads or official paths. Like landmarks, they are repurposed for longer or different routes. Even the childhood paths described earlier in this chapter followed lanes and roads, but moved from one to another to create a route to school, or to the shops. Sometimes, routes may become official in the landscape, with waymarkers or bus stops; although, as Konstantinos Papangelis found when he studied a particular bus route, the marked stops on the ground may be a historical record of past routes that have ceased, and the current stops may not be marked [324]. Routes may also be formalized outside the landscape itself in guidebooks or mobile apps.

There is a core difference between waymarked routes, which have become inscribed in the landscape, and personal wayfinding, where features of the landscape are used by the traveller to reach their own objective. Even when the latter are formalized in guidebooks, they remain invisible, part of the information landscape only. While landmarks are fixed places in the landscape, instructions using church steeples or pubs rarely expect you to pray or drink beer, they are appropriated and repurposed for route-finding. This repurposing is critical where the same space is used for multiple purposes. In the digital world, Murray-Rust and colleagues talk about *meshworks*, intertwining patterns of human movement overlaid on the raw network of the digital landscape [301].

Psycho-geographers revel in this insubordination of the formal, drawing arbitrary routes on maps that have no relation to recognized features, or following hidden features such as the buried waterways of London [34]. Like counter tourists (Box 10.3), they seek to understand a place by turning their back on the accepted interpretations.

Even when there is no formalized path, the traces that people leave, footprints on sand or worn patches on grassland, can create long-lasting marks on the physical landscape. For the non-waymarked route, such marks can be an essential part of wayfinding. In the digital world these patterns of wear and passage need to be explicitly designed. Murray-Rust and colleagues report how users of a bulletin board appropriated the comments mechanism to leave breadcrumbs [301], deliberate traces for others, rather like the Romany patrin. Amazon's recommender system has something of this feel, though with a very commercial intent, and numerous web trackers are more ominously reminiscent of the manhunt: following threads caught on branches and mud trails on the ground.

Whether we follow formal roads, transcend them with guided tours, or even cut across uncharted lands, we each take our own journey. A road, a route, a path, a guided tour are all ways that can be followed again, but each journey, each traversal, is unique. As we saw earlier, literature is redolent with stories of journeys, and today we seek to capture them with GoPro and GPS trackers. As we saw in the last chapter, modern physics regards the world as defined less by abstract space and more by the spaghetti-like reality we take with us: one thread through space-time, one unretraceable path across the landscape.

The Built Environment

13.1 Introduction

The computer has made its mark on the world, particularly in urban spaces. For example, the metaphorical footprints that show us someone has been to a place before and the wayfinding methods mentioned in Chapter 12 have their digital counterparts. This chapter focuses on the relationships between the physical environment and the various digital informational augmentations that have been added to it over the years, increasing our understanding of space and perhaps time. Most of these digital 'layers' have positive attributes, such as the convenience of location-aware apps that tell us when the next bus home is due, the joy of hunting virtual Pokémon in the local park, the right to warn other customers of a particularly rude Uber driver or the ability of our sat nav to find a parking space [393]. Negative aspects are not hard to find, however. The same sat nav can also be used to check whether we've been speeding, or whether we've parked where we shouldn't; the Uber driver can rate us too, potentially making getting a taxi more difficult next time it rains, and the safety concerns surrounding Pokémon GO are well publicized. Here we discuss the existing and future digital layers on our cities, and their existing and potential pros and cons.

13.2 Physical–Digital Layers

One of the more unexpected aspects of the Internet age is that the interrelation of the physical and digital worlds has become blurred. Take the case of MonmouthpediA (Figure 13.1) [296]. Monmouth is a small market town on the border between Wales and England.

Figure 13.1 MonmouthpediA plaque on a wall in Monmouth

Crossing the River Monnow, and entering through the medieval gateway, the pattern of centuries-old streets is still evident despite the modern shop fronts. Like all such towns it has had its battles and bloodshed, local heroes and celebrities; it is the site of the first theatre in Wales and where the last men in Britain were hung, drawn, and quartered. However, if you linger you may notice something different: small ceramic plaques on buildings, lamp posts, and shops. Each plaque has a snippet of historical or topical information and a Quick Response (QR) code. QR codes are now common, but in Monmouth they are ubiquitous. Every location of any renown, and even of none, is digitally labelled and links to special WikiMedia pages: MonmouthpediA.

Monmouth is the world's first Wikipedia town.

Monmouth is unusual in its density of QR codes, but links embedded in the physical world are now commonplace. Again using Wales as an example, around the borders and especially in north Wales you will find HistoryPoints [220]: small plastic-coated cards glued to posts and buildings, which, like the plaques of MonmouthpediA, link to a special website with further historical information. Elsewhere, information signs may have a QR code or simply a web address to connect to, and nearly every commercial lorry and van has an associated Uniform Resource Locator (URL) painted on the side. Not only places but the objects around us often have digital connections: barcodes on books and tins of beans, and again the ever-present URL.

Some years ago, Alan described barcodes as one of the great success stories of computer-supported collaborative work (CSCW). There are other technologies that more obviously support collaboration, such as shared document editing and communication, but the barcode is unusual in relating the physical and digital worlds:

> The barcode is a form of deixis relating the physical artefacts and the logical artefacts which describe them ... it relates the world of work to the world of communication—it allows us to talk about the things with which we are working. [104]

Whether we are using digital communication to talk to one another about physical things or interacting directly with digital technology in connection with the physical world, it is essential that there is some way to connect the two.

There are two sides to this:

1. physical identifiers of digital things
2. digital identifiers of physical things

Either on its own can create a connection, but the richest experiences often involve both.

Examples include the likes of IKEA Place, which lets customers see what furniture looks like in their home by using their phone or tablet to display an augmented reality view showing furniture *in situ* [246]. In this case, an augmented reality (AR) marker provides the physical identifier of a digital thing, and our view of the space is then occupied onscreen by a digital marker of a physical thing—a computer model of, say, a chair apparently sitting in our living room.

This digital–physical experience of shopping extends further to another kind of mixed reality experience—digital–physical–digital—especially for major purchases. Many of us now look online until we find something we like, then check the reviews of people who have already bought it. If we are minded to purchase, we tend to visit a convenient shop, and if we like what we see, buy it elsewhere online. This has been blamed for the destruction of city centres, which rely on shopping trade. There are upsides, however. Gumtree and eBay, for example, have helped to fuel a rebirth of the concept of reuse, and provided a range of new business opportunities, frequently based on flexible working practices with consequent benefits.

This mixing of the digital and the physical goes further. The modern urban environment is overlaid with myriad digital layers, mediated by computers of varying types. An obvious example is a networked bus stop computer that 'knows' where each of the company's buses are and which number each bus is carrying at a given time. It uses the data to provide passengers with an estimated wait time at their particular stop. Uber works on similar underlying principles: the location of the passenger and the mode of transport are known. In Uber's case an additional demand-value layer calculates price according to how many passengers want to travel, while an additional 'social layer' deals with review ratings that allow the driver to decide if they want the passenger's business and vice versa.

Other obvious digital–physical layers are provided by 'location-aware' applications such as Google Maps. A interesting aspect of Google Maps is that it both forms a digital layer on the physical world, and is itself several layers 'deep'. The *Terrain* layer represents the physical world in an easily understood manner by using a range of accepted mapping semantic codifications, including some of those discussed in the previous chapter. Layers of detail are removed or codified, while boundaries of greater importance are enhanced: road routes, for example, are easier to discern. The *Satellite* layer represents exactly the same views as *Terrain* but using photographs to give what in some senses is a richer picture of a given area but with less navigational value in most cases. In many areas we can also see an entirely different photographic view in *Street View*, which represents the physical world in a way much more closely linked to how most of us experience the world most of the time. OpenStreetMap also allows multiple layers displaying public-contributed content on

Figure 13.2 Digital layers in OpenStreetMap

different topics including effective cycle routes and public transport (Figure 13.2).

Still other layers within mapping applications allow users to filter search results according to location so that a search for, say, 'hotels' will return only those results within the area being viewed on the screen. These digital layers augment what Lynch called the 'legibility of the city' [269] by which he meant the extent to which an urban environment could be structured and identified by its inhabitants. Selected areas of interest are also represented in three dimensions, allowing further virtual exploration. This concept has been taken further by the so-called Scottish Ten group, which has made LiDAR (Light Detection and Ranging) scans of large sections of Edinburgh and very detailed laser scans of such UNESCO Heritage treasures as Mount Rushmore, the Sydney Opera House, and Rosslyn Chapel (Figure 13.3) [17].

Figure 13.3 A 3D laser scan point cloud image of the Forth Bridge, digitally documented by Historic Environment Scotland and the Glasgow School of Art © Historic Environment Scotland

Google Earth takes the layers concept still further, allowing us to look up (Google Sky), and out (*Google Moon* and *Google Mars*, which use data acquired by orbital and landed spacecraft to construct virtual facsimiles of the two bodies.) Presumably missions such as *Cassini* and its successors will provide the data for similar facsimiles of other planets in the solar system and, in time, beyond.

So far we have been discussing data sourced and grouped by a commercial entity, but some layers are crowdsourced, either knowingly, like user-uploaded pictures of particular places, or less knowingly—how many of us read the terms and conditions when we download a 'free' app? The ethical pros and cons of these issues are not particularly straightforward, by the way. Many users might be pleased to be able to avoid traffic jams by using other users' data, but simultaneously unhappy to realize that they are effectively carrying a tracking device. These digital 'footprints' have had clearly negative consequences, particularly on young people. Generation Y have grown up with social media, a consequence of which is that the evidence of their mistakes is recorded on servers beyond their control and available to be used by anyone from peers to prospective employers. Other vulnerabilities include our credit card and password details and the fact that our world views can easily be seen by those in authority. For example, access to our social media accounts is now being routinely requested by US immigration.

This lack of privacy also generally has an upside, although sometimes it is almost comically minor: all the data on what you buy, and when and where you buy it, sold for profit to whomever wants to purchase it in return for a few points on your store card, anyone? Other upsides are more unexpected. For example, Uber drivers like the fact that drug dealers don't use their vehicles. What drug dealer wants to give their bank details and a clear and accurate record of places they have been and the times and dates they visited? Yet in certain circumstances users are quite happy to advertise their precise movements, for example via Map my Ride and Strava, or as Alan did when he walked round Wales covered in biometric sensors and Global Positioning System (GPS) monitoring equipment [120]. Sometimes this is a mistake: Strava data gave away the location and shape of a secret US military base because soldiers ran the perimeter and then posted the data online, thereby providing a 'heatmap' that outlined the base's precise location [207].

13.3 Temporal Layering

Digital layers also enable temporal layering. Google Mars, for example, allows users to view the development of our knowledge of Mars over time by viewing global models of the planet created from historical data such as Giovani's map of 1890.

Other layers are hybrid affairs. A few years ago Steve and his colleague Ingrid Murphy created a kind of digitally mediated physical–temporal layering experience. They got involved in setting up a geocache for the Isle of Tiree's school children involved in the Duke of Edinburgh Award, an international youth achievement scheme. One of the concepts behind this particular geocache was that it would provide a very basic 'window' into Tiree's recent past, with the digital layer providing the means by which to locate it. Each geocache contained a picture taken a few decades earlier at a spot close to where the geocache was hidden (Figure 13.4). Having found the picture, geocachers would try to find the precise spot on which the original photographer was standing, allowing them to compare the contemporary scene with how it looked when the picture was

Figure 13.4 Temporal layers

taken, the idea being to connect participants with the past by creating a pseudo-physical connection.

To some extent, we can also find wholly physical equivalents of temporal layering. For example, the Spanish city of Zaragoza was originally Roman—'Zaragoza' is a corruption of 'Caesar Augusta', after the Emperor who had it built. The ruins of the Roman city lie under the modern metropolis and are often found during construction or repair to the urban fabric (Figure 13.5). In some parts of the city, the newly uncovered Roman infrastructure pokes up through the modern landscape. The amphitheatre, for example,

Figure 13.5 Physical temporal layers: The remains of Zaragoza's amphitheatre as found *underneath* the modern city (left) and the outline of Lucca's Roman amphitheatre preserved *within* the contemporary cityscape (right)

is now mostly uncovered. Under the basilica a different approach has been taken. The modern city is propped up on pillars to allow tourists to visit the Roman layer beneath. The Roman ruins are themselves layered too: foundations, hypocaust, and sewers. Ancient structures can, in some senses, be preserved even after their physical removal. The shape of the Roman amphitheatre in Lucca has been preserved because locals built houses within its ruins (Figure 13.5). While the walls of the amphitheatre are long gone, the boundaries of the buildings have persevered, recording its outline in the modern city [41]. Other examples of urban temporal layering effects can be found in British cities like Bristol and Newcastle upon Tyne, where layering has more to do with overcoming underlying geography. In medieval times, Newcastle upon Tyne was divided by tributaries of the River Tyne. These hampered communications and development, so as the town expanded they were rerouted through culverts to allow the city to connect over the top of them. Such temporal layering effects are not exclusively urban over rural. Archaeologists have long used aerial photography to search for civil engineering buried below the rural landscape, with ancient roads below farmers' fields frequently betrayed by the way they affect drainage patterns.

There are obvious possibilities for furthering the use of digital layering to explain and reveal existing temporal layering or to create new layers. One example would be using augmented reality to allow us to look behind walls, underground, or back in time.

13.4 Digital–Physical Playgrounds

Mixing computer gaming environments and real-world context has been another use for augmented reality approaches. This is not a new concept. As far back as 2003, Flintham and colleagues [166] used early versions of these games to examine player behaviour. They concluded that the context of the games was more socially than technically constructed, a finding that continues to make sense now. In 2006, Diepenmaat and Geelhoed created an interesting take on augmented reality gaming in the form of a GUI less computer game called Nexus (Figure 13.6) [101]. The game employed a location-aware computer, headphones, and a handheld haptic device to create an immersive 'mediascape'. Players chased virtual elephants and mice around real-world locations by listening for them and 'catching' them with a handheld haptic device. The game was a forerunner to the Nintendo hit of 2016, Pokémon GO, which allows gamers to see and catch virtual 'Pokémon' in the real world.

Figure 13.6 Diepenmatt's Nexus concept and Pokémon GO

13.5 The Conquest of Space

In some senses, digitality has given us the ability to conquer physical distance, even to the extent of transmitting physical objects (or at least the data with which to construct them). This ability, with the digital manufacturing technology that enables it, is one component of what has been called Industry 4.0 or the fourth industrial revolution. These technologies, because they are flexible and do not need labour-intensive processes, promise to create disruptive change in the world. Much of the rise of the so-called BRIC countries (Brazil, Russia, Israel, China) has been based on the availability of cheap labour. Removing it from the equation resets the paradigm and might eventually have very powerful effects on manufacturing infrastructure and urban landscapes across the world.

The concept of using three-dimensional (3D) printing as a production rather than prototyping method is not fanciful. It is already a fact in high-value, low-volume applications such as rocket engines and Formula 1 car components. What might a full-scale implementation of Industry 4.0 look like? Will factories exist at all in their current sense or will the 'product' become the digital information, with the device itself produced at a hub close to where we live or even by our own 3D printers? The city of the future might be shaped by the way in which the products on which it relies are made and distributed. Like other aspects of our digital present and possible futures, the promise of Industry 4.0 is both an exciting blue-sky vision and a dystopian nightmare in waiting—who will be able to afford all these products when AI-controlled robots have taken all the jobs?

The same pros and cons exist around the desirability of eroded physical and power structures. The Internet has, to some extent, allowed the voices of the disenfranchised to be heard across borders and at the expense of more traditional establishment outlets such as radio, TV, and newspapers. While opinions will vary regarding their desirability, it is hard to deny the influence or the power of digitally enabled populist movements facilitated by the likes of *Breitbart* or pro-Brexit social media. At the time of writing it is still probable that these movements will have physical results on our living environments. The UK's legal separation from Europe, for example, has real-world consequences for where people live and work, as does a physical barrier between the United States and Mexico. The same properties that overcome physical distance for legitimate outcomes also apply for murkier approaches to the same issues. At the time of writing, issues related to the Mueller investigation into Russian government interference in the 2016 US election are being hotly contested [300], and there are reasons to believe that Twitter accounts such as that of 'passionate Brexit supporter' David Jones, are the work of a 'troll factory' based in St Petersburg [94].

13.6 Computer Mediation

All this digital content is of course mediated for us by computers of some kind, particularly the now near-ubiquitous smartphone. The power of the phone in this regard is multiplied by physical infrastructures such as third-generation (3G) and fourth-generation (4G) cells, providing access to the worldwide web, and by precise location data via networked satellites. This powerful combination is amplified by concerted efforts by the likes of the Open Data Institute to make large datasets, such as weather, mapping, and a wide range of government data open access and therefore available to app developers. The Internet's democratic traditions allow users to share information freely—sometimes without them realizing, as we have seen. All this has made the phone a primary tool for navigating the urban environment. A phone provides actual navigational data—think Apple Maps, Google Maps, TomTom app, geocaching. It is a portal to the kind of digital-urban playground applications we have discussed, such as Nexus and Pokémon GO, and it allows users to add their own digital layers—photos, reviews, Strava, and Map My Ride routes and times. Attempts to replace the phone as the prime digital layer access device have so far failed. Google Glass and other AR and VR devices such as Microsoft HoloLens have so far failed to revolutionize our navigation of digital layers. Efforts continue, however, and Google are known to have invested more than $0.5 billion in 'Magic Leap', a glasses-based augmented reality system that is rumoured to allow animated 3D models to appear within the physical world, including on our person [272].

13.7 Digital Culture

The cultural hubs of any major city are one of its defining components: museums, galleries, concert halls, and so on. Creativity, particularly in the arts, has generally been thought of as an area

Figure 13.7 'The Next Rembrandt': a computer-generated 3D printed 'painting' in the style of Rembrandt

of *human* strength, but recent developments place this in question. Might the cultural institutions of the future display digitally created and manufactured pieces? Maybe. In 2016 researchers used detailed scans and analysis of a number of Rembrandt masterpieces to 3D print a 'new Rembrandt', right down to the maestro's brush strokes (Figure 13.7) [44].

Other revolutionary changes in the cultural landscape are less disruptive and driven more by a move towards openness and democratization. Some of the world's biggest museums are making their collections available online in various forms, from digitally scanned archives to 3D printing files that allow anyone to 'handle' valuable cultural objects, the originals of which generally reside in glass cases. Some research has gone further. In 2013, Younan [431] explored the value of making museum artefacts available to artists via photogrammetric scanning (Figure 13.8). The project raised some interesting issues around ownership and intellectual property, issues all the more germane now that off-the-shelf mobile phones offer 3D scanning capability [20].

Box 13.1 Digital–physical–digital display: the Wooden Mirror

In the late 1990s and early 2000s, artists and designers experimented with displaying digital information via physical objects. A good example is Rozin's *Wooden Mirror* (1999), which used small pieces of wood to represent pixels. The angle of each 'pixel' was controlled by motors, actuated by a camera/computer combination, which rotated each piece at an angle to a light source. As result, each piece of wood appeared darker or lighter according to its angle, so that the image caught by the camera was roughly portrayed on the surface of the 'mirror'.

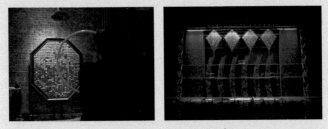

Wooden Mirror and *Digital Waterfall*

Like the Wooden Mirror, the Digital Waterfall uses physical matter to create pixels. In this case a series of water droplets are released in a coordinated fashion, by a computer, to form patterns as they fall, creating a short-lived physical image made of water and light.

In an ever more complex intermingling of the digital and the physical, players in *Second Life* pay currency with real-world value for virtual art, furniture or property [402] and have been known to get a real-world divorce having paid a 'Second Life private detective' to uncover virtual infidelity [151]. In sport, racing drivers

Figure 13.8 'Digital taxidermies'. Clockwise from top right: original piece; photogrammetric model; texture map (Source: [431])

like Max Verstappen are also members of the virtual racing world [343] where they develop skills, practice overtaking manoeuvres, and try different engine, suspension, and aerodynamic car se-tups. The more sophisticated racing games use real-world data based on the physical world, in algorithmic terms (e.g. the down pressure for a given aerofoil setting) and in more direct terms (e.g. laser scanning of the race track surface to create an accurate digital model of the physical track. That this level of accuracy allowed real skills to be built exclusively online was proven by placing top virtual racer Greger Huttu in a racing car with impressive results—even though he didn't have a driving licence [236].

Simulators are not new, of course. They were, for example, used extensively by NACA and later NASA. Most of these simulators relied to some extent on computing technology though the balance between the digital and physical varied enormously. Sometimes computers were used to directly affect real-world interactions with real-world consequences. The Space Shuttle Orbiter's training aircraft was a converted business jet with a fly-by-wire system and one-half of its cockpit controls designed to mimic the Orbiter's. By flying nose down with engines in reverse thrust and landing gear deployed, it was possible to match the Orbiter's flying characteristics. In contrast, one of the more commonly used simulators for the earlier Apollo missions was a computer-based simulation with some real-world interactions added to enhance the simulation. The Lunar Lander simulator used giant hand-painted spheres and scaled models made to depict the lunar surface accurately from various altitudes, while a computer oriented the simulator in relation to these models with regard to height, velocity, and orientation. The view from the appropriate model was recorded by a TV camera and projected on a screen outside the window of the simulator.

Box 13.2 Digital humanity

Steve's colleague Ingrid Murphy is a maker. Originally a ceramicist, she has, over the years, developed an interest in the potential of physical-digital interactions. Like many researchers in the art field, Ingrid's work is curiosity rather than application-driven. One interesting departure from that approach was her computer-embedded tea cosy.

Ingrid's Dad lives by himself overseas. He has an emergency contact device, which he wears around his neck, so that in the event of an emergency he is able to call for assistance. It seemed to Ingrid that a more elegant, less visible, more human approach might be possible.

So she hacked her Dad's tea cosy.

Ingrid noticed that one of the first things her Dad does every morning is to make a pot of tea, kept warm by a tea cosy. Ingrid installed a thermo-triggered Arduino in the tea cosy that sent a tweet on reaching temperature. Back in the United Kingdom, Ingrid has modified two 1960s Teasmades (one for her, one for her sister). When her Dad's tea

continued

Box 13.2 *continued*

cosy sends its tweet, both Teasmades make tea. Knowing that their Dad is up and about, this normally triggers one of the two sisters to call him and have a chat.

13.8 The Internet of Things

The integration of the digital and physical is seldom more obvious than in the so-called Internet of Things (IoT)—computer-embedded products connected to the Internet. These have already had a significant effect on the way we interact with the built environment, given the way we can monitor and control our homes from a distance. As we know, IoT products range from Internet TV devices such as Roku or Apple TV to Internet kettles, cameras, thermostats, and lights, including Firefly (Box 2.1). These devices let us boil the kettle before getting out of bed, switch the heating on while we're on holiday should a deep freeze threaten the pipes, or check that the house is OK via a remote camera while we're at work. There's also the Internet of moving things: networked bike lights that know where junctions (and therefore peak danger points) are and so change their lighting patterns. They even work together to build up a picture of where and when potholes are forming [353]. Cloud analytics firms such as Splunk use a range of data to allow organizations to respond with more agility. For example, a major motorway accident will likely lead to a glut of late and panicked passengers at airports some way from the scene of the accident. By knowing this in advance, airports can prepare appropriately. City authorities in Los Angeles reduced congestion by 10% by using data on peak travel to change traffic light settings.

Other datasets are less formally managed and tend only to be coordinated for special purposes such as solving a specific crime. In many urban environments in the developed world, video cameras have become ubiquitous, even without counting the two—or more—cameras on every smartphone. Closed circuit TV Cameras (CCTV) on public streets and buildings, pubs, shops, restaurants, and businesses record our movements many times a day and are supplemented by those on buses, taxis, and trains and even police officers. While—phones aside—they are not yet installed on each of us, they are voluntarily adopted by drivers, cyclists, and motorcyclists in the form of dash and helmet cams. Most of these devices are not location-aware, except in the sense that a fixed camera is in a known location and hence anything it records is too. Combine all this data with automatic number plate recognition, the ability remotely to track any phone and the location and time that credit cards, debit cards, and smart watches are used, and it is easy to argue the case for a surveillance layer on the modern built environment. Little wonder there is increasing interest in living 'off grid'. All of the above are backed by case studies, but much more may be happening without our knowledge.

Like all computers, IoT devices are vulnerable to hacking and smart homes often raise fears of hackers hijacking cameras to spy on you, or criminals analysing the pattern of Internet-connected kettle usage to choose a good time to burgle. These fears are not unfounded.

IoT devices need to be cheap and easy to connect, two factors that do not lead to high security. In principle, cheap devices do not have to be low security; high volume can drive down the cost of necessary hardware and amortize development time. Indeed some IoT boards include special cryptographic hardware. However, the combination of the need for easy configuration and a level of ignorance has meant that even higher-value applications are easily hackable.

Some threats are similar to those facing larger computer systems. For example, many IoT and industrial devices have a default admin password that is rarely changed after installation. However, there are also special threats, for example the fact that you do not explicitly log in to a small device means that you may not even be aware that it can be hacked. There are also new threats. For example, several car-key fobs use low-strength or poorly coded encryption that leaves them open to attack.

With the exception of celebrities and politicians, attacks on household IoT are unlikely to be focused on an individual; they are based instead on fairly random probes of vast numbers of devices. A hacker from China is not going to burgle or even spy on a home in Columbia, but compromising vast numbers of IoT devices can create a 'bot army' of devices that can be commanded to perform a simultaneous DDoS (distributed denial of service) attack. This is precisely what happened in October 2016 when the websites of several major companies, including Twitter and Spotify, were brought down by a massive global DDoS attack launched from household devices [157].

Of course, DDoS and other attacks can be targeted at otherwise secure physical installations, possibly to demand a ransom to restore service. For example, a few weeks later in 2016 a DDoS attack brought down the central heating system in two apartment buildings in Lappeenranta; this was in late October/early November, a cold time of year in Finland [240]!

For devices taken out of the home, issues such as 'overhearing' become critical. For example, if devices authenticate to one another through flashing screen or audio, this can be picked up and replayed later. A slightly different variant saw Apple phones hijacked in public places by attackers playing back the owner's voice, shifted to the ultrasonic range where the phone could 'hear' the commands but people could not [433].

As the history of such attacks grows, which it will, this also means that there will be known threats that you have to deal with. However, as a developer, the crucial thing is to understand the particular threats your device is likely to encounter. Is it in the home, in the office, or in the street? Can it be accessed over the Internet or via wireless? Can it be physically stolen?

The whimsical nature of some IoT devices somehow increases the spookiness of their vulnerability to attack. We know that a *Hello Barbie* doll *could* be hacked to record conversations [306] and teddy bears already *have* been hacked to do just that [189]. On a more adult note, sex toys have been found to be reporting how they're used [81]. Meanwhile that best-known and most ubiquitous Internet Thing, your mobile phone, could be listening to your conversations [251]. It shouldn't be much of a shock; after all, we know that TVs have been caught doing just that [82].

Cars, heart implants, and nuclear power stations are also vulnerable [254, 257]. In 2007, the wireless function of Dick Cheney's pacemaker was deliberately disabled because of its vulnerability to hacking—and therefore the (then) US Vice-President's vulnerability to assassination by laptop. In 2010, researchers at the Universities of Washington and California successfully remotely hacked the internal WiFi of a standard production model of car. They were able remotely to control the locks, ignition, engine, brakes, and instrumentation. They were also able to track the car using its own GPS and listen in on conversations within the vehicle using its own hands-free phone. More worrying still are vulnerabilities in nuclear power plants. In 2010, the Stuxnet cyberattack on Iran's Natanz nuclear facility spun several centrifuges until they broke. In 2016, Dr Patricia Lewis, Research Director of International Security at the UK's independent policy institute, Chatham House, told the *Independent* newspaper that not only could state-sponsored cyberattacks potentially trigger reactor-core meltdowns but that nuclear weapons were also potentially vulnerable to cyberattack [249].

Devices in our built environment do not need to be Internet capable to be hacked, either. In 2015, Alan postulated that your lightbulbs could be spying on you [123]. Although written half in jest, all the technology is available or near horizon. Incandescent bulbs have filaments that are very sensitive to vibration, including sound. Given that they are connected to the electric grid, the only obstacle to listening to the conversations in any given home is extracting the high-frequency signal from the power line, which simply needs a lot of computing power—hardly beyond the reach of the National Security Association (NSA)! You might think that the increasing popularity of light-emitting diode (LED) lightbulbs would end this vulnerability, since the 12-volt step-down transformers between the light and the mains process out useful information, but in fact you only need more computing power and more sensitive listening equipment. If all of this seems far-fetched, then consider MIT's 2014 experiment demonstrating how video of crisp packets and pot plants could be used to extract sound good enough to listen in on a conversation [91]. And there's more. Because LEDs detect as well as emit light, they output these data as small changes in DC current, so if you have several LEDs they can be used to make a rudimentary camera [33], and because each LED lightbulb usually contains a number of LEDs, they could—theoretically—be used to form a very-low-resolution video camera, a bit like a fly's compound eye.

Having painted such a bleak picture of technology's misuse, let's end on a more positive note.

Figure 13.9 Left: The Dancing Traffic Light. Right: Traffic management Hans Monderman style

13.9 Human Technology

Technology, digital or otherwise, tends to work best when it is designed to work with and for humans. Hans Monderman [394] was a Dutch traffic engineer who pioneered a new form of traffic management system based on drivers' social sensibilities. Monderman broke convention by mixing pedestrian and vehicular traffic, removing signs, rights of way, pavements, and safety barriers. He believed that people's social skills and intelligence would more than make up for the lack of rules—and he was proven right. Both drivers and pedestrians were happier; they felt safer, and studies showed they *were* safer. Meanwhile the traffic flow was improved and traffic junctions even *looked* better. What Monderman did was essentially to accommodate and exploit the human condition to the benefit of all, including the local authorities who paid for and maintained the systems. Digital technology can perform a similar humanizing role. The Dancing Traffic Light (Figure 13.9) [424] was an experiment in effecting behavioural change using humour and curiosity to persuade pedestrians to wait for the 'green man' before crossing. Cameras in a temporary structure with a small dance floor translate the real-time movements of members of the public into the movements of the 'red man' in the traffic lights. Smart Cars, who ran the experiment, claim that 81% more people stopped at the red light as a result. Contrast these two approaches, which rely on human curiosity, humour, sociality, and intelligence, with the employment of networked digital motorway signs used to tell drivers that visibility is poor, that it is raining, or that driving drunk is a bad idea.

Digital Augmentation of Space

14.1 Control over Space

In the twenty-first century we have the privilege of seeing nature as benign, something to be enjoyed, cherished, protected, even venerated. However, for much of human existence, nature has been both provider and enemy, the chaos from which the order of early civilization emerged. Even our ancient ancestors left marks on the landscape, from hand prints to schematic maps and undoubtedly stories and names.

Although there are some stories that offer a closer connection with nature, many of our oldest myths see nature as chaos. Even in Genesis, where God declares the creation of the world and nature within it as 'very good', still part of Adam and Eve's punishment is banishment from the ordered garden of Eden into the wilds beyond.

From the earliest hut circles and agriculture, we have found ways to control space. We:

- *Enclose it*—buildings and boundaries;
- *Traverse it*—transport;
- *Describe it*—maps and plans;
- *Transcend it*—communication, action at a distance.

Digital technology extends each of these. In the built environment, computer-aided design (CAD) systems and laser levels have allowed vertiginous skyscrapers that appear to defy gravity, and, paradoxically, more organic structures that mirror the shapes of nature. In transport, the same technology has allowed road and rail tunnels, drilled to extend for many kilometres and yet meet with millimetre accuracy, closed-circuit television (CCTV) and sensors for traffic systems (albeit sometimes ineffective), and driverless cars. In cartography, the combination of GPS and satellite imagery has allowed us to bring the whole world into a mobile phone. Perhaps most radically, we can now feel in continuous touch with friends and work colleagues continents apart.

Time, however, has been harder to control. We cannot stop it or wall it, the dreams of time travel are in science fiction, and when we want to chat in real time with Antipodean friends, we must carefully work out times when all are awake. Our only success with time is in description, where line graphs and timetables transform time into space, and to some extent transcend the passing of time through memory technology, writing, and stories.

If anything, technology has broken the relationship between time and space. In the past, and still today in remote areas, when asked the distance to a place, the answer would be in terms of days' travel. Communication technology, from signal beacons to transatlantic telegraph and the Internet has meant we can at least communicate simultaneously, while transport technology, from Roman roads to bullet trains, has shrunk the temporal impact of distance. The promise of sub-space hypersonic travel may soon mean that travel to even the most distant reaches of the earth will be possible within a few hours (well, at least to the cities and for those with sufficient money).

To some extent, digital technology has merely amplified the effects of previous waves of technological development, but there is a fifth means of control, or perhaps a thread that runs through the other four, which seems qualitatively different.

The computer now *infuses* space.

From the digital clock on the electric cooker, to optical cables running through the street, sensors and CCTV cameras everywhere, automatic doors and lighting, the very fabric of space and materiality has become computational, a digital medium. The Ancient Greeks saw dryads in the woods and naiads in the streams. Now it seems that we are creating a pixelated legion of nymphs in our smart buildings, and soon, as these interconnect through the Internet of Things, a pantheistic world where Google, Amazon.com, and Apple are omnipresent.

14.2 Mobile Phones and Mobile Applications

As we saw in the last chapter, the smartphone has become something akin to Sherlock Holmes' magnifying glass: the means by which many of us examine and encounter the space around us.

There are two kinds of applications on mobile devices:

1. Those where location doesn't matter;
2. Those where it does.

At first this sounds like a tautology, but these represent very distinct uses of a mobile device with respect to space.

The first category includes email, social media, and office productivity applications. The whole point of having a word processor on a laptop is so that you can type anywhere. Similarly, making a phone call or sending a text is about doing something where your location is immaterial. You do not have to be at your desk in your office, you don't have to be standing next to your friend. This is mobile technology that *transcends* space.

The second category includes route directions, local information, 'check-in' applications, and augmented reality such as Pokémon GO: applications whose spatial location is fundamental to their operation. This is mobile technology that *describes* space and enables *interaction with it*.

Of course, as with any category, a single application may have features of both, so this distinction is perhaps more about the individual features, or even how they are used. You can use your mobile phone map to see where you are or to plan a journey beforehand, and social media apps that allow cross-continental communication also often include spatial check-in.

While the first kind of use is important, with regard to space it is, of course, the second that is most critical.

The Wales Coast Path (WCP) runs for 1400 kilometres around the estuary and sea coast of Wales. When it was opened in 2012, one of the major points was that it was a complete *waymarked* route. You could follow the route on a map, guide books have been written, and an app released, but along the way, on gates, lampposts, and sometimes sunk into pavements, are small WCP roundels. In contrast, the Cambrian Way, which cuts across mid-Wales, has no waymarks on the ground. You follow it entirely through maps and guides.

Note the difference: signposts, waymarks, mileposts, and boundary stones are all *inscribed* on the landscape, whereas maps and guidebooks *describe* it.

Inscribed navigation is always available, and is especially useful for those without map-reading skills, but it requires some level of ownership or access to the land itself, and can be confusing if there are multiple kinds of simultaneous signposting. In the United Kingdom, the Department of Transport has had numerous projects and publications on reducing traffic sign clutter [75, 98], and in collaboration with the Chartered Institution of Highways & Transportation has presented Reducing Sign Clutter Awards [66].

In contrast, to create an external map, guide book, or location-based mobile app you do not need to own the land. Indeed you may even map enemy land. During the Second World War, signposts were removed in rural areas of the United Kingdom to make it more difficult for an invading army to navigate, though whether this would have seriously hampered a Nazi advance we will never know. Those who plan new housing developments on 'brown-field' sites in the United Kingdom now often consult Soviet maps from the Cold War period as these include details of many industrial buildings, such as chemical works, that are now demolished but may form a potential hazard for new buildings. Notably, some of these were not described in as much detail on publicly available British maps of the same era, and were entirely absent in some cases, if they were deemed secret.

It is possible to have as many external maps and guides as there are potential purposes or ways of seeing the land. In days gone by you might have had layers of clear plastic or translucent paper that you laid on top of a map to draw different kinds of features: pipelines, footpaths, geological features. Now the same can be provided as 'layers' on a GIS (geographic information system) at the press of a button.

This potential multiplicity of views is also a facet of augmented reality systems. Imagine two people looking at the high street of a small market town using augmented reality. One, a tourist, sees a medieval view of the street superimposed on the present-day shop fronts. The other, an engineer, sees the pattern of buried pipes and cables that lie underneath the road.

Such external descriptions of space have their disadvantages. It is becoming increasingly common to find road signs that say 'Don't follow sat nav'; indeed, a relative of Alan's pointed out a mud track where she had recently been routed by her sat nav; fortunately she had a four-wheel-drive car! Note the paradox of such signs: a *physical inscription* on the landscape, pointing out errors in an external *digital description* of it. Even physical signs may be erected with little regard to their meaning, but at least someone sees the sign in place, whereas the digital map on the sat nav may have been checked only by someone on the other side of the world—the external description lacks *local knowledge*.

The nature of the representation also interacts with the user's cognitive map of their spatial location. A map, whether on paper or a phone screen, invites engagement and internal mapping of the local environment, but map reading is a complex learned skill. In contrast, following route instructions is more like being a passenger in one's own walk or drive. It requires little skill, but neither does it develop spatial understanding. This becomes particularly evident when technology fails. Mountain rescue services are increasingly receiving call-outs because walkers have got lost when their mobile has run out of battery or lost signal. Again there is an interesting paradox here. The *description* of the space where someone is currently located is delivered by communications that *transcend* space—when they work. A paper map may also fail, for example if it blows away or is dropped, but the continual engagement with the material will have given the walker a better idea of their location and how to reach safe ground.

14.3 Pervasive and Public Displays

Recall from Chapter 2, that Mark Weiser's vision of ubiquitous computing [416] was based largely around displays from inch scale to yard scale. This has certainly come to pass: in the home, almost every kitchen and media appliance has its own display, not to mention sewing machines, individual heaters, and radiators. In public spaces we see ticker-tape displays at bus stops showing the next bus, touchscreens in railway stations to plan journeys, and vast digital advertising hoardings or town-centre public displays.

Weiser's inch (3 cm), foot (30 cm), and yard (1 m) sized displays related to the office and home environments, but public displays like departure boards and billboards often exceed these scales. These have been termed (following Weiser's use of imperial lengths) perch scale (6 m) and beyond [389, 135].

The size of a display is related to the size of the area it inhabits, so it is not surprising that a railway station can support larger displays than a living room. Indeed, Times Square has displays bigger than a block of flats. However, it is a little more complex than that. Any display defines an area over which it can be easily viewed. For example, a phone-sized display is not much use across a room unless it shows something simple but very large, such as the current channel for a set-top box, and if a display subtends more than about 30 degrees you need to start moving your head to see the ends of it, and text and images become distorted by the viewing angle (Figure 14.1).

In other words, for any display size there is a 'hot' area from which it is easily viewable, which also defines the number of people who can easily view it at the same time. If you want a lot of people to be able to view a whole display, you make it large and position it so that people can stand well back from it to see it. However, if a display is intended for the use of only a small group of people (such as a 'plan your route' display), you make it smaller (yard scale, 1 m or so). If privacy is also an issue (as with an automated teller machine (ATM)), you may make it smaller still so that the user blocks the screen.

Understanding the hot area of a public display is crucial if you want it to be noticed and also for understanding how it will affect the flows

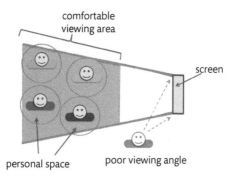

Figure 14.1 Public display comfortable viewing area [389]

Figure 14.2 Firefly lights in perch scale display

of people in the space. Displays are not only embedded in space; they form an integral part of the dynamics of the space.

At the other end of the spectrum, Firefly (Box 2.1) extends Weiser's imperial measurements at the small end: 'poppyseed' scale devices. However, the purpose of these tiny single pixel computers is that they are wrapped over surfaces or suspended in three-dimensional

(3D) structures to make non-flat two-dimensional (2D) and 3D displays. Once camera images are used to triangulate the position of every pixel, the surface or space becomes a single, potentially vast display. This technology has been used in perch scale public displays (see Figure 14.2), but the scale could be larger still. Imagine a path through a public park with lights strung around every tree. The people on the path see moving patterns of colour around them, but from high above the whole park displays a moving image.

Similar technologies have tiles or strips of lighting that can be used to coat simpler structures, either to make the large screens used at pop concerts, or to turn buildings into display surfaces. Looking forward, nanotechnology versions of Firefly could be used to spray paint displays onto any surface.

14.4 Interacting with Public Displays

Interacting with smaller public displays is relatively straightforward. The interfaces must be particularly intuitive as many users will be interacting with them for the first time (so-called walk up and use interfaces). However, small displays can easily utilize familiar keyboards, buttons, and touchscreen interactions.

However, some screens may be too inaccessible to be touched, such as the TV in a pub or bar, or so large that to approach them close enough to touch brings you out of the hot area for viewing. Most current screens of this scale only provide information on a fixed schedule, but more experimental or artistic displays may include some sort of interaction. The most common kinds are:

- *fixed and/or bespoke device*—for example, a podium with a keyboard or trackpad. Most useful for a performance.
- *gesture or body movement detection*—a common choice for shop window displays that react in some way to the movements or even eye-gaze of passers-by.
- *second screen*—for example, inviting people to SMS or tweet to the screen, or using specialized apps for more sophisticated control such as multi-person games.

Interactive public displays face common problems. To begin with we have to communicate to people that they can interact at all. This is less likely to be an issue for fixed devices, although those who are most likely to approach a podium in a public space may be those you least want to be in control of the public surface! For personal devices it is more difficult, and usually some form of QR code or explicit 'how to' notice is required. Gesture-based interfaces often have some kind of reaction to proximity, to catch the attention of passers-by, and then move to more direct interactions once they are engaged.

The first interactions are often the hardest to elicit. Once some people start to interact then the potential becomes more obvious to others. This is very evident with gestural interactions: as soon as people realize they are interacting, they use exaggerated gestures that tend to attract attention. This is sometimes called the honeypot effect. It is less likely to happen with second screens, which are more private, but an updating feed shown on screen can help to alert other people to the possibility of interaction. Often some form of priming may be used; for example, one might display a selection of the previous day's tweets to a public screen.

Even when people have realized *that* they can interact, they need to know *how*. Given that public screen interactions differ so much and are non-standard, this can be a particularly complex challenge, especially for gestural interactions, where there are few universal gestures. Some systems show small stick representations so that people can tell which parts of their movements are being tracked; others may even show some sort of mini-tutorial of gestures, or have instructions. However, neither of these are very effective for relatively short 'walk up and use' interactions. For artistic and game-based installations, the 'how do I use this' phase may be part of the playful interaction, but that is less acceptable for more goal-oriented behaviour. This is less of an issue for second screens. To send an SMS or tweet only requires the users' own familiar phone applications; even if a special app or website is accessed via a QR code or web link, it can be organized on the second screen in a conventional fashion.

Visual accessibility, especially for older people, is one of the big drawbacks of any second screen interaction. Even those with perfect vision, or younger people with corrected vision, may experience some discomfort or inefficiency, constantly shifting focus back and forth. From middle age on, however, most people experience a reduction in accommodation, meaning that eventually different glasses are required for close and distant vision. This can be a problem even at living room distances, making it difficult to relate actions on the remote control (using one pair of glasses) with those on the screen (having swapped to another pair). With public displays this problem is exacerbated, suggesting that interactions on the second screen should either be complete in themselves (e.g. selecting content to display on the public screen) or not require visual inspection (e.g. using the phone screen as a touchpad for large screen interactions).

Binding, making the connection between the small device and screen, can be another major issue. For in-home devices this tends to be a one-off connection process, and may include setting wireless passwords, or simply using the WPS (Wi-Fi Protected Setup) single-press facility. However, it can be a lot more complicated for public displays if you want 'walk up and use' access but also have a level of security to avoid remote spamming. Solutions may exploit locality of wireless access using Bluetooth or a special local WiFi hotspot for the display, or may involve scanning a QR code or entering a special key displayed on screen. We will return to this issue in more detail in Chapter 18.

Finally, public screen interactions have to deal with scale, from the first tentative uses to the simultaneous interactions of many people. If there is a physical interaction device or small hotspot for gesture interaction, this limits the number of people who can simultaneously interact, and could lead to individuals hogging the display. Second screens do not have this problem, but then the software has to deal appropriately with large numbers of requests. For example, in a bar one might allow people to share holiday photos on a public screen, but what if everyone wants to do this? Solutions might include majority preferences (e.g. for channel selection) or queuing (for personal photos). The second screen can form part of the solution. For example, if there is a queue of items for a public display, the second screen can show where the user's preferred items are in the queue and when they are expected to appear.

One way of dealing with scale is through low intention interaction [108, 126]. For example, one might change the kind of media being displayed depending on whether people are rushing by on a rainy day, or relatively static (for example eating lunch in the sunshine in a public square). This raises privacy issues. Social media applications already have your location and knowledge about your behaviour and interests. You can imagine that in the future they might sell anonymized information to owners of public spaces about the aggregate media preferences of those in the space so that public displays can tailor their content to the audience.

14.5 Public Roles, Privacy, and Intrusion

Interaction in a public space creates roles [135]:

Performer—the person interacting with the public display or other public installation. In some cases the 'performer' may not be aware that they are interacting: an *unwitting performer*. For example, at a sports event or concert where the camera scans the crowd and there is that moment of realization when the person on camera discovers that everyone else is looking at them.

Audience—the performer(s) are expecting these people to see the effects of an interaction. In the case of small public displays there may be no intended audience, or just the performer's travel group. However, for a town-centre pubic display the audience may be hundreds of people.

Bystander—those who are watching or hearing the effects of the performer's actions, but are not the direct intended audience. For example, while using a medium-sized train route planning screen, someone else may notice that you are going to the same place as they are and read the information you intended for yourself and your travelling companions.

Passer-by—people who are not actively observing the effects of the interaction, but may notice or be peripherally aware.

Note that some of the interaction issues we have mentioned concern transitions between roles. In particular, we may be seeking to increase engagement, so we design interactions that turn passers-by into audience or performers; or we may deliberately try to make it easier for bystanders or passers-by to see the performer's actions in order to increase the honeypot effect.

For example, we have mentioned the potential problem that because second screen interactions are private, they do not create such a strong honeypot. We might design the interaction so that periodically the user has to hold their phone up and wave it at the screen: a flashing pattern on the phone screen could be detected by cameras, verifying that they are indeed near the second screen, but with the side effect that others become aware of the potential for interaction.

Of course, the opposite can sometimes be the case: we want information in public spaces to be private. For example, a hospital emergency department could have a 'self check-in' screen where you enter your details and symptoms to streamline service for those who are not too sick. In this case you would want to design details such as the size of screen and the places where people stand so that it is hard to be a bystander. You might make similar decisions for a railway information system, to avoid stalkers.

Even where the results of the interaction do not need to be private, some people do not like being the centre of attention. They may wish to interact with the public display, say to give a preference for a channel to be displayed, but they prefer to do so discreetly. In other words, we may have public and private interactions with a display in a public place and public or private information on that display (Figure 14.3).

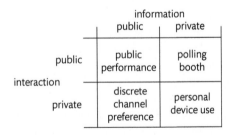

Figure 14.3 Public interaction and information

others want to see

		yes	no
performer wants others to see	yes	public use of display	intrusion anti-social behaviour
	no	privacy security staking	accidental interaction

Figure 14.4 Privacy and intrusion

There is an opposite problem, *intrusion*, where the performer is happy to project material to an audience, bystanders, and passers-by, but those who see it are not so happy (Figure 14.4). Offensive material is an obvious example, or when someone hogs the TV remote control in a pub and chooses to show a football match with a team that no-one else cares about.

Although we have used the term 'intrusion' for this, there is in fact no widely accepted term for this phenomenon, even though it is common. Of course, because there is no word, it is more difficult for it to become a part of formal requirements.

One of the most common solutions to the problem of intrusion is to have some sort of human moderation of content, although it may be that automatic algorithms, refined for social media policing, become used for this purpose. Another alternative is to constrain interaction strongly. Examples would be a game like Tetris where the user can only play set moves, or a screen where a user can choose between preselected media such as particular sports or news channels, but not upload arbitrary text or media.

If interactions are public, this may itself be sufficient to control behaviour. In the Introduction we briefly mentioned the Hermes system of small messaging screens beside office doors (Figure 14.5) [65, 64] and how no offensive messages were ever left, even though visitor messages were anonymous. It is believed that this is because visitors leaving notes did so in a public corridor. They would know that if they had left an offensive message, they might have been spotted going in and out of the corridor [131].

Figure 14.5   Hermes office door display: (left) in corridor; (right) close-up

This *auditability of space* depends critically on the design of the system, the nature of the social situation (a gang of youths in a city centre may want to be seen to be offensive), and crucially the spatial location and layout of displays and interaction devices.

14.6   Space as Interface

We have looked at interactions with screens, but the movement and placement of objects and people can itself be a form of interaction.

In the early 1990s, Pierre Wellner put together a number of emerging technologies to form an envisionment of the DigitalDesk [417]. At the time there had been a number of research systems that involved touch-style interfaces, not unlike those found on tablets and touchscreens today. However, DigitalDesk was not simply a clever screen showing software objects; it was a vision of how physical paper and desktop objects could combine with projected displays and vision technology. When paper was placed on the DigitalDesk it was immediately scanned. Or you could write using a pen on real paper, but then copy the image you had drawn and reproduce it or edit it using digital software. The physical presence and placement of objects and the physical actions on them were intimately interwoven with digital representations.

The DigitalDesk was an envisionment, combining technologies and system fragments, each of which worked, into coherent videos that pointed the way forward. More than fifteen years before Ishii's coining of 'tangible bits', DigitalDesk prefigured many of the computational interactions with physical objects that are now common in the Tangible User Interface research community (see Chapter 2). The projection and touch-detection technology that was a major work of engineering in the early 1990s is now available for less than the cost of a laptop [25], though it is still not trivial to install and calibrate reliably.

Spatial location is crucial for many people's desktops—listen for the cries of anguish if a new cleaner has not understood this and 'tidied' a colleague's desk! More recent digital office research prototypes also include the ability to locate files using QR codes [399], though of course many people know just where to find things despite apparent disorder. It is not only their location that is important but their *disposition*, how they are located in space—aligned, angled, propped up. Alan had a bad 'cleaner' experience when a pile was simply 'straightened'. The higgledy-piggledy nature of the papers on the top of the pile had been an implicit cue that they had not yet been dealt with—letters remained unanswered for weeks!

Surface-based computing is of course now common. The original Microsoft Surface was a large table-top display using PIR to allow multi-touch and multi-person interactions on large surfaces. Early marketing videos showed it being used in bars but it is still rare to see these kinds of products in use beyond research labs and museums. This was originally because of the cost, yet even though costs have dropped, they have not been taken up in bars, offices, or the home.

At first this seems surprising, given that flat surfaces are such an important part of work and leisure, but of course the thing about flat surfaces is that they usually have things on them: beer glasses, newspapers, staplers. Even Wellner's DigitalDesk envisionments, which combined physical and digital obects, were always filmed on otherwise clear desks. We are yet to crack interaction on cluttered surfaces.

In contrast, whole-body interaction in the home has become accepted, with first Wii and now Kinect, even though it often requires moving of furniture to make space.

Wellner was working at Xerox research labs in Cambridge, a hotbed of novel interaction design. For a period the employees all wore infrared badges so that they could be tracked through the building. The data was then used by the Pepys system to make personal diaries for each person [307]. At the end of each day the system analysed the logs, and if two people spent more than a certain amount of time in the same location the system recorded this as a 'meeting'. Here the interaction was low intention, people just did their everyday jobs, but their movement incidentally had an effect [108, 126].

The Pepys meetings were based on the relative locations of the people. A meeting did not have to be in a designated meeting room, it could be in an office or even the corridor. Proximity or mere presence in an area can be important interaction mechanisms. Often a combination of physical proximity and near simultaneity can be used as a way to establishing bindings. For example, the WPS system for connecting smart devices to WiFi requires the device to be within range of the WiFi router, and the WPS button on the router and some button on the device must be pressed within a short time of each other. A more sophisticated variant of this involves holding two devices together and shaking them; the proximity allows a short-range wireless connection and the simultaneous identical movement confirms they are the devices to be paired [284].

At a larger scale, geocaching and Pokémon GO use physical movement in the world as their means of interaction. If you want to find something, you have to go there. More prosaically, location-based tourist or shopping applications do the same, giving you information based on where you are; to find new things you have to move. Some artists have made use of this by tracing out images using their movements over large areas so that the GPS trace becomes part of the artwork. There have been attempts to use the same mechanism for mobile games, but this has proved less popular than simple catch 'em type games!

Location-based narrative has been more successful, for example as a form of guide, taking people through fixed locations with some kind of historical, documentary, or fictional narrative emerging along the way.

14.7 Mixed Reality—Real Space Meets Virtual

Consider again the type of scenario we discussed in Chapter 13. You are standing in a busy town square checking TripAdvisor comments about a restaurant. As you read the comments, two children rush past seeking Pokémon characters, looking at the world through their mobile phones, while images of the twinned town are projected onto a fountain in the middle of the square.

In each case, digital and physical worlds are mixed or superimposed in different ways. When this happens, we see three spaces emerge (Figure 14.6) [139]:

- *real space*—the locations, dispositions, and extent of people, movable objects, and fixed buildings and structures in the physical world. For Trip Advisor, this would be your location and that of the restaurant; for Pokémon GO, the children's location, or to be precise the location and orientation of their mobile phones.
- *measured space*—the way the real space has been captured as data. This includes the GPS traces of your own phone and the children's phones, the location of the fountain and projector (to work out mappings), and geographic coordinates of the restaurant, from a map or postcode or from people previously checking the location.
- *virtual space*—the things that only have digital representations: TripAdvisor comments, the Pokémon characters.

The measured space is the way in which real and virtual spaces meet for the computer, a representation of the physical world in the digital world. They also meet, of course, back in the physical world you experience, as you look at the images on screen or possibly some sort of auditory output.

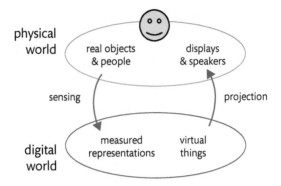

Figure 14.6 Real, measured, and virtual spaces

In practice there may be different forms of measured space, for example digital maps, current GPS coordinates, or location as estimated from WiFi base stations. Even simple latitude/longitude may vary in terms of precision, but there are also radically different kinds of digital spaces:

- *coordinates*—some form of Cartesian points in space, precise, although not necessarily accurate.
- *zonal*—simply that you are within some area, for example in the range of a particular IR sensor, in a room, etc.
- *relative*—where location is reported relative to some other object.

Mappings between these may not always be trivial. Latitude/longitude is reported using a number of different standards that can differ by as much as a few hundred metres from one another, and things get more complex when trying to make connections between digital spaces of different kinds. For example, knowing that someone's phone is within a particular cell may only locate them 'somewhere' in an area ranging from hundreds of metres in a city to many kilometres in the countryside, and typically this is not a circular area, since it depends on intervening buildings and landforms.

This means that it is often not sufficient simply to translate everything into a single coordinate system. For example, if someone is playing a multi-player game on the seat-back display in an aircraft, you know precisely which seat they are in and therefore whether their opponent is in front, behind, or beside them. However, if you tried to translate their location into world coordinates using the GPS location of the aircraft and their physical location relative to the aircraft, even a fraction of second difference in calculating their locations would completely destroy their relative position.

When discussing public displays, we looked at the way a display creates a 'hot' area where it is easy to view it; audio, similarly, has an area over which it can be heard. However, when displays project virtual or augmented worlds, such as virtual characters or images of the buildings in a past era, they create a virtual projected space that extends *behind* the visual surface on which it is displayed. This is true even of your TV at home: in a way it creates a porthole into worlds that, if it were really a window, would project far beyond the borders of your living room. With a TV we are, of course, aware that this is not real. We do not put our hand behind it and expect our fingers to encounter the objects we see on screen, but augmented reality systems aim to create precisely this illusion, layering the virtual images on the real world.

There has been a long tradition of virtual office shares, large screens in an office or coffee area that connect to buildings and offices far away. In these, cameras and microphones are carefully positioned in relation to the screen to create a virtual window between the spaces. There are also virtual meeting rooms, which can achieve a sense of almost 'being there' by carefully creating furniture and arranging screens so that people are located virtually where they would be physically (Figure 14.7).

However, this is more difficult when people can move around in the space. Putting your head close to a real window between offices allows you to see more of the space on the other side. Although there have been some experiments tracking head movements with desktop displays using Wii-mote [260], in general virtual windows do not behave like real windows. Users may move outside the (often narrow) range of the camera, and parallax effects reveal that the virtual window is clearly not really a way into another space.

Figure 14.7 The Teliris VirtuaLive Telepresence System

Oddly, the illusion of presence can sometimes be made greater by adding distance. MRACells (Mixed Reality Architectural Cells) does not attempt to connect offices in this way but instead positions individual offices as movable vehicles in a virtual space [349]. Offices can be steered in this space. They can be positioned well away from each other so you can just see movement, giving a sense of co-presence, rather as if you could see someone in an office in an adjacent building. On the other hand, you might move your office so that its window is positioned close to another person's office window. When the offices are close enough, you can hear as well as see each other. However, even when positioned like this there is still a small virtual space between the rooms, rather like talking to another driver while waiting alongside at traffic lights. This means that you expect the near corners of the other room to be hidden, as you effectively cannot get close enough in the virtual world to peek.

14.8 Computational Space

Let's look with a focus on computational space at some of the ideas we introduced in Chapter 2.

We said that when you step into a lift you are effectively getting inside a robot. When you press the buttons, the lift does not always go straight to the floor you have selected. It may stop at intermediate floors to pick up more passengers; it may even take you temporarily in the opposite direction from the way you want to go. When it is empty, with no pending requests, it may return to the ground floor. Multiple lifts in a large building may coordinate based on past usage patterns, waiting at intermediate floors at certain times of day to minimize the expected wait time.

A lift is autonomous and moves, albeit in a bounded vertical shaft. The buttons are merely your communication with it—a robot.

We have become so used to lifts that we do not think of the complex sensing and planning that runs behind the surface and indeed differs markedly between lifts. Elements of the space around us are becoming computational, a trend that is set to continue as smart objects are linked together in the Internet of Things: manual things become automated, and fixed programme automation becomes more dynamic using multiple sensors and stored data.

Alongside the obvious examples of embedded intelligence, such as driverless cars, think about the less obvious, such as traffic lights in smart cities, where the lighting pattern is planned and replanned moment by moment as current traffic is sensed and past data is analysed.

Although humanoid robots are still emerging from science fiction, they have a level of comprehensibility—identifiable artificial creatures that may be more or less smart and more or less capable. It is harder to conceptualize intelligence that is embedded into the environment around us—even something as familiar as a lift.

Recall the 'myHouse' scenario in Chapter 2.

You get home and as you walk through the door you hear the kettle boiling. Your phone knew when you left the office and told your home computer. It consulted your diary and the live Metro information to predict exactly when you would be arriving, and it started to adjust the heating to be the perfect temperature when you stepped inside. Your phone continued to update the house with your current position until three minutes before you were due to arrive, when it switched on the kettle so that it was ready for a hot cup of tea.

How do we make sense of a world where the very walls are alive?

One way is to explicitly anthropomorphize it, give it an identity. HAL in '2001' was the voice of the ship, and similarly in 'Star Trek' the invocations to 'Computer...' were many people's first introduction to the idea of voice interfaces in the 1960s. We now have a number of voice-operated home controllers including Amazon Echo and Google Home. Interestingly, these also have a physical form, helping to build the idea of an embodied agent that is controlling the house, rather than the house being diffusely intelligent. Some designs for driverless cars include a robot-like embodiment, not robot hands turning the steering wheel but a small device sitting on the dashboard that acts as a focus for attention; early studies suggest that this 'presence' gives passengers more confidence in the self-driving operation [309].

14.9 Designing Intelligent Spaces

The use of the word 'computer' before each command in 'Star Trek' was probably a dramatic device to tell the viewer that the ship was being addressed, but it also highlights one of the common problems of both voice and gesture sensing systems: how does the system know that you are addressing it rather than simply talking to someone?

This is one of five challenges that Victoria Bellotti and colleagues identified for sensing systems [24]:

- *address*—How do I address one (or more) of many possible devices?
- *attention*—How do I know the system is ready and attending to my actions?
- *action*—How do I effect a meaningful action, control its extent, and possibly specify a target or targets for my action?
- *alignment*—How do I know the system is doing (has done) the right thing?
- *accident*—How do I avoid mistakes?

Note how each of these is relatively straightforward to achieve on a well-designed GUI device, even if there are occasional problems, such as pocket dialling (an *addressing* failure). For voice, we have seen that addressing can be problematic and usually requires a key phrase or explicit 'turn on voice commands' action, but at least voice feedback can solve some of the problems, for example providing commentary on what has been done when this is not apparent (you do not need to hear 'the TV has been turned on' when it is facing you, but you may need 'the heating has been turned up'). However, all the challenges get a lot more complicated if one wants to rely purely on gesture or other sensing.

One way to deal with these issues is to make systems so automatic that you don't even realize they are operating. In a lift you explicitly press buttons but have only a vague idea of its scheduling behaviour; it does its job. When you walk up to an automatic door it opens; when you open the fridge the internal light comes on. In some of these cases you may be aware that something has happened (the door opening), even though you did little to make it happen; in others you may not even realize that anything has happened at all (the fridge simply appears to be always illuminated).

These are *low-intention/low-attention interactions*: you do have an influence, but do not have to explicitly take action (low-intention) and may not even be aware that you have had an effect (low-attention) [108, 126].

Intention and attention are not binary attributes; we have different levels of each.

On the intention side, you may make an explicit *intentional action*, for example pressing an 'open door' button. However, you may simply throw your hand up as if to push the door (which could be huge) and this gesture triggers the automatic door opening, an *implicit interaction*, which you may hardly be aware you have done even though the initiative comes from you. Requiring less intention still are *expected interactions*. For example, as you approach the door it opens; you know that it will do so and would be surprised (and hurt your nose) if it did not. Finally, *incidental interactions* are where you do something and may not even be aware that this is being used by the system to initiate autonomous action or modify some future interaction. For example, when the lift doors open it may appear that all the fire doors in the library archive corridor are open, allowing an unrestricted view, but in fact they are normally closed and only open when someone is in the lift and approaching the floor.

Regarding attention, when you click on an email you very explicitly see it open and read it. But when things happen in your peripheral vision you have some vague, possibly subconscious, awareness of them but would be hard-pressed to say exactly what you have seen. In the case of the fridge light, there may be the merest flicker as you open the fridge that lets you know it is not on all the time, but otherwise you never think about it being on—unless it fails.

The idea of the task or activity is central in much of interaction design: what is the user currently trying to achieve and how do we redesign this activity or aid it to make it as easy or pleasurable as possible? For low-intention interactions we typically need to look at two tasks, or the same task from two viewpoints:

- *sensed task*—understanding the user's actions, intentions, or mental state based on what they are doing.
- *supported task*—later using that knowledge to act on behalf of the user or aid the user's actions.

The library archive lift is a good example of the system acting on behalf of the user: the user presses the lift button to get to the desired floor (sensed task), and when they get there the fire doors are already open (autonomous action) to make navigating the corridors easier (supported task). As an example where the user is aided in an explicit action, imagine that on a train journey home from work the user has been having a social media conversation about a television series (sensed task). When they get home they turn on the TV (explicit action in supported task) and on the 'home screen', among the ever changing suggestions for viewing, there 'happens' to be the TV series they were discussing (modifying the explicit action).

Autonomous system actions involve decisions on what is needed. Some of these may use predesigned rules based on typical behaviour. For example, a car courtesy light goes on when the door is opened, then automatically fades after a fixed time. However, more intelligent systems will try to modify their behaviour over time to match the inferred patterns of behaviour of specific users. Such machine learning can be very powerful, allowing highly personalized behaviour, but it has the potential for disaster, especially as users also adapt their own behaviour depending on the way systems behave. Good design can both minimize conflicts and help obtain the information that the system needs to adapt.

14.10 Fruits of Success

Imagine yourself in a small village 150 years ago. You knew your neighbours and they knew you, perhaps even knew too much! You heard about big national events—celebrations, wars, elections—but only when the newspapers came or when someone had travelled on business or for war. There was an inverse relationship, roughly, between information and distance: you knew most about the people and places closest to you and only a little about those far away.

Of course, there have always been traders and travellers for whom this is too simple a view. Even in Neolithic times European trade routes flowed deep into the heart of the continent down rivers and along coasts, and from the Mediterranean out to the shores of Britain. Before the Roman Empire opened up overland routes, Phoenician wines found their way to Britain, and Cornish tin is believed to have underpinned the entire European Bronze Age. However, even for such traders, information travelled at the speed of foot, hoof, and sail.

It is difficult to appreciate this level of locality in the age of mass media and the internet. We expect instant live footage (itself an anachronistic word) of major world events, and television news often shows amateur mobile phone coverage of distant disasters before the reporters have had time to reach them. Whether through phone, Zoom, or social networks, we can keep contact with friends and family far away, and indeed may have many Internet friends whom we have never met in person.

Even before the web, the ubiquity and space-warping effects of media gave rise to the term 'global village'. Utopian visions imagined that the gradual dissolving of language and cultural barriers would

usher in an age of peace and tolerance, but sadly the constant images of war-torn, disease-stricken, and hungry people beamed to our
living rooms have only occasionally led to fitful compassion. The
utopian dream seems even further away now that mass media has
given way to Internet 'news bubbles', where we each hear news tuned
to our personal interests and entrenched opinions. Rather than a
single global village, we are more like separate insular communities, as deeply separated by the fractured geography of cyberspace as
were isolated mountain villages in the days before television and the
motor car.

If the topography of cyberspace is divided by digital arête and gully,
it sometimes seems that unseen but unassailable barriers equally
fragment physical space.

Step back again to the 150-year-old rural village, or for that matter some more remote rural locations today, and not only did you
know your neighbours but your parents knew their parents, and indeed it was likely that you were distant cousins. Even at that time,
if you found yourself instead in an industrial city or mining settlement, you might have known your neighbours, but without the
same shared roots and history. The Industrial Revolution and ur-
banization started a process that continues today, where families are
scattered and not only is the person next door not a relative, they are
a total stranger. Even before the ubiquitous mobile phone provided
an excuse to stare anywhere but at another's eyes, the studied blank-
ness of faces on mass transport, and the steel shell of the commuter
car were emblematic of the isolation of the crowd.

It is not so much that virtual social networks are replacing face-to-
face relationships, but more that they are filling the void that already
exists. We live in a global village but need passports to visit next door.

14.11 Hyperlocal

If digital connectivity can connect us to communities far afield, can
it reconnect us to the community we live in?

In 1995, Craig Newmark began an email list for his friends, sending updates on events in the San Francisco Bay area [422]. Over time

this developed into a web classified listing serving cities and communities in seventy countries. Although the current Craigslist is a commercial company, it maintains a strong community-focused ethos. The Freecycle Network is more radical again [169]. Freecycle was founded in 2003 by Deron Beal, who was seeking an easier way to distribute unwanted items to community groups who could use them. The network enables local email lists where people can advertise things that they want to give away for free. Crucially, the central website is used simply as a way to point people to these local lists; the lists themselves are managed entirely locally.

In both cases the global connectivity of the web and email is used to find out about things that are very local to you. The term 'glocal' is sometimes used for this kind of service—a hideous word for an important idea. In many ways services such as Uber operate in this space. Uber allows you to find a taxi nearby: a single global app to connect you to someone round the corner. However, there are great differences in terms of local control and autonomy between Uber and Freecycle!

'Hyperlocal' is an alternative term that captures the way in which digitally enabled services can work at a level even finer than traditional media. Radio and television typically have a combination of national and regional broadcasting and news. Newspapers often bring this to a finer level with small newspapers for small towns. However, with digital media it is possible to access news at the level of a street or block of flats.

We started this section focused on the isolation of urban environments, but in fact rural environments often need similar technology. On the remote Isle of Tiree few people lock their doors and it is hard to keep a secret, but the 650 residents are scattered over an area of 78 square kilometres, so it is surprisingly difficult to inform people about events. If you sit in the Cobbled Cow, a café near the island airport, an LED ticker-tape displays weather, tide times, transport information, island events, and other local information (Figure 14.8). It is part of an island data infrastructure that draws partly on web sources such as the weather forecast, BBC news, and ferry status,

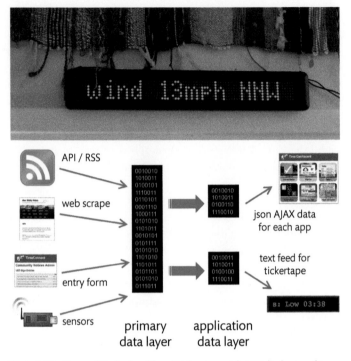

API / RSS

web scrape

entry form

sensors

primary
data layer

application
data layer

json AJAX data
for each app

text feed for
tickertape

Figure 14.8 Tiree public display: (above) ticker-tape-style LED display in café; (below) community data infrastructure

and partly from a community event diary and other locally sourced information. This is then used to feed the café display and a web-based 'dashboard' [143].

Computation
and
Information

Representation and Language

15.1 Fire

In the introduction we listed elements of the natural world and of the human constructed environment. We started with solid things such as stones and tools but ended at the numinous end of the spectrum with wind and fire (on the natural side) and information, language, and computation on the constructed side.

As we said, fire is the strangest. A modern scientist would consider the others as representing the three states of matter: liquid, gas, and solid. Almost any modern element can exist in any of the states depending on pressure and temperature. Indeed, the 'triple point' of water, the precise temperature and pressure where the three states can simultaneously coexist, is still used as the definition of the international temperature scale (Figure 15.1):

> The kelvin, unit of thermodynamic temperature, is the fraction 1/273.16 of the thermodynamic temperature of the triple point of water. Bureau International des Poids et Mesures [48]

Some fire is feral, like the huge plumes rising from a bonfire; other flames, like a candle, are tamed. But what is a candle flame? If you know your physics you might think burning vapour and glowing gases, and indeed this is the physical process. The heat of the flame melts the wax at the top of the candle, which rises in liquid form up the wick by capillary action. When the liquid wax in the wick is in the hottest part of the flame it vaporizes. Simultaneously the rising column of hot gases generated by the candle flame draws in air from below, which mixes with the hot flammable wax vapour and burns, generating heat, which maintains the process.

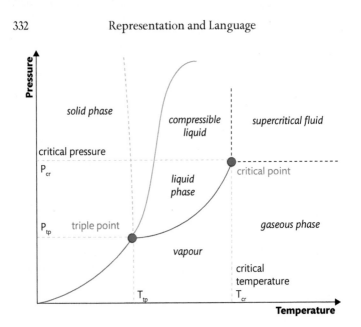

Figure 15.1 Triple point—gas, liquid, and solid can coexist

Although the candle itself and the wick are of fixed substance, the flame itself, the definable thing that you see, is in perpetual change (Figure 15.2). The physical molecules of wax vapour, air, and glowing gas are constantly flowing away, while others take their place. And yet we call it 'the' flame, a definable visual 'thing' occupying physical space.

Think too about the words of a book. They have no inherent physical form, only in the ink on the page or, in older times, the raised type on the plates that struck down again and again as the printing press stamped out the copies. Yet, when we talk of *The Wind in the Willows* or *War and Peace*, we often mean the abstract text, the disembodied words that are yet still identifiably a 'thing', not the specific volume we have in front of us.

Whether in words on a page, electronic bits in computer memory, neuron connections in a brain, or the faint reverberations of air molecules between lovers' lips and ears, pure information only exists in representation, and indeed constant repetition as the physical

Figure 15.2 Candle flame—constant yet ever changing

form decays. The earliest writing was simply an *aide mémoire* for oral culture. Semitic scripts had no vowels, even though these are more critical than in European languages, because the reader already knew the words. The text was simply waymarks along a well-trodden route.

15.2 Representation

Douglas Shiell recalls a colleague being stopped at customs with a deck of punch cards: When he was asked if it had any value, he showed the official the cards, and said "no, they've been used" and was allowed to pass. Feedback, *New Scientist*, 30 Nov. 2013, p.66

When you choose a newspaper from a newsstand, you may choose which newspaper (*The Times, The Washington Post, Le Monde*), but you do not care which copy of the newspaper you have unless one is marked or damaged. Similarly when, as a student, you borrow a textbook from the library, you do not care which copy of the textbook you get—assuming you do not write notes in library books! The physical book is important because of what it *represents*.

Similarly, your photos on Instagram or files in Dropbox may be copied in multiple data centres and moved multiple times, but you do not care about the physical disks on which they are stored, only about what is stored. However, like the candle flame, the information only continues to exist when represented in physical form. If Instagram ceased its service, or Dropbox had a catastrophic failure in its data centres, the photos or files would cease to exist except in your memory of them (unless you kept your own backups).

This is not to say that the physical representation of information may not accrete its own value: the CD that you were give as a birthday present, the treasured book you have had since childhood or the copy of the textbook with your personal notes in the margin. But the *initial* meaning of a physical form is in the information that it represents.

Box 15.1 Stories on the page

While Alan was walking round Wales in 2013, he visited the Roderic Bowen archive in Lampeter. While there he was shown two books side by side.

One was George Borrow's *Wild Wales*, where he tells of his journeys around Wales, largely on foot, in the late nineteenth century. He visited the archive (newly formed at that time) and saw a manuscript, which had been barely rescued when the Saxons attacked a monastery in the seventh century. He describes the bloodstain of the monk that saved it, still visible on the page.

'A manuscript Codex containing a Latin synopsis of Scripture which once belonged to the monks of Bangor Is Coed. It bears the marks of blood with which it was sprinkled when the monks were massacred by the heathen Saxons'. [37]

Beside this was the very manuscript that Borrow had seen 140 years earlier, with the dark-red mark still visible on the vellum. Alan touched the surface of the page where Borrow's fingers had touched.

In fact, modern scholarship has revealed that this is really a thirteenth-century copy of an older original, and the stain is most likely to be claret [119, 401].

This said, it would be wrong to think of a physical representation as simply a passive container of information. The physical manifestation may have additional properties: the attractiveness of a book cover, the convenience of an ebook. The nature of the representation may make the meaning more or less accessible—from the language in which it is written to the alignment of tables. Even a permanently sealed book contains information, though it is not usable.

Furthermore, the information may not be merely what is initially inscribed in the physical material. Some representations allow annotation or wear, explicitly or implicitly adding knowledge about use. The 'accidents' of its physical location and orientation are also important—think of the example of Alan's pile of paper being 'tidied' by a new cleaner in the last chapter.

So we see that information is often not merely to be consumed but is part of activity. Psychologists have repeatedly found how important the choice of representation is in solving problems and facilitating action. Indeed the most creative step in a problem-solving activity often involves the appropriate point to switch between representations or to discover new ones.

When designing devices or applications to store, transmit, or visualize information, we need to keep in mind the ways in which the information may be used actively. It may be part of study or research, in which case annotations and the ability to cross-reference are crucial. It may be just-in-time knowledge for practical activity, in which case it is important to have a form suitable for being consulted in the work environment, which may be wet, dusty, or poorly lit.

15.3 Ideas

As well as designing devices to store information, the product of the act of creativity or design is often information itself. In some creative endeavours, such as a novel or poem, the ideas themselves and the words that express them are central. But in the case of design ideas it is not the idea *per se* but the thing that is created from the idea. For example, the idea of the Model T Ford may have been recorded in writing, specified in plans, discussed in meetings, but the real goal of the idea was to have physical cars rolling off the production line.

These different kinds of ideas often have different protection under patent and copyright law. For example, whereas in the United States you can patent an algorithm or business process, in the United Kingdom you cannot patent the idea as such. It needs to have an embodiment. In practice the difference is less extreme, since patent lawyers have developed ways to have default embodiments of algorithms by simply positing a generic computer with memory and communications containing the algorithm. In contrast, copyright is all about the idea itself.

Patents are often seen as restricting innovation and use, at best yet another tool of big business, at worst immoral, not least when applied to life-saving drugs. Paradoxically, however, patents were originally designed to engender innovation, partly to help the patentee to be rewarded for their idea and hence be spurred to further innovation, and also because the patent is supposed to contain a full and faithful disclosure of the idea. Rather than keep an idea secret, and risk the knowledge dying with the individual, the inventor is encouraged to share the idea, feeding the innovation of others.

In many ways, this epitomizes one of the core differences between the world of physical objects and the world of ideas and information. If you buy a CD from a shop, the shopkeeper may have more copies but does not have *that* copy. If you later give the CD to a friend, then you no longer have it. In contrast, when someone downloads a song from iTunes, it is no less present in Apple Store than it was before, and they then have the potential to copy the MP3 to a friend's computer without losing it themself.

We will revisit these issues of reproducibility in Chapter 16. Suffice to say here that the move to digital goods and an information economy has fundamentally challenged the nature of economics and business in ways that we are still struggling to comprehend. On the positive side, ideas feed ideas and data shared becomes greater than the sum of its parts. In other words, we have non-zero sum economics: by giving freely we are all collectively the richer. On the negative side, we have still to work out ways to reward adequately those who create open materials, whether software, music, educational resources, or data. Often the collective good accrues unequally to the already powerful.

None of this, neither the complexities of open-source economics nor the accessibility of representations, applies until ideas are formulated. Sometimes this happens in conversation with materials, as a sculptor responds to the structure of stone; sometimes the idea is fully from within. Often, however, the initial idea is tacit, there in your head, but not in a form you can talk about or even recognize that you know.

15.4 Externalization

Whiteboards, scribbled diagrams, models, even using salt and pepper pots as surrogate cars as you tell a friend about a recent near-accident—human communication is full of external forms of ideas, memories, and imaginings. This is very evident in design, where sketches, blue-foam models, CAD diagrams, and functioning prototypes are all used to communicate design ideas within a team or to clients.

The standard way to think about such external representations is as a form of information transfer, first formalized by Shannon and Weaver in their classic formulation of information theory [359]. An idea in one person's head is translated into an external form (words, signs, diagrams), which is then heard or seen by the second person and becomes an idea in *their* head.

This model of communication is very powerful, and the measures of information content underpin all our computer and telephony networks. However, it does not account for all the ways external representations are used both in groups and individually.

Have you ever been writing about a topic, or even telling someone about it, and when you reread what you wrote or hear the words you are saying you think, 'I didn't know that before?' It is as if in articulation new knowledge is formed, even though the words come 'from your head'. If writing is about communicating, then where did the idea come from?

Some of these 'new' ideas are to do with the difference between tacit and explicit knowledge. Unless you are very forgetful, you know your name, or your birthday. This is explicit knowledge, things that you know that you know. However, you also clearly 'know' how to run and how to find your way round your home in the dark, yet would find it very hard to explain to someone exactly how you do this. It was not until Muybridge's stop-frame photographs at the end of the nineteenth century that the nature of gait and the precise movements of ordinary actions such as walking and running began to be understood. Today sports trainers use video recordings in order to help athletes improve their performance.

It is not only physical actions that are tacit. 'Expert systems' is the area of artificial intelligence that attempts to replicate or aid expert decision-making. One of the challenges is that while a doctor makes diagnoses every day, they find it hard to articulate precisely the 'rules' they use. They clearly 'know' how to diagnose but do not know how to explain it. This is also a challenge for educators in more mundane areas.

In Chapter 5 we saw the way that external representations, such as adding up using pencil and paper, can act as a form of extension of the mind, allowing us to perform cognitive tasks that would otherwise be difficult or impossible because of limited memory or imagination.

This is again particularly important in physical industrial design. Seeing a mock-up, prototype, or scale model allows us to try things out, squint along the wall line of an architectural model, run our hands along the curve of a new car. Sometimes this is about obtaining an emotional understanding of the feel of things. Sometimes it is about precise measurements on a scale model, or dynamic properties, such as whether a door would open freely. The act of making is an integral part of the conceptual work of design.

Thinking of such examples in design, research, and everyday life, we can identify four functions of externalization:

informational—This is the obvious explicit–explicit communicative function of writing, noted earlier. You have some existing thoughts or ideas and set these down on paper so that someone else can understand the same things that you do (Figure 15.3). Similarly

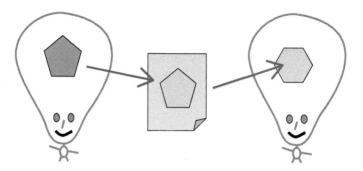

Figure 15.3 Informational—passing on already formed ideas to others

an architect may make a scale model or virtual reality simulation in order to convey the shape, appearance, or experience of a building to a client. Note that this process may not be perfect. The words or pictures on the paper, or model on the table, may not fully capture the idea or picture in your head, and the impression that it creates in your readers' or clients' heads may be not be the same as in your own. However, while not a perfect act of communication, it is achieving a communicative purpose.

formational—Most writers have noticed the phenomenon we described above, that they know more after they have written than they did before. This is odd if one regards externalization solely as an act of communication (Figure 15.4). The act of writing demands a particular word, the need to sketch demands that the location of a door is specified. What had been vague or fuzzy thoughts becomes specific and concrete; the very process of elaboration of thoughts changes the thoughts. Rather than pre-existing ideas being *re*-presented in an external form, the idea is itself *formed* in the process of presentation. This can be problematic, leading to premature commitment, hence the need at some stages of design for deliberately fuzzy representations. For example, Buxton [52] emphasizes the importance of the way sketched lines are imprecise and often don't join at the corners.

transformational—While the informational function is most obvious when considering communication media, for those involved

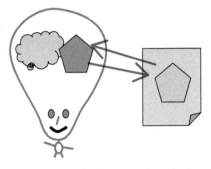

Figure 15.4 Formational—vague ideas becoming clearer by the process of externalization

in craft or industrial design the most important thing is that the external representation has properties that can be used to help in understanding or planning the eventual outcome (Figure 15.5). We may measure lengths on a scale diagram, add up lists of numbers, play back a tune, or simply feel the planned shape of the wing of a car. Sennett [357] talks about the relationship between craftsman and material as a form of conversation, and Schön [350] refers to the 'back talk' of the situation, part of knowing in action. In problem-solving research it is well known that changes of representation can offer obvious solutions to what appeared to be intractable problems, and perhaps this move from internal to external is the most radical transformation of all. It is this function of externalization as an augmentation of cognitive activity that is critical in distributed cognition accounts and the study of embodiment.

transcendental—This final meta-cognitive function is the least obvious, but ultimately perhaps the most powerful[1]. Because our thoughts have been expressed externally we can peruse them as if they were any other thing. This is most obvious when we capture the abstract aspects in some way: concepts, arguments, criteria, etc. In a mind map one can see both the names of concepts written down

---

[1] Note that 'transcendental' is being used here in its meaning as a different (higher) plane or level of reasoning, not in any mystical sense.

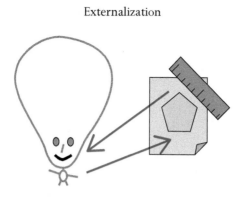

Figure 15.5 Transformational—thinking using materials

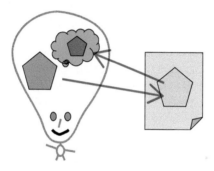

Figure 15.6 Transcendental—our thoughts and ideas become the object of thought

and also the relationships between them as connecting lines and clustered word bubbles. In an academic book, like this, one can analyse the way an argument is structured and recognize its strengths and gaps. This function is most common with symbolic representations such as words, as the symbols in some sense 'flatten' the conceptual landscape: the word 'stone' is similar to the word 'concept' or 'efficiency'. Talking about thoughts, and thoughts about thoughts, become little different from talking about feet or walking.

Without minimizing the importance of communication in the informational function, or the embodied cognition of the transformational function, we will shift our attention to the formational and transcendental aspects as it is in these that embodiment and reflection meet.

15.5 From Knowing to Knowing about Knowing

It is the transcendental function of externalization that we see at work in accounts of professional reflection. Often this is via the resistances felt through interactions with others or with the world, which then force reflection. Quist is a tutor architect in Schön's *The Reflective Practitioner* and Petra is Quist's student [350]. Quist and Petra are discussing her initial ideas for a site and her problems. Quist says, 'You should begin with a discipline, even if it is arbitrary, because the site is so screwy'. The odd patterns of contours in the site, its 'screwiness' forces Quist to step back, consider, and explicate higher-level heuristics. However, the screwiness itself was evident not from walking the terrain but from the representation in terms of contour lines on the page. The externalization allows Quist's *tacit* understanding of the spatial characteristics to operate. He notices the site feels 'screwy', and then, by articulating this, makes it available as an *explicit* issue to be faced.

'There are known knowns ...
We also know there are known unknowns; ...
But there are also unknown unknowns.'
Donald Rumsfeld, 2002

At a larger scale, Alexander's pattern language is doing just this, reflecting on centuries of craft knowledge made external in buildings and streets, and extracting from that the patterns of events and spaces that make these 'work' for people [4]. Furthermore, by making these patterns explicit, one can not only apply and teach them but also discuss them, perhaps debate whether a particular pattern is right or how patterns fit together. Similarly, by naming his six 'S's (site, structure, skin, services, space plan, and stuff), Brand was able to analyse and articulate the aspects of traditional buildings that made them able to evolve [41]. Likewise, in music theory, Magnusson describes how the need to create code means that digital instruments make explicit the knowledge that was implicit in traditional analogue instruments [273].

At an even higher level this can be seen as the ultimate success of language and the symbolic. Words allow us to talk about things and so to collaborate. However, words are also things in themselves, identifiable on the page, and yet remarkably similar in form no matter whether what they represent is concrete or abstract, verb or adjective. Recall in Chapter 4 how, in his use of archaeology to uncover past human and pre-human cognition, Mithen identifies the importance of *cognitive fluidity*, the ability to work between multiple modular intelligences (social, physical, etc.), which arose somewhere between 30,000 and 60,000 years ago [294]. This fluidity is necessary for material symbolism, and therefore essential for language; thus language cannot be the sole source for it. Alan has argued that imagination acts as an alternative cognitive connection between these modules, a pre-linguistic form of cognitive fluidity, potentially kick-starting the process that eventually led to human language [111].

Whatever its origins, language creates an important ratchet, since symbols and words are a great conceptual leveller. Once they are external symbols, we can manipulate 'wolf' and 'worry', 'heavy' and 'health', because as words they become things of the same kind, no longer animals, ideas, or concepts. At its extreme, this is precisely the agenda of the formalist movement in mathematics at the turn of the nineteenth century, but it is also the stuff of day-to-day language use. Language is one of the core tools of the transcendental function of externalization. It turns the world of ideas into the world of material 'stuff' and thus allows us to have ideas about ideas as easily as ideas about stuff, and those ideas about ideas are named, becoming material themselves and thus the subject of discussion. At each stage the level of discourse is raised, allowing us to think more generically, more conceptually.

Andy Clark sees language within a framework of external mind, as a sort of bringing of the external world into the internal [68]. The external material symbols become available in our imagination and therefore amenable to our internal means of apprehending and dealing easily with the external material world. Some writers, such as Searle [351] stress the role of language in creating reality, especially in establishing *institutional facts* (Obama was the President of the United States, because he was *declared* to be). However, Renfrew notes that it is often 'the material reality, the material symbol, that takes precedence' [340]. It seems there is a rich interplay whereby material realities shape language, but language, while not in the end limiting thought [100], does shape it, making some things easier to say and think. This then changes material culture. The fact that we have words for 'chair' and 'table' means we see the world in these terms, and so the world becomes populated with easily classifiable chairs and tables [117].

By understanding this rich interplay, it is possible to exploit it, to expose our internal categories in our external actions, and to use external tools to challenge those categories.

15.6 Language and Learning

Often, when commentators want to emphasize the transformative nature of digital technology or the web, they compare it to the acquisition of language. In the age of steam and machines one would probably have looked to the invention of the wheel, but when considering information technology language is not just an older 'technology' than the wheel but more apposite and also more fundamental. Without the wheel we would still be human, indeed many past civilizations have coped quite well without it. In South America, wheels were put on small children's toys but not used for transport. However, language is one of the quintessential aspects of being human, possibly more so even than the opposable thumb. Without language we would have no complex culture, no nations, no cities, and certainly no Internet or books.

This is not to say we are the only species that communicates; indeed signs of complex communication are seen in dolphins and elephants, and pack animals, dogs and wolves in particular, manage complex social cooperation. However, all are rudimentary in comparison to even a three-year-old's language skills.

Language enables us to learn as individuals and as communities. The most primitive form of learning, common to all life from bacteria to rose bushes to chimpanzees, is through the information stored in our DNA, age after age of adaptation through natural selection; effective, but tediously slow. Somewhat faster are crude Lamarckian adaptations[2], changes within cells that regulate DNA and allow parents to pass on to their offspring some effects of coping with the environment, though a very limited repertoire of only the simplest kind of effects, mainly to do with chemical conditions.

More developed creatures are able to learn through their own lifetime experience, with the kinds of behavioural reinforcement discovered by Pavlov and Skinner. Although we, as humans, have more complex mechanisms, we can still be conditioned just like Pavlov's dogs, whether by advertisers trying to make us associate their brand with pleasure, power, sex, or excitement, or by therapists helping us to overcome a phobia, itself quite likely the effect of such conditioning.

More complex again are creatures that can learn by imitating others: juveniles imitating their parents, adults imitating each other. This is crucial as it allows the passing on of new behaviour and arguably a form of 'culture'. It is particularly evident in the stone tools created by early hominids, who are not believed to have had any linguistic ability, but could observe and copy each other making tools. However, the ability to learn by imitation can be seen in far simpler animals. For example, blue tits in the United Kingdom learned to break open the tinfoil caps on milk bottles left on doorsteps to get to the cream on top. The rate and pattern of spread of this behaviour showed that birds were learning by observing each other.

---

[2] For a long time dismissed as a somewhat foolish alternative to more well-known Darwinian adaptation, but in recent years found to be increasingly prevalent alongside genetic adaptation.

The mirror neurons we discussed in Chapter 8 are particularly important facilitators of such behaviours, and language depends on these other forms of learning. We have physical adaptations that make language possible (for example, the structure of throat and larynx), we learn language through imitation, and we create new language to cope with new situations during life. However, language itself creates new opportunities for passing on knowledge and experience within and between generations. While we learn behaviour through imitation, it is only through language that we can fully share the reasons and context of that behaviour. Furthermore language allows storytelling, the sharing of vicarious experience.

Crucially, the learning made possible by language can spread faster and over greater distances, transcending the germ line as the focus of selective success and replacing this with groups, societies, nations, and above all culture.

15.7 The Origins of Language

By its nature language is of the air, ephemeral and passing; its only trace, once the reverberations have ceased, the impressions in our mind. The beginnings of language are therefore unrecorded amongst stone tools and the fire circle; it is only when language is represented in writing and symbol, when it leaves behind a physical mark, when prehistory becomes history, that we can have any certainty of its form or even existence.

However, despite its lack of physical trace it is widely believed that the development of language was the key factor that drove the profound social and technological changes around 40,000–70,000 BC.

Homo Sapiens have been around since around 200,000 BC, but they had originally not behaved radically differently from other early hominids. Indeed, they are now known to have interbred with Neanderthals. A combination of physical and DNA evidence means that our understanding of this period is constantly changing, and the distinctions between Homo Sapiens and earlier hominids are now regarded as less radical than once was thought. It has long been known that crude stone tools had been used by pre-human hominids, but recent evidence even suggests that some Neanderthals produced simple art.

However, despite this relative continuity, and a long period of apparent stasis in Homo Sapiens' development, in this 'socio-linguistic Eden' around 50,000 years ago it seems everything changed. Tools became more complex. Stone axes not dissimilar to those used by ancient ancestors millions of years earlier gave way to complex multi-part tools, such as axe-heads tied onto wooden shafts. Representative art began to appear, with early cave painting and carved 'Venus' figures, and the physical remains of settlements suggest larger and more complex social structures. However, these behavioural changes have no concomitant changes in the physical brain, as far as can be discerned from the inside of skulls. The change was not about what was in our heads but how we used it, and the assumption is that this was language.

We said that language leaves no physical trace, yet it is likely that its origins in both human and pre-human communication are, paradoxically, deeply physical.

The earliest beginnings can be seen in other animals. Dogs are unusual in that they can follow a pointing finger. Almost every other animal, including most apes, will look at your pointed finger, but a dog will look at what the finger is pointing towards. It is easy to see how this skill developed. A class of shooting dogs are called 'pointers' because they spot prey, such as a grouse on the moors, and silently point their noses towards it, helping the hunter to identify a target. This skill has been developed by careful breeding, but has its origin in the hunting pack.

A wolf spots prey and naturally looks towards it, but it is important not to frighten the prey away, so initially the animal is quiet and still. The rest of the pack notice the first wolf's behaviour and locate the potential prey, and they hunt it together. The crucial step is the ability to *interpret* the first wolf's behaviour as a sign.

While it is natural to think of the complexity of language being in its production—being spoken—in fact it is no use speaking without an audience. Anthropologist and linguist Robbins Burling has argued that in fact it is the *comprehension* of language that is more

critical than its *production* [50]. It is the ability to interpret initially un-
conscious and natural signs that makes it worthwhile learning to
produce more developed and artificial actions and sounds.

This effect is very obvious if you watch a parent and child. When
interacting with even the tiniest baby, the parent will treat even
the slightest grimace or sound as meaningful. This becomes more
pronounced when the young child begins to vocalize. An outsider
listening to the child's sounds may not even recognize words, and
yet the parent will appear to be able to understand every utterance.
This is partly because they are used to the particular sounds of their
child, but also because even partial attempts at communication are
interpreted in the context and the parent makes informed guesses.
In other words, the parent is using sophisticated ability to interpret,
which then amplifies the small child's attempts at language.

Returning to the wolves, once the ability to notice the natural
turning of the head and eyes is widespread, it becomes advanta-
geous for a wolf to emphasize this initially natural movement. In
the pointer breeds of dog, we have artificially developed this ability,
but this exaggerated pointing is not so different from similar exaggerated human actions. Many people who do not wear a wrist watch
will mime lifting their hand up to glance at the back of their wrist
when asked the time; the action is ineffectual, but serves as a sign to
the other.

The wrist lifting is an example of *onomatopoeic action* [116]. In spoken
language onomatopoeic words are those where the word sounds like
or emulates the thing it refers to, such as 'bang' or 'wheeze'. The turn
signals on a car have a similar role, positioned to suggest the direction
of movement, and indeed these car signals had their beginnings in
the hand signals used by early drivers, pointing the way they intended
to go. More complex is the tendency, when driving down a road, to
pull slightly towards the centre of the road when you are about to
turn into a turning (Figure15.7). If you are turning into an entrance
on the other side of the road, and the road you are on is not wide, you
have to steer out towards the edge of the road in order to get a good
'swing', so the central positioning is not ideal for the manoeuvre but
effectively tells the driver behind that you are about to turn.

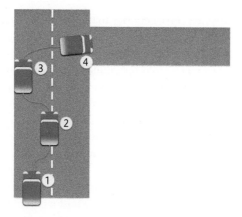

Figure 15.7 Turning right into a narrow road (from [116]): (1) normal road position; (2) initially move towards centre of road; then (3) move to the left ready for (4) swing into the narrow entrance. Step 2 is the onomatopoeic action to alert other road users of your intention.

Many of our onomatopoeic actions have become cultural norms. Indeed in the case of the turn signal the action is embedded in the car itself. Others develop more dynamically. Steve noticed that he would tend to leave the light on in his office when he left it for short periods. While this was not good from an energy conservation point of view, he realized he had been unconsciously leaving it on as a sign to say, 'I am in the building'. In some ways we are recapitulating the earliest development of language through action and gesture in our modern habits and even machines.

15.8 Interpretation

Burling's shift of focus from production to comprehension puts interpretation at centre stage. It is no good representing information if the representation cannot be interpreted—that is no better than the sealed book at the beginning of the chapter.

Semiotics is the study of the 'signs' that underpin human communication. In semiotics the term 'signs' encompasses everything from the words and sentences of language to the use of icons in a train station showing where to find the toilet, or indeed the onomatopoeic actions discussed in the last section.

Saussure, the French philosopher and father of semiotics, elaborated on the dyadic relationship between signifier (e.g. a word) and signified (the idea the word represents), but Pierce, the American pragmatist, added a third element: the interpretant. By this term Pierce (confusingly) did not mean the person who interprets but more the process of richer elaboration and eventually the 'effect actually produced on the mind' [10].

Barthes and other Postmodern philosophers increase the emphasis further towards the role of the person who does the interpretation in their distinction between readerly and writerly texts. The former, the readerly text, refers to the traditional notion of a text where the writer's meaning is paramount, and the reader passively receives that meaning, whereas the writerly text is one where the reader is expected to take an active role, effectively inscribing their own meanings and interpretations. The terms can be slightly confusing but refer to the role of the reader; Umberto Eco uses the terms closed text (fixed interpretation) and open text (multiple interpretations possible by the reader), which are somewhat more clear.

When these terms were coined they were intended to emphasize the radical nature of Postmodern writing, but if Burling is right then it is the writerly language (if not text) that is more primitive, and the active role of the writer or producer that developed later.

With the exception of totally experimental writing, even in the most writerly text the author does not write down random words but seeks a level of common meaning with the future reader. When you point, your companion may take this to mean 'look there' or 'go there', but it would be perverse to point in the opposite direction to the one you intend. Paul Grice talks about a cooperative principle in language, and Herb Clark about the way participants in conversations work towards a common ground, a shared understanding that is sufficient for the purpose or task at hand [70, 201].

When engaged in face-to-face conversation, there is a constant process of testing the meanings we have of one another's words.

Indeed, our responses even to a direct question often include a reformulated version of our interpretation of the question, and possibly also additional information. For example, imagine the British Airways desk of a London airport. If a customer says, 'I'd like a flight to Paris', the reply might be 'The next direct BA flight to Paris is in three hours. Shall I check if a seat is available?'. The reply assumes that the customer wants a direct flight, served by BA. The reply at a regional airport where there are fewer direct flights might be quite different.

When the communication is indirect, it is far more difficult to create a physical or digital representation of information or to frame words in an utterance, since there is no opportunity to test and correct misinterpretation. There needs to be an explicit or implicit sense in which the producer prefigures the act of interpretation, imagines the potential meanings and effects of the representation, and tunes it accordingly.

Of course this is equally true for the person doing the interpretation. They may second-guess the intended meaning, trying to work out why the utterance was made. The better the communication the less explicit this is likely to be. If the alarm sounds at an airport you simply scan for the green signs (which you normally ignore) and follow the arrows saying 'Exit'.

Of course, we are usually unaware of the many stages and cues that take place during the interpretation of the simplest sign. First we make decisions about whether we even need or are supposed to interpret something. How often do you read the page near the beginning of a book that lists the publisher, ISBN, etc? In an airport the signs with small letters implicitly say 'for staff eyes'; the green signs, 'for emergencies only'. Interestingly a lack of labels on a door or stairwell usually carries an added meaning: 'do not enter'!

Then, once we have decided the message is for us, we need to work out the language or symbolic system being used. Airports and train stations often use semi-realistic icons that may be part of internationally agreed sets, so there is minimal confusion. However, the same icons transposed to a different setting may have a different meaning: a picture of a plane on a road warning sign typically means 'beware of low flying aircraft', but on a direction sign shows the way to find the airport. The physical location of a sign is often part of this: the words 'Steve Gill' on a door may mean 'this is Steve Gill's office, knock if you want to find him', whereas the same words on a pigeonhole mean, 'these are Steve Gill's letters—don't peek'!

The nature of the materials also carries its own meaning. A rough cardboard notice, 'Steve Gill', may mean a temporary or new office; the same notice printed on laminate or a engraved brass plate says something about permanence or status. Going back to the examples at the beginning of the chapter, you probably don't care on which particular physical servers Instagram stores your photos; it is the photo itself that is important. However, whether your photos are on Flickr, Instagram, Facebook, or in a physical photo album speaks volumes about you and your intended audience—as Marshall McLuhan famously wrote, 'the medium is the message' [289].

It can be harder to replicate these subtle cues of context in digital media, where to some extent everything looks the same. This is one of the reasons for the problem of 'fake news': it is hard to distinguish reliable sources from cranks or clickbait advertisers. It is also why organizations often have draconian web policies. There is a clear difference in formality and authority between the glossy official university publications and the stapled sheets produced by an individual, but if everything is just pixels then everything must be subject to the same branding and quality control.

15.9 Internalization

The huge growth of humanity—it is hard to call it 'success', given that unfettered growth has brought the planet virtually to its knees—is largely because of our cognitive, social, and cultural powers, not physical strength or speed. This, with the fact that commentators, philosophers, and historians are, by their nature intellectuals, has often led to a cerebral focus. Descartes' introspective thought experiments and 'I think therefore I am' are often seen (or caricatured) as epitomizing this position. It is precisely this focus that proponents of embodiment challenge, albeit at the risk of sometimes underestimating the internal life.

Whatever one's philosophical position on current human cognition and actions, it is evident that in the early days of humanity, and certainly in the development of all other animals, the brain was the servant of the body, its function to enable the body to thrive. Even today, if the body is not cared for, not fed, watered, and kept from cold and harm, then the body will die and the brain with it. Although the exact mechanisms are not known, and maybe will never be known short of time travel into the distant past, our innermost cognitive capacities have developed in order to function in the external world and are likely to be internalizations of that external world.

As we saw in Chapter 10, neurophysiologist William Calvin regards the skills needed to throw discus-like stone hand 'axes' as both the driving force to larger brains in Homo Erectus and early Homo Sapiens, and crucial in developing the ability to perform complex sequences of actions [56]. These sequencing skills are of course essential not only for our current physical dexterity in craft or sport but also for language, where the ability to stream together multiple sounds and utterances is central.

Prehistorian Steven Mithen hypothesizes that communal singing and rhythms of dance gave rise to proto-language in the Neanderthals [295]. Again sequence is crucial, but also the sense of sharedness: that one person's feelings and actions link to those of others, a precursor to the way a great author or orator can get inside your head.

15.10 The Development of Self

It is also possible that the very idea of self, the ability to say 'I', develops initially from the outside in.

One explanation for the way our stream of thought feels almost like listening to oneself talking is that this is precisely how it originally formed [97]. Imagine the early human talking to others and hearing the words, then beginning, when alone, to use that talking to oneself as a way to order complex activities. In many of our senses the neurological impact of the intention to act is very close to the action itself, so that after a while the quieter and quieter whispering to oneself disappears: the loop from mouth to ear is bypassed internally and we talk endlessly to ourselves as a stream of consciousness.

If this explanation sounds a little stretched, listen to a small child chattering to themselves while they play.

Logical reasoning, the crown jewel of cognitivism, is also likely to have started outside the head. Imagine you are a hunter 40,000 years ago. You have the idea of getting the fastest person in your hunting group to goad a woolly mammoth and then run from it, to lure it to a place where the rest can kill it. Food for half the winter in one short hunt. However, although you have the idea, how do you convince the fast hunter to run in front of an eight-ton mammoth? Once plans become complex you not only have to express them, but also convince others that they are a good idea.

For one's own actions, or even for deciding what would be good for others to do, logic is not necessary, but actually to convince others some form of argumentation is needed: dialogue precedes logic. Of course, once one has developed the skill of expressing logically to others, this can be internalized, perhaps initially in rehearsing persuasive arguments, until it becomes recruited as a skill in its own right. One can then argue with oneself in order to check whether complex intuitive ideas make sense, or to lay out options.

Perhaps most radically, the whole idea of self may have developed early on as part of this need to be cooperative social beings [125]. If you are chasing a rabbit, it can be useful to get inside its head, to guess how it might react as you start to chase it, to foresee its actions in order to forestall its attempts to escape and win yourself a rabbit supper. Likewise when interacting with other people it is worth having some understanding of their possible reactions. This is 'first-order' theory of mind: modelling other people's and other animals' mental states.

However, the rabbit has at best a very rudimentary understanding of you, whereas when you interact with other people, they also have a model of you. So as part of your model of them, it is also helpful to have some idea of how they understand you: second-order theory of mind [277].

This is commonly seen as an inside out mechanism, because other people are similar to you and you have intentions, ideas, feelings that you project onto others, seeing them as if you were inside their heads. Clearly we do have internal models of our own bodies, so that if we feel a pain in our foot, we are able to modify our gait to avoid it, or maybe look down and pull out a thorn. Damasio argues that consciousness and complex emotion develops precisely from this inner body image into an image of self that encompasses the more cognitive and affective aspects of our being [88].

The extension from physical to cognitive and emotional self-modelling seems reasonable; cognitive development usually proceeds by adaptions of existing neural mechanisms. However, it is not so clear why early humans needed to understand themselves in this way. In contrast, the need to understand others is clear in any social situation.

Some philosophers distinguish between 'I', the first-person view of the world, and 'me' the way other people see us. They then usually posit the inner to outer movement from 'I', to 'you', to 'me'. However, the fact that we need to understand other people's model of ourself suggests the opposite: that we first understand others' actions, then build models of how they think, then begin to understand their models of us, 'me', and thus indirectly create a model of ourselves, 'I' [125]. In other words we really do see ourselves through each other's eyes.

The idea that individuality and consciousness of self emerge through sociality may sound unexpected, but in fact these abilities develop at exactly the same time in small children, a process developmental psychologist, Alison Gopnik, termed *developmental synchronies.* [277, 193]. The concept of theory of mind has been particularly important to researchers in autism, which causes problems in understanding both the beliefs and intentions of others and one's own emotional state [14].

Reproducibility

In some ways reproducibility is at the heart of digitality. The very notion of digital information and formal definitions of information theory is that an item of information is independent of physical form. The words of a book may be printed on paper, displayed on a screen, or stored in magnetic properties of a disk, but they are the same words. Hence there can be one copy of a book, or a thousand, or a million, or a billion. Each copy of *Harry Potter* is a different physical thing, but the same 'book'.

Books and text are not an arbitrary example. They are iconic of the power of reproduction of information. One of the major tasks in early seats of learning was the copying of manuscripts by monks who spent innumerable hours bent over writing desks, copying word by word. The results, such as the *Book of Kells*, are often highly individual masterpieces of artistic virtuosity, but the words are, as far as possible, identical from copy to copy. If anything, the precise copying of the Koran is even more critical than for the Bible and other Christian texts, since the precision of reproduction of the text over generations is a core element of Islam.

While reproduction was always an element of the notion of text, it was elevated to new levels with the invention of the printing press, which is often seen as a parallel to the twentieth-century digital revolution. The reproduction and distribution of information enabled by print was crucial not just in putting existing text, notably translations of the Bible, into many more hands but in accelerating the diffusion of new ideas, from the religious tracts of the Reformation to the penny newspapers of the Industrial Revolution.

Of course, rapid dissemination brought with it consequent dangers: social upheaval and political dissent, but also simple errors.

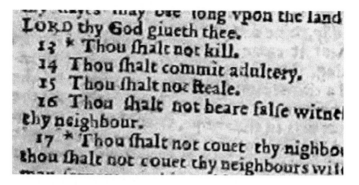

Figure 16.1 The Adulterous or Wicked Bible.

In 1631, during the typesetting of the Bible, the word 'not' was accidentally omitted from the seventh commandment (Figure 16.1). Copies of this 'Adulterous Bible' had to be recalled and destroyed quickly, and the printers were fined £300 (a lot of money in 1631) for their mistake!

The Bible is unique in terms of the number of translations, editions, printings, and versions (even discounting the occasional error), but of course other books, not least textbooks, have multiple printings and editions. When we talk about the Eiffel Tower, there is a unique physical construction in Paris to which we are referring. In contrast, when we talk about *Huckleberry Finn*, there is no such clarity. Library and bibliographic experts have developed a whole vocabulary for talking about these variations: the *work* (the central idea) may have different *editions* if it is updated, amended, or illustrated, may have multiple *printings*, or appear in different *formats* (hardback, paperback, audiobook, ebook), but in the end a library holds a particular physical copy.

In *Languages of Art*, Goodman's account of the meaning and development of musical notation [191], a central element of his argument is the way the delineated stave and notes discretize the music, making it possible both to perform it and to say with certainty whether a particular piece conforms to the written work. That is reproducibility.

Note the role of discretization here. On an analogue instrument such as a violin or trombone, it is possible to play a continuous range of notes. Within these, a certain range would be regarded as being 'C sharp', another range as 'C'. There is thus a difference between playing badly or out of tune (the note is some way from the perfect C sharp) and playing the wrong note (closer to a C).

Linguists also emphasize the importance of binary distinctions that enable one to distinguish, say, a 't' sound from a 'th' sound, or to be able to say, 'yes this is a ball' or, 'no this is not'. These distinctions allow clarity of communication and, again, reproducibility. Of course this process is not perfect, as anyone who has played Chinese whispers will know, but it increases the likelihood of successful transmission. Where ideas needed to be preserved over multiple retellings, bards would use poetic forms to increase both the *redundancy* and the memorability of the words.

Box 16.1 Redundancy

In everyday speech, to say something is 'redundant' means it is unnecessary and often unwanted. In contrast, in communications theory, redundancy is a positive term. If the same thing is said more than once, it is less likely to be lost or confused if part of the message is omitted or corrupted.

English is unusual in not having a 'double negative'. In many languages there are two words which together tell you the statement is negative, but English only has the word 'not'. For example, in French both 'ne' and 'pas' together tell you that a statement is negative. This means the Adulterous Bible would not have been possible in French, where the seventh commandment reads 'Tu ne commettras pas d'adultère'—if either the 'ne' or the 'pas' are omitted it is clear that there is something wrong.

In digital encodings redundancy is often explicitly added. For example, in barcodes and book ISBN codes a special check digit is appended. In the thirteen-digit ISBN code the first twelve numbers are alternately multiplied by 1 or 3, added together, and then 10 minus the last digit of the answer is used as the thirteenth digit.

continued

Box 16.1 *continued*

For example, for ISBN 13:9780130461094 take the first 12 digits 978013046109 and calculate the check digit as follows:

$1 \times 9 + 3 \times 7 + 1 \times 8 + 3 \times 0 + 1 \times 1 + 3 \times 3 + 1 \times 0 +$
$3 \times 4 + 1 \times 6 + 3 \times 1 + 1 \times 0 + 3 \times 9$
$= 9 + 21 + 8 + 0 + 1 + 9 + 0 + 12 + 6 + 3 + 0 + 27 = 96$

The last digit of 96 is 6, so the thirteenth digit of the ISBN is $10 - 6 = 4$.

If any single digit of the ISBN (including the check digit) is corrupted then the check digit will not correspond to the sum and hence you know there is a problem, even if you can't tell which digit is corrupted.

More complex forms of redundancy allow you to correct as well as detect certain kinds of errors.

16.1 Moulds, Plans, and Mass Production

When books are printed the pages come out the same because they are printed with the same plates. In the earliest presses these were woodblocks. Later presses used movable type on a matrix, but whatever the technology it is the plate that defines the text. Note that the physical form of the plate is not the same as the book. Not only is it metal rather than paper but the letters are mirror images of the final text. However, the reflected text on metal represents the same information as the ink on the paper; it is the information that is reproduced.

In the Stone Age each flint axe was individually knapped, albeit in large numbers on an almost industrial scale. They were effectively reproduced, but from knowledge in the head of the skilled flint worker. Archaeologists who have relearned the art of flint knapping have discovered quite how skilled you need to be to see the axe or arrowhead in the flint and create it blow by blow. Perhaps the closest equivalent today is the jeweller cutting gems; one false move and the precious diamond becomes worthless shards.

Once we get to the Bronze Age, we see the very earliest metal moulds, and each bronze axe from a single mould was identical.

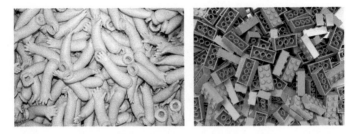

Figure 16.2 Mass production of identical items

Stone axes had been reproduced from knowledge in the head applied through the hands, but now that knowledge was reified in the stone mould from which the axes were cast. In some ways this can be seen as the forerunner of mass production, just a short hop from bronze axes to Barbie dolls (Figure 16.2).

Moulds and printing plates directly encode a design into a physical medium in such a way that it can be reproduced by inexpert or inanimate means. In contrast, plans and patterns represent a design so that someone else can reproduce it. Whereas the mould is a very direct representation of the final item, the plan is more abstract, requiring intellectual transformation: perhaps scaling, or turning a schematic drawing with measurements into a precise shape. In both there is an element of deskilling—that key move from craft to technology.

Lying somewhere between moulds and plans are scale models and templates. The former are a direct representation requiring only a systematic scaling of the elements; the latter are of the correct scale but are incomplete. The skilled craftsperson must still know how to shape a boat's timbers, for example, around the cross-sectional templates for the hull.

To some extent the Computerized Numerical Control (CNC) machine tool, laser cutter, or 3D printer is merely an extension of the plan. Instead of a human reproducing an artefact based on the plan, the job is done by a machine. The shape and design of the physical artefact is represented in bits.

From the Bronze Age mould to the MakerBot, the design is, in various ways, abstracted away and represented separately from the ultimate physical artefact. That is to say, design is essentially about information, whether that information is in the neurons in the designer's head, in moulds and templates, in plans and instructions, or in bits in computer memory. The story of the separation of design from artefact is the story of reproduction and mass production.

Adam Smith's analysis of pin-making in the eighteenth century created a conceptual vocabulary for understanding the role of technology in the manufacturing process. Division of labour was at the heart of this process, with each worker doing a simple subprocess again and again. This was valued for its efficiency, the worker becoming faster and faster at the mindless task:

> The greatest improvements in the productive powers of labour, and the greater part of the skill, dexterity, and judgment, with which it is anywhere directed, or applied, seem to have been the effects of the division of labour.
> Adam Smith, *Wealth of Nations*, opening words of Chapter I [370]

Smith introduces the idea in the work of the pin-making shop but then notes that this has been the founding principle of economic activity since the earliest days when people specialized in farming, metalworking, and other trades. Crucially, however, for the production line of the Industrial Revolution, there had to be uniformity, not only to create a standard product but so that each person performed their task on a known base. This became even more important as mechanical parts were put together. One example of this was the development of the standard screw thread, which vastly simplified manufacture and maintenance [219].

> He proceeded to dilate upon the importance of the uniformity of screws. Some may call it an improvement, but it might almost be called a revolution in mechanical engineering, which Mr. Maudslay introduced. Before his time no system had been followed in proportioning the number of threads of screws to their diameter. Every bolt

and nut was thus a specialty in itself, and neither possessed nor admitted of any community with its neighbors. To such an extent had this practice been carried that all bolts and their corresponding nuts had to be specially marked, as belonging to each other. Any intermixture that occurred between them lead to endless trouble and expense, as well as inefficiency and confusion, especially when parts of complex machines had to be taken to pieces for repairs.

(part of James Nasmyth's description of his apprenticeship with Maudslay in the early eighteenth century [369])

While Adam Smith created the intellectual roots of mass production in the late eighteenth century, the iconic image of this industrial push to standardization and reproduction was the Model T Ford (Figure 16.3), nearly 150 years later in the early twentieth century: 'any color . . . so long as it is black' [167]. Standard products are not only easier and cheaper to produce in volume but they simplify the supply chain: you know what you are getting. Twentieth-century consumerism therefore saw the sacrifice of choice in exchange for availability and cheapness.

Figure 16.3 The Model T Ford production line

16.2 Singularity and Scarcity

If a core quality of the digital and information world is reproducibility, the converse is also true: singularity is part of the essence of physicality. At the non-quantum scale, no two physical objects can occupy the same place at the same time, and each stone, leaf, and butterfly is unique. Even a pile of books fresh from the printing press, while identical, are also unique. If one is dropped and its cover scuffed, none of the others are affected. They are produced identical, but inherently singular.

As intimated, this is not necessarily true at the quantum scale. Indeed, the core difference between bosons (the most well known being photons) and fermions (including protons, neutrons, and electrons) is that while the former retain their identity, the latter are only distinct if their properties are distinct. No two identical fermions can be in the same 'state' (called the Pauli exclusion principle). This turns out to be essential for the existence of the universe. The only reason orbiting electrons do not all gradually lose energy and sink into the nucleus is that only one can be in each state (of energy and spin). The complex pattern of electron shells, which determines the properties of elements on the periodic table, occurs because each electron in an atom has to be different. If the sub-atomic scale behaved like the human scale of stone and steel, then there would be no human-scale objects, and indeed no humans.

We have seen how reproducibility is not only an essential quality of the digital world but also central to the development of mass production and the consumer society. Amazon.com was able to develop in the late 1990s because the goods it sold, books, were identical. If each book were different, you would need to look at a particular copy before you bought it. Mail order and Internet shopping would not be impossible but would certainly entail a far larger number of returns.

We have seen that the move from craft to technology has run parallel to the rise of mass production. The crucial difference is the removal of the unique role of the maker. This process began in the late medieval period, but came to fruition in the Industrial Revolution, leading to the cog-like role of the industrial worker, glorified for its efficiency by Adam Smith and Frederick Taylor, and condemned by Marx for the way it alienated workers from the products of their work.

Commoditization and uniformity has had other critics. John Ruskin, William Morris, and those in the Arts and Crafts movement sought a return to traditions of craftsmanship, not only for the sake of the worker but also for the purchaser or owner of the objects created. One almost wants to write 'consumer' here, but the notion of the 'consumer' assumes that products are 'consumed', whereas people in ages past preserved crafted items, often from generation to generation. Now the relatively costless nature of mass-produced items makes them also worthless, discardable: new fashions each year, a new phone when the contract runs out.

In both the economic and aesthetic spheres, scarcity leads to value. That is, ease of (re)production reduces value compared to the intrinsically singular nature of certain works of art or hand-crafted items. Haute couture is the antithesis of high street fashion (even if it sometimes drives it), and raku pottery and shibori dyeing glory in the not wholly predictable nature of physical processes and human imperfection.

Box 16.2 Shibori

[The actions of shibori—manipulation, compression] 'create a record of the resist-dyeing process—the imprint of the interaction between the hands and the material'
From: Yoshiko Iwamoto Wada. 'The sou-sou impulse' [406]

Printing and metal casting are iconic in the reproducibility of physical products but they have their own variants that emphasize the scarcity or singularity of the final product. Limited prints of artworks use similar techniques to large-scale printing but the number of prints is guaranteed to be strictly limited. This allows the artist to distribute multiple copies of the same work, while still retaining the cachet of scarcity.

Monoprints are produced by painting ink onto a surface, then using it as a printing block or plate to create one or more prints. Although the original inked surface may be reused more than once, the design becomes indistinct with use, so that every print is slightly different, from a sharp first print to increasingly broken and faded subsequent prints. Once the original ink has been used up a fresh, unique pattern has to be drawn.

In metalwork, lost wax techniques have a similar nature. An object is crafted in wax and then covered in heat-resistant clay. When the clay has hardened it is heated so that the wax melts and flows out. The resulting mould is then filled with metal, and when the metal cools the mould is broken off, leaving an exact replica of the original object but in brass or gold rather than wax. This is rather like the way a fossil is created. In some variants either the wax is itself produced from a mould or the mould made from the wax is cut so that it can be reused. So, while the technique can be used for mass production, the process also lends itself to unique castings.

The fact that value is associated with scarcity can be a problem for digital goods; whereas physical mass production requires large-scale capital infrastructure, digital reproduction happens at the click of a mouse. The software and music industry have struggled with this: digital rights management (DRM) attempts to prevent duplication at the level of hardware and operating systems, whereas the Federation Against Software Theft (FAST) uses the threat of legal action. In software the registration code attempts to recreate the uniqueness of a physical copy, while the music industry has simply made legal copies sufficiently cheap and easy (yet more reproduction) to compete with informal (illegal!) copying.

The closed nature of many ebook platforms has so far made this less of a problem for the publishing industry (certainly less problematic than the monopolistic dominance of Amazon.com). This may change, however, partly because of complaints that ebooks are less flexible than physical books: you can read the book on any of your devices, but can't lend it to a friend. In an odd twist, ebook publishers are even attempting to recreate the wear and tear of a physical copy by insisting that libraries are only allowed to lend an ebook a fixed number of times. The publishers argue that a heavily used physical copy would simply fall to pieces.

So digital reproduction destroys the intrinsic uniqueness of a physical copy, undermining the traditional sales channels and forcing new forms of distribution and pricing. However, its impact on physical production is no less dramatic.

Even Model T Fords were not all black, and car manufacturers today offer varied colour choices and numerous accessories and options, to the extent that for some products there are more potential combinations than potential customers. We are sold choice and individuality. Oddly, it is standardization that allows both manufacturers' customizations and third-party add-ons; the identical size and shape of every iPhone is precisely what enables the industry of cases and covers to flourish.

However, the use of digitally controlled machinery and the ease of digital transmission of choices are enabling even greater levels of customization and personalization of products. A traditional printer would produce thousands of copies of the same book and put them in a warehouse until they were sold. With print-on-demand, the configuration of machines is managed automatically. Precisely because physical reproduction encodes information in moulds and plates it necessitates slow changes and thus large runs. In contrast, reproduction based on digital information can be switched at the speed of a network connection or disk access. Furthermore the encoding of form in bits means it is more malleable, allowing, for example, the printing of one-off storybooks that include a particular child's name, birthday, friends, and family. The most reproducible technology paradoxically facilitates a new era of personalization.

16.3 The Irreproducible and Impermanent

There are some aspects of physical things and events that are irreproducible, or at least cannot be reduced to pure information: the feel of wood under your fingers, the sensation of being at sea, the buzz of a music festival. While we can list the items performed, listen to a recording, or watch it on television, none of these can reproduce what it is like to be at the Last Night of the Proms.

This is partly to do with the physical sensations, which can sometimes at least be mimicked in a 'reproduction'. Museums recreate artefacts that have already perished, or allow visitors to handle copies of objects where touching would damage the original. However, there is also something about the momentariness of experience that defies reproduction.

In jazz and improv theatre there is no attempt to follow a set score or script; instead it is the interplay of performers at a particular moment that matters. Likewise, while performance art may be thoroughly prepared, it is all about a specific performance at a specific place and time. In the fine arts the singular works of artists are presented in galleries or exhibition spaces. While not reproduced physically on the printing press, they are reproduced temporally, static, unchanging, and endlessly presenting the same face to every visitor.

Many forms of installation art seek to break this pattern, with interactive works that react to the visitor, bringing them into the work of art. Other artists take the transience of nature as part of their aesthetic, for example Andy Goldsworthy's sculptures that use twigs, leaves, and even icicles to create works that fade and decay.

While this move towards transience is recent in the fine arts, music, and drama have always valued both the timeless work of the composer or playwright and the significance of the performance. The trainee musician, and indeed the professional also, practices endlessly, developing skill and precision (for reproducibility), yet also seeks to develop interpretation and virtuosity (for irreproducibility). We recall great actors, conductors, soloists, and singers as well as composers and playwrights.

However, while the transience of the natural world means that few physical things are ever permanent, the same softness that allows decay also leaves traces and marks of the ephemeral. Enlightened landscape architects may deliberately plant grass with no paths and then watch where the natural wear patterns fall; the tracker will note a broken twig or paw-print in the earth. Books start out as identical clones from the presses, but soon have thumbed pages, notes, and underlines. And in musicology, the ephemera of concert programmes and newspaper adverts have become the subject of serious academic study alongside the composer's score.

Of course, these signs of wear often become part of the aesthetic of objects even if they are not deliberate. The restoration of fine antique furniture often seeks to create an as-if-new appearance, but in an old cottage or castle the hollow in the doorstep where countless feet have trodden sends a small tingle down the spine. In Kington, near the Welsh–English border, a portion of a yew tree bulges through an old stone wall. It is as if wall and wood grow out of each other and when you touch the wood, as touch you must, it is smooth, polished by innumerable fingertips, as if it were a sacred monument.

A sense of the importance of 'touching the past' or preserving things touched by others can be seen in all kinds of ways. For example, the recently rebuilt *Bluebird* K7 hydroplane has been very, very carefully restored, using about 85% of the original parts, painstakingly gathered from the bed of Coniston Water in England's Lake District, identified, catalogued, cleaned, and straightened before being reassembled and painted to look almost new. Three areas have been left un-retouched: the Union Jacks on either side of the tail fin and a small patch on the front of the fin where it meets the fuselage: the place where *Bluebird*'s famous pilot, Donald Campbell, used to rest his hand as *Bluebird* was pulled from the water following a run. By leaving these areas unrestored, the restoration team have sought to add extra *connection* and a kind of *authenticity* to a very carefully rebuilt machine.

What authenticity even means is not always very straightforward. Some years ago Beatrix Potter's much-loved books were reprinted in a fresh edition that went back to her original illustrations and the master plates. This caused uproar. Reprinting after reprinting had worn the plates from which the books were produced, lending a soft edge to the illustrations. The new images were crisp and bright, less of the misty-eyed nostalgia of the adult reader and more like the sharp-eyed child. Despite the fact that this new edition was as

Potter had intended, and what the first readers would have seen over 100 years ago, many protested because 'their Beatrix Potter' was that of the aged worn plates.

In the Sistine Chapel there was similar disquiet when the ceiling painted by Michelangelo was cleaned. For 500 years candles had burned there and the soot gradually coated the ceiling. A small square has been left uncleaned and it looks black and indecipherable against the bright Renaissance painting, but for many the brooding, smoke-blackened, indistinct image *was* Michelangelo, and the restoration sacrilege.

And of course, each battered Barbie doll is individually loved.

16.4 Recording

While the effects of wear and ageing accidentally leave marks of the transient, humans deliberately record, trying to capture the singular moment or singular object and reproduce it. The very word 'capture', often used when framing a photograph, betrays the almost feral quality of the singular: caged and ready to be brought out at will like a songbird in a Victorian drawing room or a tiger pacing at the entrance to a circus ring.

Whatever the sensory medium, we have devised ways to transform experience into information: drawings, text and transcripts, tape recorders, photographs, and Instagram video clips.

This is nothing modern in this. Forty-thousand years ago, cave dwellers, maybe even Neanderthals, blew pigment over their hands to leave ghostly traces of long-dead digits [390]. The Romans carved histories of victories in stone columns and triumphal arches, and Norman ladies bent for long hours over the Bayeux Tapestry.

These early forms of recording, and indeed most forms of non-textual representation, including photographs, differ from digital recording in that they are analogue in both senses of the word: they are continuous rather than discrete, and they have analogous physical form to the thing they represent.

The earliest forms of recording were also largely mediated by human eye and hand; they were an abstraction. Digital sensors are both ubiquitous and of high fidelity, enabling us to capture images more precisely than the eye, and 'see' things that would previously have been invisible, from heart rhythms and brain scans to sub-atomic events and the cosmic background. Ubiquity is evident not only in the number and scope of sensors, but in the almost constant recording of some sort taking place around us, from traditional weather stations to closed-circuit television (CCTV) and Nike wrist bands. Some of it, like the recording of old, is manually instigated or created: think of Facebook posts and Instagram photos. Some is automated, such as medical sensors or the lorry driver's tachograph.

Lifeloggers and those who belong to the 'quantified self' movement embrace this ubiquitous recording culture, seeking to capture as much of their day-to-day existence as possible. The MyLifeBits project at Microsoft has collected the historic and ongoing activities of Gordon Bell, creating database software and visualizations so that they can be cross-linked, searched, and navigated in every conceivable way [21, 302]. In a similar way, Chris Dancy (billed as 'Most Connected Human on Earth') uses combinations of software and hardware recording to enable him to detect patterns and trends in his own life; for example, discovering that he ate more calories after binge-watching TV shows but fewer if he mixed shows [89, 38].

Box 16.3 Data from a long walk

In 2013 Alan walked around the periphery of Wales: more than 1500 kilometres along rivers and mountains of the Welsh–English border and around the cliffs, estuaries, islands and beaches of the Welsh coast. There were many reasons for the walk, some personal, some research [121]. Crucially, the walk involved collecting a lot of data including the most extensive electrocardiogram (ECG) trace in the public domain [120]. Some of the data were captured implicitly by devices while he walked, some recorded explicitly:

location—GPX (GPS Exchange Format) from multiple devices, although constant issues with batteries and the occasional very odd readings

continued

Box 16.3 *continued*

bio-sensing—ECG (heart), EDA (Electrodermal Activity) (skin), and accelerometers

audio and images—captured 'in the moment' including 19,000 photographs

text—over 150,000 words of blog entries, most written in evenings and mornings during the walk, a few filled in from memory afterwards

For Alan this was a one-off exercise, but large numbers of people are now gathering and sharing extensive material every day. Alan's location was constantly available via the SPOT satellite service. Walking in remote parts of Wales this seemed innocuous, but would he have been as happy walking the streets of a large city broadcasting his position with tweets and blogs that made it clear he was carrying expensive technology? The ECG trace was gathered for research purposes, but what are the implications of this? Might a life insurer in the future use the data as part of a risk assessment, or to claim that a medical condition was pre-existing?

Given the ubiquity of recording and sensing one wonders if there are any limits. David Bell, in his discussion of Derrida's 'Mal d'archive' [99], introduces the idea of the 'infinite archive' [22]. Bell is commenting on the French obsession with memory and history, and in particular Pierre Nora's seven-volume *Les Lieux de Mémoire*, a history of France focusing on the 'sites' (places, books, events) that make the nation what it is. While Bell introduced the term to emphasize the futility of universal recording, it has become a theme in the humanities as they seek to cope with the cascading volumes of ephemera, local and personal archives that would once have been lost, if they had been collected at all.

Nora himself wonders at the value of such recording:

> Imagine a society entirely absorbed in its own historicity. It would be incapable of producing historians. Living entirely under the sign of the future, it would satisfy itself with automatic self-recording processes and auto-inventory machines, postponing indefinitely the task of understanding itself. [311]

To be fair, Dancy has used his lifelogging to gain some personal understanding, at least in regard to health, but there is a clear danger that in our efforts to photograph, share, and tweet each moment the record overtakes the experience itself.

Furthermore, Mayer-Schönberger suggests that, for privacy, personal sanity, and maintaining our public face, the critical issue for the twenty-first century is not the ability to record but the ability to delete [283]. Already we have seen people lose jobs or be forbidden access to countries because of Facebook posts, or Internet searches revealing what would once have been simply forgotten as the foolishness of youth. In 2014 the European Union Court of Justice upheld the rights of people to demand that Google and other search giants remove links to material that is irrelevant or outdated, the so-called right to be forgotten [18, 158]. However, this builds on longstanding national law that protects people from being required to divulge certain personal information, for example a criminal conviction, once a suitable period of time has elapsed.

While digital recording seems to be the ultimate shift from transience to permanence, libraries and museums are having the opposite problem, the risk of a new digital Dark Age. The British Library maintains rooms full of old or re-engineered computers, tape readers, and floppy disk drives to cope with the plethora of outdated formats they are receiving in recent personal archives. In the past a person of eminence would leave behind diaries and letters. There were physical preservation issues to prevent the paper from decaying, but otherwise you could simply read the letters. Now, not only can the physical medium that holds information decay, but the logical formats also age—a Microsoft Word document written ten years ago is often unreadable in the latest versions of the software.

The World Wide Web Consortium takes this seriously, considering long-lived bodies with whom to file standards for long-term preservation for centuries or millennia. The only candidates are a few old banks and the Vatican. However, despite their best efforts, widespread variations in the interpretation of standards and proprietary extensions mean that a ten-year-old web page is only marginally more readable than a ten-year-old word processor document. For books the situation is, if anything, worse, as minor titles become ebook-only publications and Digital Rights Management (DRM) prevents copying from the original platform.

In general, the combination of physical decay of media and the need to transform data to more up-to-date formats means that preservation of recorded information is only possible through periodic copying from medium to medium, the digital information constantly re-represented in new physical form. In Celtic Britain, bards went from hall to hall reciting tales and training their apprentices, and in numerous societies dances and songs are repeated from parent to child or elder to youth. Likewise, in the digital twenty-first century, permanence is only achieved in constant motion.

16.5 Decontextualization

We discussed earlier the way we often talk of a photo 'capturing' a scene or an event, as if the wild transience of the moment were in some way tamed in celluloid or Secure Digital (SD) card, held behind bars to be viewed later on a computer screen or video projector. As with all subjugation, whether the once proud stag's head over the doorway, or Marie Antoinette's twee *Hameau de la Reine*, in any recording there is always loss.

Tracey Emin's 'My Bed' caused significant controversy when shortlisted for the Turner Prize in 1999. The key issue was not whether it was good art (although that was certainly disputed) but whether it was art at all; there was no paint on canvas, no cast bronze, nor even constructed clay[3]. The problem with 'My Bed' was not how it was depicted but that it was simply Tracey Emin's own unmade bed; it could have been any bed on any day. Quite literally, if she had 'made' her bed in brass or acrylic there would have been no question of it being art.

What makes a great photograph? The subject matter is of course important: a spectacular mountain view, beautiful flower, or impressive building. However, not every 'snap' of the same subject by a tourist would count as a great photograph. To take a stormy sea, or dawn-washed landscape, the photographer might wait days, choosing the right weather or right time of day, and maybe return home many times frustrated, unable to find that perfect shot. Even when the conditions are right, the photographer carefully chooses a precise angle, a focus that sets some parts sharp and others indistinct, and a field of view to include some things and not others.

Alan has a photograph taken in the early morning at the Spanish Steps in Rome (Figure 16.4). Because of the time of day, the steps, usually crowded with tourists, are empty. Except that they were not: halfway up the steps the street cleaners had left a pile of black plastic refuse sacks waiting to be collected. They are not apparent in the photograph because the image is taken from the square below and the prow of the boat-shaped fountain cuts across the view, precisely blotting out the unwanted sign of the twenty-first century.

---

[3] Although it was several years later before the first pottery won the Turner Prize—craft finds it harder to be regarded as 'art' than old bed linen.

Figure 16.4 Spanish Steps in early morning

Photography is all about framing, choosing what to focus on and, equally important, what to omit.

Tracey Emin's 'My Bed' is not a random unmade bed; it was chosen for its aesthetic as well as personal significance. In the gallery we see not only the bed but also the detritus of several days spilling out over the blue bedside rug; not the whole flooring of the room, not the windows or walls, and crucially not the artist herself. The Wikipedia image of 'My Bed' is taken while Tracey Emin is (re)making it in the gallery, her shoulder visible over the back of the bed as she carefully manipulates the sheets to recreate (or create) the image of the 'unmade' bed.

Until the advent of social history, traditional history was often criticized for telling the past through the lives of kings, queens, and the rich, not ordinary people. However, that is precisely because the written records are the records of the powerful, deliberately— or simply negligently—leaving out the 'unimportant' details. All information is selective. Like Borges' map, the record of everything tells you nothing. The power of information (and art) is in what you choose to leave out.

Yet this loss, though essential, is problematic.

In Plato's *Phaedrus*, Socrates criticizes the way the written word loses the immediacy of the moment that it relates. Given that Plato is committing the words of Socrates to writing, there is an irony in *Phaedrus*, which it is hard to believe Plato did not intend but seems largely ignored by commentators. This said, the point stands, whether of the written word, or even the spoken word; any retelling is distant from the thing it tells. Moreover when a third party tells the story, or when the story is committed to print, there is a lacuna, with no person present who was there, who could reconnect the words to life.

In digital recording this danger is even greater. The apparent fidelity of the medium belies the ease of tacit or deliberate bias in selection, let alone editing.

During the 2003 invasion of Iraq, a short video clip was circulated on social media. The clip was filmed through the back of a US Army truck driving through the streets of an Iraqi town. Through the open back you could see children excitedly following. If you stopped the video at this point the message was obvious: Iraqi children fêting the liberating heroes. However, if you watched right to the end, intentionally or otherwise, at the edge of the frame you caught sight of a water bottle being held enticingly. Now the message is different, cruel soldiers taunting poor war-weary children with fresh water in towns where the infrastructure has been destroyed by the invading army. But maybe this is still only half a story. Perhaps moments later the truck pulls up and starts to distribute bottles of clean water: benevolent soldiers offering essential humanitarian aid.

Loss of context is also an important issue for privacy. Almost all discussions of digital privacy are about reducing or controlling the flow of information. The assumption is that less information exposure means less of a threat to privacy. However, we are also aware of the danger of things taken 'out of context' and there are many occasions where less information is a greater threat to privacy because of the danger of misinterpretation. Imagine a businessman who has told his wife he is 'working late' but in fact has been with a young woman. If his wife should learn this fact he might also want her to know that the woman is a silversmith who is making a necklace for a forthcoming wedding anniversary [147].

These 'less is more' issues also occur with more diffuse information:

> A parent may drive his child 100 metres down the road to school because the road is unsafe to cross. On the way, he passes an observer measuring road usage. Because the road is used such a lot it is widened, attracting more traffic and thus making it more dangerous. [147].

Of course, as Socrates pointed out, physical preservation also has dangers of loss of context. A wild animal in a zoo or safari park, or an archaeological exhibit in a museum, can lose its meaning when taken out of its original environment. In this case the ability of digital materials to record and replay may serve to reduce this loss of context. For example, a zoo could have videos of animals in the wild alongside their enclosures, or an archaeologist might use digital scans and GPS to record the precise location of an object when it is uncovered.

So, while the danger of digital information is that context is lost it is also possible to use digital means to keep track of where information came from and how it has been processed. The representation of this *provenance* information has become an area of study in itself with its own challenges of data representation and visualization.

17

Embodied Computation

17.1 The Physics of Information

It is obvious that if you create electronics to do computation, it is bound to use energy, and, in general, the faster you run the clock of a processor the more energy it uses and the more heat it generates. While manufacturing processes have constantly reduced the physical size of chips, the dissipation of this heat has become more and more critical. At a small scale, computers have to be carefully designed, rather like a building for a hot summer's day, with heat sinks, fans, and natural convection paths. At a larger scale, data centres are being built in Iceland and similar countries in order to minimize cooling costs, and the Semiconductor Industry Association has estimated that by 2040 data computers and data storage will consume more energy than the world can generate [368]. Given the need to reduce carbon footprint, this is clearly not sustainable!

To some extent these concerns are about current technology. There is some work on using DNA for data storage that can last almost indefinitely, and quantum computing has moved from theory to practical engineering. However, there are fundamental limitations.

Shannon and Weaver's development of information theory in the 1950s showed that the information capacity of any communication channel was governed by the ratio of the power of the signal and the level of noise: if you want to be heard in a noisy room, you have to shout louder. While noise can be decreased with better materials, quantum uncertainty means that there are inviolable limits beyond which it cannot be further reduced, which consequently limits the amount of information that can be transmitted. Similar arguments put a limit on the amount of information that can be stored in a given amount of space.

Computing itself is more complex, partly because we have no measure of computation in the sense that we do for information. Computation is effectively about transforming representations of information. It never creates information[1]; however, it can lose it. Think about a simple whole-number adding machine. Given the input $\{2,3\}$ it outputs '5'. The numbers that go in uniquely determine the result, but you cannot work out what they were, given the result '5'. It could have been $\{3,2\}$, $\{1,4\}$, or $\{4,1\}$. A whole-number multiplying machine clearly does more complex computation, and also loses information, but it actually loses less than an adding machine, since there are typically fewer possible inputs for any output. Indeed, in the case of a prime number (such as 41) there are precisely two possible inputs ($\{1,41\}$ and $\{41,1\}$).

This loss of information is important because, paradoxically, the physics of entropy means that losing information requires energy. The more information you lose, the more energy you need. Because of this, some theoretical computer scientists have investigated *reversible computing* (also called *adiabatic computing*), computations where you can always recover the input from the output. For example, instead of a simple adder you would have a machine that outputs both the sum and the difference. The idea is that if there is no information loss, there is no theoretical limit to how little energy you need.

In practice, of course, even reversible computations consume energy and happily we are still many orders of magnitude from the point where these theoretical limits become the real constraints. Indeed, in many ways it is in physics itself that they are more critical.

The connection between information and physics goes back many years; the use of the term entropy in both is no accident. In the nineteenth century, mathematicians were trying to work out the fundamental limits of mechanical systems and steam power, addressing

[1] The possible exception to the 'not creating information' rule are true random number generators such as ERNIE [316], which used to allocate winning numbers for the UK Premium Bonds.

both theoretical and practical issues of whether it was possible to create a perpetual motion machine, and how much power you could extract given a certain amount of burned energy. Of particular importance were the exiled father and son Lazare and Sadi Carnot, who developed the first insights into what is now called thermodynamics, and later Rolf Clausius who coined the term 'entropy' and the second law of thermodynamics that entropy (disorder!) always increases.

A key insight from Clausius is that you can only do useful work from heat where there is a difference: if two steam vessels are at an identical temperature, no matter how hot, you cannot use them to drive an engine, but once there is difference in temperature between them you can extract power. The connection to what we would now call information was made more explicit by Ludwig Boltzmann; in the theory of 'statistical mechanics', he related entropy to the number of possible states of a system:

entropy $= k \log(N)$
where
    N = number of states
    k = Boltzmann's constant 1.38×10^{-23} Joules/Kelvin

In the 1950s, when Shannon was first developing the ideas of information theory, the early computer pioneer John von Neumann suggested that Shannon called one of his measures 'entropy' partly because of the parallels with the thermodynamic definition, and partly because 'no-one understands entropy'!

Going back to the nineteenth century, Maxwell posited a thought experiment to break the second law of thermodynamics and hence potentially create limitless power.

He envisaged a demon (Maxwell's demon) who can open and close a tiny door between two steam vessels (A and B). If the demon spots a molecule in vessel A that is travelling slower than the average speed in vessel B, he opens the door to let it through to vessel B. When he sees a molecule in vessel B that is faster than the average speed in vessel A, he opens the door to let it through to vessel A. Over time, vessel A becomes hotter (more energetic molecules) and vessel

B cooler, thus reducing entropy and creating the potential for usable work.

While in the nineteenth century this was a purely philosophical idea, it is now close to realizable as nanotechnology creates molecular-sized machines. But very early it was surmised that the act of measuring the speed of the incoming molecule would cause an increase in the entropy of the demon. In other words, the work done to measure and open and shut doors would be more than the work gained through the temperature difference. In the early twentieth century this was made precise, using the identical arguments that give rise to the fundamental limits for computation described earlier.

At a more normal scale, effects not dissimilar to Maxwell's demon underlie the sonic boom when an aircraft breaks the sound barrier, and put a limit on how fast you can send speech through air: the speed of sound. The speed of sound in air is determined from equations relating pressure and movement in a fluid, effectively the bulk physics of octillions (millions of millions of millions of millions) of air molecules. However, just as with Maxwell's demon, some molecules will travel faster than the speed of sound. One might think that these could pass messages faster than sound travels in the bulk material, just like someone running quickly through a slow-moving crowd, and indeed this is true, but only over a tiny scale. The mean free path of a molecule in air, the distance before it is likely to bump into another, is less than a ten-thousandth of a millimetre. If the collision is head on, then the forward energy is preserved. However, glancing collisions mean that some of the forward energy is turned into sideways movement in effectively random directions. Within a millimetre any information carried by the original fast-moving molecule will have been diluted a trillion-fold.

You hear the sonic boom because the air ahead of the aircraft cannot know that the plane is coming!

Information is also central in both quantum mechanics and Einstein's theory of relativity.

In quantum mechanics, we have all heard of the Heisenberg uncertainty principle: you cannot perfectly measure both the momentum and position of a particle at the same time. The more you know about one, the less you know about the other. Furthermore, the act of observation has almost uncanny effects (not least Schrödinger's unfortunate cat), which physicists and philosophers still debate. Observation, information, and knowledge, not only intimately part of theoretical debate, but intimately involved in the equations and experiments of fundamental physics.

At a cosmic scale, Stephen Hawking used laws of thermodynamics and information to argue that black holes cannot swallow information and hence that they must in fact not be black but instead emit 'Hawking radiation'. This has not yet been observed, although to some extent our lives depend on it, since physicists at CERN use this as part of the safety argument that if tiny black holes were to be created in the Large Hadron Collider they would (in theory!) immediately evaporate because of this effect.

Other aspects of the curious relationship between information, relativity, and quantum mechanics can be observed in the lab. It's often said that nothing can happen faster than the speed of light, but more accurately it is *information* that cannot be transmitted faster than this. Experiments using quantum entanglement and the strange effects of observation show that there can be effectively instantaneous effects at a distance. It is just that you can only tell that they happened after the event; there is no information transfer. Although this sounds very esoteric, in fact these same curious 'action at a distance' effects are being used to prevent eavesdropping in quantum-based encryption and communication systems.

These interconnections are leading some physicists to propose that information is not only a useful way to talk about physics, but in some sense *is* physics.

> Understanding space time, and the route to a more unified picture of nature generally, lies in treating information—not matter and energy—as the most fundamental thing in the universe. *New Scientist*, September 2016 [71]

17.2 Turing Machine or Touring Machine?

The Turing Machine is one of the most iconic elements of computer science. Alan Turing worked on the practical aspects of creating machines for code-breaking at Bletchley Park during the Second World War. This was informed by his more theoretical investigations of the fundamental nature of computation. He tried to imagine the simplest possible computing machine, what is now called the Turing Machine.

A Turing Machine consists of an infinitely long tape, containing rewritable cells, each of which can be one of a finite number of symbols. In Figure 17.1 they are drawn as binary 0s and 1s, but any small finite set has effectively the same power (albeit that the representation on the tape is longer if they are restricted to 0s and 1s). The 'machine' itself sits on the tape, and can inspect a single cell at a time, rewrite it if desired, and move the tape back and forth a cell at a time under it. Inside the machine there is a single finite state memory, and a rule table with rules of the form:

current state—current tape symbol= >new state—new tape symbol—movement direction

Turing believed that a Turing Machine with a suitable set of rules could also compute any problem that it was possible to calculate mechanically or electrically. This belief was reinforced when Turing and Alonzo Church showed that Turing Machines were equivalent (in power) to Church's Lambda calculus (one of the other foundations of computer science), which addressed the similar issue of mathematical computability but from a completely different direction (more like a modern programming language).

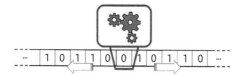

Figure 17.1 The Turing Machine—tape moved depending on rules

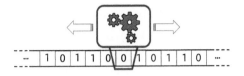

Figure 17.2 A touring machine—the Turing Machine moves while the tape is still

It is assumed in computing that it is indeed the case that these do represent the fundamental limits of computation, but that is strictly still an open question, known as the 'Church–Turing thesis'. However, what is certain is that all modern forms of digital computer are effectively 'equivalent' to suitable Turing Machines—as long as you have a *very* long tape and don't mind *how long* you wait for the answer.

So far so good, but just imagine a Turing Machine that is going to solve a real problem. Think of the tape, whether paper, as would probably have been in Turing's mind, or magnetic tape, lots and lots of it. Big coils would pile up near the machine as it pushed and pulled the tape back and forth, but every so often it would need to pull on a taut end of the tape. A relatively short tape would be fine, but to solve harder and harder problems the tape must get longer and longer, and thus heavier and heavier, and pulling on it would snap the tape near the read head. In fact a real Turing Machine would almost certainly need to be a touring machine (Figure 17.2), with the machine moving back and forth over the tape, or perhaps, like a giant game of hopscotch, writing and rewriting symbols on the ground.

17.3 Physical Locality of Computation

The Turing Machine as touring machine is not just whimsy but reflects the deeply physical nature of all computation.

1. only a finite amount of data can be stored in a physical space—in the case of the Turing Machine, large amounts of data require long tapes, which in turn are physically heavy

2. only a finite amount of computation can occur in a physical space—the Turing Machine has a relatively simple rule set; the complexity of calculation happens through repeated computation over time. Other variants of Turing Machines can have multiple machines working on the same tape, rather like some massively parallel super computers, or some cloud-based data processing platforms such as Google's Map-Reduce [93].

3. for computation to occur, the computational engine, the data, and the code must all be present in the same place and the same time. In the case of the Turing Machine, the machine (engine) and rules (code) are together, and the tape (data) is pulled until it is under the read/write head (data moves to code + engine)

While the computational engine is usually fixed in one place (actual 'touring' machines are rare!), you can see many variations in the way code and data move around networks. In a PC, both data and code are fetched from the disk (and from random access memory (RAM), at a finer scale) to run on the computer processing unit (CPU) (code and data go to engine). In many database-powered web systems, SQL queries (code) are sent from the web server to the database server (data and engine) to execute (code goes to data). However, the results of the query are then typically sent back to the web server for further processing (data goes to code) [337].

17.4 Time and Distance

The need to constantly shift code and data around creates delays; transmission always takes time, whether through electrical current in a wire, light along an optical fibre, radio waves bouncing from a satellite, or stretched string between tin cans.

For wireless or optical fibre connections, the raw transmission speed is close to the speed of light: about 30 million km per second. For electrical connections, the speed is typically between 0.5 and 0.75 of the speed of light: up to 20 million km/s. This all sounds fast until you think about a modern processor running at up to 4GHz. In the

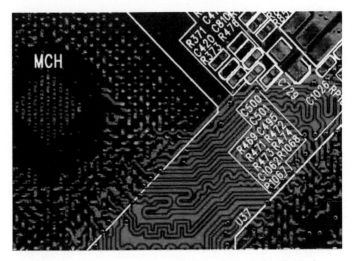

Figure 17.3 Circuit board showing meandering tracks to equalize electrical propagation delays

time of one clock 'tick', light travels just 7cm and electrical signals 3–5cm.

The external bus in a computer typically runs a little slower than the processor itself, but still it is clear that if a circuit board is badly designed so that the copper tracks are not made as short as possible, it becomes less like a face-to-face conversation between components and more like communication by carrier pigeon. Paradoxically, if you look at a circuit board you can sometimes see wires that apparently meander (see Figure 17.3); however, this is so that multiple tracks between two components end up the same length. Delays are bad, but far worse if signals are not in time with each other.

Human-to-human communication is not quite as sensitive as chip-to-chip, but the distances that we deal with are orders of magnitude larger. You notice this sometimes on an international telephone call, or on TV when a reporter in the field is talking to a presenter in the studio via satellite link. If the delay is no more than 200 milliseconds (ms) we don't really notice it, but above that it becomes harder and harder to communicate because the natural small

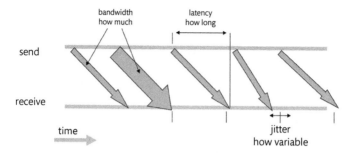

Figure 17.4 Network measures: bandwidth—how much can be transferred in a given time; latency/delay—how long do you have to wait; jitter—how variable is the delay

breaks we use in speech to synchronize one another and 'pass the floor' to each other are only a fraction of a second long. News presenters and reporters become quite skilled at managing the gap, sometimes even trailing a word or two after a question in order to cover the momentary silence, but without training or experience it can lead to breakdowns in communication.

You might think this is just poor technology, but in fact it is a fundamental limitation caused by the speed of light and the size of the earth that can *never* be entirely removed (Figure 17.4). Imagine talking to someone the opposite side of the earth using a dedicated unbroken fibre-optic telephone line. It takes approximately 70 ms for a beam of light to get halfway round the world; that is, the absolute minimum delay is about 1/14 of a second. The round-trip time, the minimum time before the other end responds and you hear the response is twice that, about 1/7 of a second or 140 ms. This is very close to the 200 ms limit. In addition, we notice breaks in lip synchronization of just tens of milliseconds, so it is important that video and audio are packaged together.

Of course, this is a theoretical limit, with imperfect optical transmission, repeaters, routers, and copper-based networking all slowing the actual time. In practice, land-based communications can get close enough to this limit so that the delays are not really noticeable, but satellite-based communications have to take far longer routes up to the satellite and back down again, leading often to a second or more of delay, hence the expertise needed by the TV presenters.

Again note that the 150 ms round-trip time is the absolute minimum. The only way to speed this up would be to drill a hole through the centre of the earth, which would undoubtedly have its own problems and still only reduce the delay by a third. However, we should also be grateful that the earth is just 12,700 km in diameter. If we could live on Jupiter, which is ten times wider than the earth, the round-trip delay would be 1.5 seconds, and long-distance telephony would be almost as uncomfortable as the 250 mph winds.

17.5 Finitude and Moore's Law

While we already operate near the physical limits of the speeds of data transmission, processors just seem to get faster and more powerful all time. In 1965 Gordon Moore, co-founder of Intel, graphed the transistor density of microprocessors over time. He noticed an approximate doubling every twenty-four months, and conjectured that economic drivers and technological improvements would see this continue for the foreseeable future. This exponential reduction in size and growth in power is now called Moore's Law, although the period usually cited is eighteen months, because of another Intel executive who factored in improvements in performance as well as density.

Fifty years on, this prediction has largely stood the test of time, with a modern-day phone having more raw computing power (and a lot more memory) than the earliest supercomputers. There are arguments that the rate of growth will slow, for a variety of reasons, and requirements such as power consumption may take centre stage in microprocessor development as mobile devices become more important. However, whether it doubles every eighteen months, twenty-four months, or three years, computers have relentlessly increased their power to size ratio, and will continue to do so.

On the one hand this means that desktop computers have become steadily faster, at least in raw processing speed, with progressively larger disks. In the early 1980s, a 360 KB floppy disk was 'mass storage', whereas thirty years later a 360 GB disk is standard and a terabyte hard disk is a cheap upgrade. In other words, a million fold increase in thirty years, exactly doubling every eighteen months.

Networks, despite having fundamental limitations on delay, have also undergone similar changes with increased speed and decreasing costs. Thirty years ago, thirty characters per second (300 bits/s) was deemed a good communications speed. Even around the turn of the millennium during the years of the dot.com boom and massive growth of the web, domestic Internet speeds were measured in hundreds of bytes per second (ps) and 1 KBps was considered fast, whereas now a typical (urban) broadband speed might be 10–50 Mbps, a near doubling every eighteen months over the last twenty years.

Box 17.1 Bits and Bytes

Memory sizes are almost always measured in bytes, where 1 byte stores approximately one character. So a terabyte disk stores approximately a trillion bytes, enough to store 300,000 copies of the Bible, or the contents of a medium-sized library.

Network speeds are a little more confusing, as they are sometimes measured in bits per second and sometimes in bytes per second. The former is written as bps and the latter Bps—as we said, a little confusing! Strictly there are eight bits in a byte, but in practice there are a few bits used for starting and stopping, so the real difference is closer to 10:1. Therefore a 50 Mbps network (50 million bits per second) is delivering approximately 5 MBps (5 million bytes per second). If your finger slips on the shift key it makes a big difference!

Of course, this does not mean that the applications we use are a million times faster, nor that we actually store a million times more stuff. The amount of data storage needed for the 'same' thing, for example a word processor document, also seems to rise exponentially, although fortunately more like every two to three years. This is partly because of higher resolutions in images and movies and greater use of images in documents, and partly more verbose data storage formats. In the early days, when disk memory was

computation.docx	18:47	139 KB	Microsoft Word document
computation.rtf	18:47	942 KB	Rich Text Document
computation.txt	18:45	10 KB	Plain Text Document

Figure 17.5 Different storage mechanisms for the same text

tight, data formats were highly optimized with dense proprietary binary formats. Now, Microsoft Word, for example, uses XML and similar formats. At one point during the writing of this chapter, while the plain text was a mere 10 KB, the Word document was 139 KB, fourteen times bigger (Figure 17.5)—the majority of which is due to the document 'thumbnail' for use in previews, weighing in at 100 KB.

Code is subject to the same profligacy. Because processors are faster it is possible to do more than would have been possible thirty years ago (e.g. real time spell checking), and at a higher display resolution, although the latter has only grown by a factor of 10 or so over the period. However, the main reason that all technology is not lightning fast is that, like document storage formats, the code of applications is written in ways which are easier to engineer but require more processing power and more memory, necessary because the increasing complexity of added features would otherwise make software even more fragile than it is. An interesting example of this is the way many desktop applications are partly written in JavaScript, the 'web page' language, which is powerful and easy to program, but very hard to run efficiently.

17.6 Smaller and Smaller, More and More

Recall the 'How many computers?' exercise in the Introduction. Some of the objects around your home might simply not have existed without digital technology, notably the mobile phone. Others, however, have simply changed their form, for example car keys or cameras. Sometimes the use of digital technology allows new functionality (e.g. editing the images on your camera); at other times it is simply cheaper, or an alternative or more convenient way of doing the same thing, like opening your car door.

The proliferation of digital technology arises from Moore's Law: the trend that gives us more and more powerful computers for the same cost and size also means that the same power of processor gets smaller and smaller. Computation has infiltrated almost every area of modern life and an increasing number of material objects, a process Adam Greenfield calls 'Everyware' [199]

There are two ways in which this works out. The first is in the digital augmentation of individual objects, such as a liquid crystal display (LCD) weight display built into a kitchen spoon, a smart salt-shaker, or near-field communication (NFC) chips in packaging to enable easy checkout at supermarkets. The second is in the way individual small devices can communicate, either point to point or via the Internet.

While the chip in the can of beans does not need any interaction or instruction beyond the checkout till, designing for digitally augmented devices poses major challenges. Although there may be instructions when you unpack your digital kitchen spoon, it needs to be self-explanatory as you actually cook. With computer tasks you can often break off the task to check a how-to video, but if you did that with a kitchen spoon, the milk would have boiled over, and anyway, explanations are difficult with a tiny screen or no screen at all.

In the dystopian future of the 2002 film 'Minority Report', while the hero eats breakfast the cereal packets speak and display advertising messages. There are still a few years to go before this becomes reality, but think about speaking greeting cards and numerous children's toys: digital technology is already not just ubiquitous but disposable. In some ways disposable technology deals with one of the main problems for ubiquitous computing—power. A single use, soldered-in battery can last until the greeting card (or cereal packet!) is discarded. The downside is that the disposal of electronic waste is already a major issue. Applying cradle-to-cradle design thinking to a laptop computer is difficult enough without needing to consider every cereal packet.

We can see that the digital augmentation of individual objects has enormous impact and design opportunities in itself, but it is potentially even more transformative when such objects are able to communicate with one another.

This technology has been used in industrial applications for many years with remotely controlled and monitored pipelines and chemical plants, and sensor networks, hundreds of tiny sensors that talk to one another to create large-scale views of, say, a river flow for environmental protection, or troop movements in a military situation. While this technology has become crucial to the management of many areas from energy to agriculture, it has largely been 'behind the scenes' for ordinary consumers. However, applications are becoming increasingly apparent, for example bus stops that can tell you when the next bus is due.

In the home itself, the Internet fridge, heralded and indeed manufactured for twenty years, has been very slow to mature. Services such as Nest are changing this, often starting with home heating, where there are obvious benefits in terms of greater control. While we saw some of the potential for bad uses of this type of device in Chapter 13, the true good/bad balance is yet to fully emerge.

Imagine you have a home assistant such as Alexa, and that kitchen spoon with the integrated light-emitting diode (LED) weight display. If you are in the middle of cooking you could ask Alexa, 'how do I change the spoon to show ounces instead of grams?'. Even without direct connection, it is possible to ameliorate some of the potential usability issues of embedded devices. However, now imagine the spoon is network connected (perhaps inductively recharged in your electronic utensil jar). You are in the middle of cooking and you ask Alexa, 'what is this in grams?' or even, 'how many spoonfulls have I put in so far?'.

Note how this potentially both improves the user experience with the spoon and removes any need for it to have a separate display, reducing components and probably making it easier to have the electronics fully encased and hence washable.

We have previously seen various ways in which the Internet of Things is vulnerable to misuse. Stuxnet, which was used to attack Iran's nuclear enrichment programme, was the first and in many ways most successful cyber-weapon to date. However, it did not even need a network connection, but spread through universal serial bus (USB) drives [432]. Stuxnet is generally believed to have been the product of a clandestine Israeli and US programme, but the technical ability to perform such attacks is now widely available, not only to governments but to criminal and terrorist groups, among others.

Part of the threat arises from lack of awareness. Developers and users of computer software are used to thinking about malware, but until recently industrial devices were either disconnected, or on closed networks. However, there are instrinsic issues, cost being an obvious one. The effort one might put into securing an Internet-connected fridge is easier to justify on a £1000 price tag than on a £10 digital spoon. That may change as off-the-shelf electronics becomes more standardized, with large enough volume to offset the low cost per item. More fundamental is the trade-off between security and usability: a relatively complex but one-off procedure may be acceptable to connect a smart TV, but not for an Internet-connected greeting card you will discard in a few days.

Spoons and cards may seem small as candidates for digital augmentation, but they are still relatively large compared with other current and emerging technologies. Recall Firefly intelligent lighting (Box 2.1), which puts a tiny network-enabled computer behind every LED in large-scale display lighting. A typical display may have tens or hundreds of thousands of computers. At first this sounds like profligacy but in fact it can reduce costs and even potentially environmental impact. While adding a computer to every light seems like technological overkill, the fact that this is mass manufacture reduces the cost substantially. Note that in Firefly the complexity has been *commodified*—this will be an increasingly common story as the Internet of Things market grows, and we will return to it in Chapter 21.

Researchers at Georgia Tech are taking this a stage further with work on computational skins. We have already discussed some of the power issues of larger and larger demand for computation. Currently, the world production of silicon wafers, the raw material for all kinds of semi-conductors from solar cells to processor chips, is about 10,000 million square inches (the standard measure) [356]. This is a large figure, the area of a medium-sized town, but world glass production is a thousand times greater in terms of the surface area produced.

Those researching computational skins are considering the potential applications of covering large-area materials such as glass, roofing, and wall cladding with relatively low-density computational circuitry. While it might be used simply to make the material smarter, perhaps helping environmental control, it could also be utilized for actual computation. Low-density computation could scavenge energy from the environment.

While it is odd enough talking to your teaspoon through your voice-activated house computer, it is even less clear how we design ways to talk to a smart wall, or for that matter 100,000 digital lights. With Firefly we talk, not about the lights going on, but in terms of their effect, 'I want that area of space lit up'. Perhaps we need a whole new way of thinking about communicating with and about computers.

17.7 Stand Up and Walk—Robots Come of Age

Although we have seen that all computation is ultimately physical and embodied in the world, the most obvious form of embodied computation is the robot.

Once the dream of science fiction, and then for many years bolted to the factory floor, robots are now coming of age, from autonomous vacuum cleaners and mowers to self-driving cars and the inevitable sex-bots.

The boundary between automation and robotics is blurred. In Chapter 2 we discussed the ways in which lifts might be considered to be robots. The level of autonomy in a lift is quite low; in some ways it is more like a light switch: you press the button and it does what it is told. Parcel delivery drones and driverless vehicles, however, need to include sophisticated artificial intelligence. In the latter, this will include implicit or explicit 'moral' decisions. For example, if someone steps into the road in front of a self-driving car that is carrying passengers, does it endanger the passengers by swerving, or the pedestrian by continuing straight?

The embedding of values in computation is not new, of course. When a banking system refuses to make a rent payment, this may lead to eviction. The decisions Facebook makes about which posts to show you may affect your behaviour, mood, and mental health. It is the direct physical effects of robotic actions that seem different. The potential for physical movement makes the need for coherence between physical and digital design even more important than for more passive digital devices. Sometimes this may involve a trade-off between whether you design certain eventualities into physical or digital aspects. For example, a robotic vacuum cleaner could be a trip hazard. Do you choose to colour the device bright yellow and black so that people can easily see where it is and avoid it, or do you design the sensors and software so that it quickly scurries out of the way when a person approaches? If its motor is reasonably noisy, you might simply ensure it is always moving when it is in the middle of the room, and rely on that to make it audibly present.

Note how design here is about not only the robot, but the way the robot fits into the household ecosystem. This is equally true for self-driving cars. On the one hand, the car needs to understand the way other road users behave, including the ones who don't quite keep to the official rules. On the other hand, the behaviour of the car needs to be predictable for others; recall how human drivers use *onomatopoeic action* to alert others to their intentions (Chapter 15).

Household assistants, such as Alexa, while they do not move themselves, have physical effects on the house, controlling lighting, heating, or other appliances. As we saw in Chapter 14 , they are there to give us a focus. They are typically abstract in design, more like a vase or an ornament than a robot. They are neither anthropomorphic (imagine a head sitting on the table, complete with moving lips!), nor completely disembodied like the 'Star Trek' ship computer. The former would be creepy, but in some ways the latter might seem a more obvious design choice, requiring no physical space in the room, with no risk of clashing with the household aesthetic, and more directly corresponding to the distributed nature of the services and appliances it is controlling.

The robots of science fiction, however, usually look like humans, and indeed there are good reasons for designing robots this way (though for dramatic effect they may just be meant to look creepy).

17.7.1 Environment

The first reason is that robots have to operate in a human environment. Current robot vacuum cleaners usually can't climb stairs, but a general-purpose robot helper would need to be able to do that, to go through doorways, reach cupboards designed for human heights, and use appliances and utensils designed for a human hand. This does not mean a robot needs to look exactly like a human, but to function in a human environment a humanoid robot is the obvious option.

Once released from the close confines of the home, on a factory floor, or in public places, some of these constraints can be lifted, even for general-purpose robots. For example, for rough terrain four-legged (somewhat insectoidal) robots may perform better and move faster (just as a horse is faster than a person), or for built environments or factories, combinations of legs, wheels, and body and arm positions that are definitely not human may be better.

Note that in both cases, robot design is ecological. The nature of the environment and the other agents, human and robotic, all need to be considered. In a factory or warehouse with many robots, the environment (shelf heights, passageway widths, etc.) may even be deliberately designed to be suitable for robot rather than human use.

17.7.2 Embodied communication

The second reason for designing robots with human attributes is to do with human communication and empathy. Give us a machine, from car to kettle, and if it behaves in any way that appears to be intransigent or benign, we talk to it, admonishing it or opening our heart to it. In some airports you may be greeted by a full-size human projection giving instructions, carefully filmed so that the person moves, but always stays exactly the same shape as the cut-out onto which they are projected. On the web, chatbots engage in vaguely human-like conversations. Unsurprisingly, it is often meet-and-greet-style interactions that are the focus of work on the most realistic robots, especially on robotic faces that can create expressions beneath artificial skin.

Occasionally these robots step perilously close to the *uncanny valley*. The idea of the uncanny valley was identified in 1970 by a robotics professor, Masahiro Mori [297]. He noticed that as robots (of the time) were made more and more human-like, they initially had more positive appeal, until there came a point when there was a dramatic reversal. The very human-like feels odd, uncanny (a key example was a prosthetic hand). Parallels are often drawn with zombie films: the most disturbing beings are those that seem almost human and yet unhuman in some respect.

There are debates about whether this effect is simply about mismatch: if different aspects all approach human-ness in the same way, the uncanny feeling may not occur. And will the idea of what level of human-ness feels uncanny change with culture and exposure to robotics? Even in his original paper, Mori includes *Bunraku* puppets, a traditional Japanese life-size puppet, which he considers to have come out on the other side of the uncanny valley: a sufficiently human-like robot might appear human enough to no longer feel uncanny.

Mori focuses on a number of features that may create the effect, noting especially that movement intensifies the valley. He also notes that there certain examples, including the *Bunraku* puppets and carved movable wooden hands, which seem less uncanny than prosthetic limbs, perhaps because they are more clearly not flesh to begin with. One way robot designers typically avoid the uncanny valley is to base their designs on animals, cartoon characters (big eyes), or simply things that are obviously robots and yet in some way friendly or endearing (often more big eyes). Often such robots are not apparently very 'intelligent', but respond more empathetically, for example showing signs of pleasure at being stroked or looked at.

17.8 Money

Fifty years ago, money was very physical for most people, a pay packet at the end of the week full of notes and coins, tills in the corner shop, and a purse to pay with. Now money is increasingly digital. Bank accounts moved from paper ledgers to computers in the 1970s, credit cards replaced cash, and now we have online banking, cashless payments via our mobile phone, contactless debit cards, and crypto-currency.

However, money has always sat on the edge of the information world. The banker's note is a record of a promise and even a coin is only of value because the government says it is. Crucially, as we shall see, money has for hundreds of years been both a carrier of 'value', itself a numinous concept, and also, less obviously, a carrier of information. This latter role is being replaced by digital means: the nature of money is changing.

17.8.1 Money as value

Although there were early currencies that were purely tokens, such as the use of cowrie shells, for a large part of history money has been made of rare and precious metals, and literally 'worth its weight' in gold or silver. Sometimes other rare materials were used, including the use of salt to pay Roman soldiers. Official hammer-stamped coins served to make it easier to assess the value of small pieces of precious metal, enforced by heavy penalties, and 'clipping' the edges of coins was made more difficult by adding the tiny grooves, or reeding, round the edge of the coin.

However, for the past few hundred years these metal-based value coins have been replaced by tokens, where the value is determined by government edict or mutual trust. These are primarily produced by governments, or banks under government licence, though there have also historically been more localized 'truck systems', employers paying workers in their own tokens which, of course, could only be redeemed in their own stores.

Token value coinage and notes sit curiously with respect to some of the properties of physicality and information we have discussed.

On the one hand they should be reproducible, and to a large extent indistinguishable—every pound is equally worth the same. Although there are sometimes differences in terms of the decoration of the coins, particularly evident in the euro with its national designs, each coin is effectively identical. However, money has to be hard to reproduce. This comes for free at one level with a physical coin. When one person pays another the physical money changes hands; the payer has less money, the payee more.

That irreproducibility has to be recreated when money becomes virtual, and here the clash with the reproducibility of information becomes apparent. Most bank notes have a unique serial number that identifies them. You could imagine a system where you did not keep physical notes, just a list of numbers in a notebook. When you want to pay someone, you simply cross the number out of your notebook, and they add it to theirs. Fine if everyone is honest, but there would be nothing to stop you giving the same number to lots of people.

Older forms of information-based payment, such as cheques, relied on the mutually trusted bank, and the same is true of credit cards and many forms of cashless payment, with the added benefit of an instant network. In the end it is the bank's ledger that defines whether you have money, not coinage in your purse, and of course the bank knows not only how much you spent but where you spent it.

As there is no actual bag of gold held for you by the bank, only numbers on a computer, they are free to do exactly the 'duplicating money' trick—and they do. For each pound, dollar, or euro deposited as savings in a bank, they will typically lend four to six times as much to others. It is very apparent when governments print more notes, but the vast majority of money created is virtual: the banks lending more than their deposits, or governments using quantitative easing to manage interest rates. This matters because every pound, dollar, or euro created means that your own pounds, dollars, or euros are worth less. Of course, this is all heavily regulated by governments, so they in the end decide just what your money is worth!

Cryptocurrencies such as Bitcoin attempt to recreate the irreproducible nature of physical currency without the need for a trusted third party, while retaining the anonymity of cash. Effectively they use a variant of the paper notebook with lists of note serial numbers, but instead of keeping track only of your own transactions, you have a copy of every transaction—they do away with the need for a trusted third party by broadcasting the ledger to everyone! In order to maintain anonymity, the ledger (called a 'blockchain') is processed cryptographically so that it is possible to verify that the person you are transacting with 'owns' the Bitcoin they say they do, without being able to see who they are or what transactions they have made.

At the core of Bitcoin lies the solving of a series of harder and harder cryptographic problems. These solutions are used both to digitally validate the ledger, and to pay the solver of the problem, in Bitcoin, as part of the algorithmic process. The problem-solving addresses a number of issues as well as cryptographic validation. By generating new coins it allows the growth of the currency (hence avoiding runaway inflation), its computational difficulty means this happens slowly (maintaining scarcity and hence value), and it rewards those who do the ledger validation.

A side effect of the growth of Bitcoin and other cryptocurrencies is that they give an explicit monetary value to computation. Whole server farms are dedicated to Bitcoin mining (the solution of the problems). This is highly wasteful both of computation and of the energy used to accomplish it, but some have suggested making a virtue of this by Bitcoin-powered heating. You replace your radiators with special ones containing tens or maybe hundreds of processors. When you turn on your heating, these processors start to do Bitcoin computation and their waste energy heats your room; furthermore, you earn money for the computation—it beats burning pound notes.

17.8.2 Money as information

While it is evident that money is used for value exchange, its role in information exchange is perhaps less obvious. We live in times when some level of inflation is accepted, but for large tracts of history prices were more or less stable. For 100 years after Nero, legionary pay scales did not change, and from the eleventh to the sixteenth centuries in

England inflation was never more than 1%. This was partly due to underlying socio-economic conditions, including the large amount of goods traded locally, and an agrarian lifestyle that was close to subsistence.

This stability also arose from—or gave rise to—a sense of a 'fair price'. Indeed, as instability began to grow it led to popular revolt including the Flour Wars in France in 1775 [39], bread riots in England in 1795 [395], and, as late as 1837, the Flour Riot of New York [171]. EP Thompson saw these riots as expressing the belief of the populace in a 'moral economy' in the face of a growing market economy [395]. This was not just a popular myth, it was part of policy in many nations where regulations controlled the production and pricing of bread, and indeed in the Bible, where the price of land or bond-slavery was determined by a fair price based on years of productive use before redistribution at Jubilee (*Lev. 25*).

Variation in price is not simply an unfortunate consequence of market economies; it is the quintessence that makes the 'hidden hand' function. If demand outstrips supply, prices will rise, triggering efforts to increase production (to obtain the higher price). If supply outstrips demand the reverse happens. In other words, in a market economy many people make numerous transactions, which somehow 'computes' the best value—the economy is a physical computing system! It is money and pricing that are the means by which information is transmitted to make that computation possible.

However, while it is the information role of money that is crucial for the functioning of market economies, it is in fact a very *poor* transmitter of information. Imagine you go into a (very traditional) shop one day and pay one pound for a tin of beans. At the point you pay, the shopkeeper knows that you wanted a tin of beans and that you were prepared to pay a pound for it. However, unless the shopkeeper has a very good memory, that will soon be forgotten. The only traces of the transaction are your pound coin among many others in the shopkeeper's till, and a tin-of-beans-sized gap on the shelf, among all the other gaps left by purchased tins. When the shopkeeper next prepares their order for the wholesaler, they

Figure 17.6 Diversity density in a kitchen cupboard (left) and supermarket shelves (right)

will order tins of beans and pay for them, and their payment will join with many other shopkeeper's payments as the wholesaler, in turn, buys tins of beans from the importer. As you move up the supply chain, the indistinguishability of money means that the precise information about who wanted what, and where, is lost into the agglomerate.

This loss of information is also reflected in *diversity density* (Figure 17.6) [107, 136]. Go into your kitchen and open your food cupboard or fridge. Different items jostle amongst each other; few packets have the same contents. A typical 1 m × 60 cm × 25 cm wall cupboard may contain 50 to 80 items of many different kinds. That's around 400 items per cubic metre. Now go into a supermarket and look at the shelves. Wide swathes contain effectively the same item, with maybe some variations in brand or flavour. The diversity density may drop to only a few tens of items per cubic metre. Go into the warehouse and on the shelves there are whole boxes of tins of beans; now the diversity density is only one or two items per cubic metre. This drops further in the delivery lorry and further still once one gets to the supplier's warehouse where there will be pallet-loads of the same product stored together.

Diversity density is a physical measure of stored goods but it is also a measure of entropy or information. Imagine playing a game with a friend where you cover a packet or tin in your store cupboard and ask them to guess what it is. They would have little idea, so when you take off the paper bag and they see it is a tin of beans they are surprised: there is information. Now imagine playing the same game

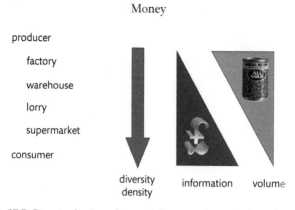

producer
factory
warehouse
lorry
supermarket
consumer

diversity
density   information   volume

Figure 17.7 Diversity density and money information flow in traditional supply chain

in a supermarket. Your friend would almost always win. Taking the bag off and saying 'it's a tin of beans' would hardly be a surprise; there is no information that is not already provided by the presence of all the other tins of beans around it.

So both the information implicit in storage and the information carried by money reduce as one moves up the supply chain (see Figure 17.7). This is no accident. What is stored on the shelves reflects the information about demand that is being passed up the chain by money. Furthermore, the reason we have such centralized logistics of supply is in large part because of the paucity of information about who wants what and where.

However, this picture is really a depiction of the 1960s and has been gradually changing over the last half century because of information technology. Through various means from customer loyalty cards in supermarkets to Amazon Internet sales, the information about who wants what where (or when) is being preserved throughout the supply chain.

Perhaps the most famous example of this is to do with lager and nappies. When supermarkets began to analyse sales receipts and work out which products were related to one another, they found that nappy sales were often related to lager sales. At first this puzzled

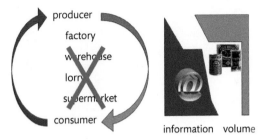

Figure 17.8 Direct information connection in Internet sales

the market analysts until they realized this was because of new fathers shopping and slipping in the odd pack of lager.

At one level this additional information is good, allowing companies to make more efficient use of resources. On the Internet, however, it can also be used to create differential pricing, where different people are charged a different price for what is effectively the same product (Figure 17.8). This is an existing offline practice. For example, airlines may charge more for returns with no Saturday night stay, since these are more likely to be business customers who are willing to pay more, and insurance companies may charge more or less depending on where you live. However, on the Internet, where a website may have tracked your behaviour over time, this practice can lead to personalized pricing and potential discrimination, a matter of concern especially when combined with fears about privacy [60] or that AI systems and machine learning may amplify existing forms of discrimination.

Most significantly, this flow of information without degradation completely changes the role of money and opens up the potential for new forms of economic activity. We saw that centralized distribution was related to the 'lossiness' of money as an information transfer mechanism. Vegetables from the farmer 5 kilometres away may be transported hundreds of kilometres to a central warehouse and hundreds of kilometres back to the shop next door, simply because the old market didn't know enough about who wanted what, where and when. When more information is preserved it enables better matching of supply and demand and the potential for more sustainable local systems to develop. Hyperlocal systems (see Chapter 14), such as Craigslist, Freecycle or Facebay, offer ways to connect to people selling or giving away goods or services in your local area using the global Internet.

Connecting Physical and Digital Worlds

In Chapter 13 we described MonmouthpediA, the first Wikipedia Town. The quick response (QR) codes that are ubiquitous in Monmouth create a connection between the physical and digital worlds. We saw there were two sides to this:

1. physical identifiers of digital things
2. digital identifiers of physical things

Each can create a one-way connection, but often the richest experience combines the two.

In this chapter we will further explore the way physical and digital worlds meet.

18.1 Visual Identifiers

The examples we've already discussed—QR codes and barcodes—are visual markers, so they can be read by any device with a camera, and they are also obvious to the human user. This visibility is both an advantage and a problem.

On the positive side, if we can see that an item is marked, we can choose to use a digital reader (phone camera, barcode scanner) and know where to point it. Compare this with digital graffiti applications that use mobile phone cameras and image recognition to identify buildings and places, and then allow users to add comments and have those comments shared with others who look at the same building. Without knowing which buildings are marked, you'd need to point your camera speculatively at everything in the hope that you find a comment; not very exciting, especially in the early days of adoption when comments are sparse.

In short, an obvious visual marker makes the *presence* of a digital connection evident.

Note that an indication of presence is not always necessary. In the graffiti application, seeking out obscure comments could be part of the experience. Alternatively, if the same technology were to be used in an archaeological site where everything had some form of initial marking, there would be no problem; everywhere you point your phone you find information. Or, with some technologies, for example an augmented reality headset like Google Glass, the camera is always scanning everything and pops up information when it spots something, so you yourself don't have to know where it is.

So, the advantage of visual markers is that they are obvious and you can see them—but this is also a disadvantage: visual markers both signal presence, but also alter *appearance*, potentially for the worse.

Initially there was a certain cachet to QR codes, which indicated that the product or the company was digitally savvy. Now they are usually tucked away in the bottom corner of a poster, easy to find, but placed to avoid spoiling the aesthetics of the image. There have also been attempts to modify QR codes to make them inherently more acceptable. Sometimes, as in the ceramic plaques in MonmouthpediA, this is simply a choice about the medium on which they are reproduced. However, QR codes are error-correcting: they can be altered quite radically and still be readable, even if some parts are damaged or obscured. Software applications can utilize this to create pixelated images that still function as barcodes.

Such images still have a very 'techy' aesthetic, but other forms of visual code allow more flexibility. 'Artcodes' (Box 18.1) use patterns of enclosure to encode sets of digits [331]. The rules are flexible enough that artists can incorporate codes into visual designs in ways that are not evident to the viewer. Indeed, subtle differences, such as leaving a curve very slightly open, change the encoding so that images that look almost identical, can encode different information. Of course, this improvement in *aesthetics* consequently reduces the identification of *presence*.

Box 18.1 Artcodes

Artcodes consist of connected regions surrounded by closed boundaries and containing blobs. The number of blobs in each region creates a code. The regions are not ordered, so the image below codes 1:1:2:3:3 rather than 2:3:1:3:1 (left to right reading).

(Image: Mixed reality lab, University of Nottingham)

Within these constraints the creator of the image can do anything. Blobs outside regions are ignored, as are incomplete boundaries. By allowing small gaps in boundaries, or having blobs slightly touch a boundary so that they are considered part of it, it is possible to subtly modify images to engineer a specific code, and this allows a lot of freedom to create images that are both pleasing to the artist and yet encode information. In addition, one can create images that look visually very similar, but represent different codes.

Spot the difference!

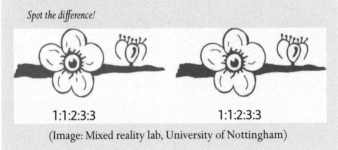

(Image: Mixed reality lab, University of Nottingham)

18.2 Electronic Tagging

If you have a credit card or travel card it is likely that it will contain a chip that can be read by simply swiping it over a reader. These are sometimes referred to as radio-frequency identification (RFID), which was one of the early technologies, but are now more generically referred to as NFC (near-field communication). You will also find these electronic tags used in hotel keys and as security devices on clothing and other items in shops. Indeed, the ubiquitous tagging of commodities is starting to open up opportunities for smart devices in the home that can, for example, detect what food you have in your cupboard without you having to scan it in and out.

Whereas the wireless technology in a phone or computer uses a large amount of power, NFC is compact, cheap, and passive, with no battery or fixed power source. Instead the reader creates a small burst of electromagnetic radiation, which is picked up by the aerial in the NFC chip. This transmits just enough energy to the NFC for it to be able to communicate with the reader for a short while. NFC devices sometimes simply broadcast an identifier, for example when they are attached to clothes to prevent shoplifting; in other applications, they may perform computation such as debiting the cash balance on your travel card.

NFC, as its name suggests, requires the tags to be close to or in contact with a reader. In contrast, more active devices may use wireless, infrared, or ultrasound in order to communicate over larger distances, even potentially using mobile networks or satellites to be accessible globally. Power has long been an issue for ubiquitous computing research into smart devices, but low-power versions of Bluetooth and careful use of power-saving technologies for other kinds of network mean that it is possible to have small tags with several years' battery life.

Whether NFC is 'close to or in contact with' depends on the power used by a reader and the precise kind of NFC. This can be used to create different forms of interaction. Non-contact tags (close but not necessarily touching) mean that applications can, for example, interrogate many devices simultaneously: imagine smart paperclips that enable a filing cabinet to 'know' what is inside it. In contrast, making contact requires a deliberate action, such as swiping your card at a ticketless station barrier. Indeed, the physical design of ticket barriers means that not only can you be reasonably certain that a travel card has been deliberately swiped but also that it was the person standing in the barrier entrance who did the swiping.

The 'nearness' of NFC means that you effectively get location for free. Wireless and other non-contact devices often make use of other means to establish location, if that is important; for example, using ultrasound or wireless time of flight indoors, or a Global Positioning System (GPS) for outdoor tracking. Determining indoor location often requires some form of instrumentation of the environment, either transmitting signals that devices can use for location, or receiving signals and embedding location tracking into the building's computational infrastructure.

Wireless and NFC tags are often invisible, so their presence may not be obvious to the user, especially when first used. Many cards have some sort of icon, and in hotels new guests are often given a short 'how to use the room key' tutorial! However, electronic tags may also include visual or audible elements. For example, every Light-Emitting Diode (LED) in the Firefly intelligent lighting system (Box 2.1) flashes its identity during initialization, allowing the calibration system to work out the location of each individual light.

Adding some form of electronic tag to an object can form a powerful combination when the object can also include sensors and computation. The cashless card is an example where the card holds the current balance and updates it; this is a largely digital transaction, though the physical form of the card is important. However, there are more interesting examples where computational and physical aspects interact more strongly; for example, smart food labels may record the storage temperature history and so allow more precise indication of freshness than a static 'use by' date.

Qraqrbox (http://qraqrbox.com/) is an extreme case where devices with small solar panels are left in remote tourist locations. The device does not just broadcast an ID or URL (uniform resource locator) so that it can be linked to web information, but includes a mini-webserver so that it can be used even when there is no mobile or WiFi signal. It contains all the information within itself.

18.3 Intrinsic Properties

For some purposes we measure ages by technology: the Stone Age, the Iron Age, the age of steam, of the motorcar, of the Internet. However, in history books and in personal memories it is often the wars that punctuate the centuries. And of course the two are not independent: the twin drivers of technology have often been commerce and armaments.

The First Gulf War in 1991 was one such moment. The images of the rout and slaughter on the Baghdad road out of Kuwait were largely too graphic for television and even newsprint, but we did hear and see iconic images of precision ordnance, cruise missiles flying down the avenues of Baghdad itself.

Unlike the radio-controlled drones of today, early cruise missiles had to operate entirely autonomously once fired. The crucial technology was a combination of digitally stored maps matched against ground radar and cameras. Roll on ten years or so and in Afghanistan and later Iraq, the smart bombs and missiles fell under the guidance of GPS, delivered to exact locations with chilling accuracy. In neither case did the targets advertise their presence with electronic tags or specially painted signs, 'bomb me'. Instead it was the intrinsic properties of the target, its location, appearance, or surroundings that were used.

Happily, not all such technology revolves around death. We have already described the digital graffiti applications that use image recognition to connect comments to buildings, and some phones use fingerprint recognition to control use. Properties used for identification may also be dynamic, for example gait or patterns of typing.

In some ways visual markers and intrinsic properties are opposites. A QR code typically encodes a URL. A generic QR-code reader on your phone reads the code and directs you to the website, based on the address alone. The digital part, the website, does not need to be altered and does not need to know about the QR code. In contrast, if you use an intrinsic property like visual appearance you need a digital application to do the image matching, but the physical part, the object, does not need to be altered, and it is not apparent that it is in anyway linked to information.

18.4 Marking the Environment and Media

Xerox's core business has historically been about paper: printing, photocopying, faxing. When you print information from the digital world it becomes physical, but thereafter the digital and physical worlds largely diverge. In the late 1980s and early 1990s, a group at Xerox wondered what would happen if paper were not only an output but also a way to input, if the physical world of paper and the digital world of information were more intimately interwoven.

Their solution, PaperWorks, was a system to print small marks, glyphs, at the top of each sheet of paper [242]. The marks consisted of slashes and back slashes ('/' and '\'), and were specially designed to survive being faxed, which at the time often distorted the image or lost scan lines. If the paper were ever scanned, the system would be able to identify the precise sheet of paper from the marks and know exactly where and when it was printed and furthermore exactly what had been printed on it. Knowing that, it could also recognize any differences, anything that had been written on the paper between printing and scanning. If the paper contained a form to fill in or a survey, the responses could be gathered and used to populate a database. If the paper was simply text, any comments or mark-up could be identified and each annotation associated with the appropriate point in the digital document.

Twenty-five years on, paper technology has added to this early work. PaperWorks glyphs were very visible, but now printers often use very low intensity colours to print a unique code on each printout to help police track things such as ransom letters or, in a different kind of nation, track dissident leaflets back to their source.

In another application, Anoto (http://www.anoto.com) is a brand of pen that uses paper with an almost invisible pattern of small dots all over the surface, so that in each small area there are sufficient dots to identify both the sheet and the location on the paper. The pen can use this to associate audio notes with the thing you were writing when you made the note, or to create digital versions of handwritten notes, without the need to scan. In some ways this digital paper is similar to a can of beans with a bar code on it. However, the sheet of paper is both an object to be traced and also a medium in which other marks are made.

The Artcode markers described earlier can be used singly to mark an object such as a plate but can also be printed onto wallpaper, so that each patch of wallpaper has its own unique code. Imagine a wallpaper printed all over with QR codes (Figure 18.1), or perhaps in a factory setting one might imagine printing floor tiles with QR codes to help robots navigate. However, for home use, the crucial thing about Artcodes is that they can be designed to be attractive!

As well as visual markers, physical spaces may include digital markers. For example, the insides of buildings may be populated with small wireless or ultrasonic pingers to allow devices to know where they are (see Chapter 21). Even the satellites that enable GPS can be seen as a form of digital marking of the globe.

Figure 18.1   Artcode wallpaper, from [331].

18.5   Digital Identifiers of Physical Things

Inside databases, fields often refer to physical things, probably the most common being people or locations. When referring to real-world entities in databases there has always been a tension between more meaningful or descriptive identifications and more arbitrary ones.

For people, fields may contain names, addresses, some form of tax or national identity number, an email address, username, internal system ID, and so on. Note that some of these references to people, such as names, are primarily for human consumption, whereas others, such as internal identifiers or tax codes, are more for system identification. Likewise, places may be recorded using addresses, postal codes or geographic coordinates such as latitude–longitude. While a good map reader will understand the latter, on the whole the address tends to be more meaningful for the human reader, and geographic codes are more useful for a device or system.

Meaningful information may change. For example, a person might change their name or move their address. Even placenames can change over time. Arbitrary identifiers are fixed and uniquely identify the object or person, but may need some separate mechanism to match the ID to the actual object or person, typically some sort of descriptive identifier! Some databases try to encode intrinsic physical properties that are believed to be invariant. For example, for identifying people, various forms of biometrics are used from fingerprints and retinal scans to DNA, with more or less success.

There is another distinction to be aware of: an address is about a meaningful place, whereas a single geocode could represent a town, a building, or even a room in a building, a problem exacerbated by the fact that few geocodes include any sense of scale. Indeed, as we saw in Chapter 11, the number of digits in the longitude and latitude recorded by Google Maps appears to have a precision of near molecular scale—not at all reflecting the accuracy of recording.

It is possible to add some idea of scale. In Frasan, a mobile app showing historical information for the Isle of Tiree [396, 122], geocodes have latitude–longitude, but also a precision descriptor: township (about 100m), building (about 10m), and rock (about 1m).

The need for a mapping between arbitrary identifiers and what they represent can be turned to advantage. For example, in MonmouthpediA (see Chapter 13), shopkeepers and those responsible for historic and civic buildings were asked which web pages they wished the QR codes attached to their property to point to. Some chose an existing web page, for some a new Wikipedia page was created, and some ended up pointing to barely relevant material; for example, one fish and chip shop had a QR code pointing to the Wikipedia page for fish!

Imagine if instead a shop owner's QR code pointed to an entirely arbitrary URL, say http://mpedia.org/{id}, where {id} is some sort of number or code. By default these would redirect to the shop owner's chosen web page, but if the shop later changed hands or the shop owner created a new web presence, the code could be remapped without altering the physical plaque. The mapping might also adapt to the viewer. For example, if a child was registered on a site for a historical building, the QR code might trigger information in a format suitable for the child's age.

Electronic devices often have some form of identifier burned into their electronics in the factory, notably the MAC address for Ethernet and WiFi connected devices, which is used to refer to them in databases. While these IDs are useful to uniquely identify a network-connected device, they are not usually helpful in actually communicating with it, so we have other levels of identifier, such as IP address (based on network topology) and the Internet domain name (based largely on organizational units).

We have already mentioned a tension between meaning for humans (a person's name) and meaning for computers (a tax code or username). This series of relationships (MAC address—IP address—domain name) reveals a different tension in purely computational meaning within networked devices. MAC addresses are unique and persist for the lifetime of the device, whereas IP addresses are less persistent (if your laptop connects to a new network, it gets a new IP address) but, while they persist, are useful for routing messages to a particular device.

This tension between persistent identity and transient location is rather similar to 'Steve Gill', the person, who is the same person whether he is in Cardiff, Nepal, or the Isle of Bute, and Steve's address in Cardiff where it is useful to send him a letter. However, unlike a MAC address, there may be several Steve Gills; indeed for legal documents the name is usually included *with* an address, the residence at the time of the document, in order to uniquely identify the person.

Semantic web researchers and practitioners wrestle with this problem. We are all familiar with the URL, the unique web address of a particular page or service; using the URL we can refer precisely to that web page. However, the aim of the semantic web is to make the web more 'computer readable', and in particular to be able to say things like:

<Steve Gill> <lives in > <Cardiff>

For people and physical things (and in fact for non-physical things such as ideas), the semantic web requires a unique identifier similar to the URL used for web pages. There may be existing identifiers for specific kinds of things already; for example, for British people there is the National Insurance number. The semantic web, however, wants a universal solution and URIs (Uniform Resource Identifiers) fill this gap [253]. A URI could be an existing URL, for example your home page might be used to identify a person, but it does not have to correspond to an actual web page. For example the URI http://physicality.org/uri/people/steveg may not exist as a web page, but can still be used to refer unambiguously not just to anyone called 'Steve Gill', but to the particular Steve Gill who is an author of this book. However, those who advocate 'Linked Data' suggest that URIs should in fact be actual URLs pointing to web-based data resources that describe, in a machine-readable form, the properties of a person or other entity.

18.6 Bringing Them Together

We've seen a variety of ways in which physical objects can be marked or tagged in order to give them a digital identity or reference, and ways in which physical entities may be described within a database or other form of digital resource (Figure 18.2). Of course, these are only useful when they are linked. This linkage may use some sort of universal scheme, for example, the geographical coordinates or URLs we've been discussing, or the (Digital Object Identifier) DOI of a journal article. Alternatively, it may be local to an application or situation. For example, police cars often have numbers on their roofs to help helicopters identify them, or an interactive tabletop may use the x–y coordinates of an object on the table. For visual markings the distinction is particularly important, as a universal scheme requires more bits of information, and hence more physical space to encode. QR codes can encode sufficient data to refer to most web page URLs, but Artcodes, for example, are largely decorative, typically encoding far less information and thus only usable as a local identifier.

In some cases the identifier in a physical tag, such as the URL on a QR code, directly leads to an associated digital code resource. Likewise certain kinds of digital identifier, such as geographic location, can be used to find an object or place. However, in many cases some sort of index or matchmaking application may be needed. This is

digital database

physical resource	intrinsic property	id of physical resource	digital res. has id	arbitrary id
nothing	✔ (a,b)	✘ (c)	✘ (c)	✘ (c)
id of physical resource	✘	✔ (b)	✘ (c)	✘ (c)
id of digital resource	✘	✘ (c)	✔ (b,d)	✘ (c)
arbitrary id	✘	✘ (c)	✘ (c)	✔ (b)

a – may need special reader

b – need to know appropriate database

c – may be able to use broker service

d – special cases for URL, DOI, or similar forms of global resources with access scheme

Figure 18.2 Connecting physical and digital identifiers

particularly evident where an arbitrary identifier is used, but it is also true for other kinds of identifier. For a specific application, it may not be an issue. For example, in a bookshop the application that scans a barcode would automatically link to the relevant stock control database, but a generic barcode scanner on a mobile phone would need some means to find and connect to the various web applications and databases where ISBNs can be used.

Connections are often dynamic, changing as objects move physically. For example, some interactive tables or public displays allow users to connect their own smartphone, what is often known as 'bring your own device' (BYOD). This requires a way for the table or display software to know which devices are to be connected. For the initial connection, the fixed system might detect devices automatically using Bluetooth, or ask the user to enter some special code or URL into their phone. If the location of the device is important, the phone, once connected, might display a QR code or some other sort of pattern on its screen, not unlike the way a fixed visual marker might be used. Note that this second-stage identifier can be a local scheme, whereas the initial connection will probably need to use a global identifier such as the phone's Bluetooth address.

Of course, dynamic connections can create obvious (or not so obvious) security or privacy issues. Some of them are obvious. For example, if you go to a café with a public display and it asks you to download an app via Bluetooth, how do you know that the app is not malicious? If you are the café owner and you installed the display so that customers could share photos with one another, how can you prevent someone posting obscene images?

Often physical location or proximity can help to solve some of these problems, at least in part; recall the importance of physical placement of light switches and cooker controls in Chapter 9. Some applications require physical touching; for others, being located within a single context is all that is necessary. The *RoomWizard* meeting room booking system by Steelcase is a good example (Figure 18.3). Each room has its own networked *RoomWizard* device, which communicates with the room booking system. Each RoomWizard has a light to show whether the room it belongs to is booked or available, so if a series of meeting rooms are next to each other it is easy for the user to see from a distance which ones are unoccupied. They can then book any available room by connecting to the RoomWizard device physically located there, either directly or from their computer or smartphone. Disputes over who has a room booked are easier to resolve because the appliance is located with the room, and the convenience of *ad hoc* booking is maintained alongside the assurance of planned meetings booked centrally ahead of time.

Some scenarios require proximity of a device and a person. WPS (Wi-Fi Protected Setup, or Push 'n' Connect) allows home appliances such as smart TVs to connect easily to WiFi routers. The device needs to know a special code that is on the router and this has to be entered within a short period of the WPS button being pressed on the router, or buttons on both device and router need to be pressed almost simultaneously. This makes it difficult for someone to connect

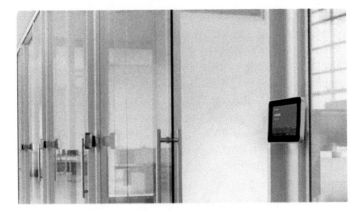

Figure 18.3 The RoomWizard by Steelcase

a device unless they have physical access to both the device and the router.

Think about how this might work in the café public display example. Customers could download a special app using a QR code that is hard for anyone to tamper with, for example behind the serving counter or in a sealed frame. The physical security of the QR code would mean that as long as they trusted the physical owner, they could trust the digital app. In order to post photos to the screen, the app could require the customer to enter a PIN or scan a QR code shown on the actual display; if this code changed over time, then only people physically present in the café would be able to post photos. Note that this would not *prevent* customers displaying inappropriate images; it would mean they would have to be present, and could be asked to stop—just as if they had acted inappropriately in any other way.

18.7 Doing Things

Sometimes the connection between physical and digital worlds is all that is needed. For example, finding information about something physical via a URL in a QR code or locating a monument or building in the world using a geocode in a database. However, there are also times when the connection is just the first stage of 'doing something'.

This 'something' might lie largely in the digital domain. For example, the location of your mobile phone might be used to make a map of your travels. This digital activity can be sophisticated and may involve multiple devices, for example learning about urban micro-climates by combining detailed crowdsourced weather reports with temperature sensor data from smartphones.

Conversely, the digital information may feed into the physical device or environment. When you follow a map on your phone, the physical location is obtained using GPS satellites, the map downloads from a web server over the mobile phone network, and on the map there may be estimates of the time to reach your destination, built up using live and historic tracking data from other mobile phone users.

Somewhere between the two is where the virtual representation in some way overlays or is projected into the physical environment. In augmented reality (see Chapter 2), some form of fiducial marker or image recognition allows objects and people to be recognized, and information or virtual objects to be displayed in special glasses or on the camera view of a phone.

Perhaps the most interesting cases are where actions and reactions of the physical objects have digital counterparts. This happens in augmented reality, where moving an object with a marker attached will typically move some virtual object also; or it may occur in games, where swinging a controller may swing a tennis racket on screen. It is also a key feature of tangible user interfaces (TUIs, Chapter 2), where the relative locations and connections between objects are often significant. For example, in some children's coding systems physical Lego-like connections are used to create executable programs. Note that in a tangible user interface such as this, the physical objects are *proxies* for digital objects. For example, one tile may represent an 'if-then-else' structure, another a dataflow; actions on the physical proxy, such as touching and connecting, are then treated as representing actions on their digital counterparts.

Connections between objects and fixed equipment or devices can also be important. We've seen prosaic examples of this, including travel cards at turnstiles and swiping a hotel room key, but research systems have used similar technology to enable rich interactions. For example, Seewoonauth and colleagues created a map with NFC tags beneath, whereby touching a phone with an NFC reader onto different cells on the map enabled location-specific interactions [354].

18.8 Ways of Knowing

Sometimes the only thing that matters about an object is its *identity*, as determined by a tag ID or its appearance. This may be sufficient on its own to draw down information about the object, as when a book's barcode is scanned. In more sophisticated examples, the *location*, *orientation*, or other physical aspects of the object may be important, either in absolute terms or relative to other objects. All of these can be obtained passively, where the object is simply recognized or tracked in some way.

However, in the most sophisticated examples, the objects themselves are active and include an element of *computation* or *interaction*, based either on networked access to an external system or using some form of local connection (physical, visual or wireless). If an object has a level of computation, it often needs to know something of its environment, its own location, and other physical factors. There are different ways in which it can find out about and share these with other objects (see Figure 18.4):

1. The object has sensors for itself
2. The object has sensors and tells the network or other things about the readings
3. The object first determines its location and then talks to a remote system that uses third-party sensors to understand the environment and properties of that location
4. The object connects to another device that does the heavy lifting, using its own sensors or other means to provide information

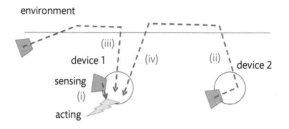

Figure 18.4 Ways devices find out about their environment

In a simple household heating system, (1) would be a thermostatically controlled heater and (4) would be a room heater that talks to a wall-mounted thermostatic controller. In a cloud-based domestic environmental control system, (2) would be the various temperature, moisture, PIR (passive infrared), and other sensors around the house, which then talk to the central server, which then tells the heaters and air conditioners (3).

These different options can be used to help when designing a novel device or system. Imagine you have decided to create a smart raincoat using electroluminescent materials, which shine to remind you to take it when rain is forecast. Any embedded electronics in the raincoat itself would need to be tiny, so rather than have it try to have its own sensors (1) and contact web weather services itself (3), it could be designed to work in conjunction with intelligent coat hooks. The coat hook could act as both power source and local wireless router (meaning the coat needs less electronics). The smart raincoat then finds out about potential rain from a house computer which itself uses an Internet weather service and talks to the house security system to find out when there is movement in the hallway, and hence when it needs to shine (4).

Location is of particular importance. Many of the examples in this chapter concern spatial location. Sometimes a global location is needed, such as GPS coordinates. However, for many purposes relative location is more important: where one object is in relation to other mobile objects, or to fixed objects such as a table top, or to spaces such as rooms in a building.

Although it sounds like scientific overkill, Newton's laws of motion mean that it is impossible to tell for yourself either where you are or even how fast you are moving (see Chapter 11). In other words, mode (1) does not work for location. You might think that your phone knows for itself where it is using its GPS, but in fact it is using mode (4), positioning itself relative to the GPS satellite network—hence GPS doesn't work indoors!

For some purposes, simple closeness or contact are what is needed; for example, in a historic house to give information about the room you are in. Others need more precise positioning: in the historic house an example would be to see which particular exhibit you are near. These more accurate systems almost always use some set of things at known locations, such as camera locations or ultrasound or radio beacons. The object's location is worked out relative to the fixed items, either at the object itself (e.g. GPS using radio) or by an external system (e.g. Kinect using an infrared camera). However, all these systems, especially camera-based systems, have problems with occlusion or objects acting as barriers or reflections.

Even if an object has some means of determining its location, there can be advantages to having an external check to recalibrate or increase accuracy. Many three-dimensional (3D printing) systems are based on open loop control (see Chapter 5). A stepper motor moves the head and so its position is known precisely. However, if the machine is knocked and the partially constructed object shifts, even slightly, the printer keeps on working regardless, adding fresh plastic to the wrong place. If the printer also has a camera to view the work piece, it can correct for any movement. Moreover, it can be used to add printed 3D extensions to existing objects, allowing repairs or objects to be built up using different processes and materials.

Just as we saw that a physical object can be a *proxy* for a digital entity, physical objects can act as proxies for one another, allowing properties of one to be inferred from the other. For example, because your mobile phone tends to be on your person or close to you, for some purposes it may act as a proxy for you. In particular, an app may use the phone's location to mark *you* on a map. In a similar way the IDs of WiFi routers may be used as a proxy for physical places, and even NFCs effectively act as proxies for the objects they tag.

Box 18.2 Tracking and surveillance

Of course, the information gathered from and about physical objects may also be used to track your activities, and for the commercial or even criminal purposes of other parties.

Even in the 1960s there were the beginnings of digital marking of physical objects. Harvey Matusow campaigned against this nascent computerization of society. In his 1968 book *The Beast of Business* [282], he suggested disabling magnetic ink on cheques using demagnetizers designed for wiping computer disk packs.

Although the technology has changed, the issues are still live. Shops can track customers using the Bluetooth IDs of their phones, and there are concerns that advertising screens or your own phone may read NFC tags in your shopping basket to profile you for targeted advertising.

part VI

The Theory
and Practice of
Physicality

19

Design Lessons and Advice

19.1 Introduction

In this chapter we will look at the tools and approaches available to designers of computer-embedded devices, and how some of the theories of physicality and computing discussed so far can be leveraged in the design process. We will use five lessons to investigate the various uses physicality has for us in design terms. Lesson 1 concerns the role of four common design tools—sketches, computer-aided design (CAD), computer-aided manufacture (CAM), and hand-built prototypes—as *thinking* tools in the design process. (We have already considered their better-known *externalization* role in Chapter 15). In Lesson 2 we examine the role physicality and context play in design, from wind accelerating skyscrapers to toilet locks and coffee bars. Lesson 3 deals with the use of the physical as a tool to facilitate a human approach through a stronger appreciation of the way we interact with artefacts in our daily lives, including doors, books and music players. Lesson 4 moves us from the literal physical world and its role as a design tool to more abstracted uses of physicality. Finally Lesson 5 takes us back to some previously explored aspects of physicality in computer-embedded devices and how these can play out in the design world.

19.2 Lesson 1: Prototype a Lot

In 2010 Tom Wujec conducted a series of tests aimed at understanding the ways in which design teams performed when set a simple task. The vehicle for these tests was a group brief devised by Peter Skillman called the 'Marshmallow Challenge' [429]. The rules of the

Marshmallow Challenge allow teams of four people 18 minutes to build the tallest freestanding structure they can. Each team is given twenty sticks of spaghetti, 1 metre of tape, and 1 metre of string. The completed structure must support a marshmallow at its top.

Wujec ran around seventy workshops with a wide variety of groups and found that 'recent graduates of business school' were among the *worst* performers. Perhaps more surprising, 'recent graduates of kindergarten' were among the *best*. Not only did young children build towers that were around a third higher than the average, they also produced some of the most creative approaches. Why?

Essentially, the adult teams spent too long negotiating, competing, discussing, and theorizing, which reduced the amount of time they had to build an effective structure. The well-known effects of design by committee notwithstanding, the core of the issue here is that the physical world is a great deal more complex than almost anyone appreciates, so predicting the ways in which even apparently simple structures like those of the Marshmallow Challenge will behave is significantly more complex than most people know. The kindergarten 'graduates' in Wujec's tests solved complex problems the natural way: they went straight to work developing prototypes, managing several iterations before arriving at a well-resolved solution. As a result they solved problems in the best way, because the physicality-based iterative approach is often the most practical solution for physicality-based problems such as the Marshmallow Challenge.

One of the reasons adults don't do what children do is that they have been systematically trained not to. Crawford contends that this is the result of 'concerted *efforts* (our italics) to separate thinking from doing' [80]. He postulates that as the Industrial Revolution matured in the early twentieth century, and craft and making skills became less valued, new theories evolved which essentially held that *making* and *thinking* are not connected. This devaluation of making, its role, and its importance in society was fiercely contested at the time, notably, as we have mentioned, by Ruskin, Morris, and the Arts and Crafts movement. Unfortunately, in the Western world at least, and despite the evidence (see Chapter 5), it is now generally accepted that doing and thinking are separate activities, and we are educated accordingly. There are exceptions: countries such as Finland invest in a holistic educational system that places equal value on arts, humanities, science, physical education, and the interactions between them (with enviable results). Unfortunately, however, young children in many of the world's countries are inducted into an educational process that slowly moves learning to an entirely theoretical process with inevitable attendant issues, including the poor problem-solving methodologies displayed by many of the adults undertaking the Marshmallow Challenge.

In fact, as we've noted previously (Chapter 5), physicality and thought do interact. Have you ever been asked by a friend or colleague for help to phrase a piece of writing, and struggled to the point where you grab a pen or keyboard and start to write? If so, you already know that we don't simply have thoughts in some disembodied way and then transfer them into text. There is a direct and natural interaction between our thoughts and actions. In his book *The Post-Human Condition* [328], Pepperell points to the evidence for the brain as we know it being only part of a wider network of consciousness that extends to our whole body and even beyond. So it should be no surprise that doing and thinking are related activities. Take the case studied by Clark [67] of a baseball player catching a baseball: the traditional model for understanding how the fielder catches the ball has the brain doing the work of calculating the ball's trajectory and predicting its eventual location, followed closely by instructions to the muscles to co-locate the ball and the player. Clark, however, convincingly argues that in fact the process *starts* with physicality. In his model our fielder begins to run as soon as a ball looks likely to be headed roughly in their direction and *before* they know where it is going to land. As they run they adjust their path to keep the ball travelling in a straight line within their field of vision (which lets them know it is heading straight towards them). Once they have correctly positioned themselves they are able to execute a catch.

This coordination between our cerebral and physical interactions to arrive at decisions and insights is a prime reason why physicality is key in both design interactions and design process. The modern designer's problem-solving armoury in this regard essentially comes down to four types of tools with physicality elements (all of which can also be used together):

1. Two-dimensional sketching (whether on paper or via digital means such as a tablet)
2. 3D CAD
3. 3D outputs via CAM
4. Iterative, hand-built prototypes

All these processes are used for iterative development. Sketching is the fastest method of recording and developing ideas, but industrial design is a three-dimensional (3D) activity and physicality is at the core of good industrial design practice. Even the most experienced designers need to trial their ideas physically, in 3D. Lawson notes: 'The drawing offers a reasonably accurate and reliable model of appearance but not necessarily of performance. Even the appearance of designs can be misleadingly presented by design drawings. The drawings which a designer chooses to make whilst designing tend to be highly codified and rarely connect with our direct experience of the final design' [258]. Which is another way of saying that frequently only designers can understand the drawings they create, and that these drawings can fool everyone including the designer that a design solution has been reached.

The physical world is a complex place, and 3D and material physicality can rarely be successfully modelled in the mind or the sketch pad. In physicality terms, sketching's key strength is that it facilitates cognition through movement (Figure 19.1). Unfortunately sketching also has some severe limitations and, like CAD, has serious weaknesses compared to prototyping (see below). The reason for sketching's ubiquity are four fold: it is fast, flexible, accessible, and cheap (with the last being crucial because it costs schools, universities and industry next to nothing to facilitate, and it comes with neither the real nor perceived dangers of a workshop environment). Almost anything can be drawn, which makes sketching a powerful tool with a serious flaw: it is surprisingly easy, even for experienced

Figure 19.1 Sketching at the heart of design

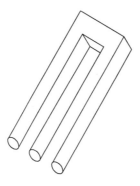

Figure 19.2 The impossible trident

designers, to sketch convincing solutions that are literally physically impossible (think of the 'impossible trident', Figure 19.2). Sketching 3D artefacts that don't yet exist requires an understanding of enormously complex interactions of scale, materials, mechanisms, forces, and textures, too complex for the human mind to fully comprehend.

So to develop form, proportion, aesthetics, and structure, designers supplement two-dimensional (2D) sketch development with *maquettes* (scale models, generally of large products) or *soft models*, typically using card or modelling foam. Soft models (Figure 19.3) often create the first opportunity for a user to interact with the product's physicality, and this is a key component of the design process, where a concept will frequently stand or fall. Ulrich and Eppinger note:

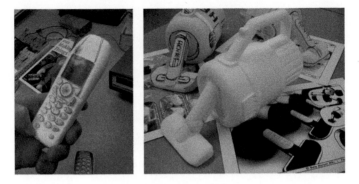

Figure 19.3 Foam prototypes

'industrial designers build models of the most promising concepts. Soft models are typically made in full scale using foam' [400]. The other 3D development technique, the rig (sometimes also known as the prototype), is used to develop the mechanical aspects of a design. Rigs don't always prototype the whole of the design and they sometimes won't look like the design concept. Their function is to test a concept, its mechanical properties, mechanisms, or user interactions: 'prototypes are built to test and validate the design' (Figure 19.4) [430]. For example, a rig of a chair concept would be strong enough for users to sit on and adjustable so that the designer could swiftly act on observations regarding seat height, angle, comfort, etc., but it wouldn't necessarily look like the finished article.

3D CAD methods (for simplicity's sake we're referring to 'solid modelling' systems when we write '3D CAD') don't have the immediacy and creative freedom of sketching, but they are powerful tools, better than sketching for correctly sizing components, for example, or ensuring that parts can interact with one another. Like a real prototype, the three-dimensional nature of a 3D CAD system means it is more difficult for the designer to fool themselves regarding product proportions and fits, so it caters well for some aspects of a design's physicality. Most 3D CAD systems also provide data on centre of gravity and weight for a given density of material, and can even be used to test mechanisms virtually. What they won't do is give the designer a sense of scale (other than relative scale *between components in*

Figure 19.4 Full-size prototypes

the same model), feel, fit, or ergonomics. *Knowing* weight, size and balance mathematically and *feeling* them are entirely different things, and designing a product directly in CAD, for example an ergonomic hand grip, is challenging at best. One way to leverage the strengths of 3D CAD while maintaining the advantages of physical prototypes is to use a 3D printer or other Computerized Numerical Control (CNC) device to output. This method would seem to have the best of all worlds, but generally speaking, is usually best done only in the later stages of the design process. The reasons for that include cost, speed, choice of material, and limitations of scale (or else high investment costs to attain larger scales).

Of course the greatest degree of physicality is provided by handmade prototypes. The advantage of physical prototypes is that they are not an interpreted version of a real-world artefact, they *are* a real-world artefact, and so carry information about scale, fit, ergonomics, weight, balance and real-world interaction that is difficult to fake, intentionally or otherwise. In the making process, designers are using physicality to develop an innate understanding of the problems they are dealing with in order to impose an elegant solution. Both Schön

Figure 19.5 Internet-enabled Swiss army knife (left)—oops, thumb on the display (right)

[350] and Alexander [4] use scientific language when talking of this: the concrete design as an 'experiment' or 'hypothesis'. Certain limitations are only realized when an appropriately sized prototype is introduced to the real world in a way not possible with sketching or CAD (although possible to some degree with CAM).

Alan once had a discussion based around the concept of an Internet-enabled Swiss Army knife (Figure 19.5). The idea was that useful tips could be shared via a website and step-by-step instructions for using the different blades would be displayed on a small screen on the side of the knife, using the toothpick as a stylus. Verbally this sounded fine (as it most probably would if sketched) but when acted out with a scale model it quickly became apparent that at a critical moment the fingers holding the knife would obscure the display [183].

As we saw in Chapter 4, the nature of the materials and tools the designer uses at the point of concept formation can have a profound impact on the designs they produce. The other role of physicality in a prototype can be transformational [134] (see Chapter 15) in that the properties of the external representation can be used to help in understanding or planning the eventual outcome. For example, we may sit on the rough prototype of a seat and find that an element sticks uncomfortably in our back. We may learn that a particular material does not have the right degree of 'give' or softness, or we may simply run our hands over the prototype wing of a car. This brings us back to Sennett's 'conversation' between craftsperson and material [357]) and Schön's 'back talk' and 'knowing in action' [350]. In problem-solving research it is well known that changes of representation can offer apparently obvious solutions to what appeared to be intractable problems, and perhaps this move from internal to external is the most radical transformation of all. It is this function of externalization as an augmentation of cognitive activity that is critical in accounts of distributed cognition and embodiment and, by extension, physicality; and in the use of prototypes by designers of 3D objects.

19.3 Lesson 2: Context Offers Complications *and* Solutions

Designs don't have a life of their own. They exist for their mechanical, visual, aural, tactile, social, and olfactory connections with people. This is why the physical context of a design's use has a dramatic impact on the design itself. As a purely physical example, people can be injured by the high winds caused by the interaction of large buildings with local wind conditions (tall buildings can accelerate wind speeds by a factor of 9 [325]), so wind tunnel testing of models of proposed skyscrapers within their intended context is now standard architectural practice.

Other interactions are more subtle. For example, many trains in the UK have electrically powered toilet doors, designed to make facilities accessible to disabled passengers (Figure 19.6). The door functions are computer-mediated and button-activated: a button on the outside opens the door and another on the inside closes it. A second internal button activates the lock.

When you push the 'Lock' button it lights up to indicate that the lock is active and the door is locked. In theory this should work well; it produces confirmation in accordance with Shneiderman's 3rd Golden Rule of Good Human Computer Interface (HCI) design:

Figure 19.6 Typical toilet door lock setup found on a UK train; unlocked (left) and locked (right)

Offer Informative Feedback [365]. Unfortunately there are few occasions when you feel as vulnerable as when you are sitting on a toilet in a public place with your underwear around your ankles. Most people would prefer some physical evidence that the door is locked, rather than trust their dignity to a little light. How do we know that the door is locked? The usual way to find out is to try and open it, because if we can't open it than neither can someone on the other side. Unfortunately the designers followed a different logic path: 'If (they reasoned) a passenger wants to leave and the door is locked, why not have the 'open' button over ride the 'lock' button?' This reduces the number of button presses by 50% so it would usually be good design practice—but it won't feel like good practice to the person in the toilet. The issue is further compounded by the lack of physicality in the locking process. The system works via a software algorithm that temporarily disables the 'Open' button on the outside of the toilet. This means that the user has not been reassured by the sound of a lock firmly engaging to keep intruders out of the toilet.

So even a simple, non-life-threatening design that follows seemingly logical thinking can be a bad design. The lesson here is to *start* in the physical world and work one's way back to the studio. Very few designers would disagree that this is indeed the best way to design, but in practice it rarely happens that way.

The two alarm clocks in Figure 19.7 are good case studies of both context and physicality in design. The one on the left is a recent model belonging to Steve's partner. It has a radio and allows you to play music from your phone; it has different alarm settings for

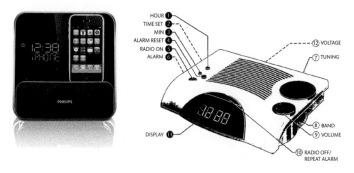

Figure 19.7 Two Philips alarm clocks

weekdays and weekends and a summer +1 hour setting. It even tells you the time and date. What it doesn't do is work very well. Nearly all alarm clocks are used in bedrooms. Bedrooms, particularly bedrooms at bedtime (when one normally sets an alarm clock), tend to be poorly lit. If you share the room with someone who is already asleep when you set the alarm, there may be no light at all. The alarm clock on the left has buttons on the top and behind the main fascia that are small and labelled in small, low contrast text. They are similarly sized and shaped, and most of them are difficult to access without sitting up and tilting the alarm towards you and towards the bed light (particularly if you are over about 30 and so not great at seeing well in low light conditions). Even after a year of ownership, it could take five minutes to set the alarm to a new time. In all probability the situation was exacerbated because Steve's partner, like many people on the verge of sleep, tended to be tired when she set the alarm.

Now consider the alarm on the right. It is of 1980s vintage and not as attractive to modern eyes as the one on the left. It doesn't do much, but it is designed for context, which is why after 30 years it is still by Steve's bedside. The switches are all labelled, not only with text but by position, shape, and texture, and it takes around 30 seconds to set in pitch dark conditions. It is an excellent example of physicality being used appropriately in design to suit the context of a product's use.

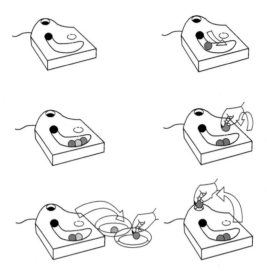

Figure 19.8 'Marble Answering Machine' by Durrell Bishop (1992)

Durrell Bishop's Marble Answering Machine (Figure 19.8) [335] is a rather more radical and disruptive example of physicality-based design. The answering machine contains marbles that it releases to represent messages—a kind of physical—digital proxy (see Chapter 18). Users know how many messages await them by looking at the retrieving tray and counting the marbles. Messages can be played back in any order and each marble is digitally tied to the message it represents: placing a marble in an indentation on the machine triggers the machine to play back a specific message, and to return a call the user drops the marble into another indentation. Undeleted messages can be kept outside the machine in a separate receptacle.

If the physicality and context of a design is important, it follows that conducting physical testing *in context* as early and as often as possible is also important. In other words, just as the Marshmallow Challenge demonstrates the importance of physically testing a design proposal, so the examples above demonstrate the effect that context and physical environment interaction have on the efficacy of a design solution. Unfortunately, while this is easily said, the route to achieving it is not always immediately obvious. This is because the iterative prototyping methodology that we and others advocate necessarily results in a whole series of explorative but roughly developed outputs that might be described as 3D sketches. Making a sophisticated, well-finished, fully working device runs counter to the reason for producing this type of output, because the whole point is to slowly problem solve your way, with increasing understanding and detail, towards a finished solution.

Sometimes testing ideas in context is easily achieved by skipping the more demanding prototyping challenges in favour of getting to the heart of the physical and contextual issues. Remember the concept of the 'device unplugged' from Chapter 9. Figure 19.9 shows a basic mock-up of a phone design being tested in context. Many of the design features of this concept can be tested with a surprisingly basic model, and this exercise and others like it have gathered a lot of very rich design insights. In other words, 'the device unplugged'

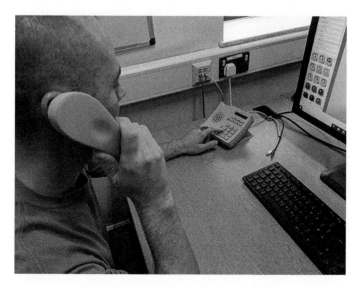

Figure 19.9 Testing a basic prototype in context

is delivering important insights without ever actually performing its core task.

However, sometimes testing is far less straightforward. This might be because the real context is not suitable for testing. For example, testing a medical device prototype in an actual hospital setting is difficult for a number of practical and ethical reasons. It might be that the intellectual property of the device is highly sensitive (it is by no means unusual to have strict confidentiality issues surrounding a new design), or it might be that the prototype itself requires a lot of support. This would be the case for many methods of prototyping computer-embedded devices, which often require high levels of computer support via wire, Bluetooth or Wi-Fi (see the next chapter).

One solution is to prototype the context as well as the device itself. Steve and several colleagues have worked for some years on contextual prototyping [194, 427]. Their latest solution is the Perceptual Experience Laboratory (Figure 19.10) (PEL). PEL contains a 6.5 × HD, 180° wrap-around screen and a digital surround sound system. Air conditioning systems allow temperature to be varied as required, and fans allow air movement within the lab to be controlled. Scents

Figure 19.10 An early iteration of the Perceptual Experience Laboratory (PEL)

(e.g. disinfectant in a hospital mock-up) are used to increase immersion further, while actors and physical props can be used to complete the illusion of immersion. The eventual aim is to apply an algorithm that will dynamically modify the linear perspective photogrammetric images into an experiential perspective via eye tracking, so that a participant in PEL should have a very strong feeling of presence in the simulated environment. When it is fully developed PEL should allow an environment to be mimicked to a high degree of realism in less than a day, allowing more realistic prototype testing than is generally possible in a lab setting while continuing to benefit from the computer support, observation techniques, and confidentiality security offered by a laboratory environment.

PEL represents a technique through which a well-established design method called *Experience Design* [29] can be executed. Experience Design can be quite extensive, for example IDEO's case study of a study of passenger experience in Business Class for *Lufthansa* (see Figure 19.11). In that case study, designers created a mock-up of an airliner interior and adopted the roles of passenger and crew in order to explore the issues surrounding key moments in a flight. Once they had refined their thoughts they progressed to tests in a real airliner and with real passengers and crew.

Figure 19.11   IDEO's Experience Design process in action

19.4 Lesson 3: Be Human-centric

It may seem obvious to say so, but designs are mostly aimed at use by humans, and even when they are not, they tend to be developed to solve a problem faced by humans (e.g. a cat feeder is used by a cat, but only so its human owner doesn't have to persuade their neighbour to feed it).

Appropriate use of physicality is frequently at the core of systems that are truly human-centric. Conversely, an absence of appreciation for physicality's importance is frequently at the heart of poor design. Consider the second, third, and fourth generations of iPod Shuffle. Like the first-generation model, the second-generation Shuffle had buttons. These were 'designed out' in the third-generation, in keeping with Apple's drive for a clean and minimal aesthetic. They were then designed right back into the fourth-generation model. The advertising strategies were essentially, and respectively, 'iPod Shuffle with no buttons!' and 'iPod Shuffle: Now with buttons!' We can't definitively say why Apple revised their approach, because their design processes and even their designers (with the notable exception of Sir Jonathan Ive) are a very well-kept secret. A little consideration provides some possible reasons, however. The iPod Shuffle was small enough to be kept in a pocket or clipped to clothing. It had no screen, so there was no need to see it to operate it—as long as it had buttons. It could also be operated through clothing (e.g. if it were being used below waterproofs while walking or cycling on a rainy day)—as long as it had buttons. In other words, its interaction depended more on touch and physicality than most electronic products, and its physicality may well have been critical to its previous success. The switch back to physical controls certainly suggests so.

The inappropriate door handle and the button-less iPod Shuffle are both examples of a misunderstanding of physicality's importance, and, perhaps more importantly, they are a misunderstanding *by* humans *of* humans. In the case of the door we see a lack of understanding about physicality's influence on our behaviour, and in the case of the iPod Shuffle we see the creator of a successful product misunderstanding the importance of physicality to their customers, and where and when those products fit into people's lives. The way people interact with the physical world and the artefacts in it is subtle, complex, and surprising, leaving room for innovation in even the simplest interactions.

Steve's daughter Lauren recently rearranged the bookshelf in the family study by colour, which, while aesthetically pleasing, does not at first seem to make much sense (Figure 19.12). The books had previously been alphabetized (by Steve's mum, Iris), and before that they were grouped by category (by Steve's wife, Diane). Both Iris and Diane's methods are typically used in bookstores and libraries, but the thing about a personal book collection is that one tends to have read most or all of the books in it, so when looking for a book one tends to recall its physical attributes (colour, shape, size). Grouping them by colour tends to make it much easier to locate a book, even when one can't recall the title or author, and this makes it a nicely human-centric way of designing a filing system for this particular context.

Figure 19.12 Books filed by colour

19.5 Lesson 4: Highly Abstracted and Selective Physicality Can Be Powerful

In 1933, Harry Beck designed a revolutionary map. London Underground had commissioned Beck, an electrical draughtsman, to draw a new map of their underground rail network. Previous maps had sought to represent accurately the physicality of the geography and the lines' relationship to it, which made them difficult to use. Beck reasoned that people travelling in a tunnel were less interested in the geography of their journey than how to get from one location to another. Drawing on his draughtsperson training, he drew a diagram that filtered the representation of the physical world according to whether it was useful. So directions are very rough, line routes are artificially straight, and scales are disposed of altogether. On the other hand, the stations where one can change from one line to another are displayed in a heavily codified but essentially accurate representation of physical reality. This diagrammatic way of representing the physical world according to need has had a powerful effect, and nowadays nearly all transport maps borrow on the concept to some degree.

Among the people who have borrowed the general concept is Steve. A few years ago he designed a virtual learning environment (VLE) for use by design students in his university's School of Product & Engineering Design. The first problem he faced was making the students *want* to interact with it. He called it the 'Virtual School' and based its filing structure on a real-world model (Figure 19.13). Like Beck, he did so in abstract terms: the environment was a series of 2D webpages linked together in a rough spatial analogy of the campus, with a campus map forming the index page. Users navigated by pointing the mouse at areas where they expected to find 'rooms' (webpages). Each 'room' was connected to its function in the real world and to other 'rooms' in the same way as their real-world counterparts. A number of conventions were used to make the physical world more convenient. Scale was abandoned and building plans simplified and resized, with unused spaces reduced dramatically. The

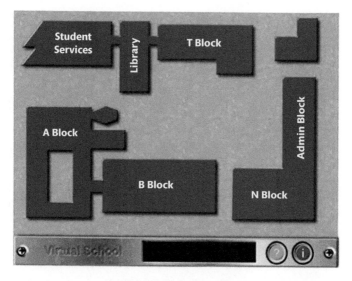

Figure 19.13 The Virtual School

system was mutually reinforcing by being 'face-and space-based'. People could be contacted if any two of the following were known: where they work; their name; what they look like. Students could learn who was who either through real-world contact or through the virtual environment, or a combination of the two. The idea was that it would help students 'navigate' both worlds: if you knew where to find the nurse on the campus you could find their room in the VLE, and vice versa. Faces were used, rather than more straightforward text hyperlinks, to help students contact people and know who was who. Lists of students and their contact details were displayed in the appropriate 'studio' to help year groups communicate in a pre-Facebook era (Figure 19.14).

Product semantics were used to convey the idea of a physical product in a slightly over the top, vaguely humorous way. Text appeared displayed on screens, buttons were set into surfaces, and instrumentation was designed to reflect a machine aesthetic to the extent of including screw-on panels.

Figure 19.14 Staffroom and first year studio

Figure 19.15 Skoda Octavia controls

While this approach may seem frivolous, it was in fact a calculated attempt to engage students, often at the expense of efficiency, by using abstracted and codified physicality. It worked, and the Virtual School was operational for 10 years, long after a much more sophisticated but less 'human' system had been implemented in the rest of the university—which brings us to the next lesson.

19.6 Lesson 5: Sometimes Using Physicality Just Makes More Sense

In a more physical context, could more physicality make a difference to our driving experience, and in particular, could it make it safer?

According to the World Health Organization, road traffic accidents caused the deaths of 1.25 million people in 2013 [428]. There will of course be a range of reasons for those accidents, but fundamentally driving carries risks because it allows us to travel at speeds we are not evolved to cope with. The only reason we can manage car-level speeds at all is that we have created for ourselves a massively simplified physical world of roads and signage systems to compensate for our inadequacies in this area. Given that, and the potentially lethal consequences of even minor errors, it would make sense for driving to be as natural a process as possible, which, as we've seen, generally involves including physicality wherever we can. In many ways that is exactly what car designers have achieved. Although we respond to what we see on the other side of the windscreen, the actual driving controls themselves are experienced through touch (because our visual senses *should* be concentrated on what is on the other side of the windscreen). As mentioned in Chapter 5, driving can be thought of as a *cyborg* activity [109], because to a surprising extent we treat the car as a literal physical extension of ourselves.

Car designers have long understood that the driver treats the car as a physical extension, so for decades the basic car controls have been standardized (e.g. clutch on the left, brake in the middle, accelerator on the right) and we use them without looking at them. Later additions, such as indicator controls, were also eventually designed to be primarily experienced through physicality. They are mounted concentrically with the steering wheel so that we can locate them by moving our fingers into position using the physical reference of the wheel as a guide. Steadily, however, cars have 'evolved' to have more and more controls, and not all of these are well designed to be operated by the driver while their eyes are focused on the road. Figure 19.16 is an analysis of the controls in a 2014 Skoda Octavia (which happens to be the car Steve drives).

Box 19.1 Adopting limbs

Knowing where our own body is—*proprioception*—is a key way in which we root ourselves in the world. As we saw in Chapter 5, it is surprising how easily our sense of self can be extended (section 5.5). We are also, it turns out, quickly fooled into adopting even physically unattached, inanimate objects into our proprioception.

Readers may be familiar with the Rubber Hand Illusion [73], in which a participant's hand is placed out of sight and a rubber hand put in close proximity to where their real hand is. A researcher simultaneously strokes the middle finger of the real and rubber hands, with the result that the participant quickly comes to feel as if the rubber hand *is* their real hand. If that seems hard to believe and you don't have a rubber hand lying around, try this (you will need a mirror and a volunteer).

Ask a volunteer to place their arms either side of a mirror and their head such that they can see one of their arms and its reflection, but not their other arm. Stroke both their hands simultaneously for about 10 seconds. Now take hold of both hands at once, pause for a beat and then firmly and slowly lift the hidden arm and watch their reaction. It will immediately be clear how quickly an innate sense of physical ownership has extended to include what the volunteer is perfectly aware is only a reflection.

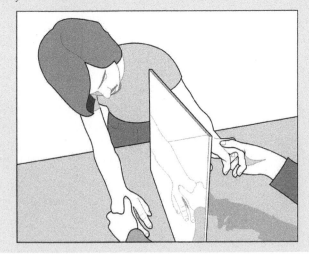

Mostly or exclusively physicality oriented	Mostly or exclusively visually oriented
Steering wheel Horn Foot pedals (3) Hazard lights Handbrake Steering wheel-mounted phone and stereo controls (11) Window controls (5) Indicators (3) Door Catch Air vent direction and opening (6) Wipers (9) Cruise control (5)	Wing mirror adjustments (8) Door lock Light controls (8) Ventilation controls (6) Computer console buttons (physical) (9) Computer console buttons (touchscreen) ≈ 150 Engine cutout and driving mode controls (5) Dashboard-mounted stereo controls (23) Ventilation controls (15)
TOTAL: **53** (51 operated while driving)	TOTAL: **229**
Grand total of controls available to the driver while driving: **282**	
Percentage that can be operated without (much) visual input: **19%**	

Figure 19.16 Analysis of the controls in a 2014 Skoda Octavia

There is a distinct pattern visible in the controls that fail to exploit physicality as a primary interaction method: most of them are mediated by computer and are relatively recent arrivals on the dashboard. It is difficult to miss the fact that previously well-understood lessons on the importance of physicality as an interaction method for car controls have been forgotten.

Porter and colleagues [330] proposed a solution to this very issue with the BIONIC project, which sought to utilize drivers' sense of touch and semi-autonomous spatial awareness of their physical environment to reduce visual load. BIONIC controls are deliberately placed out of the driver's line of sight to encourage interaction via tactility (see Figure 19.17).

Joep Frens (Figure 19.18) [170] also postulated how physicality-based interactions might humanize computers. As part of his PhD he developed an experimental digital camera concept where 'all interactions are natural'. To copy a picture to the memory card, for example, the user physically moves the display of the picture towards the physical memory card. To zoom, they physically move the lens backwards and forwards.

Figure 19.17 Porter et al.'s BIONIC Project [330]

Figure 19.18 Joep Frens' camera with rich interaction [170]

A quick disclaimer: this was a rough study to provide an illustration, not a robust piece of empirical research. There are a number of clear limitations. For example it was hard to know which controls to count at times, most especially with the touchscreen inputs where at times the number of actual options was not clearcut. For example the car's computer imports all phone contacts from whichever phone is connected to it via Bluetooth and so they appear as calling options, but it would be unreasonable to count these. Defining 'mostly physicality oriented' controls is also a judgement and no doubt different people would make different arguments here.

Prototyping and Tool Support

20.1 Introduction

In the previous chapter we explored five ways in which physicality can be leveraged in the design of computer-embedded products. In this chapter we will discuss some of the ways in which the physicality of our interactions with the world affects, drives and is exploited in the design process. We will briefly discuss standard design approaches that exploit physicality before exploring some of the problems that digital technology creates for those processes. Lastly, we will discuss some of the methods we and others have developed to return physicality to the development process of computer-embedded products.

20.2 The Problem with Digitality

Computer-embedded products (those products which have computers at their core) pose unique problems for designers. The sketching and prototype development and testing processes discussed in the previous chapter work well for 'traditional' products like chairs and lemon juicers, but are not so well suited to products that rely on a computer to mediate our physical interactions. As we mentioned, the designer's toolkit essentially consists of four types of tools, which can be used individually or in parallel. As a reminder, they are: two dimensional (2D) sketching; three-dimensional Computer-Aided Design (3D CAD); 3D outputs Computer-Aided Manufacture (CAM); hand-built prototypes. These have worked well for many years. For example, if an industrial designer has been briefed to design a chair, (a simplified version of) the process they follow would be something like this:

1. Produce a number of concept sketches through which form, structure, colour, mechanisms, and proportions are explored—**2D sketching**
2. At the appropriate juncture, produce a series of *maquettes* or soft models to further develop promising sketch concepts into physical forms—**hand-built prototypes**
3. Build (an) adjustable prototype(s) that allow(s) the exploration of ergonomy, structure, comfort and scale—***hand-built prototypes*** and/or **3D outputs CAM**
4. Test and iterate the prototype(s)
5. Build a facsimile of the design—**3D CAD** and/or **3D outputs CAM**
6. Work with manufacturers to develop the design for mass manufacture—**3D CAD**

In fact the process is not as linear as that, and many of the activities occur at several points in the process, but as a rough description it will suffice. It is a process that has been honed and evolved over many years and it works well. The trouble is that products with computers in them create a whole series of problems to which traditional methods are ill suited.

Let's say our designer has been tasked with designing a camera, rather than a chair. They can use concept sketches to explore form, structure, colour, proportions. They can make maquettes or soft models to further develop promising sketch concepts in physical form, and build the design in CAD to develop it for mass manufacture. But how do they build a *meaningful* prototype? Modern cameras are entirely computer mediated. In fact, in some senses they are more computer than they are camera. Designers are not electronics engineers, computer scientists or human computer interaction experts, and yet an effective prototype of a camera involves utilizing skills more generally associated with those professions. So, while our designer has been happily sketching and modelling the physical aspects of the camera, the thing that makes a good camera design is actually the effective partnership between its physical form and the computer at its core. That aspect has effectively been completely ignored, because what choice does the designer have?

This means that not only is there no prototype but there is also no other mechanism taking its place as the vehicle for exploration of the human–product–computer interface. Furthermore, while the prototype is indeed only one part of the process, it is a vital one. It is where a designed artefact first comes into contact with people, and of course products that function well with people are the most critical component of a good design. One might argue that this is all a bit of a red herring. After all, design is not the only discipline in the world; the prototype is only one component of the design process and there are lots of other methods here that are employed perfectly well. Why not simply employ a bigger team involving people with the right skillsets?

Unfortunately, as logical as that approach seems, it doesn't really work. When Steve commissioned research into this some years back, researchers found that in most cases even design teams that included all the right skillsets weren't able to work together effectively [187]. In a nutshell, what happens in real-world scenarios is that it's rarely possible to make the right skillsets available at the right time within any given project. If too few projects are running it is impossible to keep everyone employed; if too many run, the 'pinch points' quickly misalign, meaning the right expertise isn't available at the right time. In practice it seems that a happy medium is almost never found. However, even if it did work, there is good reason not to be tempted to go down that route, because it artificially separates issues that should be connected.

The reason for connecting everything together in a single place is because that's how we human beings operate. We don't experience the world by assembling the data coming into our heads from our various senses through separate channels. It used to be thought that our eyes gathered light projected onto the back of the retina like a movie camera projecting onto film, and that these pictures were sent to the brain, which saw them, more or less, like a projected moving image. Meanwhile, it was thought, our eardrums were vibrated by sound waves and the resulting patterns were processed as sounds that were then added to the moving pictures in an independent stream.

But that's not actually how we experience the world.

While our eyes really do gather light on the retina and our eardrums really do gather sound when they are vibrated, it has long been known that what happens with the information after that is much more complex. Actually we understand the world as a whole through a rich and mixed stream of interrelated information sets. The evidence for this mixed information model lies in a number of scientific studies, such as those carried out by McGurk and MacDonald [287] in the 1970s. They proved that in certain instances we can't differentiate what we see from what we hear. The so-called *McGurk Effect* was found by showing participants two film clips. In one clip a woman mouthed the sound 'ga' over which the sound 'ba' had been dubbed. In the other she mouthed the sound 'ba' with the sound 'ga' being dubbed. Most participants 'heard' the sound being mouthed rather than the actual speech. At a literal level, they didn't really *hear* the sound, they *saw* it. We mix other senses too. There is, for example, a proven effect of sound on taste, and Heston Blumenthal famously proved that a farmyard soundtrack in his restaurant made bacon-and-egg-flavoured icecream taste more strongly of bacon and egg [378]. Food industry researchers at Steve's university know very well that we frequently mix what we see with what we taste [51], so they employ coloured lights to prevent sight bias in taste-based food trials (see Figure 20.1).

In design terms, we also know that our senses are influenced in all kinds of other ways: social pressures, past experience, and deep animal instinct. We know, for example, that the more a wine costs the better we think it tastes, the more a small product weighs the higher the perceived quality, and we know that a bag by Gucci or a car by Ferrari look better than similar products without the brand association. We also find it easier to interact with a product if we love it (or at least we think we do) [313]. Last but not least, we know that a product's physicality and users' interactions with it are deeply linked

Figure 20.1 Taste-testing booths in Cardiff School of Sport & Health Sciences' Zero2Five Food Industry Centre

(see the *Equinox* study below). Designing usable products people love, enhancing a sense of quality and dealing with brand perception are all core industrial design skills, and because they all work in combination it makes sense to deal with them together and holistically.

So let's look at the skills gaps. In the case of the camera, the designer can build a prototype through which to explore reach, scale, grip, and so on, but because much of our interaction with cameras is in fact computer interaction, the traditional prototyping process is insufficient for the task. Designers don't traditionally deal with HCI, and unfortunately HCI practitioners don't deal with physical appliances as such, tending to focus instead on the screen interface. The upshot is a disconnect between the digital and the physical, which causes problems. It was long ago realized that industrial designers were the right people to deal with these issues; Weed, for example, identified this very thing in the mid-1990s [415]. The problem was that while the design profession had *many* of the skills needed for the job, they didn't have *enough*. As a result, new skillsets developed, some rooted in design but others borrowed from elsewhere.

Variously referred to as User Experience (UX), User Centred (UCD), or Interaction (IxD) Designers, the discipline involves entire user experiences with the made world, including the interactions between humans and computer-embedded products. As with HCI, the practice is grounded in the development of understanding of the way users behave in the world through observation and testing. Unlike HCI, physical interactive prototypes are common tools of these professions.

Physical artefacts respond to user input mechanically; there is a direct connection between the user and the product which produces innate understanding via mechanistic linkages. In computer-embedded devices the responses have to be 'designed in', because computing is invisible to us (see Chapter 2) and allows linkages which are, for practical purposes, infinite. To design them in effectively requires iterative sets of prototyping and user testing, which is where the problems arise. Remember the train toilet lock in the previous chapter? A series of apparently sound design decisions led to a bad design, and the only way we could have discovered those flaws would have been through testing, which would have required prototypes.

20.3 Interaction Design Tools

In this section we will look at the 'designer friendly' tools and methods available to enable physicality and context to be explored in computer products in much the same way that 'traditional' products are designed now. We have started by attempting to group the various tools described according to their equivalency and position within the standard designers' toolkit (see Figure 20.2).

At the start of this chapter we made the point that the physical design and computer interface of a computer-embedded device are both facets of a single user experience. Industrial designers' traditional sketching skills don't allow them to explore interface design. But other disciplines have created methods that are either suitable or can easily be evolved to fit neatly within the designer's standard toolkit. Below we discuss a few of them, most of which have been either borrowed or developed—and sometimes both!—by Steve's UCD Research group.

Box 20.1 The *Equinox* study

In 2008 we published research findings of physicality's effects on hand-held product interactions [185]. Among other things we attempted to define the level of fidelity required in a prototype to obtain a tangible degree of accuracy in user trials. In order to have a datum, we selected a real product, a phone called the *Equinox*. We then reverse engineered three 'prototypes' of it: high fidelity, low fidelity (Sketch), and pure software.

Two of these prototypes used the IE Unit (a hardware component of the IE System, described below). The IE Unit transformed button presses on prototype devices into keystrokes that could be used to drive various forms of computer software.

The high-fidelity prototype was as close to the real product as we were able to make it (in fact we used real mouldings). An *IE Unit* connected to the phone mouldings triggered a high fidelity *Flash* mimic of the *Equinox*'s interface on a computer screen. We used this same Flash-based interface mock-up as the basis for a wholly touchscreen-based prototype which we called 'Software' (wholly screen-based prototyping was common in design consultancies at the time).

Equinox prototypes (from left to right): low fidelity (Sketch), high fidelity, real product (Equinox), and touchscreen (Software)

Lastly, we developed a low-fidelity *Equinox* prototype, which we called 'Sketch'. Sketch was modelled in blue foam, a common designers' soft modelling material. The buttons were tipped with cardboard cut-outs to give them the right shape and graphics. Sketch was connected to an IE Unit in the same way as the high-fidelity prototype, but the interface was a much simplified Flash file made up of hand-drawn sketches. Overall we estimated that in a real-world design exercise, the *low-fidelity* prototype would have taken about 80% less time to create than the *high-fidelity* prototype, and 60% less than the *software* prototype

continued

Box 20.1 *continued*

on its own. When the results of the user trials were compared we found that both the *high-fidelity* and *low-fidelity* prototypes performed in a more similar fashion to the real phone than the pure *software* prototype. At no point did 'Software' outperform either of the tangible prototypes, and it was sometimes much poorer.

Having proved that a low-fidelity tangible prototype clearly out-performed the industry standard prototyping method while taking less than half the build time, we decided to lower the fidelity further. This time we reduced the physical prototype to a block of the right dimensions. We printed a picture of the phone on paper at 1:1 scale and stuck it to the top surface of the prototype, covering the physical buttons in such a way that pressing the picture of, say, the '1' key activated the physical button beneath it. The new prototype was linked to the interface originally developed for *Sketch* and the tests were rerun. The results were not encouraging: the prototype compared badly to the real Equinox.

So what happened? Essentially the user could no longer easily feel the buttons' edges and that was enough to badly erode the advantage of having a physical prototype.

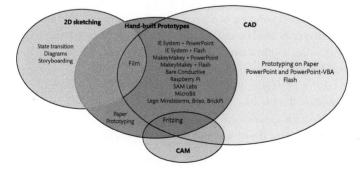

Figure 20.2 New interaction design tools and their equivalencies in the 'traditional' design toolkit

20.4 State Transition Diagrams

State transition diagrams have been around for a long time. Originally created by the computer science community, they are used to describe system behaviours and the triggers for them. There are many different types of state transition diagram, but the overall concept is similar in each case. Each 'state' of a system (e.g. 'off' state and 'on' state) is described diagrammatically and linked by a transition that is triggered by an 'event', which might be, say, a user input (pressing a 'power' button) or a sensor reading (the time is 17:00 so a timer triggers the oven to switch on). The *Physigrams* in Chapter 9 (also in Figure 20.3) are a type of state transition diagram. Like design sketches they can be high or low fidelity, but crucially they are an efficient and flexible way to explore digital behaviour.

Steve's design researchers and students generally use the 'Post-it® Note' model. In this version designers sketch each product state on a Post-it® Note and attach these to a whiteboard of a large sheet of paper (on the right in Figure 20.3). The states are then linked with arrows that point to the state change and also show the event that triggers it. In Figure 20.3 we see state changes triggered by button press events (e.g. pressing the 'OK' button on Post-it® 1 takes us to the state shown in Post-it® 2) but it's very easy to make it work with a range of mechanical controls, gesture commands, time, sensor, or any other event. Because the state transition diagrams are treated as the equivalent of a sketch, they are informal documents, used as part of the design development process to explore interaction issues. They are often only used by the designer themselves or as a device to explore issues within a small team, and this means that they are often used flexibly, roughly, and creatively.

Like other forms of 2D sketching, state transition diagrams are extremely flexible: they are very malleable, and almost anything is possible with some creativity. Of course, this means that they suffer exactly the same drawbacks as 2D sketching, discussed in Chapter 19:

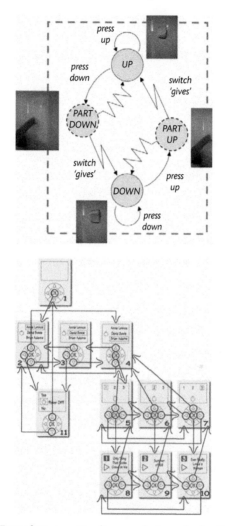

Figure 20.3 Types of state transition diagrams: physigram (top) and Post-it® Note (bottom)

isolated from the social and physical contexts of a product's interaction, with their extreme and often subtle complexity, the designer will quickly run into problems if they rely entirely on state transition diagrams.

20.5 Storyboarding

One of the easiest early-design-stage tools through which to engage with contextual issues is the storyboard (Figure 20.4). Storyboards originated in the film industry (the Walt Disney Corporation is usually credited [332]), where they have been used for decades as a tool for sketching out what a particular scene will look like. In a way, they are a film-maker's design tool. These days, however, software designers, service designers, user experience experts, and other professions also benefit from storyboarding as a tool.

Figure 20.4 Storyboarding for design

From the perspective of a computer-embedded device designer, a good storyboard will focus on how a user interfaces with the device, which is always at the centre of the story. This type of storyboard tends to have a start and an end, with characters who have a task to complete and a context within which to complete it. The storyboard will show the characters interacting with the device in its intended context of use in order to deal with whatever task the story requires. There are several ways in which this helps the design process:

- It places the user and the product within a relevant context and forces the designer to think about the social and physical aspects of that space and the product interactions happening in it.
- It helps designers 'get under the skin' of people who have different needs and likes from themselves.
- It is an excellent communication tool to promote discussion within the design team, and to aid communication with and input from a client.

There are a number of tools available that make storyboarding easier. They include tangible tools such as 'Scenes' by SAP User Experience [348] and software solutions such as Storyboard Fountain for Mac [381].

20.6 Paper Prototyping

There are not many tools for interaction designers that are directly analogous to the traditional rigs, maquettes, and soft models toolsets. This is usually because some kind of digital application is required, as we will see with most of the tools discussed below. The one exception is paper prototyping.

Paper prototyping (Figure 20.5) [376] is a little like a low-tech version of the *Wizard of Oz* technique described below, in that a

Figure 20.5 Paper prototyping

person plays the role of a computer, interpreting a user's interactions, and translating them into state transitions and other computer responses. There are two key differences, however. First, paper prototyping can be carried out using hand-making skills alone, and second, in paper prototyping the 'Wizard' is not hidden from the user but is an active and visible participant in any participant trial.

To create a prototype the designer would normally use their standard soft modelling or CAD/CAM techniques to make the physical device. Replaceable elements are then created, for example sketches of a touchscreen and LEDs. In a participant trial, the participant is given the appropriate task to complete. One of the facilitators will then watch the participant's interactions with the device and make the prototype 'respond' accordingly. So, for example, if a participant touches a particular part of the 'touchscreen' or tilts the device in a particular direction or speaks to the device, that might lead to a change in the device's state. The facilitator will then action that change (e.g. change the paper sketch of the screen so it displays a new graphic). It is a surprisingly powerful technique that can uncover key insights without going to a huge amount of time and effort. Aside from this, its particular strengths are its flexibility—it is very easy to make quite significant changes in seconds or minutes and then try them out—and the fact that it can be used just as effectively outdoors as indoors (which many of the much more sophisticated approaches below cannot). Lastly it can in many instances be employed in context, which is a huge advantage. Its key weakness is the fact that it is only as good as the facilitator playing the part of the machine, and even the best facilitator is not going to respond at computer-like speeds. This may not sound like a big problem, and often it is not, but sometimes accurate response times down to milliseconds can really make or break human–machine interactions—recall Alan's problems with his old multi-tap mobile phone from Chapter 9.

Box 20.2 Physical fidelity

How important is physicality in the design of digital physical devices, and to what fidelity level should that physicality be prototyped? Jo was asked to create a hypothetical information appliance to work with the photo-viewing site *Flickr*. A series of these *Flickr Friend* prototypes were made, their standard of construction dictated by the time within which the designer was allowed to create them. The initial hypothesis was that fidelity would have an effect on user feedback and usability. Analysis showed that there was, in fact, little difference at the concept stage. Rather, a layered picture emerged that suggested that physicality is radically more important in some areas than others, and that pointed to the need for firm designer guidelines for digital–physical devices. Even the Level 1 paper prototype seemed to produce usability data in line with the higher fidelity ones. Perhaps simply having a tangible model to interact with produces usable results.

continued

Box 20.2 *continued*

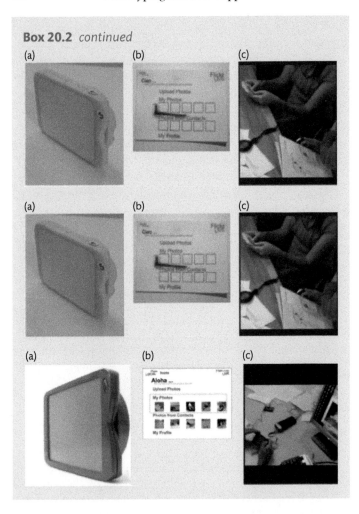

Paper prototyping works very well with state transition charts, which can be used to map the paper prototype's interface, and with storyboards, which help refine a design before taking it as far as a prototype. Paper prototyping also works well with *prototyping on paper* (Figure 20.6) (see section 20.8) and can be used in Experience Design scenarios (see the previous chapter).

Figure 20.6 Prototyping on paper

20.7 Video

One of the most effective ways of both exploring and communicating is by using video. Now that smartphones can be equipped with 4K sensors and excellent low light capability, and a range of phone-based video editing software is available, video has become a very accessible option. The most straightforward way to integrate video into the interaction design process is simply to use the storyboard for the purpose for which it was invented: the design of a film. Combining the power of a narrative and the most basic level of stop motion filming will put a paper prototype into context and give a very good indication of how a real device would work (for an example see [305]).

20.8 Software/Hardware Hybrid Approaches

Sometimes the best approach is to combine the quick, handmade prototype approach with a digital tool. 'Prototyping on Paper' (PoP [279]) is an iPhone app that exploits this type of approach, enabling paper-based drawings to be made into touchscreen prototypes. It is a handy but more limited technique than the seemingly less sophisticated paper prototyping approach. In the case of PoP, the designer draws all the states of the device on paper and photographs them with the phone's camera. They then create areas of the screen that, when touched, will move from one photograph (state) to any other. The idea is similar to Lin and colleagues old DENIM concept [262], which allowed the rapid trialling and iteration of prototypes. In some senses PoP is an automated state transition diagram and really only suited for touchscreen interactions. You can create 'virtual buttons' on pictures of a tangible product, but the lack of physicality will likely cause misleading results (see the *Equinox* study, earlier). In the right circumstances, however, it can be used to create sophisticated prototypes in very little time, because an iPhone can be embedded into a prototype where it will behave like a touchscreen. Like paper prototyping, PoP-type approaches work very well with hand-drawn state transition diagrams—in fact images of the states from the state transition diagram can be photographed and used in the prototype in the way described earlier.

20.9 Serious Toys

Subverting products made for one thing and applying them in a completely new context is a common approach in the design field. In fact, storyboarding is an example of that. Toys are another, and some of them can become powerful tools. Lego has long been regarded in this vein, as Cambridge University's appointment of a Lego Professor of Play illustrates [161]. In 1998 the computer arrived for Lego in the form of their Mindstorms product. This includes a series of stepper motors, and colour, infrared, and light sensors, all of which are programmable via an easy to use drag and drop visual programming environment on a desktop or laptop computer. Those with greater expertise can create more advanced prototypes by programming in Java, and a range of compatible kits are also now available which

Figure 20.7 LEGO Mindstorms and BrickPi

vastly increase the flexibility and scope of Mindstorms, including BrickPi which allows it to be linked to a Raspberry Pi (Figure 20.7).

20.10 Bespoke Kits

Various researchers have proposed bespoke toolkits. One example, StickIT (see Figure 20.8), was a system built by Ian Culverhouse as part of his PhD [83] and described in a conference paper [85]. StickIT worked using a system of passive RFiD tags and was designed in response to a challenge laid down by Steve [184], to design a system that would enable a tangible electronic prototype to be produced from scratch in two hours or less (a feat it achieved with relative ease). The system's roots lie in three different systems: Avrahami and colleagues' *Switcheroos* [13], Villar and colleagues' VoodooIO [403], and Cardiff's own *IE System* [186]. StickIT was designed to overcome issues that made each of the three systems that inspired it less fit for purpose. *Switcheroos* used passive RFiD readers to do away with the need for an internal power source, but the size of each antenna made the form factor too large to be useful for handheld devices. VoodooIO used a clever co axial pin and substrate combination for both power and networking, but the substrate had to be wired in, which meant it couldn't be moved. The IE system was wireless but only worked with a small set of input devices and required an internal power source, though its keyboard outputs gave it a lot of flexibility. StickIT used VoodooIO's conductive substrate to allow the sharing of a single RFID antenna pinned into the substrate. When a control input pinned to the substrate was activated, it completed the circuit, linking the control to the antenna and making it available for power and ID recognition. A wearable RFiD reader delivered the power to

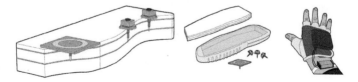

Figure 20.8 StickIT

the antenna, and a Bluetooth module enabled the detected tag's ID to be relayed to a computer in the form of keyboard strokes (just like the IE System, section 20.12). A set of 'drag and drop' *Adobe Flash* software components completed the toolkit, removing the need for ActionScript to trigger an interface design. StickIT could therefore be used without requiring any knowledge of programming, internal power, wiring, soldering, or electronics, and the only hardware needed in the prototype was the conductive substrate and the single antenna.

20.11 Office Software

Humble, everyday software can make surprisingly powerful tools. Microsoft PowerPoint is a good example (Figure 20.9). The slideshow metaphor it employs is analogous to a state transition chart's description of the states of a computer-embedded device, with each slide showing a single state of the appliance. PowerPoint's shape hyperlinking feature makes it easy to move from 'state' to 'state' and it is possible to develop surprisingly sophisticated prototypes employing graphics, sound and moving images.

20.12 The Power of the Keyboard

Many years ago, Steve's colleague Tek Jin Nam saw the potential of Visual Basic for Applications (VBA) to increase the power and

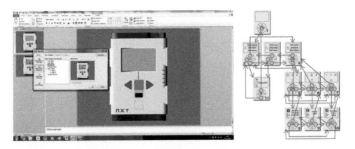

Figure 20.9 PowerPoint as a prototyping tool

Figure 20.10 IE4 and MakeyMakey

flexibility of PowerPoint prototypes through the keyboard. He commissioned a modified keyboard that allowed prototypes to trigger screen changes via embedded buttons which controlled the PowerPoint slideshow. This 'fooled' the computer into thinking it was receiving keyboard commands.

In later years, Steve's group developed this approach into the IE System, culminating in the IE4, by Alex Woolley, shown in Figure 20.10. The IE4 is a small battery powered unit with an embedded Bluetooth keyboard chip. It plugs into a shield into which the designer wires their prototype input devices so that the prototype can communicate wirelessly with the computer.

Like the IE System, MakeyMakey outputs keystrokes, allowing users to exploit the power and flexibility of a PC from a prototype of their own design. What sets it apart as a system is that 'switches' can be made from an almost infinite variety of conductive materials, including tin foil, playdough, water, and people!

20.13 Programmable Boards

Electronic prototyping has become more and more accessible over the past few years with a range of boards available, the best known of which is probably the Arduino. Arduino's power lies in its vast open-source community, which lends support and coding free of charge to anyone wishing to engage, increasing its accessibility enormously. Arduinos are programmed via a desktop or laptop computer but can then operate on their own. While they are extremely powerful

Figure 20.11 Bare conductive, BBC micro:bit, and Arduino

and flexible in the right hands, they do require a level of comfort with basic programming that is beyond some novices. Interestingly, however, Arduinos are at the centre of other prototyping tools.

Bare Conductive boards are Arduino-based units with a similar flexibility on the input side. Bare Conductives are specifically designed for sound output and, as with all Arduinos, are programmed via a PC or Mac but are then capable of operating independently—adding another dimension of flexibility.

The BBC micro:bit is a successor to the very successful 1981 BBC Micro-computer. The micro:bit is surprisingly powerful and flexible. It has programmable on-board buttons, a twenty-five LED grid, accelerometer, compass, and a series of input–output connectors. It also has Bluetooth connectivity and is compatible with a series of other devices including Arduino and Raspberry Pi.

20.14 Internet of Things

Yes, Internet of Things (IoT) solutions extend to prototyping, with the SAM Labs offering being a prime example (see Figure 20.12). Like

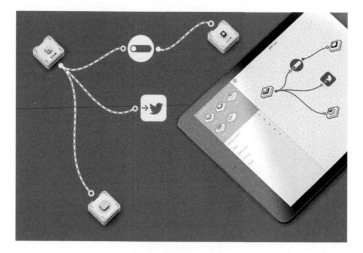

Figure 20.12 SAM Labs

Mindstorms, SAM Lab kits come with a range of inputs and outputs that can be linked and programmed using a computer. These include light, pressure, tilt, heat, and proximity sensors, RGB (red, green, blue) lights, buttons, sliders, dimmers, servos, and buzzers. Like a number of the tools described here, it cannot operate without the support of a laptop or desktop computer, but unlike some, it does so wirelessly at a range of up to 30 metres. There are two elements to the kit: the physical—essentially mini-computers with their own power source and Bluetooth connectivity—and the virtual, where those physical components that are switched on and within range appear as avatars: another example of the physical–digital proxies first mentioned in section 18.7. Programming of the physical component is achieved through its software avatar. Components in the physical world behave in an identical way to corresponding components linked in the virtual world and can communicate through the Internet, for example through Twitter or Facebook.

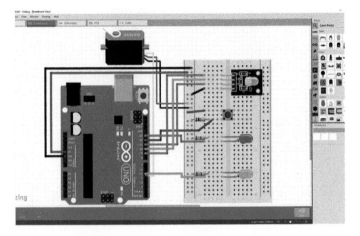

Figure 20.13 Fritzing

20.15 Automated PCB Design Tools

One of the obstacles that used to face designers who had got as far as rigging up an electronic prototype was the need to convert their ad hoc lash up to a proper circuit board. This is where tools such as Fritzing come in (see Figure 20.13). Fritzing is an open-source software tool that allows users to create schematics and PCB designs directly from breadboard layouts. Once a breadboard prototype has been built and tested, a facsimile can be constructed in *Fritzing*. The software will simultaneously build a schematic of the breadboard design, and when the breadboard facsimile is complete, the components can be arranged on a virtual PCB. When the components are placed to the designer's satisfaction, the software will auto-route connections to create a PCB which can be produced in the normal way.

Box 20.3 Case Study: *Globa-Pharm*

Steve and Ian Culverhouse (who designed the StickIT system mentioned above) were once commissioned to carry out a consultancy [84]. The project was set by a company whose details can't be revealed under

continued

Box 20.3 *continued*

the terms of a non-disclosure agreement (NDA) so we'll refer to them here as *Globa-Pharm*. *Globa-Pharm* needed a set of interactive prototypes for use within a formative usability study. Though we can't discuss the design or the product type, the brief essentially required interactive prototypes of a new handheld medical device. Each prototype was the same design, with slight physical and user interface differences. User feedback was given by coloured LEDs and a variety of haptic outputs.

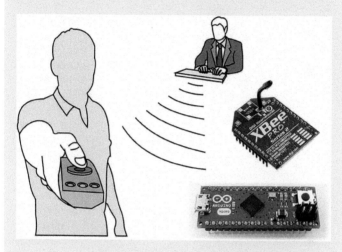

'Wizard of Oz' via Arduino + Zigbee

Globa-Pharm's usual approach to this type of trial was to use *Adobe Flash* prototypes showing onscreen animations of the user interface (UI). Where they deemed it necessary to have a physical device, they would commission a high-fidelity mock-up to help users understand what the completed product would look and feel like. It is clearly imperative that medical devices are easy and safe to use. We convinced the client that we could deliver more effective prototypes to a tight timeline and for much less cost. To some extent we regretted this when they challenged us to be as good as our word and deliver four working prototypes for user trials commencing in three weeks! The units did

continued

Box 20.3 *continued*

not need to work insofar as they were not going to deliver any medication. However, they did need to give appropriate feedback to allow those commissioned to run the user trials to assess the effectiveness of each interface. The *Equinox* trial results had convinced us of the value of 'medium visual fidelity'/'high physicality fidelity' prototypes and we determined to produce prototypes in line with those findings. Making them work was beyond either what was required, what we could afford, what we had time for and, indeed, our designerly expertise. Instead we elected to adopt a version of a classic HCI method: the 'Wizard of Oz' technique, first used by Gould in the 1980s [195].

The devices were CNC machined from *Globa-Pharm*'s CAD files. Meanwhile Ian used an *Arduino Mini* prototyping platform in conjunction with *Zigbee* modules to allow the prototype to be remotely triggered. One of the great advantages of this platform is that it allows for rapid 'on the spot iterations' *during* user studies.

Globa-Pharm were not actually very impressed by our prototypes. They were accustomed to a high standard of finish and were not entirely convinced of our explanations of why we hadn't felt it appropriate to go to those lengths. They were unfamiliar with the Wizard of Oz method and were concerned it wouldn't work, forcing them to reschedule some very costly user tests with serious knock-on delays to product development. Fortunately the method worked well. The 'Wizard' (Ian) covertly triggered appropriate prototype responses to specific observed user actions via Zigbee from a laptop while posing as a note-taker.

Once testing was underway, the opinions of the company representatives were entirely reversed. Participants spoke freely, making reference to important ergonomic issues and other design considerations in a way that previous methods had failed to elicit. This point was underlined when *Globa-Pharm* made a last-minute addition to the testing protocol: a secondary UI was prototyped using the standard onscreen Flash animation method. It was immediately clear that users were far more engaged with the Wizard of Oz approach than with the onscreen prototypes. Users struggled to mentally integrate the physical and virtual aspects of the devices in just the way that our research had predicted they would.

continued

Box 20.3 *continued*

It was testament to the effectiveness of the Wizard of Oz approach that out of twenty-eight users, only two thought to question how the prototypes worked. In another comforting outcome, the facilitator of the user trials noted that the low visual fidelity of the prototypes helped him convince users that they were interacting with an early prototype, which facilitated more open responses. But perhaps the ultimate indicator that the method worked was that *Globa-Pharm* com-missioned a second phase of testing and requested that the Wizard of Oz approach be used again. They did request a higher level of visual refinement but you can't win them all.

Computational Modelling and Implementation

21.1 Modelling

If designers love sketches, rigs, and prototypes, computer scientists love models, notations and diagrams, from 1960s flowcharts to UML (Unified Modeling Language [35]). We have already seen several examples of one-off architectural diagrams, including the multiple feedback cycles in Chapter 9, Figure 9.10, and the Tiree community data infrastructure in Chapter 14, Figure 14.8. The Physigrams in section 9.7, themselves a variant of state transition diagrams, are an example of a notation that can be used to specify many kinds of physical device.

Models have different purposes:

- *models to help understand a situation*—including models of the environment and application domain.
- *models to help in a design process*—including models of the device or system being deployed.
- *models to help in product development*—including representations or sketches of the design of system architecture or physical form.

However, a single model or notation may be used for a combination of these. For example, Physigrams can be used to model an existing device, to help make early design decisions, or to specify the required behaviour during implementation.

Such models may be primarily for human use or may be capable of some form of automatic analysis, verification, or simulation. In the case of use within virtual reality (VR), an executable model may indeed become the actual behaviour.

There are examples of models that address physical interaction with devices. Harold Thimbleby used models of the layout of controls on consumer and medical appliances to drive finite state simulations in order to explore the impact of Fitts' Law on interaction timings [391]. Parisa Eslambolchilar combined models of device characteristics with psycho-physical models of human action to create predictions of the conjoint cybernetic behaviour of human—device interactions [156], and Zhou and colleagues created detailed models of finger pressure on buttons [434]. There have also been models of physical movement in urban environments using variants of space syntax theory [160], of the architectures of sensors and actuators in smart environments [45], and of ubiquitous interactions [27] using the formalism of Bigraphs [293]. However, compared with screen-based interaction, this work is quite limited and the models and notations are not in widespread use.

We have already seen how Physigrams [132, 140] can be used to model the interaction potential of physical devices. Here we will briefly consider the modelling of two other key differences between traditional screen-based interaction and physical interaction: *continuity* and *intention*.

21.1.1 Continuity

Digital interactions with digital objects are usually broken down into discrete time events, whereas physical interactions are often *continuous* in time and space. For example, when you pull a bowl across the table, you do not conceive of it as a discrete series of 'move' events to intermediate locations, but as a smooth movement.

Status–event analysis [148, 137] is one way to think about this kind of interaction. It distinguishes two kinds of temporal phenomena:

- *events*—things that occur at specific times, such as your alarm going off at 7 a.m., or the post arriving—these are the things that fit relatively straightforwardly into the digital world.
- *status*—things that can be sampled at any time. What is the weather like now? What is the mouse location now? Where is the bowl now?

Internally your code may end up treating everything as events. For example, if you wish to track the bowl's movement as part of an intelligent kitchen system, you might end up taking measurements every 200 milliseconds (ms), but this should not be the way you describe it to users, nor how you think about it from a design perspective.

There are common ways in which event and status phenomena behave, which are similar across many scales of physical and social activity. One of these, *status–status mappings*, occurs when two status phenomena are linked, for example dragging a window with a mouse, or having a light track someone's finger across a wall. Another important common behaviour is the way that status phenomena are often converted into events by *polling* or by detecting *thresholds*.

21.1.2 Intention

In Chapter 14 we saw how many 'smart' environments give rise to low-intention/low-attention interactions. When you press the button on a device in your hand, you have chosen to interact with it and have some expectation of the result. However, when an automatic door opens, it may be unexpected, or if the heating automatically adjusts itself based on past behaviour you may not even know that this has happened.

We saw that such systems involve two tasks, or two aspects of the same task: the *sensed task* and the *supported task*. When we model the sensed task the crucial thing is to find ways to understand the user's behaviour based on sensors. For the sensed tasks, the issue is more about understanding what ways system behaviours could help (or not help) the user. One way in which the sensed task has been modelled uses a variant of state transition networks (STN) [126]. In this case the STN models the main states of the *user* and *world* (in contrast to the device state in Physigrams, or computer state in many computing formalisms). Figure 21.1 shows an example of such a model for a sensed task: a café open sign that has been Internet enabled by adding a small sensor.

Note that many transitions depend on the café owners' habits. Some behaviours are very reliable (they have to arrive at the café in

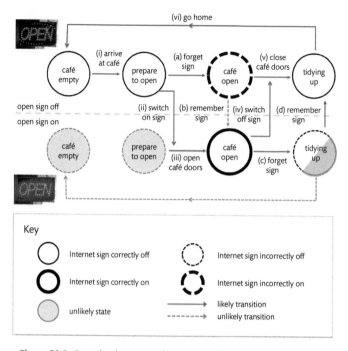

Figure 21.1 Sensed task—states of Internet-enabled open sign (from [126]).

order to open), others less so (remembering to turn on the sign). This means there are times when the sign being on is a valid indicator of the café's open-ness, but with some uncertainty—a common feature in intelligent environments.

The supported task could use one of the forms of task analysis notation, or, where the task is not complex, a simple scenario. Figure 21.2 shows an example relating to the café open sign. The customer is considering going to the café, and in the past has simply relied on published opening times, which might be inaccurate if the café owners are delayed or have a family crisis. The Internet-enabled sign allows an alternative means of checking that the café is open, by turning on a web sign when the café sign is on.

It is not good if the customer thinks the café is closed when it is really open, but it is even more critical to avoid step 5, where the

```
0. Eat out at café
        1. decide would like food at café
        2. check if open
                2.1 check current time and opening hours (old)
                2.2 look at open sign on web page (new)
        3. drive to café
        4. buy and eat food (if open)
        or
        5. disappointed and hungry (if closed)
        6. drive home
```

Figure 21.2 Supported task–café customer (from [126]).

customer travels to the café but is unable to get any food! By looking at the reliability of the sensors in Figure 21.1 it is possible to assess the likelihood of different potential outcomes and, if necessary, to consider adding additional sensors, or adjusting the way existing ones are used.

21.2 Software — Engineering, Architecture, and Security

21.2.1 *Where do you do computation?*

Imagine you are creating the software for a standalone hiker's navigation device, intended to be used in remote areas that have Global Positioning System (GPS) coverage but no usable mobile phone signal. It is clear that you have to create code that runs on the device.

Even on a standalone device like this you may still have decisions to make when you want to design the interactions to download maps, or perhaps upload Global Positioning System Exchange Format (GPX) tracks of where you have been. Should the device be self-contained with its own SIM card or WiFi receiver, or should it connect through Bluetooth to a mobile phone or plug into a laptop? If it does connect to another device, is that used merely as a connection with the actual interactions happening on the navigation device, or should the interactions be on the smartphone or laptop?

We saw in Chapter 17 that when we do computation, code and data must be in the same place at the same time. In addition, part of the 'data' is related to the user's interaction and context, from button presses to GPS location. The choice of where we do computation—on the navigation device, smartphone, or laptop, or in the cloud—has many knock-on effects:

- cost and complexity of the device;
- network traffic;
- power use of the device;
- responsiveness of user interactions.

This choice is also influenced by the ecology of other devices within which a device sits, as we have already seen with the hiker's navigation aid example.

At the simplest level of ecology, a device is completely standalone, for example a low-end fitness tracker that measures heart rate and includes a simple pedometer, all displayed on a small built-in Liquid Crystal Display (LCD) screen. Here all the sensing, computation, and display are performed on the device. A simple electronic kitchen scale is a similar example where everything happens on the device.

One step up are devices that sit within a fixed ecology, such as the remote control for a TV. The simplest remote just transmits infrared codes to the TV. It requires minimal computation to monitor the keypad and encode the key presses for transmission. However, imagine a slightly more complex remote with a small LCD screen that allows you to view the TV schedule without disturbing the programme you are watching on screen. Here you could choose to make the device itself quite simple, with most of the 'smarts' in the TV; the TV sends text or graphics to the display and the remote sends back what is selected. However, in order to improve responsiveness, you might instead choose to let the remote download each day's full TV schedule, enabling it to react more quickly to user input.

The Internet of Things (IoT) is gradually changing our mindset, shifting us from fixed ecologies to open collections of embedded appliances (smart kettles, central heating) and interactive devices (smart phones, voice-based home assistants). Tiny off-the-shelf circuit boards designed for embedding in IoT appliances include sufficient computational power for substantial computation to be performed on the device. However, it may often be easier to treat them as if they were dumb devices, so that though they gather the sensor data including user interactions, and control aspects of the environment (heating, screens), they then simply use built-in networking to offload the real computation to home computers or the cloud.

21.2.2 Where am I?

As we discussed in Part IV, spatial location can be a powerful part of physical interaction. In some cases, like a map-based smartphone application, that is self-evident, but location is also central in less obvious situations: a room thermostat should control the radiator in the room it is in, not the room next door. This would be hardly worth saying in an old, directly wired installation, but networks are no respecter of walls. Indeed, if you occasionally use the same Bluetooth mouse with two different laptop computers, you might have had the experience that the mouse appears not to be working because it has decided to connect to the other computer in the next room.

Each generation of GPS receiver is more accurate, cheaper, and, crucially, requires less power than the last, so for many purposes outdoor location is a solved problem. That said, there are exceptions, notably in forests, deep valleys, and, very important for navigation applications, densely packed cityscapes. Narrow cavern-like streets between tall buildings make it hard for GPS satellites to be visible, creating blackspots, while bounced signals can make locations inaccurate. Happily, WiFi stations are common in cities and allow backup location methods to work, which is not usually a viable solution in a forest.

Indoor location is far more problematic. There are many technologies, including ultrasound, radio beacons and camera-based techniques, but no widespread pervasive technology similar to GPS. In a closed environment, for example information tablets in a museum, you can use any of these technologies to create a bespoke location service. In this case you often have a choice about whether the device or the environment will do the location calculations.

For example, you might place radio pingers at known locations in the environment and have a small receiver in the device that uses time-of-flight to calculate its own position, or you might do it the other way round, like the Active Badge system [409], for example, which has a small infrared transmitter that sends a unique signal every 10 seconds. Networked sensors in the workspace can detect the badge in the frame and triangulate the exact location of the wearer.

However, you do not have the same level of control when dealing with a general-purpose application that needs to work anywhere. Often the best that is possible is rough proximity-based location calculation based on the closest WiFi base stations. Browser-based location often uses this and it yields relatively good latitude–longitude positioning with no GPS at all, even indoors.

In the case of static equipment, such as the thermostats and radiators in a domestic heating system, you may simply use a room plan to specify the locations, or perhaps some form of pairing procedure. As this is only done once during installation it does not need to be as automated.

The most difficult challenges arise when you would like to use the *relative* locations of devices, for example to allow you to drag a file between device screens. Here the device locations need to be accurate enough to know how they are positioned, and the relative orientations also often matter: if I 'throw' a file off the left edge of my screen, the system needs to know which other device sits at that location. For more than ten years, bespoke research systems have been available that plug into a laptop USB (Universal Serial Bus) port and allow multiple laptops, for example during a meeting, to transfer files in this manner [206]. It is also possible to use screen/camera and audio/microphone to obtain crude relative locations of smartphones [342]. However, there is sadly, as yet, no standard off-the-shelf solution; the best you can do is use Bluetooth or WiFi strength to get a measure of relative proximity.

21.2.3 Networks

Many of the development boards for embedding in devices come with some form of wireless networking (either Bluetooth or WiFi) as standard, which makes this aspect of IoT applications fairly straight-forward; indeed the greatest difficulty for embedded devices is in configuring them to use the *right* network, and reconfiguring them when the network changes. However, point-to-point communications can be a little more complex, for example when you are designing devices to be positioned around a house, where older walls, or conductive things such as machinery, trees, or people can block or absorb wireless signals.

In Chapter 14 we mentioned Hermes, a digital message system, which used WiFi to connect small digital displays beside office doors [65]. In practice, when someone bent over the Hermes display to leave a message, they sometimes blocked the WiFi signal, just when it was needed most! For similar reasons, Ambient Wood [347], a technology-rich digital experience in a Suffolk woodland, had to po-sition multiple wireless base stations because water in the trees and the summer foliage quickly absorbed signal.

Sometimes fixed connections can be used. For devices attached to mains electricity, it is possible to superimpose a signal on the power line, either using off-the-shelf powerline adapters or bespoke circuitry (with appropriate safeguards). Similarly (and more safely) low-voltage power sources can be used for signalling. For example, the first version of Firefly intelligent lighting (Box 2.1) used commu-nications over a 5-volt (V) power line. The communication signal used the full 0–5 V range, but was designed so that the signal was 'up' at 5 V a fixed proportion of the time, so that a simple capacitor-diode circuit was sufficient to create a clean voltage to power the lighting-control chip.

Sometimes an *ad hoc network* may be required. Imagine an example where each room in a house has a radiator and thermostat. The central control unit (which may also be Internet connected) can connect to nearby devices via Bluetooth or on a dedicated WiFi net-work. These devices then connect to others, and so on. So long as there is a path between every device, messages from the central unit can be routed hop by hop. This kind of network can be especially useful where there is no fixed network, or to reduce the power requirements of battery-powered devices. Sensor networks are used for environmental monitoring or for military applications. They often employ hundreds of tiny devices (sometimes called *smart dust*, see Chapter 2), each equipped with sensors, processor and low-power wireless communications. Individually they are low fidelity and localized; together they can create a detailed picture of a wide area, sometimes even floating downriver or in ocean currents. For these the lower power requirements of an ad hoc network are essential.

21.3 Working with Electronics

Working with electronics can seem daunting. If you forget to put the right resistor in line with a component, or wire it in the wrong way, with a little pop it is destroyed, or perhaps, even worse, there is no little pop and you spend hours trying to work out why the Light Emitting Diode (LED) isn't going on. Not to mention, of course, using the soldering iron, which appears to be a simple art until you try it and your circuit board ends up like a wedding cake that's been iced with a cement mixer.

Happily, much of this pain has been resolved by the numerous prototyping systems (see Chapter 20), which have been developed to serve the hobby maker movement, bespoke DIY projects and artistic installations, but often also have variants that are costed at a level suitable for widespread deployment or embedding.

Such prototyping variants typically come with a number of GPIO (general purpose input-output), which can be configured to accept either digital or analogue inputs or outputs. This means that if you want to create, say, a simple digital thermometer to turns on a sequence of LEDs depending on temperature, it simply involves wiring a temperature sensor to one GPIO pin, connecting the LEDs to some others and then—a little coding. Often the maximum output power is low enough that they cannot burn out a component, and the standard components provided cannot damage the circuit board itself. If you connect a component the wrong way round it may not work, but it will not pop!

In addition, networking functions such as WiFi and Bluetooth are often built in, and more complex circuitry that is not on-board, for example to power robot stepper motors, is often available on plug-in 'shields'. The platforms often come in several variants, some of which make initial development easy, while others are better suited for final deployment. For example, a variant of Arduino, the Lilypad series, is designed for sewing into digital fashion. Significantly, these platforms are built on open-source hardware. Since the designs are not proprietary, if there is no variant that is suitable production engineers can create a custom circuit board that has just the components required for deployment, but is still compatible with the development system.

As we discussed in the previous chapter, a design team requires many different skills. While ideally that would include electronics, it is now usually possible to postpone the need for higher levels of electronics expertise till quite late in the production process. The one exception is when you intend the final product to be very small or very cheap, in which case getting expert advice early on can help you avoid designs that are hard to scale (see section 21.5).

The very smallest and cheapest processors (costing a fraction of a dollar) only have a few hundred bytes of program memory. With this level of hardware, each byte of program code may mean you have to go for a higher-end processor at greater per-unit cost. If you are aiming at real commodity scale you will need to work in assembly code. However, even at this level there are development boards and IDE (integrated development environments) to allow you to code on a PC screen and even, with the slightly larger processors, in the C language.

For projects where you can deploy a variant of one of the more prototype-friendly families such as Arduino, or at least do early development using these, things become much easier. At a hardware level, the development board is typically connected to a PC via a USB cable, allowing a full screen IDE to be used on the PC. In some cases, notably Electric Imp, the embeddable device may connect

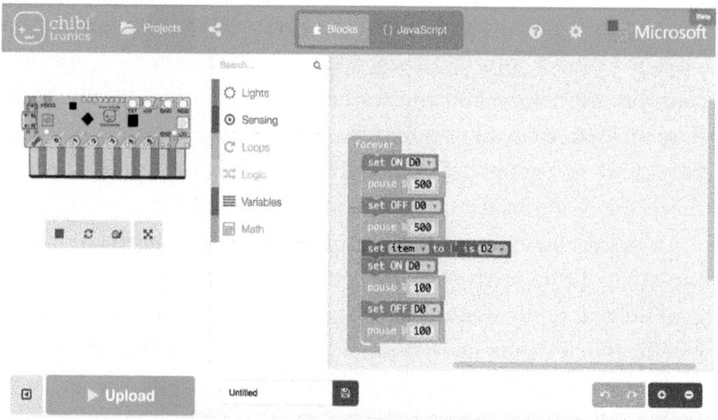

Figure 21.3 Example from Chibitronics, 'Love to Code' (https://chibitronics.com/lovetocode/)

directly through WiFi to a cloud service, enabling programming and deployment via a web-based user interface, and even allowing deployed systems to be updated with no physical connection.

In terms of coding, dedicated high-level languages, such as Processing, have libraries that allow easy access to the GPIO and other low-level features, so that controlling electronic devices is not significantly more complex than reading or writing a variable. Furthermore, the development environments include Scratch-like graphical programming (Figure 21.3) and block and link visual data-flow paradigms (such as Max/MSP) that are familiar in audio and video processing applications. This significantly lowers the barriers for development, allowing those who would see themselves as non-coders to create relatively complex interactions that can be directly deployed.

21.4 Time and Delays

If you study for an undergraduate computer science (CS) degree, the first programming classes focus on imperative command and data structures: loops, arrays, objects; always essentially straight-line coder-in-control programming, with each step following precisely from the one before, and when you put a value in a variable it stays there unchanged until you next access it. Possibly in a second or third year option you get to deal with network or real-time programming, where you realize the world is not always so clean.

If instead you took a more business-oriented computing course you might begin with Visual Basic or a similar environment that combines graphic-oriented screen construction with small snippets of code. These languages are often considered less 'hardcore' than those used in a CS course: Java, C++, or Python. However, while these courses often start with less rich data structures, they are event-driven from day one: the user presses a button and you, the coder, have to deal with it. Control is not entirely absent, of course. Within the confines of each block of event code, you stay in control and the screen does what you tell it to do. However, the larger flow is outside your control, determined by user actions and external events.

Even in user-interface programming, there are many layers of software between the real world and your code: starting with low-level drivers, then through the operating system and often multiple layers of libraries. You end up with a sanitized view of coding. Once you start to deal with network and physical computing, all semblance of this sanitized world is stripped away. In particular, you have to deal with *time*.

21.4.1 *Delay-sensitive interaction*

The classic models of early coding, described above, can lead to 'the myth of the infinitely fast machine', a sense of instantaneity that can cause real problems even in conventional user interfaces [146].

As we saw in the case of Alan and his old mobile phone (Chapter 9), even delays of a few hundred milliseconds can disrupt hand–eye coordination, and if responses to user actions, such as processing a button, take more than a second the user can lose the sense of simultaneity and agency.

Delays can occur because of the time required by complex calculations, but are most commonly caused by interactions with external devices, including network communications or accessing files. Network communication delays are especially noticeable on many smart TV apps where user actions may lead to a spinning dial, or sometimes simply a blank screen, while the next page of information loads.

The spinning dial is a common example of *feedback* that follows the first rule of interaction with delays:

- *immediate syntactic feedback when semantic feedback is delayed*—In a word processor, when a user presses ctrl-B the text immediately becomes bold. This is *semantic feedback*, and if the effect is instant it is sufficient, and best. However, if the user selects 'programme schedule' on the smart TV and has to wait for the screen to refresh, they cannot tell whether the system is waiting or they failed to press the right button. An artificial key-press sound or the appearance of a spinner tells them their action has been recognized—syntactic feedback—even if the action may take some time to complete.

Of course users become impatient, hence the second rule:

- *idempotence*—If an action takes time, users are likely to repeat it, jabbing a button again and again until it does something. If possible, make sure that actions are idempotent—doing them twice has the same effect as doing them once—so that the repeated button presses do not lead to crazy results!

Note that these rules and other advice for time-based interaction [146, 127] become even more critical with IoT devices, especially where you have decided to offload the majority of computation to more central controllers in the environment, or to the cloud. And the situation becomes even more complex when the things that are being controlled, say the temperature of the house, are themselves slow to change.

Box 21.1 Time and temperature

Thinking about time and delays might change the nature of the interactions and controls you offer.

Consider a household heating controller. Typically you have a room thermostat with a target temperature. If the house feels cold there is a tendency to set this target temperature high, partly out of a desire to 'do something' and partly because the difference between a temperature control and a heating input control is often unclear. In particular, if the householder has set the temperature higher but still feels cold a short while later, they may set it higher again, even if the system has not hit the original target temperature yet.

Imagine substituting the temperature control for a simpler up–down control. Often digital thermostats already have this: an 'up' arrow or 'plus' button means 'increase the target temperature', and a 'down' arrow or 'minus' means 'reduce it'. Suppose instead that there is an 'up' and also a 'double up' button: 'up' means 'I want it hotter than now' and 'double up' means 'I want it a lot hotter than now'. If there were an LCD display this would display the current temperature and some little 'up' or 'down' arrows showing whether the controller is trying to warm or cool the room.

With the control where 'up' means 'increase the target temperature', multiple hits may increase it to what will eventually become uncomfortably (and wastefully) hot. With the alternative control the 'up' button is *idempotent*. A second press simply means the same as the first press: 'hotter than now'.

21.4.2 Physical actions take time

The slow change in heat in a radiator system is an example of the way physical actions typically take time to complete. Imagine the 'open' button of an automatic door such as are often found on trains. This sounds quite simple: 'open' button to open the door; 'close' button to close it.

The user presses the button, your code responds by starting the motor—but what next? Well, the motor might have a start/stop relay so that it keeps on going until you tell it to stop, or, if it's a stepper motor, your code may have to periodically say 'take another step'. Then what about when it is fully open? Possibly there is a sensor and your code will have to respond to that, and of course we also hope there is a sensor to recognize when there is unexpected resistance (to avoid squashing people).

Now imagine what happens if the 'close' button is pressed when the door is not yet fully open. You have design decisions to make: do you finish opening the door fully and then process the 'close' button, or do you abandon opening it and reverse the motor?

For the door, you probably want to do the latter, but now imagine you are programming a drinks dispenser. When the flap to drop a can is half open, reversing that motor might jam the can in a half-dropped position. The decisions you make in different situations depend on the physical nature of the action being performed.

It is not only the actions of the system that take time. Think about someone approaching a door controlled by a proximity sensor. If it is a binary 'near'/'not near' sensor, then simple code might look something like this:

> when proximity = 'near' and door closed then open it
> when proximity = 'not near' and door open then close it

Now imagine a person standing just at the outer edge of the proximity sensor's range. The sensor would repeatedly flicker between 'near' and 'not near' and the door would judder back and forth, opening a bit, closing again. You have probably experienced just such a door! Recall also the Savannah game (Box 11.1) in Chapter 11, where the children were confused when small changes in GPS location made animals appear and disappear from their virtual game.

For such circumstances you normally have to introduce hysteresis into your code, making the decision to 'open' when the door is closed a little harder than the decision to 'keep opening' when the door is partially open. You might base this on time, only starting to open the door if the proximity sensor says 'near' for more than a minimum specified period, and likewise only reversing the decision, once it has started, if the sensor says 'not near' for a period. Alternately you might have a three-level sensor: 'near', 'further', 'not sensed'. You then *start* to open the door only when the system triggers 'near', but *keep* it open for as long as the sensor is either 'near' or 'further'.

These partway states are needed not only for sensors but even for the 'open' button itself. As the user presses the button, there will be a moment when it is almost making contact, just like the person standing at the edge of the proximity zone. This can lead to a whole series of press–release–press–release events rather than just one. Correcting this is called 'de-bouncing', and for a keyboard or other off-the-shelf device it is managed at a low level. However, if you are creating a device yourself, you may have to deal with this and 'de-bounce' the button in your own code using time-based triggering. However, you have to choose the timing carefully when you add delays or you may 'de-bounce' someone who tends to jab the button too sharply, losing their button press entirely (Alan always gets de-bounced by train doors).

Box 21.2 Hysteresis in an art gallery app

Imagine you are designing an app to be used in an art gallery. It will show additional information about each artwork and allow gallery users to add their own comments. You have some form of inside location sensing, and in the first prototype you simply show the closest artwork to the user as the focus artwork. However, when you come to test the app, you stand in the middle of the room and the app focus constantly flickers back and forth between all the different artworks because they are all equally close.

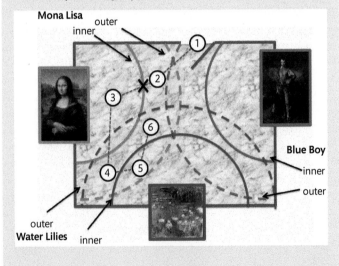

continued

Box 21.2 *continued*

In the second iteration you add hysteresis. You work out an inner and outer active region for each artwork, as in the diagram. Your code looks something like this:

```
Initially:
    focus_variable is empty
When device moved:
    for each artwork A in turn:
        if device is in inner region for artwork A
        then set focus_variable to A
    if not in any inner region and focus_variable
    is not empty
        is device still in outer region for
        focus_variable?
        if so leave focus_variable unchanged
        if not clear focus_variable
```

This code sets the current focus only when you enter the inner region of one of the artworks, then keeps this focus until one of two things happens: either you leave that artwork's outer region, or you enter a different artwork's inner region.

See how this would work for a group of visitors entering through the art gallery door at (1). Initially there is no focus artwork. As the visitors move to (2) they enter the outer region for the 'Mona Lisa', but there is still no focus artwork until they enter the inner region at step (3). As they start to move away to (4) they are still in the outer region of the 'Mona Lisa' and have also entered the outer region of the 'Water Lilies', so the app still retains the 'Mona Lisa' as the focus. Only when the visitors move into the inner region of the 'Water Lilies' at (5) does the focus change to the 'Water Lilies'. Finally, when they move to (6), they are again in the outer region of both the 'Mona Lisa' and the 'Water Lilies' (as at step (4)), but this time, because they have come from the Water Lilies the device focus stays on the 'Water Lilies'.

Note too what happens if, as they walk between (2) and (3), they stop at the moment they first see the 'Mona Lisa' come up as their focus artwork. This will be as they cross the boundary marked with a cross

continued

Box 21.2 *continued*

(X). If the rule were simply to only show the focus artwork when they are in the inner region, then it would disappear if they stepped back even a few centimetres. However, using hysteresis, even if they take a step back the 'Mona Lisa' stays as the focus because they are still in its outer region.

21.4.3 Coding it

It may be that the processor you are using for your physical device or application supports a high-level toolkit for the sensors and buttons on the device, one that operates pretty much like a standard user-interface toolkit, with call-backs or events when things happen. You still have to think about your design choices for cases such as the half-open door, but much of the low-level detail is managed 'under the hood'.

At a slightly lower level, if you are working on a processor with an operating system kernel, such as Linux on a Raspberry Pi, you may find that your code needs to respond to operating system interrupts. Interrupts may happen when a key is pressed (de-bounce managed for you), or when the input from a sensor changes. In some ways, they are like call-backs, except that many systems ensure that call-backs happen one after another, whereas interrupts (as their name suggests) can happen right in the middle of other code. In a high-level language this can even be partway through a single line of code, and if you are on a 16-bit processor, assigning a 32-bit value may involve two assembly language instructions, in which case the interrupt could happen halfway through the assignment! This may be a level you are unfamiliar with, even if you are an experienced coder, but there is an extensive literature on how to deal with this form of concurrency, including semaphores, managing buffers, etc.

If you drop to a lower level again, as you would when programming an Arduino board, for example, you have very little between you and the bare circuitry. At this level your code is often a 'busy loop', going on forever checking various things on each loop and responding to them. If you want to wait for a period between actions, even that typically involves checking the clock on each loop until the time is reached.

Whichever level you are working on, you still need to ensure that you are correctly implementing the design decisions you have made for the physical hardware. Because you are closer to 'bare metal', it is easy to make design decisions accidentally without realizing it. For example, choosing the precise delay to de-bounce a signal is apparently a low-level implementation decision, but without care the chosen delay may be long enough that the user's actions are de-bounced and ignored.

Remember that you also have to manage the partway states of the physical world: whether the door is closed, open, or part open; whether the motor is in the process of opening or closing the door. Rather like the discussion of embodied cognition in Chapter 5, you have a choice. You can manage this model of the world state within the computer; or you can manage it by re-sampling sensors within the world. The latter is more accurate (depending on the sensors), since internal models need to rely on predicting the effect of actions. Systems based on the sensor method are a form of closed-loop feedback (see Section 5.4) and hence typically more robust. For example, if the train is going round a bend the sideways force may make the door open more quickly or slowly. However, using sensors can be more costly, and adds points of failure.

Whether it is held internally using predictive models, or externally through sensors, you also have to be aware that your model of the world is just that—a model. If you use an internal model it may say the door is open because the motor ran for 3 seconds, but perhaps the motor failed, or the door is jammed. If you use sensors, they may say the door is closed, but that could be because the optical sensor has a piece of waste paper stuck over it.

Simple computing is about stasis and certitude; physical computing is about change and uncertainty. It is challenging, but rewarding.

21.5 Pragmatics

21.5.1 Resilience

Although it can be difficult to get the code right, often that is the least of your problems. Getting something to work for a demo on a desktop is one thing; having it still running after a month in the grimy, disordered real world is another!

At a software level you need to make sure your code is resilient to WiFi hotspots failing and restarting, power cycles after glitches in the power supply (no nice shutdown), and memory leaks, or other aspects of long-running computation. Yet more challenging are problems resulting from the physical environment, including heat dissipation, damp, dust, and physical damage. Each situation is different, so you will need to be ready to predict and respond to problems particular to your system. However, here is an example to give you an idea of things to look out for.

At Lancaster University the bus stop is in an underpass that runs beneath the central square of the campus. Opposite where the students wait for their buses home in the evening is a large concrete wall. This seemed the perfect spot for a large public display that would provide the opportunity to experiment with novel interactions.

Powerful projectors were ordered with outdoor-rated casings. The original plan had been to place them on the bus-stop side of the underpass and projecting across to the wall, but there were health and safety concerns about the powerful light shining through the upper windows of double decker buses, so instead the projectors were suspended from the underpass roof, above the roadway.

One consequence of this placement was that the underpass would have to be closed completely when any adjustments or maintenance were needed. However, this was not expected to be a problem as the projector bulbs and the casings with their outdoor-rated air filters were low maintenance.

Unfortunately it turned out that the outdoor-rated air filters had not previously encountered Lancaster bus diesel soot. The filters rapidly clogged, with the result that the (costly) bulbs overheated and burned out if the projector was on for more than half an hour, causing not only considerable expense but also closure of the road.

In the end the solution was found to involve cycling the projectors so that no individual one was on for too long. Unfortunately, however, far more effort was spent on these practicalities than on designing novel interactions.

21.5.2 Cost and size

Sometimes you are designing a bespoke system with a small number of devices and in that case you may choose to use off-the-shelf hardware such as Raspberry Pi. The different forms of Tiree signage described earlier in this chapter and in Chapter 14 are a good example.

However, if you are expecting large-scale use, you have to think about commodity production. Often both size and cost are critical here. To some extent they both align naturally during the design of hardware for production: large production runs reduce costs, and choices such as custom Printed Circuit Boards (PCBs) and surface mounted components reduce the size and complexity of the final device. Prototype and pilot versions can often get away with being far more costly and 'clunky'. However, the architectural design decisions you make early during development can have an impact on this final commodification stage. Although you don't have to worry about making each unit small and cheap during the early design stages, you should think about ensuring that they can be made so later.

Again we can use the Firefly intelligent lighting system as an example (Box 2.1). The first mono-colour versions had just three additional components per LED: a micro-processor, a diode, and a capacitor. This meant that an early low volume run of 5000 lights was possible, and for this the most expensive items after the LEDs themselves were the connectors, which would not be needed in factory production, as boards would be soldered directly to the wiring.

Another early decision was to design the lights to be self-addressing on 'power up'. It is possible to have chips with individual addresses assigned at the factory, or to program each chip individually with a different address. However, that would be far more expensive than having effectively identical chips with the same program burnt into each.

We mentioned in Chapter 17 how the inclusion of a microprocessor for every LED at first seems like technological overkill; however, making each light essentially a single-pixel network computer *commodifies the complexity*. Each individual light is more complex, but volume production reduces the cost of that, and because the lights are more intelligent the wiring can be simpler. Lighting control is usually achieved through having direct wire connections from controller to light fitting, but the intelligent lights need only a single power line, reducing copper use and cost. So even at prototype levels of production it turns out to be cheaper than less flexible commercial lighting that relies more on point-to-point wiring.

Theory and Philosophy of Physicality

22.1 Gathering Threads

Throughout this book we have encountered many philosophical and theoretical threads: from discussions of Heidegger in Chapter 10 to the nature of space and time in Chapter 11 and the changing role of money in Chapter 17. We have seen how fundamental physics involves information, and how computation is intensely physical with attendant environmental implications.

There are too many such points to summarize fully, but in this chapter we will draw together a few. We start with the way digital technology acts as a mirror to the nature of the material world, and by its similarities and differences reveals fresh insights about physicality. We then move on to what it means to be human, embodied in a physical and now a digital environment. Finally we look forward to the potential design future and the way all of society is being changed, and could be transformed, by a rich understanding of the interplay between our physical and digital existence.

22.2 What It Means to Be Physical

Early in this book we discussed some of the ways we can explore the limits of human understanding of the physical world. In Chapter 7, we saw how the fairy tale of the Frog Prince, which dates back many hundreds of years [212], allows us to see aspects of what are acceptable metamorphoses; insights that have been validated by experiments with small babies. In a similar way, science fiction explores both new technologies and the limits of physicality, with wormholes, transporter beams, clones, and replicants. Arthur C Clarke wrote that 'Any sufficiently advanced technology is indistinguishable from magic' [72], but no matter whether it is magic or advanced technology, the limits of our imagination tell us something about the fixed fundamentals of our physical reasoning.

On the other hand, existing technology, and in particular digital technology, has also stretched our own understanding of the physical world. In Chapter 7, we looked at three rules of physicality and saw that digital technologies (and others) systematically break them. As we examine these divergences they often cast new light on the physical world: by seeing alternatives, we see the familiar more clearly.

Consider, for example, the nature of identity. Philosophers have long pondered on what makes a thing what it is. Plato looked to a world of 'ideals' of which the things we encounter are merely shadows. Philosophical idealists see reality as confined to our own imaginings, whereas for realists the world exists and has qualities, independent of our perceptions of it. Struggling with the paradox inherent in the Catholic doctrine of transubstantiation, Aquinas distinguished the *accidents* of an object, its perceivable attributes, from its *substance*, its actual being.

We may use some of these ideas to explore the worlds of magic and science fiction. Although Aquinas developed his concepts to account for the mystery of the Eucharist they can equally be applied to the Frog Prince: although the accidents were all (talking) frog, the substance was always prince.

The subject becomes more complex when we consider the underlying it-ness of things. When we think about 'its' accidents or 'its' substance, or say 'it is really a prince', we must first think 'it'. To deal with this, traditional philosophy often looked to the physical and temporal location of an object, or in Descartes' terms, its extension [374]. Indeed mathematicians, who appear to have a belief in the fundamental existence of their abstractions, are often seen as Platonists, placing their objects in a virtual world [95].

In the digital world we see some parallels to physical objects. Memory 'locations' are metaphorically places, but they also, in simple computers, represent real physical patches of silicon or metal oxide. Relational databases define a thing's identity in terms of essential attributes, and do not allow duplicate records—rather as fermions in particle physics satisfy the Pauli exclusion principle. By contrast, the key in a NoSQL database or the URI (Uniform Resource Identifier) in semantic web-linked data [209] denotes an abstract identifier so that objects can have identical values and yet be deemed distinct. More confusingly, a single file or database object may be replicated in multiple locations or fragmented to fit into blocks spread across a disk. The parallels with physicality are yet more strained in the Smalltalk language, which allows an object to 'become' another, exchanging all of its attributes and indeed its fundamental type, and yet still be recognized as the 'same' object. And the UNIX file system doesn't even bother to store blocks of a file that are all zero, instead effectively calling them into existence when required.

By bending or breaking the familiar qualities of physical objects, the objects we encounter in the digital world offer new examples and analogies for understanding those physical objects. In addition, conceptual things such as groups, ideas, or criteria need to be given a level of explicit form when encoded digitally. To some extent this mirrors the role of language as a leveller, which we discussed in Chapter 15. Philosophically, things at quite different levels of abstraction or conceptual realism are represented in similar ways, to be manipulated by code.

At a more practical level, this bending of reality can help educationally. The alternate reality kit [373], which allowed users to manipulate forces such as gravity and friction, was an early example, and more recently physics teachers have used Angry Birds to help students understand ballistic motion [5, 49].

22.3 Ghosts of Physicality

There is a paradox. We need to understand the physical world deeply in order to ensure that digital technologies do not lose critical aspects of human life and culture. Yet it is sometimes only through the lens of digitality, the contrast between the thing and its digital alter ego, that we understand what we originally had. One of the challenges of modern society is to make certain that we learn the lessons of technology fast enough to be able to manage it safely and well.

22.3.1 Money

In Chapter 17 we saw that the essential functions of money are being disrupted by digital technology. It is not only that the physical form of money is being pushed into credit cards and electronic transfers—that is essentially the same transformation which has been happening since the first bank ledgers. It is more that money had, for hundreds of years, two roles: as representation of value and as transfer of information, and the latter role is being taken over by completely other mechanisms.

The informational role of money has been implicit in economics since Adam Smith's 'invisible hand' [370]. However, it is only as IT systems have started to replace it that this becomes truly clear.

Cryptocurrencies also cast into relief the way that even the role of money as exchange of value has been gradually displaced. In the days of the gold standard, a paper note was linked to a certain quantity of gold, but this has long since been abandoned. Share trading, futures markets, and financial derivatives are increasingly distanced from the underlying profitability of a company or the 'value' of goods. They say more about beliefs: how others view that value now or in the future. In turn, the views of these others will be based on their own beliefs and on those of yet other others. Cryptocurrencies take this to the extreme, being based solely on such mutual beliefs and having no final physical basis for value at all, except the vast quantities of electrical power needed to secure each transaction.

Of course, money also prefigured digitality by breaking the need for temporal and spatial simultaneity in trade. In the days of barter, the farmer needed to drive a goat to the carpenter to be able to exchange the goat for a new table. Money means the transfers of goat for cash and cash for table can be separated in space and time.

22.3.2 *Space*

Electrical, electronic, and digital technology have gradually eroded the barriers of space, replacing footsteps with moving photons and electrons. Again this is not a new thing in itself: exchanges of letters have shrunk distance for thousands of years, and the richness of historic correspondence shows that these have not always been simply poor substitutes for face-to-face meetings.

In Chapter 12 we discussed the distinction made by some geographers between space and place: the former a set of coordinates, or spatial location, the latter imbued with social significance. We also saw how Auge's concept of non-place [11] describes how many constructed spaces lack this significance. However, non-places rarely stay so long or for everyone—airports, shopping malls, and train stations often have rich worker cultures behind the scenes, and, as 'Brief Encounter' [259] exemplifies, they can also become places of significance for travellers.

On the one hand this leads us to ask how digital 'spaces' such as Facebook or WhatsApp can become 'places' through use. Shared experiences via instant messages, or shared photos, may create layers of meaning—but in what? Is it the idea of the app, or the particular patterns of coloured pixels? Designers need to understand this in order to create meaning in social media. Does a change in brand colour effectively demolish a social place? Psychologists and politicians need to understand this as well, in order to make sense of the rapidly altering structures of digital society.

More radically, these digital places are also altering physical space. This is quite evident when augmented reality fills the world with Pokémon characters, bringing welcome or unwelcome guests. However, sometimes it seems that digital technology, by eroding geography, is *displacing* space. In many countries the younger generation are less likely to go out to meet friends, instead relying on ubiquitous mobile phones and computers to keep continually in touch. Friendship is no longer intermittent aloneness and togetherness, but a continual peripheral connection. Alone in non-places, waiting for buses or cramped in trains; together in coffee bars or fast-food restaurants: heads are bent over mobile phones—it is no longer where one is that is significant.

Will this be the end of physical 'place', or do we need to redefine it, finding ways to understand and create social meaning in space that runs alongside location-less sociality? Movements to take breaks from social media, or abandon it entirely, may suggest design turns that alternate physical and digital social experience, or deliberately provide non-WiFi spots. However, experiences such as photo sharing in public displays [387] may offer ways to marry ubiquitous digitality and located sociality.

22.4 Embodied Cyborgs

We have seen how, from our earliest beginnings, humans are tool users. Fitts' Law, apparently a fundamental law of human cognition, is in fact a law about the technologically extended human body—we are cyborgs from the start, first with stone and wood, now silicon and steel (Chapter 5). Scientific ecology teaches us that all creatures are intimately bound with their physical environments, fitted to them and also modifying them, sometimes accidentally—sheep tracks through the moorland, and sometimes deliberately—termite mounds or birds' nests.

Human technology is undeniably *extensive*, to the degree that we threaten the existence of the entire global ecosystem. It is also *distinctive*, different to that of other animals. Yet it is, in many ways, part of our animal nature; even bumblebees have been taught to use tools [268]. This recognition that we are embedded in the physical world goes by many names: embodied mind, extended cognition, ecological psychology, distributed cognition.

Some of these are closer to empirical statements about the way in which we act in the world. In Chapter 8 we saw how Gibson's ecological psychology, which has found its way into design through the notion of *affordances*, regards our perceptions as intimately tied to actions. Affordances are about the way the properties of the world, as they relate to our ability to act upon them, are 'immediately' perceived rather than mediated through complex reasoning. When we see a saucepan handle we do not engage in a mental calculation to assess its size and shape, but simply perceive it as 'graspable'. Equally important are the ways in which *epistemic actions* allow us to explore the perceptual world, for example to turn our head towards a noise, or open a door to see what is in a room.

Likewise, in the social world, distributed cognition and numerous ethnographic studies have revealed the complex ways in which humans coordinate their actions through shared physical artefacts and achieve 'cognitive' feats that would be impossible individually (see Chapter 5).

These insights have immediate implications for design, both in the way that we *study humans*, taking into account their physical environment, actions, and social setting, and in the ways we *build devices and systems* to fit within rich human–technology ecologies.

However, embodiment has a more philosophical or metaphysical aspect. Early embodiment theorists, notably Heidegger and Merleau-Ponty, emphasized the phenomenological nature of engaged human activity, the experience of *being in the world* [211, 291]. Central to this experience are those aspects of which we are unaware including, often, the tools in our hands. Some more recent philosophers, such as Gallagher and Noë [172, 310], pursue this phenomenological approach into near-religious territory, while others, such as Clark [68], have a more pragmatic philosophical approach. The common factor is a perspective that stands against the Cartesian view, which starts with the individual and works out. In contrast, embodiment sees humans as *first and foremost* embedded in the world.

This more ecological or relational stance casts light on our origins.

Language is clearly an interpersonal aspect of our being, and we have discussed the socio-linguistic Eden, the flowering of technical, social and artistic culture some 40,000–70,000 years ago, to which many scholars attribute the development of complex language. Recent paleontological developments have suggested that the symbolic origins of language may go deeper, potentially even being shared with Neanderthals [40]. It may well be that at some level, humans have always been linguistic beings.

The way that we incorporate language into our individual cognition may be even more fundamental than its social and cultural impact. Some philosophers, including Dennett and Clark, have argued that elements of our internal reasoning and sense of consciousness are related to internalized monologue [97, 68]. Furthermore, one of the classic examples of distributed cognition is the use of pencil and paper for complex arithmetic—tool use (the pencil) in order to enable cognition to be offloaded into the environment (on paper) using symbolic language for individual thinking: a truly rich picture of the way physical and social elements are recruited as part of our thinking, even when we're alone.

It seems possible that the very idea of logical or rational thinking has external origins in our need to work together. In Chapter 15 we argued that even our sense of self evolved from social interaction [125]—by needing to understand how others are thinking about us, we develop the means to think about ourselves. Likewise our human ability to think logically may have arisen from our need to explain things to others and subsequently, in human development, that ability has been internalized.

Embodiment seems to be primarily about physical action, and is of course important for the physical design of devices. However, Gibson's concept of affordance has also been highly influential in purely digital design. Our understanding of embodiment, and indeed the word itself, stems from our physical bodies, but is more essentially about the way in which we are creatures of action. Whether engaged in writing on a word processor, playing a computer game, or chatting in Messenger, we are often, in Heidegger's terms, *thrown*, aware only of the object of our actions, not of the technology itself.

These broader notions of embodiment and its philosophical foundations have found resonance with many in interaction design, notably Dourish, whose notion of 'embodied interaction' draws particularly on Heidegger [150]. Even our interactions on the web can be seen in this light, particularly the way in which our cognitive functions are offloaded into cloud services (including our memory of phone numbers, addresses, diaries, and research bibliographies). We also collaborate in ways in which the cognitive power of the whole is greater than any of us individually [58, 204, 118].

22.5 The Limits of Embodiment

The more extreme proponents of embodiment sometimes seem to suggest that there is no inner life and no representation of the world other than the world.

To some extent this is a matter of rhetoric and language. The term 'representation' has often been used to mean a form of declarative (consciously available) knowledge. On seeing a tomato, declarative reasoning might proceed, 'I see the front of a tomato; tomatoes also have backs; therefore this tomato has a back'. However, your phenomenological experience is that you are simply aware of the whole tomato even though you can't see it all [310]. Sometimes you may have to revise that 'knowing'—the tomato might be half-eaten, with the uneaten side turned in your direction. It seems evident that while it may not be explicit or consciously available, there is something inside our brains that is delivering this phenomenological impression of 'back-ness' to the tomato.

Recall Clark's 007 principle (Chapter 5):

> In general evolved creatures will neither store nor process information in costly ways when they can use the structure of the environment and their operations on it as a convenient stand-in for the information-processing operations concerned. ([69])

We said that this parsimony cuts both ways: if it is more efficient to use internal representations, then we will do that. Indeed, experiments have shown that subjects may use their internal memories in preference to action in an interface, even when the latter would be more efficient [196].

If we have any doubt about the importance of more conscious thought, the sheer computational cost of linear thought should remind us. Recall how we saw in Chapter 17 that computation is expensive both in terms of physical space and energy. Our brains are composed of billions of neurons acting simultaneously; in computing terms, a massively parallel associative architecture. Those who build artificial neural networks have to struggle to implement them over the very fast, but largely serial, architecture of traditional computers.

However, 'implementing' a serial stream of consciousness over the brain's inherent parallel associative architecture is equally complex and costly. Nature tends to be careful about needless expenditure of energy (or at least those species that are not usually suffer extinction) so it is reasonable to assume our linear thought processes are valuable.

Historically, there were periods, especially in the latter half of the nineteenth century and early twentieth century, when science and philosophy seemed to agree that the world could be reduced to closed categorizations and formal logic. Heidegger, Merleau-Ponty, and other phenomenological thinkers were reacting against this hegemony of the mechanical and cerebral. A philosophy of human activity, especially in a digital age, needs to take seriously our dual cognitive and physical sides, not subsuming one into the other but embracing our external and internal lives as part of our embodied nature.

More pragmatically, for many years interaction paradigms have been focused on direct manipulation—emulated physicality. This has proved incredibly powerful, allowing us to make use of our innate understanding of the physical to interact with the digital. However, if we are, in the terms of Engelbart (the pioneer of so much interface design), to use computers to 'augment the human intellect' [153], we need to create physical designs that make the best use of our physical understanding of the world as we interact with digital devices. We must also go beyond that, enabling ourselves to make effective use of their computational capacity in comprehensible ways.

22.6 The Extended Genome

Richard Dawkins' *Selfish Gene* [92] introduced many people to the ideas and controversies surrounding the role of our genes in evolution. In addition, the book coined the term 'meme', creating a parallel between the way ideas spread and replicate in culture and the way genes do in our physical bodies. Since then, 'meme' has become a household word, not least in its relation to social media, from images of cats to fake news.

Although the parallel between genes and memes is a rich metaphor, the precise analogy is loose: ideas combine in more complex ways than individual genes, their boundaries less rigid, and their mutation often intentional. Arguably, genetic technology is catching up with the metaphor: CRISPR allows precise editing of DNA, and in the laboratory the very genetic alphabet has been extended to create forms of DNA and genes that are new to nature. However, the intentionality of ideas is ancient: social-media sock puppets manipulating stock prices and election campaigns are simply following patterns of manipulation and persuasion that recur throughout history, including the orators of Ancient Greece, and Aaron speaking for Moses.

Of course the importance of genes is not simply that they sit in intersecting lines on our chromosomes but that they influence our physical nature: height, eye colour, strength, susceptibility to infection, and propensity to cancer.

Similarly, ideas and culture are not simply incisions on stone, ink on paper, or images on the screen. They also affect the physical world around us. In some ways this is very obvious: there is no way we could accomplish works of engineering like a pyramid or a skyscraper without the representational power of mathematics, and no way we could manage the complexities of a modern business without rich communication and written instructions.

However, culture and language are not merely enablers of physical manipulation of our environment. They change the way we are able to describe our environment. Hence they subtly affect the kinds of artefacts we construct. When you look through a catalogue for furniture, the sections follow well-known categories: chairs, tables, cupboards. It would be hard to place the traditional 'bacon settle' [1] in a furniture catalogue, as it combines chair and cupboard. If something is difficult to classify for sale, it is less saleable, and hence less likely to be produced. This is a positive feedback effect (see Chapter 5), which will deepen the distinctions further—the things for which we have no words are less likely to exist [117].

---

[1] A *bacon settle* is a high-backed chair or bench that would be placed freestanding in a room facing the fire. The back of the chair is also a cupboard in which bacon would be hung to store it, protected from vermin.

Not only does language alter the way we are able to describe and create our environment, it also changes the very way we perceive the world. The Sapir–Whorf hypothesis [421, 252] suggests that our language, in part or whole, determines our thoughts. If we can't say it, we can't think it. As a strong statement there are certainly counterexamples of spontaneous expression of concepts in languages where these are hard to express [100], and, indeed, a really strict linguistic relativity would make neologisms impossible. However, there is also ample evidence that our native language (or even the language a multilingual person is currently speaking) changes aspects of perception, including interpretation of pictures [9] and our ability to distinguish colours [100].

We saw in Chapter 12 that what appear to be fundamental cognitive and perceptual properties, such as the Müller–Lyer illusion, in fact vary between cultures [215]. It appears that the perceptual effects of linear perspective are related to being brought up in rectilinear built environments. In short, the physical environment affects our cognition at the deepest level.

Embodiment suggests that the moment by moment boundaries of cognition and body may spread out into the environment to encompass artefacts, tools, and other people. However, these linguistic and environmental effects mean that, at a deep level, what it means to be ourselves is determined in part by the cultural and physical context in which we are brought up: our genotype is written not just in DNA but in the dull echoes of vowels in the womb, and the lines of buildings viewed from a pushchair.

As designers we clearly need to understand how the devices we create resonate with the physical and cultural understanding of our users—but we also need to know that the devices we create will be part of the ecology that reshapes who they are.

For older users most of such effects are likely to be temporary, but for small children we do not fully comprehend the long-term developmental impact of being brought up in a digital environment [118]. Certainly, many linguistic and physical skills are either fixed permanently at a young age, or are at least difficult to change when older. Whether these digitally induced changes are for better or worse is still poorly understood. However, many national health authorities recommend against screen use in the first few years of life. That does not necessarily mean no neonatal digitality, but suggests we introduce the young to a digital world in a richer physical form than flat pixels on a screen.

22.7 Hybrid Ecologies

Education has become a voracious consumer of digital technology: virtual learning systems in universities, smart-boards in schools, and MOOCs (Massive Open Online Courses) and video learning materials such as Khan Academy, which take learning to anyone who has an Internet connection.

Digital versions of textbooks are becoming increasingly popular. For students, ebooks are lighter and continually available, not subject to the recall notice from the library. For educational publishers they offer greater control over the delivery of material, effectively ending the secondhand market that has plagued profitability beyond the first few years of a textbook's life.

However, the educational value of technology in the classroom is at best unclear, and in many cases negative. Research by the Organisation for Economic Co-operation and Development (OECD) found that while some computer use in schools was beneficial compared to no access, beyond this greater availability and use diminished educational outcomes [317]. In universities, studies have found that digital note-taking is far less educationally effective than paper notes [2, 299].

This does not mean that digital technology is not at all useful in education, nor that it should be abandoned in favour of traditional physical books, blackboards, and pens. What it does mean is that we need to look carefully at the way in which old and new technologies are used. In some cases we may try to learn from our understanding of physical materials to create better digital versions, such as better ways to 'thumb through' an ebook. How might we apply this to taking notes, for example? The studies suggest that part of the problem is that when students use digital devices they simply transcribe the teacher's words, whereas paper note-taking forces a level of processing to extract the principal points. Constructive learning suggests that this processing itself helps to integrate knowledge, while more succinct notes are easier to review and revise. Knowing this, we might envisage training students to use existing digital devices more effectively, or redesign them to encourage better digital note-taking practices [47].

Furthermore, we might also look for ways to use digital and physical materials alongside one another in *hybrid ecologies*. For example, many students find it less stressful to read a physical textbook. However, the book might have an accompanying app which gives access to the text when the book is not available, or can be used alongside the book, perhaps presenting quizzes, or interactive versions of diagrams [144].

Box 22.1 A physical–digital hybrid textbook

Twenty years ago, Alan and some colleagues had just finished another book project: the second edition of a Human–Computer Interaction textbook [138]. They wanted to put the text online to enable it to be read on devices. This was in the days before ebooks; however, the authors believed that making an online edition would increase use and ultimately lead to higher sales of paper copies. The publisher did not agree!

Because the authors wanted to do something online, more than the usual table of contents on textbook websites, they were forced to ask themselves deep questions about what were the advantages of an electronic copy of the book—in other words, they had to *deconstruct the experience* of reading online and offline.

An obvious advantage of an online edition is that you can read it without having a (heavy) physical copy to hand, but this was precisely what the publishers did *not* want. Another advantage is that you can search an online text. The physical book had an index, of course, which for some purposes is better than free-text search, since index terms are more carefully selected. Indeed, a well-devised index may include entries on pages where the indexed term does not occur but

continued

Box 22.1 *continued*

the concept does. However, free-text search is also useful for different kinds of information seeking.

So the authors created an online search for the book. The user can enter search terms and the system returns all paragraphs that contain the terms, with information about where in the book to look further.

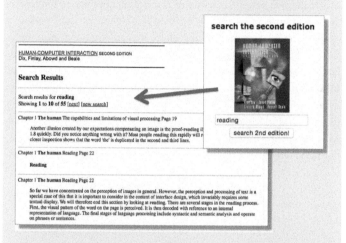

The search is useful even if you do not have the book to hand, since it includes individual paragraphs about the topics. However, the provided text is sufficiently limited to satisfy the publisher was happy (you can't easily simply read the book online), and moreover, it constantly says 'read me', encouraging users to buy the book as well. Crucially, it is also useful when you have the physical copy of the book, as it offers a way to search the text. Indeed when preparing the next edition, the authors used the search extensively to check whether they had previously covered certain topics.

More generally, thinking of the design of hybrid digital–physical ecologies can suggest ways to make the best of both. For example, some hospitals have coloured lines that lead from the reception to specific departments. Patients who arrive at the main entrance can simply be told, rather like Dorothy in the 'Wizard of Oz', 'follow the yellow line'. However, as fixed point-to-point routes, they are less helpful for patients or visitors who have to move between two departments, unless they return to the reception first.

An elegant solution to this type of issue, and one that exploits a physicality context, is *Appliance Design Studio*'s Navitile [187].

The *Navitile* system consists of a series of networked Radio Frequency Identification (RFID) enabled floor tiles. On their surface is a set of arrows arrayed on the eight main points of the compass (Figure 22.1). It is designed for large public buildings, such as hospitals, where people unfamiliar with the building are frequently asked to navigate their way through it. The system exploits 'wayfinding', which is based on the way we use the physical world to navigate by using landmarks as markers from which we orient ourselves. *Navitile* works on the premise that arriving visitors need to navigate to a particular location. In our case the hospital receptionist would give the

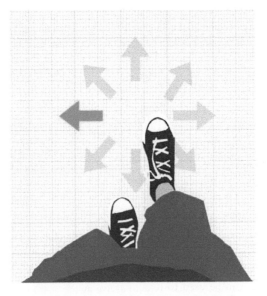

Figure 22.1 The *Navitile* by Appliance Design Studio

visitor an RFID-embedded object such as a name badge, brochure, or card, encoded with the appropriate destination. *Navitiles* are placed at key junctions, and every time the visitor reaches a junction they stand on the tile. The *Navitile* reads the RFID tag and points them in the right direction by illuminating the appropriate arrow. The system takes account of the physical context of its deployment and allows the user to interact with the world in a flexible and unobtrusive way; start and end points don't matter and the visitor does not need to know where they are to know which way to turn. A stop at the café or shop *en route* causes no problems. Unlike a map, Navitile only gives specific information about a single destination, so although the system covers any location a map can cover, it only shows the user the information they actually need.

Navitile uses quite advanced technology. A simpler system might build on the use of coloured lines along corridors that meet at major junctions. The hospital navigation device, perhaps a special purpose device or perhaps a mobile app, would initially say, 'follow the red line'. When the patient reached a major junction the device would beep or vibrate and say, 'now follow the blue line'. Sustained screen interaction would not be required, avoiding the risk of collisions and making it easier to carry bags, hold the hand of a child or push a wheelchair.

Whether using intelligent floor tiles or painted lines with a simple app, the lesson is that the whole ecology, physical and digital, can be designed together to address human problems.

Some years ago Alan led a design project to create a virtual version of the Christmas cracker, a form of table ornament found in the United Kingdom and some other countries. Crackers are pulled apart to reveal small toys, jokes, and paper hats. The experiential and functional nature of the physical experience was *deconstructed*, teased apart into different aspects, so that these could then be *reconstructed* in a different media [128]. The same technique has since been used in other projects [224, 223]. Typically the path has led to a purely digital final artefact, but the same deconstruction—reconstruction technique can be used to look at potential hybrid physical–digital ecologies, asking which aspects of the desired experience, for example lecturing a class, are best served by available physical and digital means [110].

22.8 From Object to Agent

Many of the very earliest computer interfaces used some form of command language: a 'servant' paradigm or metaphor. This was displaced in the 1980s by the direct manipulation paradigm [366, 312], which has dominated interaction design for many years. Direct manipulation essentially treats data or information objects as if they were like a virtual world. Touchscreens and tangible and gesture-based interfaces have changed the way this is embodied from mouse and pointer to more direct bodily interaction, but the computer system is largely regarded as *passive* data.

Sometimes the information objects are given metaphorical embodiments, such as folders, documents, and trashcans. However, even less physical 'objects' like the inner working of a television (channel selection, etc.) share this passive quality: you press the button and the channel changes. In embodiment terms the TV remote is *ready to hand*, invisible, almost part of your extended body.

The same happens in a car. You do not feel that you 'tell' the car what to do; you simply turn the steering wheel to turn the car. We can imagine more hi-tech versions where you could steer, accelerate, and brake by simply leaning in the driver's seat, rather like a surfer. Yet the basic paradigm is still that your control of the vehicle is 'direct', with the intention that you forget the steering wheel and just think about the road. The car is, again, part of your extended body.

Computing, however, has been experiencing a dramatic change over recent years. In many Internet-based applications, big data has been used to create various forms of recommendation or trust score. Now the computer seems *active*, not merely doing what you ask but often suggesting what you might want to do and altering your interface accordingly.

Returning to the example of the car, the way the technologies are developing is not really about drivers embodiedly surfing the motorway. It is more about sitting back, disengaged, while the autonomous vehicle drives itself. The car is still envisioned as obedient: you tell it where to go. However, it is no longer passive but instead makes moment by moment decisions for you: determining the route, changing lanes, or braking to avoid an accident. Indeed in some circumstances, the car may not even be entirely obedient. It may ignore you or modify your instructions if, for example, you ask it to do something dangerous or illegal.

Figure 22.2 shows various digital technologies along two dimensions. On the left are those where the technology takes a more passive role, such as traditional PC direct manipulation software, whereas towards the right are those where the computation is more active, such as recommendation systems. The technology at the top is more amorphous, for example cloud computation and many web technologies, whereas towards the bottom are technologies that take on a physical form, such as a TV remote or an autonomous car.

As we said, the earliest user interfaces used various forms of command-based interaction, which is agent-mediated interaction. The direct manipulation that superseded it was an instrumental or tool-based paradigm of interaction. However, now the Artifical Intelligence (AI) turn in technology is forcing a re-examination of interfaces where the computer is no longer hiding its computational power in a simulation of digital materiality.

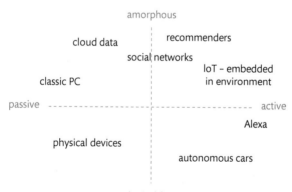

Figure 22.2 When computation becomes active

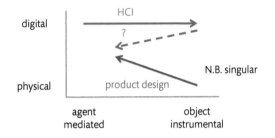

Figure 22.3 HCI and industrial design convergence (from [133])

Industrial design has taken a different route, beginning with instrumental interactions with physical objects. However, as digital technology has become incorporated into almost every object, industrial design is also beginning to engage with more agency, so that, as we have seen throughout this book, the two are converging towards new forms of physically embodied intelligent interactions (see Figure 22.3).

The bottom part of Figure 22.2 is most obviously relevant to this book on physicality. However, if we look at the bottom-right quadrant, we see that things are a little more complex. Home controllers, such as Alexa, give physical embodiment to computational elements distributed invisibly in central heating controllers, and other household appliances. Furthermore, while an autonomous car already has a clear and very physical embodiment—a ton of steel hurtling down the road—some designs nevertheless incorporate a device on the dashboard that is the locus of interaction, an embodiment of intelligence within the physical shell. The idea of being within what is effectively a robot may be a little too unnerving unless the 'clever' bit is made to have a separate existence alongside the passengers.

Intelligence is becoming spread throughout the materials and objects of our environment, creating emergent effects, rather like a murmuration of starlings. In both a home controller and an autonomous car, amorphous digital aspects are given physical form. This suggests that we need fresh paradigms or metaphors to help users make sense of active computation, and physicality has an important part to play in that.

Sometimes, especially where there is an obvious robotic element, the intelligence may be given an embodiment with which we interact directly, recruiting our linguistic communication abilities. That is the easy case. However, in human–human collaboration, we also interact with one another through the physical environment. When we act on objects we perceive the effects of our actions through feedback. In addition, those with whom we are working also observe the effects of our actions on objects, and we observe theirs. *Feedthrough*, this process of mutual observation, establishes an important channel of indirect communication through the physical or digital environment [104]. Often such collaborative activities are the most natural and fluid, for example, carrying a piece of furniture together. Direct communication is only used when something goes wrong or the task becomes especially difficult, such as navigating a narrow doorway; that is when elements of explicit collaborative problem-solving come into play.

This may well become an important paradigm of future physical interactions or even *partnership* with active digital agents. Alongside direct communication, humans and agents may share mutual observation of human and computational effects on the environment [133]. Most tangible interaction research tends towards the passive right of Figure 22.2. However, forms of feedthrough with the artificial agent are being developed in some research systems. For example, kitchen computational aids for the elderly may observe the cook preparing a meal, infer the stage in a recipe and then prompt the cook if an ingredient or step is missed [318].

22.9 Deep Digitality

As designers, technologists, or users, the digital transformation is most evidently embodied in the physical products we see around us, pick up, look at, and interact with. To a lesser extent we are aware of the digitality embedded in our homes and work places: Weiser foresaw a world full of screens made invisible by their ubiquitous presence [416]. This has become true, and yet sensors typically outnumber screens, truly invisible, and made manifest only in the tiny screens of controllers, or frugally embodied home assistants.

However, the most profound impacts of digital technology could be more far-reaching, so deeply infused through the fabric of reality that to talk of its visibility is as inane as to talk about the visibility of the world itself, and yet radically affecting that material world. The deep streams of digitality can flow through modern society as surely as the culverts of buried rivers and Victorian sewers run beneath the streets of Newcastle.

How will this 'Deep Digitality' unfold?

It is easy to see the ways in which digital technology simply reinforces traditional structures of state and business. From the 1960s onward, large central computers have streamlined processes, and in so doing often further centralized power. China is building digital profiles of every citizen and equipping each police officer with facial recognition spectacles—cyborgs of the state. High-profile leaks by Snowden and others have revealed the pervasive nature of US surveillance enabled by massive computation. Fear of terrorism has prompted many countries to press for Internet companies to reveal more to the state, often highlighting how much these global corporations either know about us, or obfuscate on our behalf.

Some risks are well known: warnings of the Panopticon of the state go back to the nineteenth century. Others were foreseeable, and yet seem to have taken us almost unawares. As long ago as 1992 Alan warned of the potential for gender, ethnic, and other biases in machine-learning algorithms [103], a reality that has now become a major issue [19, 77, 90, 190].

Other aspects are less well recognized or understood. We saw in Chapter 16 how money is profoundly changing its role. In a world that gives free rein to market forces this is more radical than winning a game of Go. The central distribution networks of large business and the mass replication of the Model T Ford were due in part to the paucity of money's information flow. As digital communication supplants cash their *raison d'être* is undermined.

Yet like the superimposed drainage patterns of the Welsh valleys (Chapter 11), the patterns of old commerce, health, and governance often seem to roll on regardless as the digital geology shifts beneath them, making only small changes at the margins to incorporate technology as part of an unrelenting behemoth.

Amazon.com embraces the ability of large-scale personal information to address each customer individually, based on the behaviour of the masses, and has created an unparalleled logistic network that is both highly centralized and yet also brings high diversity density to its cathedral-like warehouses—the factories of Ford with the customization of the village blacksmith. Uber has utilized the ability of central networks to link suppliers and customers at a very local level, and yet, together with numerous delivery firms, it seems to keep people functioning as cogs in a giant machine, no less than the Satanic mills of the nineteenth century or even the eighteenth-century slavery trade in human flesh.

Digital fabrication may simply fit into this same story, allowing more flexible and customisable manufacture and reducing the need for vast inventories of spare parts. However, it has inspired a community of grassroots makers. Is there an alternative future of digital artisanship that enables consumer choice whilst fostering producer autonomy?

Likewise in healthcare, the distinctions between specialties are driven by the information constraints of what can be learned and known as an individual, and the distinctions between doctors and community care are enforced by the physical constraint of the hospital walls. But we are beginning to see how Deep Digitality might enable more fluid boundaries between doctor and nurse within hospitals, and support attempts to create more 'joined up' care between hospital and community.

In all areas of commercial and civic life we are at a point when we can question traditional patterns of work, care, and governance. We can, and must, ask the question. Which patterns exist because we need them for safety, health, or democratic accountability, and which, like the river pattern of the south Wales valleys, are simply relics of past technological constraints [129]?

22.10 Final Call

Many of the large-scale effects discussed in this chapter are beyond our ability to control or change. Yet those of us involved in digital design can make small choices. Do we opt for closed centralized or open dispersed architectures? Do we hide complex predictive algorithms or expose aspects of them? Do we abstract people so that interaction is no more than fingers on a glass screen, or do we make computation more concrete, more physical, fitting for embodied humanity? Do we do more for people or help them to achieve more?

To what extent do the devices and services we produce transcend the purposes of titillation and desire that serve to feed and grow a consumer society? How instead can we design to nurture, enrich, and empower all the inhabitants of our digital, physical world?

Some of the transformations of digital technology in a physical world will happen, almost of their own accord, simply by the normal working of industrial and economic pressures. Throughout this book we have glimpsed the far more exciting potential futures of an emerging physical–digital technology. However, if we want these futures to become more than potential, we must think, question, and act. It is up to us to make them real.

Bibliography

1. Adams S. Traditional Christmas card 'set for decline'. *The Daily Telegraph*. 15 December 2008. http://www.telegraph.co.uk/technology/3776875/Traditional-Christmas-card-set-for-decline.html, accessed April 2022. [7.5]

2. Aguilar-Roca N, Williams A., O'Dowd D (2012). 'The Impact of Laptop-free Zones on Student Perfomance and Attitudes in Large Lectures' (2012) 59(4) *Computers & Education* 1300–08. DOI: 10.1016/j.compedu.2012.05.002 [22.7].

3. Alan Walks Wales—one thousand miles of poetry, technology and community. http://alanwalks.wales/, accessed April 2022. [11.4]

4. Alexander C. *Notes On the Synthesis of Form*. Cambridge, MA: Harvard University Press, 1964. [19.2]

5. Allain R. The Physics of Angry Birds. *Wired*. 10 August 2010. [22.2]

6. Alzheimer's Research UK (2020). Sea Hero Quest. https://www.alzheimersresearchuk.org/research/for-researchers/resources-and-information/sea-hero-quest/ accessed April 2022. [12.5]

7. Annett J and Duncan KD. 'Task Analysis and Training Design' (1967) *Occupational Psychology* 41, 211–21. [5.6]

8. Antony R and Henry J. *Lonely Planet Guide to Experimental Travel*. Melbourne: Lonely Planet, 2005. [10.5]

9. Athanasopoulos P, Bylund E, Montero-Melis G, et al. 'Two Languages, Two Minds: Flexible Cognitive Processing Driven by Language of Operation' (2015) 26(4) *Psychological Science* 518–26. Doi: 10.1177/0956797614567509 [22.6]

10. Atkin A (2013). 'Peirce's Theory of Signs' in Edward N Zalta (ed), *The Stanford Encyclopedia of Philosophy*. https://plato.stanford.edu/archives/sum2013/entries/peirce-semiotics/, accessed April 2022. [15.8]

11. Augé M. *Non-Places: An Introduction to Anthropology of Supermodernity*. London: Verso, 1992. [22.3.2]

12. Augustine of Hippo (AD 401). *The Confessions of Saint Augustine, Book XI*. (tr EB Pusey, 1876). https://www.gutenberg.org/ebooks/3296, accessed April 2022. [11]

13. Avrahami D and Hudson SE (2002). 'Forming Interactivity: A Tool for Rapid Prototyping of Physical Interactive Products' B Verplank, A Sutcliffe, W Mackay, et al. (eds), in *Proceedings of the 4th Conference on*

Designing Interactive Systems: DIS 2002, London, England, UK, June 25−28, 2002, New York, NY: ACM. 141−6. [20.10]

14. Baron-Cohen S, Leslie AM, and Frith U. 'Does the Autistic Child Have a "Theory of Mind"?' (1985) 21 *Cognition* 37−46. [15.10]

15. Bayley S and Conran T. *Design: Intelligence Made Visible*. London: Conran Octopus Ltd., 2007. [1.5.2]

16. BBC (2005). Japan's hi-tech carers. *BBC News*. 12 April, 2005. http://news.bbc.co.uk/1/hi/programmes/this_world/golden_years/4436633.stm, accessed April 2022. [2.5.1]

17. BBC (2013). Scottish Ten 3D project unveils Sydney Opera House scan. http://www.bbc.co.uk/news/uk-scotland-glasgow-west-2494 2137, accessed April 2022. [13.2]

18. BBC (2014.) EU court backs 'right to be forgotten' in Google case. *BBC News* 13 May 2014. https://www.bbc.co.uk/news/world-europe-27388289, accessed April 2022. [16.4]

19. BBC (2015). Google apologises for Photos app's racist blunder. *BBC News*, Technology, 1 July 2015. http://www.bbc.co.uk/news/technology-33347866, accessed April 2022. [22.9]

20. BBC News/Technology (2017). Sony phone app takes 3D clone snaps. http://www.bbc.co.uk/news/av/technology-41111442/sony-phone-app-takes-3d-clone-snaps, accessed April 2022. [13.7]

21. Bell G and Gemmell J. 'A Digital Life' (2007) March *Scientific American* https://www.scientificamerican.com/article/a-digital-life/, accessed April 2022. [16.4]

22. Bell D (2004). Infinite archives. (2004) 33(3), 105, *SubStance* 148−61. http://www.jstor.org/stable/3685549, accessed April 2022 [16.4]

23. Bellis M (2009). The History of Prosthetics. http://theinventors.org/library/inventors/blprosthetic.htm, accessed April 2022. [3.6]

24. Bellotti V, Back M, Edwards WK, et al. (2002). 'Making Sense of Sensing Systems: Five Questions for Designers and Researchers' in D Wixon (ed) *Proceedings of the SIGCHI Conference on Human Factors in Computing Systems (CHI '02)*. New York, NY: ACM, 415−22. DOI: http://dx.doi.org/10.1145/503376.503450. [14.9]

25. Bellucci A, Malizia A, and Aedo I. (2011). 'TESIS: Turn Every Surface into an Interactive Surface' in J Rekimoto, H Koike, K Fukuchi, et al. (eds), *Proceedings of the ACM International Conference on Interactive Tabletops and Surfaces* (Kobe, Japan, 13−16 November 2011). New York, NY: ACM. [14.6]

26. Bender B. 'Mapping Alternative Worlds' in S Clifford and A King (eds), *From Place to Place: Maps and Parish Maps*. Bridport: Common Ground, 1996, 41–51. [12.6]

27. Benford S, Calder M, Rodden T, et al. 'On Lions, Impala, and Bigraphs: Modelling Interactions in Physical/Virtual Spaces' (May 2016) 23(2). *ACM Transactions on Computer–Human Interaction*. Article 9: 1–56. DOI: https://doi.org/10.1145/2882784. [21.1]

28. Benford S, Schnädelbach H, Koleva B, et al. 'Expected, Sensed, and Desired: A Framework for Designing Sensing-based Interaction' (March 2005) 12(1) *ACM Transactions on Computer-Human Interaction*, TOCHI, 3–30. [9.5]

29. Benz P. *Experience Design: Concepts and Case Studies*. London: Bloomsbury, 2014. [19.3]

30. Bertini E, Catarci T, Dix A, et al. 'Appropriating Heuristic Evaluation Methods for Mobile Computing' in J Lumsden (ed). *Handbook of Research on User Interface Design and Evaluation for Mobile Technology*. Pennsylvania, PA: IGI Global, 2008, chapter XLVI. [2.3.1]

31. Bishop D (1992). *Marble Answer Machine*. https://vimeo.com/19930744, accessed February 2022. [2.2.1]

32. Blast Theory (1999). *Desert Rain*. http://www.blasttheory.co.uk/projects/desert-rain/, accessed April 2022. [2.4.3]

33. Blinkenlight. 20 LEDs are enough. accessed January 2017. https://blog.blinkenlight.net/experiments/measurements/led-camera/, accessed April 2022. [13.8]

34. Bolton T. *London's Lost Rivers: A Walker's Guide*. London: Strange Attractor Press, 2011. [12.12]

35. Booch G, Rumbaugh J, and Jacobson I. *Unified Modeling Language User Guide* (2nd edn). (Addison-Wesley Object Technology Series). Boston, MA: Addison-Wesley Professional, 2005. [21.1]

36. Borges J. *Del rigor en la ciencia* (tr. *On Exactitude in Science*). Los Anales de Buenos Aires, 1:3:53 (Mar 1946). [12.6]

37. Borrow G. *Wild Wales: Its People, Language and Scenery*. London: John Murray, 1862. [15.2]

38. Boudway I (2014). 'Is Chris Dancy the Most Quantified Self in America?' *Bloomberg Businessweek*, 5 June 2014. http://www.businessweek.com/articles/2014-06-05/is-chris-dancy-the-most-quantified-self-in-america, accessed April 2022. [16.4]

39. Bouton C. *The Flour War: Gender, Class, and Community in Late Ancien Régime French Society*. State College, PA: Penn State University Press, 1993. http://www.psupress.org/books/titles/0-271-01053-3.html, accessed April 2022. [17.8.2]

40. Bower B (2018). Cave art suggests Neanderthals were ancient humans' mental equals. *Science News*, February 22, 2018. https://www.sciencenews.org/article/cave-art-suggests-neandertals-were-ancient-humans-mental-equals, accessed April 2022. [22.4]

41. Brand S. *How Buildings Learn: What Happens After They're Built*. New York, NY: Viking, 1994. [13.3;15.5]

42. Brave S, Ishii H, and Dahley A (1998). 'Tangible Interfaces for Remote Collaboration and Communication' in Proceedings of the 1998 ACM Conference on Computer Supported Cooperative Work (Seattle, WA, 14-18 November, 1998). CSCW '98. New York, NY: ACM, 169–78. DOI:http://doi.acm.org/10.1145/289444.289491; see also: http://tangible.media.mit.edu/project/intouch/, accessed April 2022. [6.2]

43. Bromhall C. *The Eternal Child: Staying Young and the Secret of Human Success*. London: Ebury Press, 2003. [8.3]

44. Brown M (2016). 'New Rembrandt' to be unveiled in Amsterdam. *The Guardian*, https://www.nextrembrandt.com/ accessed February 2022 [13.7]

45. Bruegger P (2011). 'uMove: A Wholistic Framework to Design and Implement Ubiquitous Computing Systems Supporting User's Activity and Situation'. PhD Thesis, University of Fribourg, Switzerland. http://doc.rero.ch/record/24442, accessed April 2022. [21.1]

46. Buchanan M. *Ubiquity: Why The World is Simpler Than We Think*. London: Weidenfeld, 2000. [11.5]

47. Bui D, Myerson J, and Hale S. 'Note-taking with Computers: Exploring Alternative Strategies for Improved Recall' (May 2013) 105(2) *Journal of Educational Psychology* 299–309. DOI: 10.1037/a0030367 (2013) [22.7]

48. Bureau International des Poids et Mesures (2006). Unit of Thermodynamic Temperature (kelvin). Section 2.1.1.5, *The International System of Units* (8th edn). https://www.bipm.org/en/si-base-units/kelvin, accessed April 2022. [15.1]

49. Burk J (2011). 'Why You Should Wait to Teach Projectile Motion Part 2: Introducing Projectile Motion Using Angry Birds'. *Quantum Progress*. https://quantumprogress.wordpress.com/2011/02/17/why-you-should-wait-to-teach-projectile-motion-part-2-introducing-projectile-motion-using-angry-birds/, accessed April 2022. [22.2]

50. Burling R. *The Talking Ape: How Language Evolved*. Oxford: Oxford University Press, 2005. [15.7]

51. Burns-Holland N (2015). 'How Color Affects Your Perception of Food'. SpoonUniversity.com. http://spoonuniversity.com/how-to/color-affects-perception-food, accessed April 2022. [20.2]

52. Buxton B. *Sketching User Experiences: Getting the Design Right and the Right Design.* San Francisco, CA: Morgan Kaufmann, 2007. [4.6;15.4]

53. Buxton W. 'A Three-state Model of Graphical Input' in D Diaper, D Gilmore, and G Cockton (eds), *Human-Computer Interaction—INTERACT '90.* Amsterdam: Elsevier Science Publishers B.V. (North-Holland), 1990, 449 -56. http://www.billbuxton.com/3state.html, accessed April 2022. [9.2]

54. van Breemen A, Yan X, and Meerbeek B (2005). 'iCat: An Animated User-interface Robot with Personality' in M Pechoucek, D Steiner, and S Thompson (eds), *Proceedings of the Fourth International Joint Conference on Autonomous Agents and Multiagent Systems (AAMAS '05).* New York, NY: ACM, 143–44. DOI: 10.1145/1082473.1082823 [1.6]

55. van Buskirk E. 'Perspective: The Secret of iPod's Scroll Wheel'. CNET. 22 September 2004. https://www.cnet.com/culture/the-secret-of-ipods-scroll-wheel/, accessed April 2022. [7.5]

56. Calvin WH. *The Ascent of Mind: Ice Age Climates and the Evolution of Intelligence.* New York, NY: Bantam, 1990. (reprinted backinprint.com) http://www.williamcalvin.com/bk5/bk5.htm, accessed April 2022. [10.1;15.9]

57. Card S, Moran TP and Newell A. *The Psychology of Human Computer Interaction.* Hillsdale, NJ: Lawrence Erlbaum Associates, 1983. [5.6]

58. Carr L and Harnad S. 'Offloading Cognition onto the Web' (2011) IEEE Intelligent Systems, 26(1) 33–9. [22.4]

59. Cavazza S. 'Regionalism in Italy: A Critique' in J Augusteijn and E Storm (eds) *Region and State in Nineteenth-Century Europe.* London: Palgrave Macmillan, 2012, 69–89. DOI: 10.1057/9781137271303 5 [6.6]

60. CEA (2015). *Big Data And Differential Pricing.* The Council of Economic Advisers, The White House, February 2015. https://obamawhitehouse.archives.gov/sites/default/files/whitehouse_files/docs/Big_Data_Report_Nonembargo_v2.pdf, accessed April 2022. [17.8.2]

61. de Certeau M. *The Practice of Everyday Life.* (tr Steve Randall). Oakland, CA: University of California Press, 1984. [12.11]

62. Chalmers M, MacColl I, and Bell M. 'Seamful Design: Showing the Seams in Wearable Computing' 2003 IEE Eurowearable, Birmingham, UK, 2003, 11–16. doi: 10.1049/ic:20030140 [11.4]

63. Chandler A, Finney J, Lewis C, et al. 'Toward Emergent Technology for Blended Public Displays' in S Helal, HW Gellersen, and S Consolvo (eds), *Proceedings of the 11th International Conference on Ubiquitous Computing.* New York, NY: ACM (Orlando, FLA, 30 September–3 October, 2009), 101–114. DOI: 10.1145/1620545.1620562 [2.1.5]

64. Cheverst K, Dix A, Fitton D, et al. 'Exploring Awareness Related Messaging Through Two Situated-display-based Systems' (2007) 22(1–2) *Human-Computer Interaction* 173–220. DOI: 10.1080/07370020701307955 [14.5]

65. Cheverst K, Fitton D, and Dix A. 'Exploring the Evolution of Office Door Displays' in L O'Hara, M Perry, E Churchill et al (eds), Public and Situated Displays: Social and Interactional Aspects of Shared Display Technologies. Dordrecht: Kluwer Academic, 2003, 141–69. [21.2.3]

66. CIHT Awards 2016. Chartered Institution of Highways & Transportation. https://www.ciht.org.uk/news/outstanding-transport-projects-honoured-in-the-ciht-awards-2016/, accessed April 2022. [14.2]

67. Clark A. 'An Embodied Cognitive Science?' (1999) 3(9) *Trends in Cognitive Sciences* 346. doi:10.1016/s1364-6613(99)01361-3 [19.2]

68. Clark A. *Being There: Putting Brain, Body and the World Together Again.* Cambridge, MA: MIT Press, 1998. [22.4]

69. Clark A. *Microcognition: Philosophy, Cognitive Science and Parallel Processing.* Cambridge, MA: MIT Press, 1989. [22.5]

70. Clark H. *Using Language.* Cambridge: Cambridge University Press, 1996. [15.8]

71. Clark S and Webb R. 'Six Principles, Six Problems, Six Solutions'. *New Scientist*, 24 September 2016, 231(3092):28–35 https://www.newscientist.com/article/2106324-reality-guide-six-problems-physics-cant-explain/, accessed April 2022. [17.1]

72. Clarke, AC. *Profiles of the Future: An Inquiry into the Limits of the Possible.* London: Macmillan, 1973. [22.2]

73. Cohen J and Botvinick M. 'Rubber Hands 'Feel' Touch that Eyes See' (1998) 391 *Nature* 756 DOI:10.1038/35784 [19.6]

74. Cooke SF and Bliss TVP. 'Plasticity in the Human Central Nervous System' (July 2006) 129(7) *Brain* 1659–73. https://doi.org/10.1093/brain/awl082 [4.2]

75. Cooper J, Mitchell J, and Bedingfeld J. 'Reducing Traffic Sign Clutter'. Client Project Report Cpr727, Wokingham: Transport Research Laboratory, June 2010. [14.2]

76. Cosmides L. 'The Logic of Social Exchange: Has Natural Selection Shaped How Humans Reason? Studies with the Wason Selection Task' (1989) 31 Cognition 187–276. [4.4]

77. Council of the European Union (2016). Position of the council on general data protection regulation. https://eur-lex.europa.eu/legal-content/EN/TXT/PDF/?uri=CELEX:32016R0679, accessed April 2022. [22.9]

78. Cowen J. *A Mapmaker's Dream*. Boulder, CO: Shambhala, 1996. [12.6]

79. Coyne, R and Stewart J. 'Orienting the Future: Design Strategies for Non-place' in T. Inns (ed), *Design for the 21st Century*. London: Gower Ashgate, 2007, 79–90. [12.11]

80. Crawford M. *The Case for Working with Your Hands: Or Why Office Work is Bad for Us and Fixing Things Feels Good*. London: Penguin, 2010. [19.2]

81. Crist R. 'Screwed by sex toy spying? You may get $10k'. *CNET*, 2017. https://www.cnet.com/uk/news/app-enabled-sex-toy-users-get-10000-each-after-privacy-breach/ , accessed April 2022. [13.8]

82. Crossley D. 'Samsung's listening TV is proof that tech has outpaced our rights' *The Guardian* 13 February 2015. [13.8]

83. Culverhouse I (2012). 'Investigation into the Insights Generated through the Application of Interactive Prototyping during the Early Stages of the Design Process', PhD thesis, University of Wales [20.10]

84. Culverhouse I and Gill S. 'Better by Design: Safer Medical Devices Better and Faster (New Uses of Rough and Ready, Tried and Tested Techniques)', industry case study presented at NordiCHI 2012, 14–17 October, IT University of Copenhagen [20.15]

85. Culverhouse I and Gill S. 'Bringing Concepts to Life: Introducing a Rapid Interactive Sketch Modelling Toolkit for Industrial Designers' in N Villar, S Izadi, M Fraser, et al. (eds), *Proceedings of the 3rd International Conference on Tangible and Embedded Interaction (TEI '09)*. New York, NY: ACM, 363–6. DOI: https://doi.org/10.1145/1517664.1517737 [20.10]

86. Curtis P. 'Mudding: Social phenomena in text-based virtual realities' in S Kiesler (ed), *Culture of the Internet*. Hillsdale, NJ: Lawrence Erlbaum, 1997, 21–142 [6.2]

87. CuteCircuit LLC. 'The Hug Shirt'. http://www.cutecircuit.com/hugshirt/, accessed April 2022. [6.2]

88. Damasio A. *Descartes' Error: Emotion, Reason and the Human Brain*. London: Vintage, 2006. [15.10]

89. Dancy C (2014). Personal website. http://www.chrisdancy.com, accessed April 2022. [16.4]

90. Datta A, Tschantz M, and Datta A. 'Automated Experiments on Ad Privacy Settings' (2015) 1 *Proceedings on Privacy Enhancing Technologies* 92–112. Retrieved 4 Mar. 2018, from doi:10.1515/popets-2015-0007 [22.9]

91. Davis M, Rubinstein N, Wadhwa, G et al. 'The Visual Microphone: Passive Recovery of Sound from Video' (2014) 33(4) *ACM Transactions on Graphics (Proc. SIGGRAPH)*, 79:1–79:10 http://people.csail.mit.edu/mrub/VisualMic/, [13.8]

92. Dawkins R. *The Selfish Gene*. Oxford: Oxford University Press, 1976. [22.6]

93. Dean J and Ghemawat S. 'MapReduce: Simplified Data Processing on Large Clusters'. (January 2008) *Communications of the ACM* 51(1), 107–113. DOI: 10.1145/1327452.1327492 [17.3]

94. Dearden L. 'Pro-Brexit Twitter account with 100,000 followers could be part of Russian "disinformation campaign"'. Wednesday 30 August 2017, The Independent. http://www.independent.co.uk/news/uk/home-news/david-jones-pro-brexit-ukip-twitter-account-russia-fake-bot-troll-trump-disinformation-followers-a7920181.html, accessed April 2022. [13.5]

95. Dehaene S (1997). *The Number Sense.* London: Penguin. [22.2]

96. Delana. (2016) *Hoboglyphs: Secret Transient Symbols & Modern Nomad Codes.* Web Urbanist. Accessed December 2016. http://weburbanist.com/2010/06/03/hoboglyphs-secret-transient-symbols-modern-nomad-codes/, accessed April 2022. [12.12]

97. Dennett D (1988). 'Why everyone is a novelist' The Times Literary Supplement, 16–22 September, 4, 459. http://dl.tufts.edu/catalog/tufts:ddennett-1988.00007, accessed April 2022. [22.4]

98. Department for Transport (2013). 'Reducing Sign Clutter'. Traffic Advisory Leaflet 01/13. Department for Transport. January 2013 [14.2]

99. Derrida, J (1995). *Mal d'archive: une impression freudienne*. Paris: Gallimard. [16.4]

100. Deutscher, G (2010). *Through the Language Glass: How Words Colour your World*. London: Heinemann, [22.6]

101. Diepenmaat P and Geelhoed, E (2006). *'neXus—Designing a Dedicated Mediascape Device'*. Masters thesis project, Delft Technical University. http://www.hpl.hp.com/techreports/2006/HPL-2006-178.pdf, accessed April 2022. [13.4]

102. Dix A. 'Status and Events: Static and Dynamic Properties of Interactive Systems' in D Duce and G Faconti (eds), *Proceedings of the Eurographics Seminar: Formal Methods in Computer Graphics*. Geneva, Switzerland: Eurographics Association (Marina di Carrara, 1991). http://www.hcibook.com/alan/papers/euro91/, accessed April 2022. [7.3]

103. Dix A. 'Human Issues in the Use of Pattern Recognition Techniques', in R Beale and J Finlay (eds), *Neural Networks and Pattern Recognition in Human Computer Interaction*. New York, NY: Ellis Horwood, 1992, 429–51. http://alandix.com/academic/papers/neuro92/neuro92.html, accessed April 2022. [22.9]

104. Dix A. 'Computer-supported Cooperative Work—A Framework' in D Rosenburg and C Hutchison (eds), *Design Issues in CSCW.* New York, NY: Springer Verlag, 1994, 23–37. http://alandix.com/academic/papers/cscwframework94/, accessed April 2022. [22.8]

105. Dix, A. (1998). 'Sinister Scrollbar in the Xerox Star Xplained'. *Interfaces,* Summer 1998. http://alandix.com/academic/papers/scrollbar/scrollbar2.html, accessed April 2022. [12.8]

106. Dix A (2000). 'Welsh Mathematician Walks in Cyberspace (the Cartography of Cyberspace)' (keynote) *Proceedings of the Third International Conference on Collaborative Virtual Environments—CVE2000,* 3–7. http://www.hcibook.com/alan/papers/CVE2000/, accessed April 2022. [1.7]

107. Dix A. 'Cyber-economies and the Real World' in *SAICSIT'2001—South African Institute of Computer Scientists and Information Technologists Annual Conference.* Pretoria, 25–28 September 2001. Pretoria: Unisa Press, xi–xiii http://alandix.com/academic/papers/SAICSIT2001/, accessed April 2022. [17.8.2]

108. Dix A. 'Beyond Intention—Pushing Boundaries with Incidental Interaction' in Proceedings of Building Bridges: Interdisciplinary Context-Sensitive Computing, Glasgow University, 9 September 2002. http://alandix.com/academic/papers/beyond-intention-2002/, accessed April 2022. [14.4;14.6;14.9]

109. Dix A. (2002). Driving as a Cyborg Experience. http://www.hcibook.com/alan/papers/cyborg-driver-2002/, accessed April 2022. [19.6]

110. Dix A (2003). Deconstructing the experience of (e)learning for delivery ecologies. Talk given at the e-Learning Experience Birmingham Institute of Art and Design, 15 October 2003 [22.7]

111. Dix A (2003). *Imagination and Rationality.* http://www.hcibook.com/alan/essays/, accessed April 2022. [15.5]

112. Dix A (2003/2005). *A Cybernetic Understanding of Fitts' Law.* HCIbook online! http://www.hcibook.com/e3/online/fitts-cybernetic/, accessed April 2022. [5.4]

113. Dix A. 'The Brain and the Web—A Quick Backup in case of Accidents' (Winter 2005) 65 *Interfaces* 6–7. http://www.hcibook.com/alan/papers/brain-and-web-2005/, accessed April 2022. [4.3]

114. Dix A (2010). *Hidden Rome.* http://alandix.com/blog/2010/06/06/hidden-rome/, accessed April 2022. [10.5]

115. Dix A. 'Tasks = Data + Action + Context: Automated Task Assistance through Data-oriented Analysis' Keynote at *Engineering Interactive Systems 2008 (incorporating HCSE2008 & TAMODIA 2008),* Pisa Italy,

25–26 September 2008. http://www.hcibook.com/alan/papers/EIS-Tamodia2008/, accessed April 2022. [5.6]

116. Dix A (2009). 'Language and Action (2): From Observation to Communication'. http://alandix.com/blog/2009/05/18/language-and-action-2-from-observation-to-communication/, accessed April 2022. [15.7]

117. Dix A. 'Paths and Patches: Patterns of Geonosy and Gnosis' in P Tuner, S Turner, and E Davenport (eds), *Exploration of Space, Technology, and Spatiality: Interdisciplinary Perspectives*. New York, NY: Information Science Reference, 2009, 1–16 [22.6]

118. Dix A (2011). 'A Shifting Boundary: The Dynamics of Internal Cognition and the Web as External Representation' in *Proceedings of WebSci'11*. http://alandix.com/academic/papers/websci2011-int-ext-cog/, accessed April 2022. [22.4;22.6]

119. Dix A (2013) Day 63–off path visit to Lampeter. Alan Walks Wales blog. http://alanwalks.wales/2013/06/19/day-63-off-path-visit-to-lampeter/, accessed April 2022. [15.2]

120. Dix A (2013). Alan Walks Wales—data. http://alanwalks.wales/data/, accessed April 2022. [16.4]

121. Dix A. 'The Walk: Exploring the Technical and Social Margins', Keynote *APCHI 2013 / India HCI 2013*, Bangalore India, 27 September 2013. http://www.hcibook.com/alan/talks/APCHI-2013/, accessed April 2022. [16.4]

122. Dix A. 'Mental Geography, Wonky Maps and a Long Way Ahead' in B Hecht, L Capra, J Schöning, et al. (eds), *GeoHCI, Workshop on Geography and HCI, CHI 2013*. New York, NY: ACM (Paris, 27 April–2 May 2013). http://alandix.com/academic/papers/GeoHCI2013/, accessed April 2022. [18.5]

123. Dix A (2015). 'If the light is on, they can hear (and now see) you' http://alandix.com/blog/2015/04/01/if-the-light-is-on-they-can-hear-and-now-see-you/, accessed April 2022. [13.8]

124. Dix A (17 January 2015). 'Tiree Journeys. Tiree Tech Wave' accessed January 2019. https://tireetechwave.org/projects/tiree- journeys/, accessed April 2022. [12.7]

125. Dix A. 'I in an Other's Eye' (2017) 34(1) *AI & Society* 55–73. DOI: 10.1007/s00146-017-0694-7 [22.4]

126. Dix A. 'Activity Modelling for Low-intention Interaction' in B Weyers, J Bowen, A Dix et al (eds), *The Handbook of Formal Methods in Human- Computer Interaction*. Dordrecht: Springer, 2017, 183 -210 DOI: 10.1007/978-3-319- 51838-1 7 [21.1.2;21.1.2;21.1.2]

127. A. Dix. (2018). More than a Moment. Talk at UCL Interaction Centre, London, 10th October 2018. http://alandix.com/academic/talks/UCL-more-than-a-moment-2018/, accessed April 2022. [21.4.1]

128. Dix A. 'Deconstructing Experience —Pulling Crackers Apart' in M Blythe and A Monk (eds), *Funology 2: From Usability to Enjoyment.* Dordrecht: Springer, 2018, chapter 29. [22.7]

129. Dix A. 'Deep Digitality: Fate, Fiat, and Foundry' (2019) 26(1) *Interactions* 20–1. DOI: https://doi.org/10.1145/3289427 [22.9]

130. Dix A and Abowd G. 'Modelling Status and Event Behaviour of Interactive Systems' (1996) 11(6) *Software Engineering Journal* 334–46. http://www.hcibook.com/alan/papers/SEJ96-s+e/, accessed April 2022. [7.3]

131. Dix A, Cheverst K, Fitton D et al. 'The Auditability of Public Space—Approaching Security through Social Visibility. *2nd UK-UbiNet Workshop Security, trust, privacy and theory for ubiquitous computing.* 5–7 May 2004, University of Cambridge. http://www.hcibook.com/alan/papers/ubinet-trust-2004/, accessed April 2022. [14.5]

132. Dix A, Ghazali M, Gill S, et al. 'Physigrams: Modelling Devices for Natural Interaction' (2009) 21(6) *Formal Aspects of Computing* 613–641. DOI:10.1007/s00165-008-0099-y. [21.1]

133. Dix A and Gill S (2018). 'Physical Computing: When Digital Systems Meet the Real World' in M Filimowicz and V Tzankova (eds), *New Directions in Third Wave Human-Computer Interaction*, Volume 1. Dordrecht: Springer, 2018, 123–44. [22.8]

134. Dix A and Gongora L. 'Externalisation and Design', in C Hooper, JB Martens, and P Markopoulos (eds), *DESIRE 2011 the Second International Conference on Creativity and Innovation in Design.* New York, NY: ACM (Eindhoven, The Netherlands, 19–21 October 2011). 31–42 [19.2]

135. Dix A and Sas C. 'Mobile Personal Devices Meet Situated Public Displays: Synergies and Opportunities' (2010) 1(1) *International Journal of Ubiquitous Computing* 11–28. http://www.hcibook.com/alan/papers/MPD-SPD-2010/, accessed April 2022. [14.3;14.5]

136. Dix A and Subramanian S. 'IT for Sustainable Growth' (2010) 1(1) *Journal of Technology Management for Growing Economies* 35–54. http://alandix.com/academic/papers/IT-Sustainable-Growth-2010/, accessed April 2022. [17.8.2]

137. Dix A, Finlay J, Abowd G, et al. 'Modelling Rich Interaction' in *Human-Computer Interaction*, 3rd edn. Hoboken, NJ: Prentice Hall, 2004, 629-60. [21.1.1;22.7]

138. Dix A, Finlay J, Abowd G, et al. *Human–Computer Interaction*, 3rd edn. Hoboken, NJ: Prentice Hall, 2004. [22.7]

139. Dix A, Friday A, Koleva B, et al. 'Managing Multiple Spaces' in P Turner and E. Davenport (eds), *Space, Spatiality and Technologies*. Dordrecht: Springer, 2005, 151–72. http://alandix.com/academic/papers/space-chapter-2004/, accessed April 2022. [14.7]

140. Dix A and Ghazali M. 'Physigrams: Modelling Physical Device Characteristics Interaction' in B Weyers, J Bowen, A Dix, et al (eds). *The Handbook of Formal Methods in Human-Computer Interaction*. Dordrecht: Springer, 2017, 247–71. DOI: 10.1007/978-3-319-51838-1 9 [21.1]

141. Dix A, Gill S, Ramduny-Ellis D, et al. *Design and Physicality–Towards an Understanding of Physicality in Design and Use. In: Designing for the 21st Century: Interdisciplinary Methods and Findings. Designing for the 21st Century*, part 2. London: Gower, 2010, 172–89. [3.4]

142. Dix A, Leite J, and Friday A. 'XSED—XML-based Description of Status-event Components and Systems' in *Proceedings of Engineering Interactive Systems 2007* (EIS 2007), LNCS 4940, http://www.hcibook.com/alan/papers/EIS-DSVIS-XSED-2007/, accessed April 2022. [7.3]

143. Dix A, Malizia A, Turchi T et al. 'Rich Digital Collaborations in a Small Rural Community' in C Anslow, P Campos, J Jorge et al (eds), *Collaboration Meets Interactive Spaces*. Dordrecht: Springer, 2016, 463–83. DOI:10.1007/978-3-319-45853-3_20 http://www.hcibook.com/alan/papers/CMIS-chap-2016/, accessed April 2022. [14.11]

144. Dix A, Tamblyn R, and Leavesley J. 'From Intertextuality to Transphysicality: The Changing Nature of the Book, Reader and Writer. Future of Books and Reading in HCI.' Workshop at NordiCHI 2016 (Gothenburg, Sweden, October 2016). https://alandix.com/academic/papers/future-books-nordichi-2016/, accessed April 2022. [22.7]

145. Dix A, Wilkinson J, and Ramduny D (1998). 'Redefining Organisational Memory: Artefacts, and the Distribution and Coordination of Work.' Workshop on Understanding work and designing artefacts, York, 21 September 1998. http://www.hcibook.com/alan/papers/artefacts98/, accessed April 2022. [6.4]

146. Dix AJ. 'The Myth of the Infinitely Fast Machine' in D Diaper and R Winder (eds), *People and Computers III—Proceedings of*

HCI'87. Cambridge: Cambridge University Press, 1987, 215–28. http://alandix.com/academic/papers/hci87/, accessed April 2022. [21.4.1]

147. Dix AJ. 'Information Processing, Context and Privacy' in D Diaper, G Cockton, and B Shackel (eds), *Human-Computer Interaction—INTERACT'90.* North-Holland, 1990, 15–20. http://alandix.com/academic/papers/int90/, accessed April 2022. [16.5]

148. Dix AJ. 'Events and Status—Mice and Multiple Users' in A Dix, *Formal Methods for Interactive Systems.* Cambridge, MA: Academic Press, 1991, 239–73. http://www.hiraeth.com/books/formal/ [21.1.1]

149. Donaldson M. *Children's Minds.* London: Fontana, 1978. [12.6]

150. Dourish P. *Where the Action Is: The Foundations of Embodied Interaction.* Cambridge, MA: MIT Press, 2001. [22.4]

151. Edwards R. 'Woman divorces husband for having a 'virtual' affair on Second Life' *Daily Telegraph,* 14 November 2008. http://www.telegraph.co.uk/technology/3453273/Woman-divorces-husband-for-having-a-virtual-affair-on-Second-Life.html, accessed April 2022. [13.7]

152. Endsley M. 'Toward a Theory of Situation Awareness in Dynamic Systems' (1995) 37(1) Human Factors 32–64. [4.2]

153. Engelbart D. 'Augmenting Human Intellect: Experiments, Concepts, and Possibilities'. Summary Report, Stanford Research Institute, under Contract AF 49(638)–1024 for Directorate of Information Sciences, Air Force Office of Scientific Research, March 1965. SRI Project 3578; 65 [22.5]

154. Engelbart DC and English WK. 'A Research Center for Augmenting Human Intellect' in *AFIPS Conference Proceedings of the December 1968 Fall Joint Computer Conference,* San Francisco, CA, Vol. 33, 395–410 (AUGMENT 3954). [1.5.1]

155. Ericsson K and Kintsch W. 'Long-term Working Memory' (1995) 102 *Psychological Review* 211–45. [4.2]

156. Eslambolchilar P (2006) Making sense of interaction using a model-based approach. PhD thesis, Hamilton Institute, National University of Ireland, NUIM, Ireland [21.1]

157. Etherington D and Conger K. 'Large DDoS Attacks Cause Outages at Twitter, Spotify, and Other Sites' *TechCrunch.* 21 October 2016. https://techcrunch.com/2016/10/21/many-sites-including-twitter-and-spotify-suffering-outage/ [13.8]

158. European Court of Justice. An Internet search engine operator is responsible for the processing that it carries out of personal

data which appear on web pages published by third parties: Judgment in Case C-131/12 *Google Spain SL, Google Inc. v Agencia Española de Protecci'on de Datos, Mario Costeja Gonz'alez.* Press Release No 70/14 Court of Justice of the European Union, Luxembourg, 13 May 2014 http://curia.europa.eu/jcms/upload/docs/application/pdf/2014-05/cp140070en.pdf [16.4]

159. Facer K, Joiner R, Stanton D, et al. 'Savannah: Mobile Gaming and Learning?' (2004) 20 *Journal of Computer Assisted Learning* 399–409. [11.4]

160. Fatah gen Schieck A, Kostakos V, Penn A, et al. 'Design Tools for Pervasive Computing in Urban Environments' in JPT van Leeuwen, and P, HJ, (eds), *Innovations in Design and Decision Support Systems in Architecture and Urban Planning.* Dordrecht: Springer, 2006, 467–86. [21.1]

161. Ferguson D. 'Lego professor of play: apply now for the most coveted job in education' *The Guardian,* 17 January 2017. https://www.theguardian.com/education/2017/jan/17/lego-professor-play-education-job-cambridge-university, accessed April 2022. [20.9]

162. Finke R, Ward TB, and Smith SM. *Creative Cognition: Theory, Research, and Applications.* Cambridge, MA: MIT Press, 1996. [4.6]

163. Finke R. *Creative Imagery: Discoveries and Inventions in Visualization.* Hillsdale, NJ: Lawrence Erlbaum, 1990. [4.6]

164. *Firefly—the new medium of digital light.* http://alandix.com/firefly/, accessed April 2022. [2.1.5]

165. Fitts PM. 'The Information Capacity of the Human Motor System in Controlling the Amplitude of Movement' (1954) 47(6) *Journal of Experimental Psychology* 381–91. [5.4]

166. Flintham M, Anastasi R, Benford S, et al. 'Where On-Line Meets On-The-Streets: Experiences with Mobile Mixed Reality Games' in S Bødker, S Brewster, P Baudisch, et al. (eds), *The Proceedings of the 2003 CHI Conference on Human Factors in Computing Systems* (Fort Lauderdale, FLA, 5-10 April 2003) New York, NY: ACM Press, 569–76, Florida: ACM Press. [13.4]

167. Ford H and Crowther S. *My Life and Work.* New York, NY: Doubleday, Page and Company, 1922. [16.1]

168. Fraknoi A. 'How Fast Are You Moving when You are Sitting Still?' (2007) 71 (Spring) *Astronomical Society of the Pacific.* The Universe in the Classroom. https://astrosociety.org/edu/publications/tnl/71/howfast.html, accessed April 2022. [11.6]

169. freecycle.org (2017). History & background information. https://www.freecycle.org/pages/about, accessed April 2022. [14.11]

170. Frens J (2006). 'Designing for Rich Interaction: Integrating Form, Interaction and Function'. PhD Thesis, Library Eindhoven University of Technology. [19.6]

171. Fullilove C. 'The Price of Bread: The New York City Flour Riot and the Paradox of Capitalist Food Systems' (2014) 118 (Winter) *Radical History Review issue on the fictions of finance.* http://www.academia.edu/5789246/. [17.8.2]

172. Gallagher S. *How the Body Shapes the Mind.* Oxford: Oxford University Press, 2005. [22.4]

173. Gantz CM. *Design Chronicles: Significant Mass-Produced Designs of the 20th Century.* Atglen, PA: Schiffer Publishing, Ltd., 2007. [1.5.2]

174. Gardner H. *Frames of Mind: The Theory of Multiple Intelligences.* New York, NY: Basic Books, 1983. [4.4]

175. Gardner H. *Multiple Intelligences: The Theory in Practice.* New York, NY: Basic Books, 1993. [4.4]

176. Garfinkel H. *Studies in Ethnomethodology.* Englewood Cliffs, NJ: Prentice-Hall, 1967. [10.5]

177. Gaver W and Dunne A. 'Projected Realities: Conceptual design for cultural effect' in *Proceedings of CHI'99.* (Pittsburgh, PA, 15–20 May 1999). New York, NY: ACM Press, 1999, 600–7. [10.5]

178. Gaver W, Beaver J, and Benford S. 'Ambiguity as a Resource for Design' in *Proceedings of the SIGCHI Conference on Human Factors in Computing Systems* (Fort Lauderdale, FLA, 5–10 April 2003). CHI '03. New York, NY: ACM, 233–40. DOI= http://doi.acm.org/10.1145/642611.642653 [10.5]

179. Gaver W, Bowers J, Boucher A, et al. 'Electronic Furniture for the Curious Home: Assessing Ludic Designs in the Field' (2007) 22(1–2) *International Journal of Human-Computer Interaction* 119–52. [7.5]

180. Gaver WW. 'What in the World Do We Hear? An Ecological Approach to Auditory Source Perception' (1993) 5(1) *Ecological Psychology* 1–29 [7.6;7.6]

181. Ghazali M. and A. Dix (2005). *Visceral Interaction Proceedings of the 19th British HCI conference, Vol 2. Edinburgh, September 5–9.* L MacKinnon, O Bertelsen, and N Bryan-Kinns (eds), Swindon, UK: British Computer Society, pp 68–72. http://www.hcibook.com/alan/papers/visceral-2005/ [1.6]

182. Gibson J. *The Ecological Approach to Visual Perception.* Hillsdale, NJ: Lawrence Erlbaum Associates, 1979. [8.1]

183. Gill S and Dix A. 'The Role of Physicality in the Design Process' in J Adenauer and J Petruschat (eds), Prototype! Physical, Virtual, Hybrid,

Smart—Tackling New Challenges in Design and Engineering. Form +
Berlin: Zweck, 2012, 54–79.

184. Gill S, Loudon G, and Walker D. 'Designing a Design Tool: Working
with Industry to Create an Information Appliance Design Methodology' (2008) 7(2) *Journal of Design Research* 97–119 [20.10]

185. Gill S, Walker D, Loudon G, et al. 'Rapid Development of Tangible
Interactive Appliances: Achieving the Fidelity/Time Balance' (2008)
1(3/4) *International Journal of Arts and Technology* 309–31 [7.6;20.2]

186. Gill S. 'Developing Information Appliance Design Tools for Designers' (2003) 7 *Personal and Ubiquitous Computing 159–62.* [20.10]

187. Gill S. 'Six Challenges Facing User-oriented Industrial Design' (2009)
12(1) *The Design Journal* 41–67. DOI: 10.2752/175630609X391569 [22.7]

188. Gilleade K, Dix A, and Allanson J. 'Affective Videogames and
Modes of Affective Gaming: Assist Me, Challenge Me, Emote
Me' in Proceedings of *DIGRA'2005.* (Vancouver, 16–20 June 2005).
http://alandix.com/academic/papers/DIGRA2005/, accessed April
2022. [4.5]

189. Goodin D. 'Creepy IoT teddy bear leaks >2 million parents' and
kids' voice messages' (2017) Ars Technica. https://arstechnica.com/
security/2017/02/creepy-iot-teddy-bear-leaks-2-million-parents-and-
kids-voice-messages/, accessed April 2022. [13.8]

190. Goodman B and Flaxman S. (2016). European Union Regulations on
Algorithmic Decision-making and a "Right to Explanation"' (2017)
38(3) AI Magazine 50–7. arXiv:1606.08813. [22.9]

191. Goodman N. *Languages of Art,* 2nd edn. Indianapolis, IN: Hackett Pub
Co., 1976. [16]

192. Google (2016). KML Tutorial, Google Developers. https://developers.
google.com/kml/documentation/kml_tut, accessed April 2022. [11.2]

193. Gopnik A. 'How We Read Our Own Minds: The Illusion of First-
person Knowledge of Intentionality' (1993) 16 *Behavioral and Brain
Sciences* 1–14. [15.10]

194. Gordon B, Wilgeroth P, and Griffiths R. 'Emulation of Real Life Environments for User Testing' in *Proceedings of the International Conference
on Engineering and Product Design Education 2008* (Universitat Politecnica de
Catalunya, Barcelona, Spain 2008). Design Society, 699–703. [19.3]

195. Gould JD, Conti J, and Hovanyecz T. 'Composing Letters with a Simulated Listening Typewriter' (1983) 26(4) *Communications of the ACM*
295–308. [20.15]

196. Gray W and Fu W. 'Ignoring Perfect Knowledge in-the-world for Imperfect Knowledge in-the-head' in *Proceedings of CHI '01.* New York,
NY: ACM Press, 2001. 112–19. DOI=10.1145/365024.365061 [22.5]

197. Greenberg A (2012). 'McDonald's staff denies 'physical altercation' with cyborg scientist'. *Forbes,* 18 July 2012. https://www.forbes.com/sites/andygreenberg/2012/07/18/mcdonalds-staff-denies-physical-altercation-with-cyborg-scientist/#34c2ed204c89, accessed April 2022. [3.6]

198. Greenberg S and Fitchett F. 'Phidgets: Easy Development of Physical Interfaces through Physical Widgets' in *Proceedings of the 14th annual ACM symposium on User interface software and technology (UIST '01).* New York, NY: ACM Press , 2001, 209–18. DOI=http://dx.doi.org/10.1145/502348.502388 [2.6.3]

199. Greenfield A (2006). *Everyware: The Dawning Age of Ubiquitous Computing.* Peachpit Press, Berkeley, CA, USA. [17.6]

200. Greeting Card Association (2018). Facts and figures: latest figures from the GCA Market Report 2018. https://www.gca.cards/publishers-the-market-facts-and-figures/, accessed April 2022. [7.5]

201. Grice HP. 'Logic and Conversation' in P Cole and J Morgan (eds), *Studies in Syntax and Semantics III: Speech Acts.* New York, NY: Academic Press, 1975, 183–98. [15.8]

202. Grimm J W and Grimm WK. 'The Frog Prince' in E Taylor and M Edwardes (tr 1823) *Grimm's Fairy Tales* Online text at Project Gutenberg: http://www.gutenberg.org/files/2591/2591-h/2591-h.htm#2H_4_0013, accessed April 2022. [7.4]

203. Haines L. 'Chinese Black Helicopters Circle Google Earth: Mystery Military Project Wows the Crowd' *The Register,* 19 July 2006. http://www.theregister.co.uk/2006/07/19/huangyangtan_mystery/, accessed April 2022. [11.5]

204. Halpin H, Clark A, and Wheeler M. 'Philosophy of the Web: Representation, Enaction, Collective Intelligence' in H Halpin and A Monnin (eds), *Philosophical Engineering: Toward a Philosophy of the Web.* Hoboken, NJ: John Wiley & Sons, 2013, 21–30. [22.4]

205. Hayes PJ. 'The Second Naive Physics Manifesto' in DS Weld and JD Kleer (eds), *Readings in Qualitative Reasoning About Physical Systems.* San Francisco, CA: Morgan Kaufmann Publishers, 1990, 46–63. [7.1]

206. Hazas M, Kray C, Gellersen H, et al. 'A Relative Positioning System for Co-located Mobile Devices' in Proceedings of the 3rd International Conference on Mobile Systems, Applications, and Services. MobiSys '05, ACM, New York, 2005, 177–90. DOI: 10.1145/1067170.1067190 [21.2.2]

207. Hearn A. 'Fitness tracking app Strava gives away location of secret US army bases', *The Guardian,* 28 January 2018. https://www.

theguardian.com/world/2018/jan/28/fitness-tracking-app-gives-away-location-of-secret-us-army-bases, accessed April 2022. [13.2]

208. Heath C and Luff P. 'Collaboration and Control: Crisis Management and Multimedia Technology in London Underground Line Control Rooms' (1992) 1(1) *Journal of Computer Supported Cooperative Work* 24–48. [6.3]

209. Heath T and Bizer C. Linked data: Evolving the web into a global data space. Synthesis lectures on the semantic web: theory and technology. series volume 1:1, 1–136. San Rafael, CA: Morgan & Claypool, 2011. DOI: 10.2200/S00334ED1V01Y201102WBE001 [22.2]

210. Heidegger M. *Being and Time.* (J Macquarie and E Robinson tr). Oxford: Blackwell, 1962. [10.3]

211. Heidegger M. *Sein und Zeit.* Albany, NY: State University Press, 1927. [22.4]

212. Heiner HA (1999). History of the Frog King. SurLaLune fairy-tales.com. https://www.surlalunefairytales.com/a-g/frog-king/frog-king-tale.html, accessed April 2022. [22.2]

213. Held R and Hein A. 'Movement-produced Stimulation in the Development of Visually Guided Behaviour' (1963) 56 *Journal of Comparative and Physiological Psychology* 873–76 [12.1]

214. Hennig BD (2015). *Ecological Footprints.* Views of the World. http://www.viewsoftheworld.net/?p=4639, accessed April 2022. [11.3]

215. Henrich J, Heine S, and Norenzayan A. 'The Weirdest People in the World?' (2010) 33 (2–3) *Behavioral and Brain Sciences* 61–83; discussion 83–135. doi: 10.1017/S0140525X0999152X. [22.6]

216. Hereford Cathedral Mappa Mundi. https://www.themappamundi.co.uk/, accessed April 2022. [11.6]

217. Heskett J. *Industrial Design.* Oxford: Oxford University Press, 1980. [1.5.2]

218. Hillier, B (1999). *Space is the Machine: A Configurational Theory of Architecture.* Cambridge: Cambridge University Press. [12.4]

219. History of Screw Threads Sizes.com, accessed April 2014. http://sizes.com/tools/thread_history.htm, accessed April 2022. [16.1]

220. *HistoryPoints—Bringing History to your Mobile.* http://historypoints.org, accessed April 2022. [13.2]

221. Hollan J, Hutchins E, and Kirsh D. 'Distributed Cognition: Toward a New Foundation for Human-Computer Interaction Research' (2000) 7(2) ACM Transactions on Computer-Human Interaction 174–96. [6.4]

222. Home Office. The National DNA database. https://www.gov.uk/government/collections/dna-database-documents, accessed April 2022. [3.5]

223. Hooper CJ (2012). 'Designing and Evaluating Systems to Support Emotional and Social Wellbeing' in Designing Wellbeing workshop at DIS 2012, Newcastle, UK, 2012. https://clarehooper.net/publications/2012/DIS2012workshop.pdf, accessed April 2022. [22.7]

224. Hooper CJ. (2011) 'Using TAPT as an Analytical Method for Understanding Online Experiences' in Web Science 2011 (Koblenz, 14–17 June 2011). New York, NY: ACM. [22.7]

225. Hughes J, O'Brien J, Rouncefield M, et al. 'Presenting Ethnography in the Requirements Process' in Proceedings of the IEEE Conference on Requirements Engineering, RE'95 York, 27–29 March 1995). London: IEEE Press, 1995, 27–34. DOI: 10.1109/ISRE.1995.512539 [6.3]

226. Hughes M (1975). 'Egocentrism in Preschool Children', Doctoral dissertation. Edinburgh University. [12.6]

227. Hume C (2019). 'Dementia device "kind of brought my mum back"'. BBC News, 31 October 2019. https://www.bbc.co.uk/news/uk-wales-50237366, accessed April 2022. [2.5.1]

228. Hutchins E (1995). *Cognition in the Wild*. Cambridge, MA: MIT Press. [5.7]

229. Hutchins E. 'Understanding Micronesian Navigation' in D Gentner and A Stevens (eds), *Mental Models*. Hillsdale, NJ: Lawrence Erlbaum, 1983, 191–225, 1983. [5.7]

230. Hyde, M, Scott-Slade, M, Scott-Slade, H, et al. (2016). *Sea Hero Quest: The World's first mobile game where anyone can help scientists fight dementia.* Glitchers. http://nrl.northumbria.ac.uk/33970/, accessed April 2022. [12.5]

231. HYSCOM. IEEE Control System Society (CSS) has a technical committee on hybrid systems. https://ieeecss.org/tc/hybrid-systems, accessed April 2022. [7.3]

232. Ilyenkov E. *Problems of Dialectical Materialism.* (A Bluden tr) Progress Publishers, 1977. Moscow, USSR. http://www.marxists.org/archive/ilyenkov/works/ideal/ideal.htm [6.5]

233. Ingold T (2007). *Lines: A Brief History.* London: Routledge. [12.7;12.12]

234. Ingold T. *Hunters Pastoralists and Ranchers: Reindeer Economies and Their Transformations.* Cambridge Studies in Social Anthropology No 28. Cambridge: Cambridge University Press 1980. [12.12]

235. International Standard (2000). ISO 9241–9, Ergonomic requirements for office work with visual display terminals–Part 9: Requirements for non-keyboard input devices. [5.4]

236. iRacing.com 2010. The world's fastest Alien. https://www.youtube.com/watch?v=0p_sCrM1CcI, accessed , accessed April 2022. [13.7]

237. Irwin A (1996). 'When the anoraks wear mink'. *Times Higher Education Supplement,* 3 May 1996. http://www.timeshighereducation.co.uk/story.asp?storyCode=93510&sectioncode=26, accessed April 2022. [6.2]

238. Ishii H and Ullmer B. 'Tangible Bits: towards Seamless Interfaces between People, Bits and Atoms' in S Pemberton (ed), *Proceedings of the SIGCHI Conference on Human Factors in Computing Systems,* Atlanta, GA, 22–27 March 1997. CHI '97. New York, NY: ACM, 234–41. DOI= http://doi.acm.org/10.1145/258549.258715 [2.2.1]

239. Ivan Sutherland's Sketchpad, with comments by Alan Kay. YouTube http://www.youtube.com/watch?v=495nCzxM9PI, accessed April 2022. [1.5.1]

240. Janita. 'DDoS attack halts heating in Finland amidst winter', *Metropolitan.fi,* 7 November 2016 https://metropolitan.fi/entry/ddos-attack-halts-heating-in-finland-amidst-winter, accessed April 2022. [13.8]

241. Jastrzębowski, W (1857). *An Outline of Ergonomics, or The Science of Work Based Upon The Truths Drawn from The Science Of Nature* (T Baluk-Ulewiczowa tr and D Koradecka ed). Warsaw: Central Institute for Labour Protection, 2000. [3.4]

242. Johnson W, Card, SK., Jellinek H, et al. 'Bridging the Paper and Electronic Worlds: The Paper User Interface' in B Arnold, G van der Veer, and T White (eds), *Proceedings of the INTERACT'93 and CHI'93 Conference on Human Factors in Computing Systems.* New York, NY: ACM Press. 1993, 507–512. [18.4]

243. Joshi V and Srinivasan M (2015). Walking on a moving surface: energy-optimal walking motions on a shaky bridge and a shaking treadmill can reduce energy costs below normal. Proceedings. Mathematical, physical, and engineering sciences 471 (2174), 20140662. [3.2]

244. Karamouzas I, Skinner B, and Guy S. 'Universal Power Law Governing Pedestrian Interactions' (2014) 11(3) *Physical Review Letters* 238701. Doi: 10.1103/PhysRevLett.113.238701 [11.5]

245. Katifori A, Vassilakis C, and Dix A (2009). 'Ontologies and the Brain: using Spreading Activation through Ontologies to Support Personal Interaction. Cognitive Systems Research'. http://

www.hcibook.com/alan/papers/Ontologies-and-the-Brain-2009/, accessed April 2022. [4.2]

246. Keller H (2017). 'With Apple's New ARKit, IKEA created an app that could revolutionize furniture shopping' https://www.architecturaldigest.com/story/apple-arkit-ikea-place-app-that-could-revolutionize-furniture-shopping, accessed April 2022. [13.2]

247. KenGrok. Post on Google Earth Community Forums. 28 June 2006. https://googleearthcommunity.proboards.com/thread/6223/aksai-chin-terrain-model, accessed April 2022. [11.5]

248. Kennedy D. New robotic hand 'can feel'. BBC News. Sunday, 18 October 2009. available at: http://news.bbc.co.uk/1/hi/sci/tech/8313037.stm, accessed April 2022. [1.6]

249. Kentish K. 'Nuclear Power Plants Vulnerable to Hacking Attack in "Nightmare Scenario", UN warns. The Independent. 16 December 2016. https://www.independent.co.uk/news/world/nuclear-power-plants-vulnerable-hacking-attack-cyber-nightmare-united-nations-a7479546.html, accessed April 2022. [13.8]

250. Kirsh D and Maglio P. 'On Distinguishing Epistemic from Pragmatic Action' (1994) 18(4) *Cognitive Science* 513–49. [8.4]

251. Kleinman Z (2016). BBC News, http://www.bbc.co.uk/news/technology-35639549, accessed June 2017. [13.8]

252. Koerner E and Konrad F. 'The Sapir-Whorf Hypothesis: A Preliminary History and a Bibliographical Essay' *Journal of Linguistic* December 1992 [22.6]

253. Koivunen MR and Miller E (2001). 'W3C semantic web activity'. https://www.w3.org/2001/12/semweb-fin/w3csw, accessed April 2022. [18.5]

254. Koscher K, Czeskis A, Roesner F, et al. 'Experimental Security Analysis of a Modern Automobile' in Security and Privacy (SP), 2010 IEEE Symposium, 447–62. IEEE. [13.8]

255. Laird J. 'The Real Role of Facial Response in the Experience of Emotion: A Reply to Tourangeau and Ellsworth, and Others' (1984) 47(4) *Journal of Personality and Social Psychology.* 909–17. [5.3]

256. Lakoff G and Johnson M (1980). *Metaphors We Live By.* Chicago, IL: University of Chicago Press. [12.8]

257. Lauder J (2016). 'Stuxnet: The real life sci-fi story of the world's first digital weapon', http://www.abc.net.au/triplej/programs/hack/the-worlds-first-digital-weapon-stuxnet/7926298, accessed August 2017. [13.8]

258. Lawson B. *How Designers Think*. London: Architectural Press, 1997, 27. [19.2]

259. Lean D (director) (1945). 'Brief Encounter'. Independent Producers, Rank Organisation. http://www.imdb.com/title/tt0037558/, accessed April 2022. [22.3.2]

260. Lee J (2007). 'Head tracking for desktop VR displays using the WiiRemote', YouTube. https://www.youtube.com/watch?v=Jd3-eiid-Uw, accessed April 2022. [14.7]

261. Lehmann I. 'Seismology in the Days of Old' (1987) 68(3) *Eos* 33–5. [11.8]

262. Lin J, Hong JI, Newman MW, et al. 'DENIM: An Informal Web Site Design Tool Inspired by Observations of Practice' (2003) *Human Computer Interaction* 18. [20.8]

263. Lind J (1753). A treatise of the scurvy in three parts. containing an inquiry into the nature, causes and cure of that disease, together with a critical and chronological view of what has been published on the subject. (Lars Bruzelius tr) London: A. Millar, 1753. http://www.bruzelius.info/Nautica/Medicine/Lind(1753).html, accessed April 2022. [1.7]

264. Llinás R (2002). *I of the Vortex: From Neurons to Self*. Cambridge, MA: MIT Press. [9.7.4]

265. Locke. J (1690) An Essay Concerning Humane Understanding. Oxford University Press published a paperback version in 1979 [8.3]

266. Lømo, T., 2003. The discovery of long-term potentiation. Philosophical Transactions of the Royal Society of London. Series B: Biological Sciences, 358(1432), pp.617-620.

267. Lottridge D, Masson N, and Mackay W. 'Sharing Empty Moments: Design for Remote Couples' in *Proceedings of the 27th international Conference on Human Factors in Computing Systems,* Boston, MA, 4–9 April 2009. CHI '09. New York, NY: ACM, 2329–38. DOI:http://doi.acm.org/10.1145/1518701.1519058 [6.2]

268. Loukola OJ, Perry CJ, Coscos L, et al. 'Bumblebees Show Cognitive Flexibility by Improving on an Observed Complex Behaviour' (2017) *Science* 24 February, 833-6 [22.4]

269. Lynch K. *The Image of The City*. Cambridge, MA: MIT Press, 1960. 2–7. [13.2]

270. MacGregor N. *A History of the World in 100 Objects*. London: Penguin, 2012. [12.6]

271. MacKenzie, I.S., Sellen, A. and Buxton, W.A., 1991, March. A comparison of input devices in element pointing and dragging tasks. In Proceedings of the SIGCHI conference on Human factors in computing systems (pp. 161-166) New York, NY: ACM [9.7.3]

272. Magic Leap (2017) https://www.magicleap.com/#/home, accessed September April 2022. [13.6]

273. Magnusson T. 'On Epistemic Tools: Musical Instruments as Cognitive Extensions' (2019) 14(1) *Organised Sound* 168–76. [15.5]

274. Mandelbrot BB. 'How Long is the Coast of Britain? Statistical Self-similarity and Fractional Dimension' (1967) 156 *Science* 636–8. [11.5]

275. Mann S. 'Physical assault by McDonald's for wearing digital eye glass' (2012), accessed January 2019. http://eyetap.blogspot.com/2012/10/mcveillance-mcdonaldized-surveillance.html, accessed April 2022. [3.6]

276. Marmaras N, Poulakakis G, and Papakostopoulos V. 'Ergonomic Design in Ancient Greece' (1999) 30(4) *Applied Ergonomics* 361–8. http://dx.doi.org/10.1016/S0003-6870(98)00050-7. [3.4]

277. Marraffa, M 'Theory of Mind' in *Internet Encyclopedia of Philosophy* (2011) http://www.iep.utm.edu/theomind/, accessed April 2022. [15.10]

278. Martin L. 'This chip makes sure you always buy your round', *The Observer,* Sunday 16 January 2005. http://www.guardian.co.uk/science/2005/jan/16/theobserver.theobserveruknewspages, accessed April 2022. [3.6]

279. Marvel (2018). Prototyping on paper. https://marvelapp.com/pop, accessed April 2022. [20.8]

280. Marzo, A, Seah, SA, Drinkwater, BW, et al. 'Holographic Acoustic Elements for Manipulation of Levitated Objects' (2015) 6(8661) *Nature Communications* 1–7. [2.2.2]

281. Matsumoto D. 'The Role of Facial Response in the Experience of Emotion: More Methodological Problems and a Meta-analysis' (April 1987) 52(4) *Journal of Personality and Social Psychology* 769–74. [5.3]

282. Matusow H. *The Beast of Business: a Record of Computer Atrocities.* Wolfe, 1968. [18.8]

283. Mayer-Schönberger, V (2011). *Delete: The Virtue of Forgetting in the Digital Age.* Princeton, NJ: Princeton University Press. [16.4]

284. Mayrhofer R and Gellersen H. 'Shake Well before Use: Intuitive and Secure Pairing of Mobile Devices' (2009) 8(6) *IEEE Transactions on Mobile Computing* 792–806. DOI: 10.1109/TMC.2009.51 [14.6]

285. McCarthy J and Wright P. *Technology as Experience.* Cambridge, MA: MIT Press, 2004. [7.5]

286. McGrath R. 'Species-Appropriate Computer Mediated Interaction' alt.chi, ACM CHI 2009, 8 April 2009. [1.2]

287. McGurk H and MacDonald J. 'Hearing Lips and Seeing Voices' (1976) 264 *Nature* 746–8. [20.2]

288. McIntosh C. *Cambridge Advanced Learners Dictionary.* Cambridge: Cambridge University Press, 2013. [1.5.2]

289. McLuhan M. (1964). *Understanding Media: The Extensions of Man.* Routledge. [15.8]

290. Meltzoff AN and Moore MK. 'Imitation of Facial and Manual Gestures by Human Neonates' (1977) 198(4312) *Science* 75–8. DOI: 10.1126/science.897687 [8.3]

291. Merleau-Ponty M. *Phénomènologie de la Perception.* London: Routledge, 1945. [22.4]

292. Miller G. 'The Magical Number Seven, Plus or Minus Two: Some Limits on Our Capacity for Processing Information' (1956) 63 *The Psychological Review* 81–97. http://www.musanim.com/miller1956/, accessed April 2022. [4.2]

293. Milner R. *The Space and Motion of Communicating Agents.* Cambridge: Cambridge University Press, 2009. [21.1]

294. Mithen S. *The Prehistory of the Mind.* London: Thames and Hudson, 1996. [15.5]

295. Mithen S. *The Singing Neanderthals. The Origins of Music, Language, Mind, and Body.* Cambridge, MA: Harvard University Press, 2007. [15.9]

296. MonmouthpediA. https://monmouthpedia.wordpress.com, accessed April 2022. [13.2]

297. Mori M (tr KF MacDorman and N Kageki). 'The Uncanny Valley: The Original Essay by Masahiro Mori' (2012) 19(2) *IEEE Robotics & Automation Magazine* 98–100. doi:10.1109/MRA.2012.2192811. [17.7.2]

298. Movable Type Ltd. Convert between Latitude/Longitude & OS National Grid References. (2016) http://www.movable-type.co.uk/scripts/latlong-os-gridref.html, accessed April 2022 [11.3]

299. Mueller P and Oppenheimer D. 'The Pen is Mightier than the Keyboard: Advantages of Longhand over Laptop Note Taking' (2014) 25(6) *Psychological Sciences* 1159–68. doi: 10.1177/0956797614524581 (2014) [22.7]

300. Mueller RS. Report on the Investigation into Russian Interference in the 2016 Presidential Election, Vol I. US Department of Justice, Washington DC, 2019. Available at https://en.wikipedia.org/wiki/Mueller_report, accessed April 2022. [13.5]

301. Murray-Rust D, Tarte S, Hartswood M, et al. 2015. On Wayfaring in Social Machines. In *Proceedings of the 24th International Conference on World Wide Web* (WWW '15 Companion). ACM, New York, NY, USA, 1143–1148. DOI: http://dx.doi.org/10.1145/2740908.2743971 [12.12]

302. MyLifeBits. Microsoft. accessed September 2014. http://research.microsoft.com/en-us/projects/mylifebits/, accessed April 2022. [16.4]

303. Mynatt ED. 'Designing with Auditory Icons: How Well Do We Identify Auditory Cues?' in Conference Companion on Human Factors in Computing Systems (CHI '94), Catherine Plaisant (ed). ACM, New York, NY, USA, 1994, 269–70. DOI=http://dx.doi.org/10.1145/259963.260483 [7.6]

304. NASA (1996). COBE Dipole: Speeding Through the Universe. Astronomy Picture of the Day. 5 February 1996. http://apod.nasa.gov/apod/ap960205.html, accessed April 2022. [11.8]

305. Neale C (2016). Paper Prototyping Animation with Voiceover. https://vimeo.com/6085753, accessed April 2022. [20.7]

306. Newman J. 'Internet-connected Hello Barbie doll can be hacked'. (2015) PC World. http://www.pcworld.com/article/3012220/security/internet-connected-hello-barbie-doll-can-be-hacked.html, accessed April 2022. [13.8]

307. Newman W, Eldridge M, and Lamming M (1991). 'Pepys: Generating Autobiographies by Automatic Tracking' in Proceedings of the Second European Conference on Computer Supported Cooperative Work–ECSCW '91, 25–27 September 1991. Amsterdam: Kluwer Academic Publishers 175–88 [14.6]

308. Newman WM, 'A System for Interactive Graphical Programming' in Proceedings of the 30 April 30–2 May 1968, Spring Joint Computer Conference (Atlantic City, New Jersey, 30 April–2 May 1968). AFIPS '68 (Spring). ACM, New York, NY, 47–54. DOI= http://doi.acm.org/10.1145/1468075.1468083 [9.1]

309. Niculescu A.I., Dix A., and Yeo KH. 'Are You Ready for a Drive? User Perspectives on Autonomous Vehicles'. *CHI'17 Extended Abstracts,* ACM. 2017. doi: 10.1145/3027063.3053182 [14.8]

310. Noë A. *Action in Perception.* (Cambridge, MA: MIT Press, 2004). [22.4;22.5]

311. Nora P. Between Memory and History: Les Lieux de Mémoire. tr. Marc Roudebush. Representations 26, Spring 1989, University of California, pp. 7–24 [16.4]

312. Norman DA and Draper SW. *User Centered System Design; New Perspectives on Human-Computer Interaction.* Hillsdale, NJ: L. Erlbaum, 1986. [22.8]

313. Norman DA. Emotional Design: *Why We Love (or Hate) Everyday Things*. New York, NY: Basic Books, 2003. [7.5;20.2]

314. Norman DA. *The Design of Everyday Things*. Cambridge, MA: MIT Press, 1998. [9.6]

315. Nova N (2008). LIFT-Labs. tangible@home. MobiKUI2008, First International Workshop on Mobile and Kinetic User Interfaces, Fribourg, Switzerland, 13–14 October 2008. [1.2]

316. NS&I (2013). All about ERNIE. https://nsandi-corporate.com/media-resources/ernie, accessed April 2022. [17.1]

317. OECD: Students, Computers and Learning: Making the Connection, PISA, OECD Publishing. DOI: 10.1787/9789264239555-en (2015) [22.7]

318. Olivier P, Monk A, Xu G et al. (2009). 'Ambient Kitchen: designing Situated Services Using a High Fidelity Prototyping Environment' in ACM International Conference on PErvasive Technologies Related to Assistive Environments (PETRA), 2009. Doi: 10.1145/1579114.1579161 [22.8]

319. Ordnance Survey (2016). A guide to coordinate systems in Great Britain, D00659 v3.0 Aug 2016. https://www.ordnancesurvey.co.uk/documents/resources/guide-coordinate-systems-great-britain.pdf, accessed April 2022. [11.3]

320. Ormerod T, MacGregor J, and Chronicle E. 'Dynamics and Constraints in Insight Problem Solving' (2002) 28(4) *Journal of Experimental Psychology* 791–99.

321. Orwell G. *Nineteen Eighty-Four*. London: Penguin Classics, 2013. [6.6]

322. PalCom: Making Computing Palpable. 21 April 2008, accessed March 2009. https://cordis.europa.eu/project/id/002057, accessed April 2022. [1.2]

323. Paiva A, Costa M, Chaves R et al. 'SenToy: An Affective Sympathetic Interface' (2003) 59(1-2) International Journal of Affective Computing in Human-Computer Interaction 227–35. DOI: 10.1016/S1071-5819(03)00048-X [7.5]

324. Papangelis K (2015). *User Driven Design of Real Time Passenger Information Solutions for Supporting Rural Passengers in The Context of Disruption*. PhD Thesis. University of Aberdeen. http://ethos.bl.uk/OrderDetails.do?uin=uk.bl.ethos.678798, accessed April 2022. [12.12]

325. Parkinson J (2015), 'The Problem with the Skyscraper Wind Effect'. BBC News Magazine: http://www.bbc.co.uk/news/magazine-33426889 accessed April 2022 [19.3]

326. Pausch R. 'Virtual Reality on Five Dollars a Day' in SP Robertson, GM Olson, and JS Olson (eds), *Proceedings of the SIGCHI Conference on Human Factors in Computing Systems (CHI '91)*, ACM, New York, NY, USA, 1991, 265–70. DOI: http://dx.doi.org/10.1145/108844.108913 [12.10]

327. Penrose R. *The Emperor's New Mind.* (Oxford: Oxford University Press, 1990). [4.3]

328. Pepperell R *The Post-Human Condition.* Exeter: Intellect, 1995 [19.2]

329. Popper KR. 'Kirk on Heraclitus, and on Fire as the Cause of Balance' (1963) LXXII Mind 386-92. doi:10.1093/mind/LXXII.287.386 [1.4]

330. Porter M, Summerskill S, Burnett G et al. (2005). 'BIONIC–'Eyes-free' Design of Secondary Driving Controls' in the Proceedings of the Accessible Design in the Digital World Conference, Dundee, Scotland, 23–25 August 2005 [19.6]

331. Preston W, Benford S, Thorn EC et al. (2017). 'Enabling Hand-Crafted Visual Markers at Scale' in *Proceedings of the 2017 Conference on Designing Interactive Systems (DIS '17)*. ACM, New York, NY, USA, 1227–1237. DOI: https://doi.org/10.1145/3064663.3064746 [18.1;18.4]

332. Price S and Pallant C. *Storyboarding: A Critical History.* (London: Palgrave Macmillan, 2015). DOI 10.1057/9781137027603 [20.5]

333. Prinz W and Gross T (2001). 'Ubiquitous Awareness of Cooperative Activities in a Theatre of Work' in A Bode and W Karl (eds), Proceedings of Fachtagung Arbeitsplatzcomputer: Pervasive Ubiquitous Computing - APC 2001 (10-12 October, Munich). Berlin: VDE Publisher, 134–44. [1.6]

334. Prinz W, Pankoke-Babatz U, Graethe W, et al. 'Presenting Activity Information in an Inhabited Information Space' in DN Snowden, EF Churchill, and E Frécon (eds), *Inhabited Information Spaces, Living with Your Data.* (Berlin: Springer, 2004) 181–208. [12.10]

335. Quintanilha M (2007). Marble Answering Machine http://interactionthesis.wordpress.com/2007/02/01/marble-answering-machine/, accessed April 2022. [19.3]

336. Ramachandran V. *A Brief Tour of Human Consciousness.* New York, NY: Pi Press, 2004. [8.3]

337. Ramduny D and Dix A (1997). 'Why, What, Where, When: Architectures for Co-operative work on the WWW' in H Thimbleby, B O'Connaill, and P Thomas (eds), *Proceedings of HCI'97* Bristol: Springer. 283–301. http://alandix.com/academic/papers/WWWW97/, accessed April 2022. [17.3]

338. Ramduny-Ellis D, Hare J, Dix A et al. 'Physicality in Design: An Exploration' (2010) 13(1) *The Design Journal* 48–76. DOI: 10.2752/146069210X12580336766365 [4.6]

339. Reason J. *Human Error*. Cambridge: Cambridge University Press, 1990. [9.6]

340. Renfrew C. *Prehistory: The Making of the Human Mind*. London: Phoenix, 2007. [15.5]

341. Richardson LF. 'The Problem of Contiguity' (1961) 6 *General Systems Yearbook*, 139–87. [11.5]

342. Rishabh I, Kimber D, and Adcock J. 'Indoor Localization Using Controlled Ambient Sounds'. 2012 International Conference on Indoor Positioning and Indoor Navigation (IPIN), Sydney, NSW, 2012, 1–10. doi: 10.1109/IPIN.2012.6418905 [21.2.2]

343. Robinson M. Eurogamer, 2015 'F1 Driver Uses Game to Practice One of This Season's Most Audacious Overtakes' http://www.eurogamer.net/articles/2015-08-27-f1-driver-uses-game-to-practice-one-of-this-seasons-most-audacious-overtakes, accessed April 2022. [13.7]

344. Robinson S, Pearson J, Jones M et al. (2017). Better Together: Disaggregating Mobile services for Emergent Users. In Proceedings of the 19th International Conference on Human-Computer Interaction with Mobile Devices and Services (MobileHCI '17). Association for Computing Machinery, New York, NY, USA, Article 44, 1–13. DOI:https://doi.org/10.1145/3098279.3098534 [6.3;6.3]

345. Rodden T, Rogers Y, Halloran, et al. (2003). 'Designing Novel Interactional Workspaces to Support Face-to-face Consultations'. Proc CHI'03. ACM Press. 57–64 [6.3]

346. Rogers Y and Halloran J. Interaction Design: Case Studies: Supporting Collaboration for Choosing Holidays. (dated 2007/2019 http://www.id-book.com/casestudy_n_3.php, accessed April 2022. [6.3]

347. Rogers Y, Price S, Fitzpatrick G et al. 'Ambient Wood: Designing New Forms of Digital Augmentation for Learning Outdoors' in *Proceedings of the 2004 Conference on Interaction Design and Children: Building a Community* (IDC '04). ACM, New York, NY, USA, 2004, 3–10. DOI=http://dx.doi.org/10.1145/1017833.1017834 [21.2.3]

348. SAP (2016). Scenes: A New Method and Tool to Create Storyboards. https://news.sap.com/2016/03/scenes-a-new-method-and-tool-to-create-storyboards/, accessed April 2022. [20.5]

349. Schnädelbach H, Penn P, Steadman P et al (2006)., Moving Office: *Inhabiting a Dynamic Building*. In Proceedings of the 2006 20th anniversary conference on Computer supported cooperative work

(CSCW '06). ACM, New York, NY, USA, 313–322. DOI=http://dx.doi.org/10.1145/1180875.1180924 [14.7]

350. Schön D. *The Reflective Practitioner*. New York, NY: Basic Books, 1983. [19.2]

351. Searle J. *The Construction of Social Reality*. London: Penguin, 1995. [15.5]

352. Searle J. *The Mystery of Consciousness*. London: Granta Books, 1997. [4.3]

353. SeeSense https://seesense.cc/, accessed April 2022. [13.8]

354. Seewoonauth K, Rukzio E, Hardy R et al. 'NFC–based Mobile Interactions with Direct-view Displays' in IFIP Conference on Human–Computer Interaction (Uppsala, 24–28 August 2009). Berlin: Springer, 2009, 835-8.

355. Sellen A, Buxton W, and Arnott J. (1992). Using Spatial Cues to Improve Videoconferencing. Proceedings of CHI '92, ACM Conference on Human Factors in Software, 651–52. https://youtu.be/n-W7QTXG4G8, accessed April 2022. [6.1]

356. SEMI (2017). Annual Silicon Volume Shipments Remain at Record Highs. SEMI, Silicon Manufacturers Group. http://www.semi.org/en/annual-silicon-volume-shipments-remain-record-highs, accessed April 2022. [17.6]

357. Sennett R. *The Craftsman*. London: Allen Lane, 2008. [19.2]

358. Shackel B. *Ergonomics for a Computer*. (1959) 120 Design 36–39 [1.5.1]

359. Shannon C and Weaver W. *The Mathematical Theory of Communication*. Chicago, IL: University of Illinois Press, 1962. [15.4]

360. Shannon C. A Mathematical Theory of Communication. (1948) 27 *Bell System Technical Journal* 379–423, 623–56. [5.4]

361. Shaw J, Staff H, Row Farr J et al. (2000). *Staged Mixed Reality Performance 'Desert Rain' by Blast Theory*. eRENA ESPRIT Project 25379 Workpackage 7 Deliverable D7b.3. http://cid.nada.kth.se/pdf/CID-181.pdf, accessed April 2022. [2.4.3]

362. Shen C, Everitt KM, and Ryall K. UbiTable: Impromptu Face-to-Face Collaboration on Horizontal Interactive Surfaces, ACM International Conference on Ubiquitous Computing (UbiComp), October 2003, 281–288 [6.3]

363. Shepherd A (1995). 'Task Analysis as a Framework for Examining HCI Tasks, in Monk, A. and Gilbert N (eds), *Perspectives on HCI: Diverse Approaches*. Cambridge, MA: Academic Press, 1995. 145–74. [5.6]

364. Sheridan JG, Dix A, Bayliss A et al. Understanding Interaction in Ubiquitous Guerrilla Performances in Playful Arenas. Proceedings of British HCI 2004, 6–10 September, Leeds, UK [3.6]

365. Shneiderman B and Plaisant C. 'Designing the User Interface: Strategies for Effective Human–Computer Interaction. Pearson, 2009 [19.3]

366. Shneiderman B *Direct Manipulation: A Step Beyond Programming Languages,* (1983) 16(8) IEEE Computer 57–69. [22.8]

367. Shulaker M, Hills G, Park R et al. Three–dimensional Integration of Nanotechnologies for Computing and Data Storage on a Single Chip. (2017) 547(17) *Nature.* DOI: 10.1038/nature22994 [11.5]

368. SIA (2015) *Rebooting the IT Revolution: A Call to Action.* Semiconductor Industry Organisation. September 2015. https://www.semiconductors.org/resources/rebooting-the-it-revolution-a-call-to-action-2, accessed April 2022. [17.1]

369. Smiles S (ed). *James Nasmyth. Engineer. An Autobiography.* New York, NY: Harper and Brothers, 1883. http://sizes.com/tools/thread_maudsley.htm [16.1]

370. Smith A (1776). *An Inquiry into the Nature and Causes of the Wealth of Nations.* https://archive.org/details/aninquiryintothe01smituoft, accessed April 2022. [22.3.1]

371. Smith B and Casati R. 'Naive Physics: An Essay in Ontology' (1994) 7(2) *Philosophical Psychology* 225–44. [7.1]

372. Smith RB, O'Shea T, O'Malley C et al. 'Preliminary Experiments with a Distributed Multimedia, Problem–solving Environment' in JM Bowers and SD Benford (eds), Studies in Computer–Supported Cooperative Work. Amsterdam: North-Holland, 1991, 31–48. [6.1]

373. Smith RB. (1986). 'Experiences with the Alternate Reality Kit: An Example of the Tension between Literalism and Magic' in *Proceedings of the SIGCHI/GI Conference on Human Factors in Computing Systems and Graphics Interface (CHI '87),* John M. Carroll and Peter P Tanner (eds.). New York, NY: ACM, 61–67. DOI=http://dx.doi.org/10.1145/29933.30861 [22.2]

374. Smith, K (2017). *'Descartes' Theory of Ideas',* The Stanford Encyclopedia of Philosophy. https://plato.stanford.edu/archives/sum2017/entries/descartes-ideas/, accessed April 2022. [22.2]

375. Smith. F *Romani-English Glossary.* http://www2.arnes.si/eusmith/Romany/glossary.html, accessed April 2022. [12.12]

376. Snyder C. *Paper Prototyping: The Fast and Easy way to Design and Refine User Interfaces.* San Francisco, CA: Morgan Kaufmann, 2003. [20.6]

377. Spelmezan D, Gonzalez RM and Sriram S (2016). 'SkinHaptics: Ultrasound Focused in the Hand Creates Tactile Sensations' in S Choi, KJ Kuchenbecker, and G Gerling (eds), IEEE Haptics Symposium 2016, Philadelphia, PA, 8–11 April 2016. London: IEEE, 98-105. [2.2.2]

378. Spence C, Shankar MU, and Blumenthal H. 'Sound Bites, Auditory Contributions to the Perception and Consumption of Food and Drink' in F Bacci and D Melcher (eds), *Art and the Senses*. Oxford: Oxford University Press, 2011, 207–38. [20.2]

379. Standage T. (1998). *The Victorian Internet: The Remarkable Story of the Telegraph and the Nineteenth Century's On-Line Pioneers.* New York, NY: Walker & Company, see also review by Eric Goldman, 'The Victorian Internet', 16 November 2007 http://blog.ericgoldman.org/archives/2007/11/victorian_inter.htm, accessed April 2022. [6.2]

380. STELARC (official website), accessed March 2009. http://stelarc.org, accessed April 2022. [3.6]

381. Storyboard Fountain (2016). The Best Way to Visualize Your Screenplay. http://storyboardfountain.com/, accessed April 2022 [20.5]

382. Strogatz S, Abrams D, McRobie A et al. 'Crowd Synchrony on the Millennium Bridge' (2005) 438 *Nature* 43–44, DOI:10.1038/438043a [3.2]

383. Suchman, L. *Plans and Situated Actions: The Problem of Human–Machine Communication.* Cambridge: Cambridge University Press, 1987. [5.6]

384. Sutherland IE (30 January 1963). Sketchpad: A Man-Machine Graphical Communication System (PDF). Technical Report No 296, Lincoln Laboratory, Massachusetts Institute of Technology. available at http://www.cl.cam.ac.uk/techreports/UCAM-CL-TR-574.pdf, accessed April 2022. [1.5.1]

385. Sykes J and Brown S (2003). Affective Gaming: Measuring Emotion through the Gamepad. In CHI '03 Extended Abstracts on Human Factors in Computing Systems (Ft. Lauderdale, FLA, USA, 5–10 April 2003). CHI '03. ACM, New York, NY, 732–33. DOI= http://doi.acm.org/10.1145/765891.765957 [7.5]

386. TARDIS. Wikipedia page. http://en.wikipedia.org/wiki/TARDIS, accessed April 2022. [7.3]

387. Taylor N and Cheverst K (2012). *Supporting Community Awareness with Interactive Displays.* IEEE Computer 45(5), 26–32. http://dx.doi.org/10.1109/MC.2012.113 [22.3.2]

388. Teh K, Lee S, and Cheok K, 'Poultry.Internet and Internet Pajama: Novel Systems for Remote Haptic Interaction' in Proceedings of the First International Conference Edutainment 2006 (19 April 2006, Hangzhou). Technologies for E-Learning and Digital Entertainment, LNCS 3942, Berlin: Springer, 2006, 1288-91. DOI: 10.1007/11736639 161 [1.2]

389. Terrenghi T, Quigley A, and Dix A. A taxonomy for and analysis of multi-person-display ecosystems. (2009) 13(8) *Journal of Personal and Ubiquitous Computing* 583–98 DOI:10.1007/s00779-009-0244-5 [14.3]

390. Than K. World's oldest cave art found–made by Neanderthals? (2012) June 14 *National Geographic News.* http://news.nationalgeographic.com/news/2012/06/120614-neanderthal-cave-paintings-spain-science-pike/, accessed April 2022. [16.4]

391. Thimbleby H. 'Using the Fitts Law with State Transition Systems to Find Optimal Task Timings' in Proceedings of Second International. Workshop on Formal Methods for Interactive Systems, FMIS2007 (Lancaster, 3–7 September 2007). New York, NY: ACM. [21.1]

392. Thimbleby H. Ignorance of interaction programming is killing people. (2008) 15(5) *ACM Interactions* 52–57. [9.7.2]

393. Thomas, C. 2016 'New TomTom service helps drivers find on-street parking spot'. *Express*, Mon, Oct 3, 2016. http://www.express.co.uk/life-style/cars/717140/New-TomTom-service-helps-drivers-find-parking-spot, accessed April 2022. [13.1]

394. Thomas, N. 2014 'Streets Without Cars' https://streetswithoutcars.wordpress.com/tag/hans-monderman/, accessed April 2022. [13.9]

395. Thompson EP. *The Making of the English Working Class.* Toronto: Penguin Books, 1991. [17.8.2]

396. Tiree Tech Wave (2013). Frasan–Tiree Heritage app. accessed January 2019. https://tireetechwave.org/projects/frasan-tiree-heritage-app/, accessed April 2022. [18.5]

397. Tooby J and Cosmides L (1997). *Evolutionary Psychology: a primer.* 1997. online at: http://www.cep.ucsb.edu/primer.html, accessed April 2022. [4.4]

398. Treadaway C and LAUGH Team (2019). HUG by LAUGH. https://www.laughproject.info/home-2/hug/, accessed April 2022 [2.5.1]

399. Trullemans S, Sanctorum A, and Signer B (2016). PimVis: exploring and re-finding documents in cross-media information spaces. In Proceedings of the International Working Conference on Advanced Visual Interfaces (AVI '16), P Buono, R Lanzilotti, and M Matera (eds). ACM, New York, NY, USA, 176–83. DOI: https://doi.org/10.1145/2909132.2909261 [14.6]

400. Ulrich K and Eppinger SD. *Product Design and Development.* Chicago, IL: McGraw-Hill, 1995. [19.2]

401. University of Wales Trinity St David. Monks, Murder and Manuscripts, part of Walking around Wales, Online Exhibition. http://www.uwtsd.ac.uk/rbla/, accessed April 2022. [15.2]

402. Vartanian H (2007). The Brooklyn Rail, 2007 'Virtually an art market? artfully living a second life' http://brooklynrail.org/2007/4/artseen/secondlife-art, accessed April 2022. [13.7]

403. Villar N, Block F, and Gellersen H. 'VOODOOIO' in Proceedings of ACM SIGGRAPH 2006 Emerging technologies conference, Boston, MA, 30 July - 3 August 2006. New York, NY: ACM, 36. [20.10]

404. Voida A and Greenberg S (2008). Wii all play: the console game as a computational meeting place. Research report 2008-912-25, Department of Computer Science, University of Calgary, Calgary, Alberta, Canada, September. [1.2]

405. Wada K and Shibata T. 'Living with Seal Robots—Its Sociopsychological and Physiological Influences on the Elderly at a Care House' (2007) October 23(5) IEEE Transactions on Robotoics 972–80. DOI:https://doi.org/10.1109/TRO.2007.906261 [2.5.1]

406. Wada YI. The sou-sou impulse. (2008) 35(1) Fiberarts 38–9 [16.2]

407. Wallace J, Jackson D, Ladha C, et al. 'Digital Jewellery and Family Relationships'. Workshop on the Family and Communication Technologies (Newcastle upon Tyne, 24 May 2007). Available at https://www.researchgate.net/profile/Patrick-Olivier/publication/250866417_Digital_jewellery_and_family_relationships/links/0c960529a0d3c37ed8000000/Digital-jewellery-and-family-relationships.pdf, accessed April 2022. [6.2]

408. Wallace VL. 1976. The semantics of graphic input devices. SIGGRAPH Compter Graphics 10, 1 (May. 1976), 61–5. DOI= http://doi.acm.org/10.1145/957197.804734 [9.1]

409. Want R, Hopper A, Falcao V et al. The active badge location system. (1992) 10(1) ACM Transactions on Information Systems 91–102. DOI: 10.1145/128756.128759 [21.2.2]

410. Ward M. Universality: The Underlying Theory Behind Life, The Universe and Everything. London: Pan Books, (2002). [11.5]

411. Warner Bros. Pictures. You've Got Mail. 1998. http://youvegotmail.warnerbros.com/, accessed April 2022. [6.2]

412. Warwick K. A study in cyborgs. (2003) 16 Ingenia 15–22 [6.2]

413. Wason PC. 'Reasoning' in B Foss (ed), New Horizons in Psychology. Harmondsworth: Penguin Books, 1996, pp. 135–51 [4.4]

414. WDO (2017). Industrial Design Definition History. World Design Organization (formerly the International Council of Societies of Industrial Design, ICSID). accessed November 2017.

http://wdo.org/about/definition/industrial-design-definition-history/, accessed April 2022. [1.5.2]

415. Weed B. The industrial design of the software industry. (1996) 28(3) *ACM SIGCHI Bulletin* 8–11. [20.2]

416. Weiser M. The computer for the twenty-first century. (1991) 65(3) *Scientific American* 66–75. [22.9]

417. Wellner P. Interacting with paper on the DigitalDesk. (1993) 36(7) Commun. ACM 87–96. DOI=http://dx.doi.org/10.1145/159544.159630 (see also Digital Desk by Pierre Wellner: https://youtu.be/9HXp3s7x68o, accessed April 2022.) [14.6]

418. Wenig D, Schöning J, Hecht B et al. 'StripeMaps: Improving Map-based Pedestrian Navigation for Smart-watches' in *Mobile HCI 2015: Proceedings of the International Conference on Human-Computer Interaction with Mobile Devices and Services* (Copenhagen, 24–27 August 2015. New York, NY: ACM, 52–62. [12.7]

419. Wensveen S and Overbeeke K. Fun with your alarm clock: designing for engaging experiences through emotionally rich interaction' in MA Blythe, K Overbeeke, AF Monk, et al (eds) *Funology: From Usability to Enjoyment* Norwell, MA: Kluwer Academic Publishers (2004), 275–81. [7.5]

420. Wensveen S, Overbeeke K, and Djajadiningrat T. (2002). Push me, shove me and I show you how you feel: recognising mood from emotionally rich interaction. In Proceedings of the 4th Conference on Designing interactive Systems: Processes, Practices, Methods, and Techniques (London, England, 25–28 June, 2002). DIS '02. ACM, New York, NY, 335–40. DOI= http://doi.acm.org/10.1145/778712.778759 [7.5]

421. Whorf B. *Language, Thought, and Reality: Selected Writings of Benjamin Lee Whorf*, ed. John Carroll. Cambridge, MA: MIT Press. [22.6]

422. Wikipedia (2017). Craigslist. accessed July 2017. https://en.wikipedia.org/wiki/Craigslist, accessed April 2022. [14.11]

423. Winograd T and Flores F. *Understanding Computers and Cognition: A New Foundation for Design*. Bristol: Intellect Books, 1986 [10.5]

424. Winston A (2014). Interactive dancing traffic lights make waiting more entertaining. https://www.dezeen.com/2014/09/17/interactive-dancing-traffic-lights-installation-smart-car-lisbon/, accessed April 2022. [13.9]

425. Wobbrock JO, Ringel Morris M, and Wilson AD. (2009). User-defined gestures for surface computing. In Proceedings of the SIGCHI Conference on Human Factors in Computing Systems (CHI '09). ACM, New York, NY, USA, 1083–92. DOI: https://doi.org/10.1145/1518701.1518866 [9.1]

426. Wood D (ed) (2006). A Report on the Surveillance Society. Report For the Information Commissioner by the Surveillance Studies Network. Information Commissioner's Office, UK. September 2006 https://ico.org.uk/media/about-the-ico/documents/1042390/surveillance-society-full-report-2006.pdf accessed February 2022. [6.6]

427. Woolley A, Loudon G, and Gill S. Getting into context early: a comparative study of laboratory and in-context user testing of low fidelity information appliance prototypes. (2013) 16(4) *Design Journal* 460–85. [19.3]

428. World Health Organization. 'Number of Road Traffic Deaths' https://www.who.int/data/gho/data/themes/topics/topic-details/GHO/road-traffic-mortality accessed April 2022. [19.6]

429. Wujec T (2010) 'Build a Tower, Build a Team' TED Talks 2010 https://www.ted.com/talks/tom_wujec_build_a_team, accessed April 2022 [19.2]

430. Yang K and EI-Haik BS. *Design for Six Sigma: A Roadmap for Product Development*. Chicago, IL: McGraw-Hill Professional, 2008. [19.2]

431. Younan S and Gill S. (2013). Digital Three-Dimensional Copies of Museum Artefacts; Dynamics of Access, Ownership, and Meaning in the Proceedings of the Di-Egy Fest 0.1, Consciousness Reframed Series. Cairo, Egypt 27 March -10 April 2013. [13.7]

432. Zetter K. *Countdown to Zero Day: Stuxnet and the Launch of the World's First Digital Weapon*. New York, NY: Crown, 2014. [17.6]

433. Zhang G, Yan C, Ji X, et al. (2017). 'DolphinAttack: Inaudible Voice Commands' in Proceedings of the 2017 ACM SIGSAC Conference on Computer and Communications Security (CCS '17). New York, NY: ACM, 103–17. DOI: https://doi.org/10.1145/3133956.3134052 [13.8]

434. Zhou W, Reisinger J, Peer A, et al. (2014). 'Interaction-based Dynamic Measurement of Haptic Characteristics of Control Elements' in M Auvray and C Duriez (eds) Haptics: Neuroscience, Devices, Modeling, and Applications: 9th International Conference, Euro-Haptics 2014 (Versailles, 24–26 June, 2014). Berlin: Springer, 2014, 177–84. http://dx.doi.org/10.1007/978-3-662-44193-023. [21.1]

Image Credits

Index